BASIC LEGAL RESEARCH

Basic Legal Research

TOOLS AND STRATEGIES

THIRD EDITION

Amy E. Sloan

Associate Professor of Law
Co-director, Legal Skills Program
University of Baltimore School of Law

PUBLISHERS

111 Eighth Avenue, New York, NY 10011
http://lawschool.aspenpublishers.com

Aspen Publishers
Attn: Permissions
111 Eighth Avenue, 7th Floor
New York, NY 10011

Printed in the United States of America

ISBN 0-7355-5653-9

2 3 4 5 6 7 8 9 0

Library of Congress Cataloging-in-Publication Data

Sloan, Amy E., 1964-

    Basic legal research : tools and strategies / Amy E. Sloan.— 3rd ed.
      p. cm.
Includes index.
ISBN 0-7355-5653-9
1.   Legal research—United States. I. Title.

KF240.S585 2005
340.072'073—dc22

                                           2005028259

About Aspen Publishers

Aspen Publishers, headquartered in New York City, is a leading information provider for attorneys, business professionals, and law students. Written by preeminent authorities, our products consist of analytical and practical information covering both U.S. and international topics.We publish in the full range of formats, including updated manuals, books, periodicals, CDs, and online products.

Our proprietary content is complemented by 2,500 legal databases, containing over 11 million documents, available through our Loislaw division. Aspen Publishers also offers a wide range of topical legal and business databases linked to Loislaw's primary material. Our mission is to provide accurate, timely, and authoritative content in easily accessible formats, supported by unmatched customer care.

To order any Aspen Publishers title, go to *http://lawschool.aspenpublishers.com* or call 1-800-638-8437.

To reinstate your manual update service, call 1-800-638-8437.

For more information on Loislaw products, go to *www.loislaw.com* or call 1-800-364-2512.

For Customer Care issues, e-mail *CustomerCare@aspenpublishers.com;* call 1-800-234-1660; or fax 1-800-901-9075.

Aspen Publishers
a Wolters Kluwer business

For Bebe

Summary of Contents

CONTENTS

PREFACE

The third edition of *Basic Legal Research*: *Tools and Strategies* contains the following updated material:

- **Revised table of contents**—The third edition is organized much the same way the first and second editions were organized. The table of contents has been revised, however, to differentiate sections of each chapter devoted to general information on a research source, print research process, and electronic research process.
- **Fully updated sample pages and research explanations**—All sample pages have been updated. Discussions of print and electronic research have been updated to reflect the latest information on source coverage and research process.
- **Citation**—The coverage of citation includes both the *ALWD Manual* (3d ed. 2006) and the *Bluebook* (18th ed. 2005).
- **Weight of authority**—Chapter 1, Introduction to Legal Research, contains new material on court structure and weight of authority.
- **Developing search terms**—Chapter 2, on Generating Search Terms, uses a new hypothetical fact pattern that is connected with the sample pages on case research in Chapter 4 and the discussion of electronic word searching in Chapter 10.
- **Secondary sources**—Chapter 3, on Secondary Source Research, contains new material on HeinOnLine, an electronic source for legal periodicals.
- **Case research**—Chapter 4, on Case Research, contains new material on unpublished, or non-precedential, opinions.
- **Citators**—Chapter 5, on Research with Shepard's Citations and Other Citators, contains new material on Graphical KeyCite, a Westlaw feature that displays case history in chart format.
- **Statutory research**—Chapter 6, on Statutory Research, contains a completely revised discussion of electronic statutory research, including discussion of electronic popular name tables in LexisNexis and Westlaw and statutory index searching in Westlaw.

- **C.F.R. research**—Chapter 8, on Federal Administrative Law Research, contains a completely revised discussion of electronic C.F.R. research in GPO Access, including discussion of the e-CFR, an unofficial edition of the C.F.R. that incorporates changes to regulations as they are published in the *Federal Register*.
- **Electronic research**—Chapter 10, on Electronic Legal Research, contains new material on using alert or clipping services and blogs and other publicly available Internet sites for legal research.

The philosophy and the format of the third edition remain the same as those of earlier editions. The genesis of this book was a conversation I had with Todd Petit, a student in my Lawyering Skills class at Catholic University, in the fall of 1994. Todd was working on a research project, and he came to me in frustration and bewilderment over the research process. Over the course of the year, Todd ultimately mastered the skill of legal research. Nevertheless, our conversation that fall caused me to start thinking about how I could teach research more effectively, a process that ultimately culminated in this book.

I do not believe Todd's experience was unique. Mastering a skill is a form of experiential learning—learning that can only be done by doing. And the "doing" aspect necessarily involves periods of trial and error until a person grasps the skill. It is not surprising that this can be frustrating and even bewildering at times.

Having said that, however, even experiential learning has to be built on a base of information. My goal with this book is to provide two kinds of information necessary for students to learn the process of legal research: basic information about a range of research sources and a framework for approaching research projects.

This text provides instruction in a variety of legal research sources, including secondary sources, cases and digests, citators, statutes, federal legislative history, federal administrative regulations, and subject-matter ("looseleaf") services. Each of these sources is described in a separate chapter that includes the following components:

- introductory information about the source
- step-by-step instructions for print research, including textual explanations, charts, and annotated examples highlighting key features of the source
- an explanation of electronic research tools available for the source
- an explanation of citation rules for the source
- an annotated set of sample pages illustrating the research process for the source
- a checklist summarizing both the research process and the key features of the source.

The range of material in each of these chapters is intended to accommodate a variety of teaching and learning styles. The textual explanations, charts, and checklists can be used for in-class discussions and for out-of-class reference as students are working in the library. In addition, the sample pages illustrating the research process provide both instructional material and a useful summary synthesizing the information on the source from the rest of the chapter.

This text does more, however, than simply explain the bibliographic features of various research sources. It also provides instruction in research as a process, and it does this in two ways. First, Chapter 1 provides an overview of research sources and the research process. By providing a framework for understanding the relationships among different types of legal authority, this chapter sets the stage for a process-oriented introduction to research instruction. Second, Chapter 11 provides a framework for creating a research plan. By setting out a process based on a series of questions students can ask to define the contours of any type of research project, it provides a flexible approach that can be adapted to a variety of assignments. Although Chapter 11 is the last chapter in the text, it can be used whenever students are required to develop a strategy for approaching a research project.

Of course, a comprehensive understanding of legal research requires students to be familiar with both print and electronic research sources. This text explains electronic research in a way that will allow students to develop their computer research skills regardless of whether they learn about electronic research along with print research or as a separate component of the curriculum. Each chapter devoted to an individual research source includes information on the types of electronic research options available for that source. General techniques for conducting computer research, however, appear in a separate chapter, Chapter 10. Chapter 10 can be used in conjunction with other chapters at any point in the course when students begin learning about electronic legal research.

Moreover, the text provides instruction in a wide range of electronic research sources. It discusses research using commercial services such as Westlaw and LexisNexis that are available at most law libraries. But it also covers a range of other electronic research options, including subscription services and material available for free via the Internet. As part of this instruction, the text discusses cost considerations in a way not addressed in other texts so that students can learn to make informed decisions about when to use electronic sources and how to select the best electronic source for any research project.

This text seeks to provide students not only with the bibliographic skills to locate the legal authorities necessary to resolve a research

issue, but also an understanding of research process that is an integral component of students' training in problem-solving skills. I hope this text will prove to be a useful guide to students as they undertake this intellectual challenge.

January 2006   Amy E. Sloan

Acknowledgments

Many people contributed to the third edition of this book. My thanks here will not be adequate for the assistance they provided. I extend special thanks to my research assistant, Lauren Dunnock. The reference librarians at the University of Baltimore Law Library deserve recognition for their assistance, especially Joanne Dugan, who cheerfully tracked down answers to many questions. Lynn Farnan's assistance with a variety of tasks both large and small is gratefully acknowledged. A number of my colleagues at other schools contributed to this project by sharing their experiences in teaching with the second edition, both by communicating with me directly and through anonymous reviews. I am indebted to them for their suggestions. In addition, I want to thank Dean Gilbert Holmes at the University of Baltimore School of Law for generous financial support.

The people at Aspen Publishers have been incredibly generous with their time and talents. Melody Davies, Troy Froebe, Elizabeth Kenny, Carol McGeehan, and their colleagues provided everything from moral support to editorial advice to production assistance. Their guidance and expertise contributed greatly to the content, organization, and layout of the text, and I am grateful for their assistance.

I want to thank my family and friends for their support, especially Peggy Metzger, my strength and inspiration in all I do.

I would be remiss if I limited my acknowledgments to those who assisted with the third edition of the text because much of what appears here originated in the earlier editions. In particular, I would like to acknowledge Susan Dunham, Susan B. Koonin, Carli Masia, Herb Somers, Robert Walkowiak III, and Michelle Wu for their work on earlier editions of the text.

I would also like to acknowledge the publishers who permitted me to reprint copyrighted material in this text:

For computer screen shots retrieved using Internet Explorer™ Microsoft product screen shots reprinted with permission from Microsoft Corporation.

Figure 1.3   Geographic boundaries of the federal courts of appeals
Reprinted with permission from Thomson West, West's *Federal Reporter*, 3d
Ser., Vol. 381 (2004), inside cover. © 2004 Thomson West.

Figure 3.1   Index to Am. Jur. 2d
Reprinted with permission from Thomson West, *American Jurisprudence*, 2d
Ed., General Index (2005), p. 226. © 2005 Thomson West.

Figure 3.2   Am. Jur. 2d main volume entry under False Imprisonment
Reprinted with permission from Thomson West, *American Jurisprudence*, 2d
Ed., Vol. 32 (1995), p. 46. © 1995 Thomson West.

Figure 3.3   Am. Jur. 2d pocket part entry for False Imprisonment
Reprinted with permission from Thomson West, *American Jurisprudence*, 2d
Ed., Vol. 32 Cumulative Supplement (2004), p. 5. © 2004 Thomson West.

Figure 3.4   Treatise main volume entry for False Imprisonment
Reprinted with permission from Oscar S. Gray. Fowler V. Harper, Fleming
James, Jr., & Oscar S. Gray, *The Law of Torts*, 3d Ed., Vol. 1 (1996), p. 3:23.
© 1996 Oscar S. Gray.

Figure 3.5   ILP index entry
Reprinted with permission from The H.W. Wilson Company, *Index to Legal
Periodicals*, Vol. 31 (1992), p. 269. © 1992 The H.W. Wilson Company.

Figure 3.6   ILP electronic citation list
From The H.W. Wilson Co., WilsonWeb, *Index to Legal Periodicals.* © 2005
The H.W. Wilson Co.

Figure 3.7   LegalTrac citation list
From *LegalTrac*, by Gale Group. Reprinted by permission of the Gale Group.

Figure 3.8   Starting page of an A.L.R. Annotation
Reprinted with permission from Thomson West, *American Law Reports*, 3d
Ser., Vol. 97 (1980), p. 688. © 1980 Thomson West.

Figure 3.9   Later page of an A.L.R. Annotation
Reprinted with permission from Thomson West, *American Law Reports*, 3d
Ser., Vol. 97 (1980), p. 693. © 1980 Thomson West.

Figure 3.10   Section 35 of the *Restatement (Second) of Torts*
© 1965 by The American Law Institute. Reproduced with permission. All rights
resevered. *Restatement (Second) of the Law of Torts*, 2d Ed., Vol. 1, § 35 (1965), p.
52.

Figure 3.11   Entry under § 35 in the Appendix to the *Restatement (Second) of
Torts*
© 2005 by The American Law Institute. Reproduced with permission. All rights
reserved. *Restatement (Second) of the Law of Torts*, 2d Ed., Appendix through
June 2004, §§ 1–309 (2005), p. 119.

Figure 4.2   Excerpt from *Popkin v. New York State*
Reprinted with permission from Thomson West, West's *Federal Reporter*, 2d
Ser., *Popkin v. New York State*, 547 F.2d 18–19 (2d Cir. 1976). © 1976
Thomson West.

Figure 4.3   Beginning of the West topic for "Innkeepers"
Reprinted with permission from Thomson West, *West's Federal Practice Digest*,
4th Ser., Vol. 63 (1998), p. 1. © 1998 Thomson West.

Figure 4.4   Case summary under the "Innkeepers" topic, key number 10.2
Reprinted with permission from Thomson West, *West's Federal Practice Digest*,
4th Ser., Vol. 63 (1998), p. 8. © 1998 Thomson West.

Figure 4.9   Excerpt from the Descriptive-Word Index
Reprinted with permission from Thomson West, *West's Federal Practice Digest*,
4th Ser., Descriptive-Word Index, Vol. 98A (2002), p. 235. © 2002 Thomson West.

Figure 4.10   Interim pamphlet closing table
Reprinted with permission from Thomson West, *West's Federal Practice Digest*,
4th Ser., December 2004 Pamphlet (2004), inside cover. © 2004 Thomson West.

Figure 4.11   Excerpt from the Table of Cases
Reprinted with permission from Thomson West, *West's Federal Practice Digest*,
4th Ser., Vol. 102B (2000), p. 283. © 2000 Thomson West.

Figure 4.12   Words and Phrases
Reprinted with permission from Thomson West, *West's Federal Practice Digest*,
4th Ser., Vol. 109 (1999), p. 334. © 1999 Thomson West.

Figure 4.13   Example of a case in Westlaw
Reprinted with permission of Thomson West, from Westlaw, 826 F.2d 1554. ©
2005 Thomson West.

Figure 4.14   Example of a case in LexisNexis
Reprinted with permission of LexisNexis, from LexisNexis, 826 F.2d 1554.

Figure 4.16   Descriptive-Word Index
Reprinted with permission from Thomson West, *West's Federal Practice Digest*,
4th Ser., Vol. 98A (2002), p. 82. © 2002 Thomson West.

Figure 4.17   Descriptive-Word Index
Reprinted with permission from Thomson West, *West's Federal Practice Digest*,
4th Ser., Vol. 98A (2002), p. 235. © 2002 Thomson West.

Figure 4.18   Descriptive-Word Index, pocket part
Reprinted with permission from Thomson West, *West's Federal Practice Digest*,
4th Ser., Cumulative Annual Pocket Part, Vol. 98A (2004), p. 41. © 2004
Thomson West.

Figure 4.19   Key number outline, "Innkeepers" topic
Reprinted with permission from Thomson West, *West's Federal Practice Digest*,
4th Ser., Vol. 63 (1998), pp. 1–2. © 1998 Thomson West.

Figure 4.20   Case summaries under "Innkeepers" topic
Reprinted with permission from Thomson West, *West's Federal Practice Digest*,
4th Ser., Vol. 63 (1998), pp. 8-9. © 1998 Thomson West.

Figure 4.21   Digest volume, pocket part
Reprinted with permission from Thomson West, *West's Federal Practice Digest*,
4th Ser., Pocket Part, Vol. 63 (2004), pp. 2–3. © 2004 Thomson West.

Figure 4.22   Noncumulative interim pamphlet
Reprinted with permission from Thomson West, *West's Federal Practice Digest*,
4th Ser., December 2004 Pamphlet (2004), p. 882. © 2004 Thomson West.

Figure 4.23   Noncumulative interim pamphlet, closing table
Reprinted with permission from Thomson West, *West's Federal Practice Digest*,
4th Ser., December 2004 Pamphlet (2004), inside cover. © 2004 Thomson West.

Figure 4.24   343 F. Supp. 2d, mini-digest
Reprinted with permission from Thomson West, West's *Federal Supplement*,
2d Ser., Vol. 343 (2004), p. 58 (key number digest). © 2004 Thomson West.

Figure 4.25   *McCarty v. Pheasant Run, Inc.,* 826 F.2d 1554 (7th Cir. 1987)
Reprinted with permission from Thomson West, West's *Federal Reporter*, 2d
Ser., Vol. 826 (1987), pp. 1554–1560. © 1987 Thomson West.

Figure 5.2   "What Your Library Should Contain"
Reproduced by permission of LexisNexis. Further reproduction of any kind is
strictly prohibited.
From *Shepard's Atlantic Reporter Citations*, Vol. 90, No. 5 (May 2005), cover
page.

Figure 5.3   Excerpt from *Shepard's Atlantic Reporter Citations*
Reproduced by permission of LexisNexis. Further reproduction of any kind is
strictly prohibited.
From *Shepard's Atlantic Reporter Citations*, 2005 Bound Volume, Part 8, p. 521.

Figure 5.4   SHEPARD'S® entry for *Kenney v. Scientific, Inc.*
Reproduced by permission of LexisNexis. Further reproduction of any kind is
strictly prohibited.
From *Shepard's Atlantic Reporter Citations*, 2005 Bound Volume, Part 8, p. 521.

Figure 5.6   SHEPARD'S® entry for *Kenney v. Scientific, Inc.*
Reproduced by permission of LexisNexis. Further reproduction of any kind is
strictly prohibited.
From *Shepard's Atlantic Reporter Citations*, 2005 Bound Volume, Part 8, p. 521.

Figure 6.2   8 U.S.C.A. § 1431
Reprinted with permission from Thomson West, *United States Code Annotated,*
Title 8 (1999), p. 326. © 1999 Thomson West.

Figure 6.4   Excerpt from the U.S.C.A. General Index
Reprinted with permission from Thomson West, *United States Code Annotated,*
2004 General Index C, p. 117. © 2004 Thomson West.

Figure 6.6   Annotations accompanying 8 U.S.C.A. § 1431
Reprinted with permission from Thomson West, *United States Code Annotated,*
Title 8 (1999), p. 327. © 1999 Thomson West.

Figure 6.7   Pocket part update for 8 U.S.C.A. § 1431
Reprinted with permission from Thomson West, *United States Code Annotated,*
2004 Cumulative Pocket Part, Title 8, p. 47. © 2004 Thomson West.

Figure 6.8   Noncumulative pamphlet entry for 8 U.S.C.A. § 1431
Reprinted with permission from Thomson West, *United States Code
Annotated*, Pamphlet Number 3 (January 2005), p. 270. © 2005 Thomson West.

Figure 6.9   FACE Act entry, popular name table
Reprinted with permission from Thomson West, *United States Code
Annotated*, 2004 Popular Name Table, p. 495. © 2004 Thomson West.

Figure 6.10   Conversion table entry for Pub. L. No. 103-259, the FACE Act
Reprinted with permission from Thomson West, Tables Vol. II, *United States
Code Annotated*, 2004, p. 648. © 2004 Thomson West.

Figure 6.11   SHEPARD'S® entry for a statute
Reproduced by permission of LexisNexis. Further reproduction of any kind is
strictly prohibited.
From *Shepard's Federal Statute Citations*, Vol. 3, 1996, p. 240.

Figure 6.12   Three screens showing portions of 8 U.S.C.A. § 1431 in Westlaw
Reprinted with permission from Thomson West, from Westlaw, 8 U.S.C.A.
§ 1431. © 2005 Thomson West.

Figure 6.13   Westlaw U.S.C.A. Table of Contents search screen
Reprinted with permission from Thomson West, from Westlaw, U.S.C.A.
Table of Contents search screen. © 2005 Thomson West.

Figure 6.14   Three screens showing portions of 8 U.S.C.S. § 1431 in
LexisNexis
Reprinted with permission of LexisNexis, from LexisNexis, 8 U.S.C.S. § 1431.

Figure 6.15   LexisNexis U.S.C.S. search screen
Reprinted with permission of LexisNexis. From LexisNexis, U.S.C.S. search
screen.

Figure 6.16   Excerpt from the U.S.C.A. General Index
Reprinted with permission from Thomson West, *United States Code Annotated*, 2004 General Index C, p. 117. © 2005 Thomson West.

Figure 6.17   Excerpt from chapter outline, Title 8, U.S.C.A.
Reprinted with permission from Thomson West, *United States Code Annotated*, Title 8 (1990), p. 5. © 1999 Thomson West.

Figure 6.18   8 U.S.C.A. § 1431
Reprinted with permission from Thomson West, *United States Code Annotated*, Title 8 (1999), p. 326. © 1999 Thomson West.

Figure 6.19   Annotations accompanying 8 U.S.C.A. § 1431
Reprinted with permission from Thomson West, *United States Code Annotated*, Title 8 (1999), pp. 327–328. © 1999 Thomson West.

Figure 6.20   Pocket part entry for 8 U.S.C.A. § 1431
Reprinted with permission from Thomson West, *United States Code Annotated*, 2004 Cumulative Annual Pocket Part, Title 8, pp. 47–49. © 2004 Thomson West.

Figure 6.21   Noncumulative supplement entry for 8 U.S.C.A. § 1431
Reprinted with permission from Thomson West, *United States Code Annotated*, Pamphlet Number 3 (January 2005), p. 270. © 2005 Thomson West.

Figure 6.22   *Vernon's Texas Statutes and Codes Annotated* General Index
Reprinted with permission from Thomson West, Vernon's *Texas Statutes and Codes Annotated*, 2003 General Index A–E, p. 240. © 2003 Thomson West.

Figure 6.23   Texas Civil Practice and Remedies Code § 93.001
Reprinted with permission from Thomson West, Vol. 4 Vernon's *Texas Codes Annotated*, Civil Practice and Remedies Code, Chapter 93, p. 142 (1997). © 1997 Thomson West.

Figure 6.24   Pocket part entry for Texas Civil Practice and Remedies Code § 93.001
Reprinted with permission from Thomson West, Vol. 4 Vernon's *Texas Codes Annotated*, Civil Practice and Remedies Code, Cumulative Annual Pocket Part, pp. 121–122 (2004). © 2004 Thomson West.

Figure 7.1   How a Bill Becomes a Law
Reprinted with permission from Congressional Quarterly Inc., *Congressional Quarterly's Guide to Congress*, CQ Press, 5th Ed. (2000), p. 1093. Copyright © 2004 CQ Press, a division of Congressional Quarterly Inc.

Figure 7.2   Excerpt from annotations accompanying 18 U.S.C.A. § 2441
Reprinted with permission from Thomson West, *United States Code Annotated*, Vol. 18 (2000), p. 14. © 2000 Thomson West.

Figure 7.3   Starting page, House Judiciary Committee Report on the War Crimes Act of 1996

Reprinted with permission from Thomson West, *United States Code Congressional and Administrative News*, 104th Congress-Second Session 1996, Vol. 5 (1997), p. 2166. © 1997 Thomson West.

Figure 7.4 CIS Legislative Histories entry for Pub. L. No. 104–192
Reprinted from *CIS/Annual* with permission. Copyright 1997 LexisNexis Academic and Library Solutions, a division of Reed Elsevier Inc. All Rights Reserved. *CIS/Annual 1996*, Legislative Histories of U.S. Public Laws (1997), p. 315.

Figure 7.5 CIS Index entry
Reprinted from *1995–1998 CIS Four-Year Cumulative Index* with permission. Copyright 1999 LexisNexis Academic and Library Solutions, a division of Reed Elsevier Inc. All Rights Reserved. *1995–1998 CIS Four-Year Cumulative Index* (1999), p. 2073.

Figure 7.6 CIS Abstracts entry
Reprinted from *CIS/Annual* with permission. Copyright 1997 LexisNexis Academic and Library Solutions, a division of Reed Elsevier Inc. All Rights Reserved. *CIS/Annual 1996*, Abstracts from Congressional Publications (1997), p. 207.

Figure 7.10 Introductory screen for LexisNexis Congressional
Reprinted with permission of LexisNexis Academic and Library Solutions, LexisNexis Congressional introductory screen.

Figure 7.11 Search options for Congressional publications in LexisNexis Congressional
Reprinted with permission of LexisNexis Academic and Library Solutions, LexisNexis Congressional search options.

Figure 7.12 18 U.S.C.A. § 2441 and accompanying annotations
Reprinted with permission from Thomson West, *United States Code Annotated*, Vol. 18 (2000), pp. 13–14. © 2000 Thomson West.

Figure 7.13 House Judiciary Committee report reprinted in U.S.C.C.A.N.
Reprinted with permission from Thomson West, *United States Code Congressional and Administrative News*, 104th Congress-Second Session 1996, Vol. 5 (1997), p. 2166. © 1997 Thomson West.

Figure 7.17 Search options, LexisNexis Congressional
Reprinted with permission of LexisNexis Academic and Library Solutions, LexisNexis Congressional search options.

Figure 7.18 Search options, LexisNexis Congressional
Reprinted with permission of LexisNexis Academic and Library Solutions, LexisNexis Congressional search options.

Figure 7.19 Search screen, LexisNexis Congressional
Reprinted with permission of LexisNexis Academic and Library Solutions, LexisNexis Congressional search screen.

Figure 7.20   Search results, LexisNexis Congressional
Reprinted with permission of LexisNexis Academic and Library Solutions, LexisNexis Congressional search results.

Figure 7.21   Abstracts entries from LexisNexis Congressional
Reprinted with permission of LexisNexis Academic and Library Solutions, LexisNexis Congressional abstracts entry.

Figure 7.22   House Judiciary Committee report retrieved from LexisNexis Congressional
Reprinted with permission of LexisNexis Academic and Library Solutions, LexisNexis Congressional house report.

Figure 8.2   Annotations to 15 U.S.C.S. § 2056
Reprinted from *United States Code Service, Lawyer's Edition* with permission. Copyright 1996 Mathew Bender & Company, Inc., a member of the LexisNexis Group. All Rights Reserved. *United States Code Service,* Title 15 Commerce and Trade §§ 1701–2800 (1996), p. 158.

Figure 8.10   SHEPARD'S® entry for 16 C.F.R. Part 1210
Reproduced by permission of LexisNexis. Further reproduction of any kind is strictly prohibited.
From *Shepard's Code of Federal Regulations Citations*, Titles 1–20; 2004, 4th Ed., Vol. 1, p. 546.

Figure 9.1   Search screen for the LawTRIO database
Reprinted with permission from Arlene L. Eis and Infosources Publishing (2005).

Figure 9.2   Search result in the LawTRIO database
Reprinted with permission from Arlene L. Eis and Infosources Publishing (2005).

Figure 9.3   Entry for a looseleaf service in the LawTRIO database.
Reprinted with permission from Arlene L. Eis and Infosources Publishing (2005).

Figure 9.4   Excerpt from the Overview, *BNA's Americans with Disabilities Act Manual*
Reproduced with permission from *BNA's Americans with Disabilities Act Manual*, pp. 10:0003–0004. Copyright 2004 by The Bureau of National Affairs, Inc. (800-372-1033) http://www.bna.com.

Figure 9.5   Excerpt from the Master Index, *BNA's Americans with Disabilities Act Manual*
Reproduced with permission from *BNA's Americans with Disabilities Act Manual*, p. Index-1. Copyright 2005 by The Bureau of National Affairs, Inc. (800-372-1033) http://www.bna.com.

Figure 9.6   Excerpt from Public Accommodations, *BNA's Americans with Disabilities Act Manual*
Reproduced with permission from *BNA's Americans with Disabilities Act Manual*, p. 30:0001. Copyright 2005 by The Bureau of National Affairs, Inc. (800-372-1033) http://www.bna.com.

Figure 9.7   28 C.F.R. Pt. 36, reprinted in *BNA's Americans with Disabilities Act Manual*
Reproduced with permission from *BNA's Americans with Disabilities Act Manual*, p. 70:0151. Copyright 2003 by The Bureau of National Affairs, Inc. (800-372-1033) http://www.bna.com.

Figure 9.8   Cumulative Digest and Index, BNA's A.D. Cases
Reproduced with permission from *Americans with Disabilities Cases Cumulative Digest and Index*, Table of Cases, Vol. 1–6 (1974–1997), pp. v–vi. Copyright 2002 by The Bureau of National Affairs, Inc. (800-372-1033) http://www.bna.com.

Figure 9.9   A.D. Cases Topic Finder
Reproduced with permission from *Americans with Disabilities Cases Cumulative Digest and Index*, Table of Cases, Vol. 1–6 (1974–1997), p. 51. Copyright 2002 by The Bureau of National Affairs, Inc. (800-372-1033) http://www.bna.com.

Figure 9.10   Case summaries, A.D. Cases Cumulative Digest and Index
Reproduced with permission from *Americans with Disabilities Cases Cumulative Digest and Index*, Table of Cases, Vol. 1–6 (1974–1997), p. 1527. Copyright 2002 by The Bureau of National Affairs, Inc. (800-372-1033) http://www.bna.com.

Figure 9.11   *Arnold v. United Artists Theatre Circuit*
Reproduced with permission from 5 A.D. Cases 685–86. Copyright 1996 by The Bureau of National Affairs, Inc. (800-372-1033) http://www.bna.com.

Figure 10.1   Westlaw search screen
Reprinted with permission from Thomson West, from Westlaw, search screen. © 2005 Thomson West.

Figure 10.2   LexisNexis search screen
Reprinted with permission of LexisNexis, from LexisNexis, search screen.

Figure 10.5   Westlaw search results
Reprinted with permission from Thomson West, from Westlaw, search results display. © 2005 Thomson West.

Figure 10.6   LexisNexis search results
Reprinted with permission of LexisNexis, from LexisNexis, search results display.

Figure 10.7   Online Resources, American Bankruptcy Institute web site
Reprinted with the permission of the American Bankruptcy Institute, www.abiworld.org.

Figure 10.8   Entry from the CAMLaw blog
Reprinted with permission from Complementary and Alternative Medicine
Law Blog (CAMLaw Blog), www.camlawblog.com, © 2004, LexBlog, Inc.

Figure 10.9   Introductory screens for FindLaw
Reprinted with permission. © 2005 FindLaw, Inc., from
http://www.findlaw.com.

Figure 10.10   Search options in FindLaw
Reprinted with permission. © 2005 FindLaw, Inc., from
http://www.findlaw.com/casecode.

Figure 10.11   Introductory screen, Legal Information Institute
Reprinted with permission. © 2005 Cornell Law School, from
http://www.law.cornell.edu.

Figure 10.12   Search options in Legal Information Institute
Reprinted with permission. © 2005 Cornell Law School, from
http://www.law.cornell.edu.

BASIC LEGAL RESEARCH

CHAPTER 1

INTRODUCTION TO LEGAL RESEARCH

A. Introduction to the legal system

B. Introduction to the process of legal research

C. Overview of print and electronic sources of legal authority

D. Introduction to legal citation

E. Overview of this text

What is legal research and why do you need to learn about it? Researching the law means finding the rules that govern conduct in our society. To be a successful lawyer, you need to know how to research the law. Lawyers are often called upon to solve problems and give advice, and to do that accurately, you must know the rules applicable to the different situations you and your clients will face. Clients may come to you after an event has occurred and ask you to pursue a remedy for a bad outcome, or perhaps defend them against charges that they have acted wrongfully. You may be asked to help a client accomplish a goal like starting a business or buying a piece of property. In these situations and many others, you will need to know your clients' rights and responsibilities, as defined by legal rules. Consequently, being proficient in legal research is essential to your success in legal practice.

As a starting point for learning about how to research the law, it is important to understand some of the different sources of legal rules. This chapter discusses what these sources are and where they originate within our legal system. It also provides an introduction to the process of legal research, an overview of some of the research tools you will learn to use, and an introduction to legal citation. Later chapters explain how to locate legal rules using a variety of resources.

A. INTRODUCTION TO THE LEGAL SYSTEM

1. SOURCES OF LAW

There are four main sources of law, which exist at both the state and federal levels:

- constitutions
- statutes
- court opinions (also called cases)
- administrative regulations.

A constitution establishes a system of government and defines the boundaries of authority granted to the government. The United States Constitution is the preeminent source of law in our legal system, and all other rules, whether promulgated by a state or the federal government, must comply with its requirements. Each state also has its own constitution. A state's constitution may grant greater rights than those secured by the federal constitution, but because a state constitution is subordinate to the federal constitution, it cannot provide lesser rights than the federal constitution does. All of a state's legal rules must comport with both the state and federal constitutions.

Since grade school, you have been taught that the United States Constitution created three branches of government: the legislative branch, which makes the laws; the judicial branch, which interprets the laws; and the executive branch, which enforces the laws. State governments are also divided into these three branches. Although this is elementary civics, this structure truly does define the way government authority is divided in our system of government.

The legislative branch of government creates statutes, which must be approved by the executive branch (the president, for federal statutes; the governor, for state statutes) to go into effect. The executive branch also makes rules. Administrative agencies, such as the federal Food and Drug Administration or a state's department of motor vehicles, are part of the executive branch. They execute the laws passed by the legislature and create their own regulations to carry out the mandates established by statute.

The judicial branch is the source of court opinions. Courts interpret rules created by the legislative and executive branches of government. If a court determines that a rule does not meet constitutional requirements, it can invalidate the rule. Otherwise, however, the court must apply the rule to the case before it. Court opinions can also be an independent source of legal rules. Legal rules made by courts are called "common-law" rules. Although courts are empowered to make these rules, legislatures can adopt legislation that changes or abolishes a common-law rule, as long as the legislation is constitutional.

FIGURE 1.1   BRANCHES OF GOVERNMENT AND LEGAL RULES

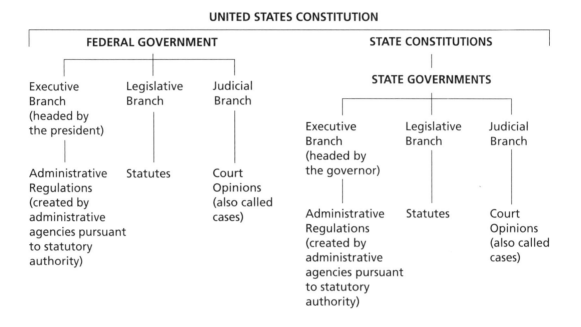

Figure 1.1 shows the relationships among the branches of government and the types of legal rules they create.

An example may be useful to illustrate the relationships among the rules created by the three branches of the federal government. As you know, the United States Constitution, through the First Amendment, guarantees the right to free expression. Congress could pass legislation requiring television stations to provide educational programming for children. The Federal Communications Commission (FCC) is the administrative agency within the executive branch that would have responsibility for carrying out Congress's will. If the statute were not specific about what constitutes educational programming or how much educational programming must be provided, the FCC would have to create administrative regulations to enforce the law. The regulations would provide the information not detailed in the statute, such as the definition of educational programming. A television station could challenge the statute and regulations by arguing to a court that prescribing the content of material that the station must broadcast violates the First Amendment. The court would then have to interpret the statute and regulations and decide whether they comply with the Constitution.

Another example illustrates the relationship between courts and legislatures in the area of common-law rules. The rules of negligence have been largely created by the courts. Therefore, liability for negligence is usually determined by common-law rules. A state supreme court could decide that a plaintiff who sues a defendant for negligence

cannot recover any damages if the plaintiff herself was negligent and contributed to her own injuries. This decision would create a common-law rule governing future cases of negligence within that state. The state legislature could step in and pass a statute that changes the rule. For example, the legislature could enact a statute providing that juries are to determine the percentage of negligence attributable to either party and to apportion damages accordingly, instead of completely denying recovery to the plaintiff. Courts in that state would then be obligated to apply the rule from the statute, not the former common-law rule.

Although these examples are simplified, they demonstrate the basic roles of each of the branches of government in enunciating the legal rules governing the conduct of society. They also demonstrate that researching a legal issue may require you to research several different types of legal authority. The answer to a research question may not be found exclusively in statutes or court opinions or administrative regulations. Often, these sources must be researched together to determine all of the rules applicable to a factual scenario.

2. TYPES AND WEIGHT OF AUTHORITY

One term used to describe the rules that govern conduct in society is "legal authority." Rules, however, are only one type of legal authority, and some types of legal authority are more authoritative than others. To understand how legal authority is categorized, you must be able to differentiate "primary" authority from "secondary" authority and "mandatory" authority from "persuasive" authority. Making these distinctions will help you determine the weight, or authoritative value, a legal authority carries with respect to the issue you are researching.

a. Primary vs. Secondary Authority and Mandatory vs. Persuasive Authority

Primary authority is the term used to describe rules of law. Primary authority includes all of the types of rules discussed so far in this chapter. Constitutional provisions, statutes, court opinions, and administrative regulations contain legal rules, and as a consequence, are primary authority. Because "the law" consists of legal rules, primary authority is sometimes described as "the law."

Secondary authority, by contrast, refers to commentary on the law or analysis of the law, but not "the law" itself. An opinion from the United States Supreme Court is primary authority, but an article written by a private party explaining and analyzing the opinion is secondary authority. Secondary authority is often quite useful in legal research because its analysis can help you understand complex legal issues and refer you to primary authority. Nevertheless, secondary

authority is not "the law" and therefore is distinguished from primary authority.

Mandatory and persuasive authority are terms courts use to categorize the different sources of law they use in making their decisions. Mandatory authority, which can also be called binding authority, refers to authority that the court is obligated to follow. Mandatory authority contains rules that you must apply to determine the correct answer to the issue you are researching. Persuasive authority, which can also be called nonbinding authority, refers to authority that the court may follow if it is persuaded to do so, but is not required to follow. Persuasive authority, therefore, will not dictate the answer to an issue, although it may help you figure out the answer. Whether an authority is mandatory or persuasive depends on several factors, as discussed in the next section.

b. Weight of Authority

The degree to which an authority controls the answer to a legal issue is called the weight of the authority. Not all authorities have the same weight. The weight of a legal authority depends on its status as primary or secondary authority and as mandatory or persuasive authority. Some primary authorities are mandatory, and others are persuasive. Secondary authority, by contrast, is always persuasive authority. You must be able to distinguish among these categories of authority, therefore, to determine how much weight a particular legal authority has in the resolution of the issue you are researching.

(1) Secondary authority: Always persuasive
A legal authority's status as a primary or secondary authority is fixed. An authority is either part of "the law," or it is not. Because secondary authority is always persuasive authority, it is not binding. Once you identify an authority as secondary, you can be certain that it will not control the outcome of the issue you are researching.

Although secondary authority is not binding, some secondary authorities are more persuasive than others. Some are so respected that a court, while not technically bound by them, would need a good reason to depart from or reject their statements of legal rules. Others do not enjoy the same degree of respect, leaving a court free to ignore or reject such authorities if it is not persuaded to follow them. Further discussion of the persuasive value of various secondary authorities appears in Chapter 3, on secondary source research. The important thing to remember for now is that secondary authority is always categorized as persuasive or nonbinding authority.

(2) Primary authority: Sometimes mandatory; sometimes persuasive
Sometimes primary authority is mandatory, or binding, authority, and sometimes it is not. You must be able to evaluate the authority to determine

whether it is binding on the issue you are researching. One factor affecting whether a primary authority is mandatory is jurisdiction. The rules contained in primary authority apply only to conduct occurring within the jurisdiction in which the authority is in force. For example, all laws in the United States must comport with the federal constitution because it is primary authority that is mandatory, or binding, in all United States jurisdictions. The New Jersey constitution is also primary authority because it contains legal rules establishing the scope of state government authority, but it is mandatory authority only in New Jersey. The New Jersey constitution's rules do not apply in Illinois or Michigan.

Determining the weight of court opinions is a little more complex. All court opinions are primary authority. Whether a particular opinion is mandatory or persuasive is a function not only of jurisdiction, but also level of court. To understand how these factors work together, it is easiest to consider level of court first and jurisdiction second.

(i) Determining the weight of court opinions: Level of court
The judicial branches of government in all states and in the federal system have multiple levels of courts. Trial courts are at the bottom of the judicial hierarchy. In the federal system, the United States District Courts are trial-level courts, and each state has at least one federal district court. Intermediate appellate courts hear appeals of trial court cases. Most, but not all, states have intermediate appellate courts. In the federal system, the intermediate courts are called United States Circuit Courts of Appeals. There are thirteen federal circuits: eleven numbered circuits (First through Eleventh), the District of Columbia Circuit, and the Federal Circuit. The highest court or court of last resort is often called the supreme court. It hears appeals of cases from the intermediate appellate courts or directly from trial courts in states that do not have intermediate appellate courts. In the federal system, of course, the court of last resort is the United States Supreme Court.

Trial court opinions, including those from federal district courts, are not mandatory authority. These opinions bind the parties to the cases but do not bind other courts considering similar cases. They are persuasive authority.

The opinions of intermediate appellate courts bind the courts below them. In other words, intermediate appellate opinions are mandatory authority for the trial courts subordinate to them in the court structure. The weight of intermediate appellate opinions on intermediate appellate courts varies by jurisdiction. Some have the ability to overrule their own prior opinions; others do not. Intermediate appellate opinions are persuasive authority for the court of last resort.

The court of last resort may, but is not required to, follow the opinions of the courts below it. The opinions of the court of last resort, however, are mandatory authority for both intermediate appellate courts

FIGURE 1.2 STRUCTURE OF THE FEDERAL COURT SYSTEM AND MOST STATE COURT SYSTEMS

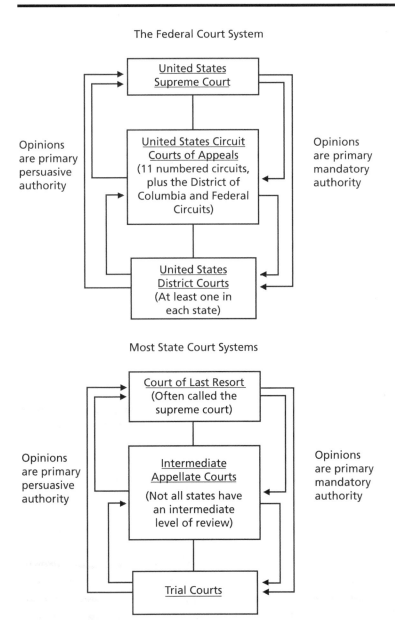

The Federal Court System

United States
Supreme Court

Opinions
are primary
persuasive
authority

United States Circuit
Courts of Appeals
(11 numbered circuits,
plus the District of
Columbia and Federal
Circuits)

Opinions
are primary
mandatory
authority

United States
District Courts
(At least one in
each state)

Most State Court Systems

Court of Last Resort
(Often called the
supreme court)

Opinions
are primary
persuasive
authority

Intermediate
Appellate Courts

(Not all states have
an intermediate
level of review)

Opinions
are primary
mandatory
authority

Trial Courts

and trial courts subordinate to it in the court structure. The court of last resort is not bound by its own prior opinions but will be reluctant to change an earlier ruling without a compelling justification for doing so.

Figure 1.2 illustrates the structures of federal and state court systems and shows how level of court affects the weight of opinions issued at each level.

FIGURE 1.3   GEOGRAPHIC BOUNDARIES OF THE FEDERAL COURTS OF APPEALS

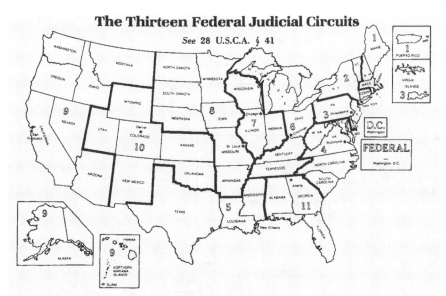

Reprinted with permission from Thomson West, West's *Federal Reporter*, 3d Ser., Vol. 381 (2004), inside cover. © 2004 Thomson West.

(ii) Determining the weight of court opinions: Jurisdiction
The second factor affecting the weight of court opinions is jurisdiction. As with other forms of primary authority, rules stated in court opinions are mandatory authority only within the court's jurisdiction. An opinion from the Texas Supreme Court is mandatory only for a court applying Texas law. A California court deciding a question of California law would consider the Texas opinion persuasive authority. If the California court had to decide a new issue not previously addressed by mandatory California authority (an "issue of first impression"), it might choose to follow the Texas Supreme Court's opinion if it found the opinion persuasive.

On questions of federal law, opinions of the United States Supreme Court are mandatory authority for all other courts because it has nation-wide jurisdiction. An opinion from a circuit court of appeals is manda-tory only within the circuit that issued the opinion and is persuasive everywhere else. Thus, a decision of the United States Court of Appeals for the Eleventh Circuit would be binding within the Eleventh Circuit, but not within the Seventh Circuit. **Figure 1.3** shows the geographic boundaries of the federal circuit courts of appeal.

In considering the weight of a court opinion, it is important to remember that the federal government and each state constitute different jurisdictions. On questions of state law, each state's courts get the last

word, and on questions of federal law, the federal courts get the last word. For an issue governed by state law, the opinions of the courts within the relevant state are mandatory authority. For an issue governed by federal law, the opinions of the relevant federal courts are mandatory authority.

Ordinarily, understanding how jurisdiction affects weight of authority is fairly intuitive. When a Massachusetts trial court is resolving a case arising out of conduct that took place in Massachusetts, it will treat the opinions of the Massachusetts Supreme Judicial Court as mandatory authority. Sometimes, however, a court has to resolve a case governed by the law of another jurisdiction. State courts sometimes decide cases governed by the law of another state or by federal law. Federal courts sometimes decide cases governed by state law. When that happens, the court deciding the case will treat the law of the controlling jurisdiction as mandatory authority.

For example, assume that the United States District Court for the Western District of Texas, a federal trial court, had to decide a case concerning breach of a contract to build a house in El Paso, Texas. Contract law is, for the most part, established by the states. To resolve this case, the federal court would apply the contract law of the state where the dispute arose, in this case, Texas. The Texas Supreme Court's opinions on contract law would be mandatory authority for resolving the case. Now assume that the same court had to decide a case concerning immigration law. Immigration law is established by the federal government. To resolve the case, the court would apply federal law. The opinions of the United States Supreme Court and the United States Court of Appeals for the Fifth Circuit would be mandatory authority for resolving the case.

This discussion provides an overview of some common principles governing the weight of authority. These principles are subject to exceptions and nuances not addressed here. Entire fields of study are devoted to resolving questions of jurisdiction, procedure, and conflicts regarding which legal rules apply to various types of disputes. As you begin learning about research, however, these general principles will be sufficient to help you determine the weight of the authority you locate to resolve a research issue.

Figure 1.4 illustrates the relationships among the different types of authority.

B. INTRODUCTION TO THE PROCESS OF LEGAL RESEARCH

Legal research is not a linear process. Most research projects do not have an established series of steps that must be followed sequentially until the answer to your question is uncovered. Although there are certain steps

FIGURE 1.4   TYPES OF AUTHORITY

TYPE OF AUTHORITY	MANDATORY (BINDING)	PERSUASIVE (NONBINDING)
PRIMARY (legal rules)	Constitutional provisions, statutes, and regulations in force within a jurisdiction are mandatory authority for courts within the same jurisdiction. Decisions from higher courts within a jurisdiction are mandatory authority for lower courts within the same jurisdiction.	Decisions from courts within one jurisdiction are persuasive authority for courts within another jurisdiction. Decisions from lower courts within a jurisdiction are persuasive authority for higher courts within the same jurisdiction.
SECONDARY (anything that is not primary authority; usually commentary on the law)	Secondary authority is *not* mandatory authority.	Secondary authority is persuasive authority.

that you will ordinarily take with any research project, the starting, middle, and ending points will vary. When you know little or nothing about the issue you are researching, you will begin your research differently than if you were working on an issue about which you already had substantial background knowledge. One of the goals of this book is to help you learn to assess the appropriate starting, middle, and ending points for your research.

With most research projects, there are two preliminary steps that you will want to take before heading out on your search for authority: defining the scope of your project and generating search terms. In the first step, you will want to think about what you are being asked to do. Are you being asked to spend three weeks locating all information from every jurisdiction on a particular subject, or do you have a day to find out how courts in one state have ruled on an issue? Will you write an extensive analysis of your research, or will you summarize the results orally to the person who made the assignment? Evaluating the type of work product you are expected to produce, the amount of time you have, and the scope of the project will help you determine the best way to proceed. The second step is generating search terms to use to search for information in various research tools. Chapter 2 discusses different

ways to do this. In general, however, you will need to construct a list of words or concepts to look up in an index, table of contents, or computer database to locate information relevant to your issue.

Once you have accomplished these preliminary steps, you need to decide which research tool to use as the starting point for your research. You will also need to think about other probable sources of information and the sequence in which you plan to research those sources. The more you know about your research issue going in, the easier it will be to plan the steps. The less you know, the more flexible you will need to be in your approach. If you do not find any information, or find too much information, you may need to backtrack or rethink your approach.

To plan your research path, it may be useful for you to think about three categories of authority: secondary authority, primary mandatory authority, and primary persuasive authority. Your goal in most research projects will be to locate primary mandatory authority, if it exists, on your research issue. If primary mandatory authority is not available or does not directly answer your research question, persuasive authority (either primary or secondary) may help you analyze the issue. For any given research project, you will need to determine the order in which you will research these three types of authority.

Because your goal will usually be to locate primary mandatory authority, you might think that you should begin your research with those sources. In fact, sometimes you will begin by researching primary mandatory authority, but that is not always the case. Secondary authorities that cite, analyze, and explain the law can provide a very efficient way to obtain background information and references to primary authority. Although they are not controlling in your analysis, they are invaluable research tools and can be a good starting point for your project. Persuasive primary authority will rarely provide a good starting place because it provides neither the controlling rules nor analysis explaining the law. **Figure 1.5** shows the relationships among these three categories of authority.

Once you determine which category of authority to begin with, you need to decide which individual sources within the category to consult. In making this decision, it is important to bear in mind that many research sources are linked together. Once you find information in one source, research notes within that source may refer you to other relevant sources. Thus, there may be more than one source that would be an appropriate starting point for your research. The trick is to be able to determine for any given research project which source is most likely to lead you in the right direction the most quickly. This book will explain the features of a wide range of research sources so you can learn to make this assessment for different types of research projects.

FIGURE 1.5   WHERE TO BEGIN YOUR RESEARCH PROJECT

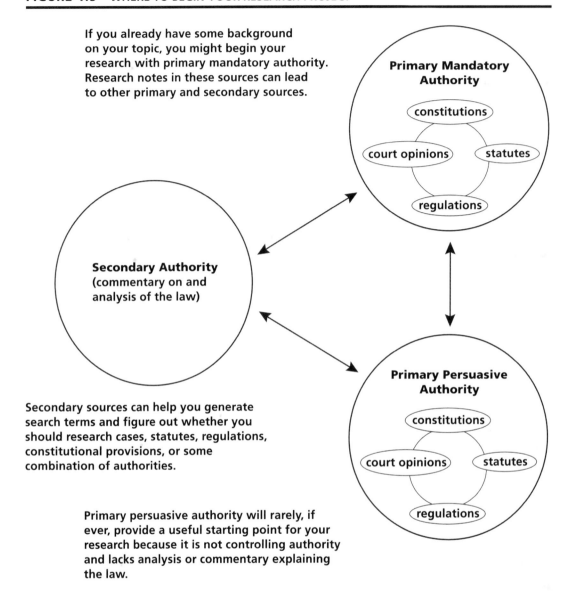

If you already have some background on your topic, you might begin your research with primary mandatory authority. Research notes in these sources can lead to other primary and secondary sources.

Primary Mandatory Authority

constitutions

court opinions   statutes

regulations

Secondary Authority (commentary on and analysis of the law)

Secondary sources can help you generate search terms and figure out whether you should research cases, statutes, regulations, constitutional provisions, or some combination of authorities.

Primary Persuasive Authority

constitutions

court opinions   statutes

regulations

Primary persuasive authority will rarely, if ever, provide a useful starting point for your research because it is not controlling authority and lacks analysis or commentary explaining the law.

C. OVERVIEW OF PRINT AND ELECTRONIC SOURCES OF LEGAL AUTHORITY

Many of the primary and secondary authorities you will learn to research are available from a variety of sources. They may be published in one or more books. Many are now also available in electronic form. Electronic research services may include commercial databases that charge each user a fee for access; Internet and CD-ROM subscription

services that libraries pay to access, but that are free to library patrons; and Internet sources available to anyone with a modem and a web browser. As noted earlier, legal research often requires research into several different types of legal authority. Therefore, you will need to learn how to use a variety of tools to be able to research effectively.

The chapters that follow explain how to use both print and electronic research tools to locate various types of legal authority. Sometimes print sources will provide the easiest and most efficient means of accessing the information you need. In other circumstances, electronic sources may provide a better avenue for research. The tools you use will depend on a number of factors, including the resources available in your library, the amount of time you have for your project, the depth of research you need to do, and the amount of money your client can spend. Often, you will find that the best way to accomplish your research is to use some combination of print and electronic tools.

Print research tools are generally organized by type of authority and jurisdiction. Thus, court opinions from Maryland will be in one set of books (called "reporters"), and those from Massachusetts will be in another set of reporters. The same holds true for print collections of statutes and other types of legal authority. Within each set of books, individual authorities, such as a case or statutory provision, can be located in one of two ways: by citation or by subject.

Each authority within a book will have a citation assigned to it. Once you know the citation, you can go directly to the appropriate book and locate the authority. For example, each court opinion is identified by a citation containing the volume number of the reporter in which it is published, the name of the reporter, and the starting page of the opinion. If you had the citation for a case, you could go to the library and locate it within a matter of minutes.

Of course, with most research projects, you will not know the citations to the authorities you need to find. You will have been sent to the library to find out which legal authorities, if any, pertain to the subject of your research project. In those situations, you will need to research information by subject, using either the index or table of contents accompanying each research tool to see what information you can find.

One challenge in researching with print sources is making sure the information is current. Most print research sources consist of hardcover books that can be difficult to update when the law changes. Some print tools are published in chronological order. For those tools, new books are published periodically as new material is compiled. Many, however, are organized by subject. For those tools, publishers cannot print new books every time the law changes. This would be prohibitively expensive, and because the law can change at any time, the new books would likely be out of date as soon as they were printed. To keep the books up to date, therefore, many print sources are updated with softcover pamphlets

containing new information that became available after the hardcover book was published. These supplementary pamphlets are often called "pocket parts" because many of them fit into a "pocket" in the inside back cover of the hardcover book. You will see pocket parts mentioned throughout this text in reference to print research tools.

Electronic research tools are organized somewhat differently. Not all electronic resources are divided by jurisdiction and type of authority. Some provide access to only one type of authority, while others provide access to multiple types of authority from many different jurisdictions. In addition, most electronic resources fall into one of two general categories: index services and services containing the full text of various legal authorities (full-text services). Both index and full-text services will allow you to conduct "word searches" that locate documents containing words you specify. Some also allow you to search by subject. The results of the search, however, will differ depending on which type of service you are using. An index service will generate a list of citations to legal authorities containing the words in your search, but you would need to go to print or other electronic sources to obtain the full text of the documents. In a full-text service, you have the choice of viewing either a list of citations or the full text of the documents retrieved from your search. Full-text services will also allow you to retrieve a document from its citation or browse a publication's table of contents, much as you would in a print resource.

The two most commonly used commercial databases are Westlaw and LexisNexis. These are full-text services with databases that allow you to access all of the types of legal authority discussed in this chapter. They charge subscribers for use of their services, although your law school probably subsidizes the cost of student research while you are in school. Other commercial and government-operated research services also provide access to legal authority. LexisNexis, Westlaw, and other electronic research services are discussed throughout this text.

D. INTRODUCTION TO LEGAL CITATION

When you present the results of your research in written form, you will need to include citations to the legal authorities you have found. One place to find the rules for citing legal authority is *The Bluebook: A Uniform System of Citation* (18th ed. 2005). Another source for rules on citation is the *ALWD Citation Manual: A Professional System of Citation* (3d ed. 2006). The citation rules in these two sources overlap to a large degree, but they are not identical. You should use whichever citation manual your professor directs you to use.

This text provides information on citations in both *Bluebook* and *ALWD Manual* format. This section provides a brief overview of the organization of both citation manuals and will make the most sense

if you have your citation manual in front of you as you read. Later chapters contain instructions for citing individual sources of legal authority. In many cases, the citation rules in the *Bluebook* and the *ALWD Manual* will be identical. Where there are differences, this text will alert you to that fact.

1. THE *BLUEBOOK*

The first part of the *Bluebook* that you should review is the Introduction. This section explains how the *Bluebook* is organized. As you will see when you review the Introduction, the *Bluebook* contains two sets of instructions for citing authority: "basic" citation rules used in legal practice and more complex rules used for citations in law journals. The "basic" citation rules apply to the types of documents most students write in their first year of law school, such as briefs and memoranda. The remainder of the citation rules apply primarily to law journals, a type of secondary source discussed in more detail in Chapter 3, although some aspects of these rules may also apply to practice documents. You are unlikely to write documents in law journal format at the beginning of your legal studies; therefore, you will want to focus your attention on the format for citations in briefs, memoranda, and other similar legal documents.

Learning to cite authority in *Bluebook* format requires you to become familiar with five items.

- the Bluepages and corresponding Bluepages Tables
- the text of the citation rules
- the Tables
- the Quick Reference examples on the inside front and back covers
- the Table of Contents and Index

THE BLUEPAGES AND CORRESPONDING BLUEPAGES TABLES. The Bluepages section summarizes the rules for citing legal authority in briefs, memoranda, and legal documents other than law journals. This section contains general information applicable to any type of citation, such as the uses of citations in legal writing. It also contains specific instructions for citing cases, statutes, secondary sources, and other forms of authority, as well as examples of many types of citations. The Bluepages Table BT.1 contains the abbreviations for words commonly found in the titles of court documents. In addition, because some jurisdictions have their own "local" citation rules that supplement or supersede the *Bluebook* rules, Table BT.2 refers you to sources for local citation rules.

THE TEXT OF THE CITATION RULES. Most of the *Bluebook* is devoted to explaining the rules for citing different types of authority. These rules

appear in the white pages in the middle of the *Bluebook* and can be divided into five categories:

1. Rules 1 through 9 are general rules applicable to a citation to any type of authority. For example, Rule 5 discusses the proper format for quotations.
2. Rules 10 through 17 contain rules for citing various primary and secondary authorities published in print. For example, Rule 10 explains how to cite a court opinion, and Rule 12 explains how to cite a statute.
3. Rule 18 contains rules for citing authorities published in electronic format.
4. Rule 19 contains rules for citing authorities published in subject-matter services. Subject-matter services are explained in Chapter 9 of this text.
5. Rules 20 and 21 contain rules for citing foreign and international materials. This text does not discuss foreign or international materials.

Some of the material contained in the rules is summarized in the Bluepages. If the information you need for the authority you are citing is contained in the Bluepages, you may not need to consult the individual rules in the white pages. If you face a citation question not addressed in the Bluepages, however, you should consult the individual rules for more detailed guidance. Most of the rules for citing specific types of legal authority begin with a description of the elements necessary for a full citation. The remainder of the rule will explain each component in greater detail.

Frequently, the rule will be accompanied by examples. Although this might seem like it would simplify things, in fact, sometimes it just complicates the citation. This is because the examples in the white pages are in the typefaces (e.g., italics, large and small capital letters) required for law journals. These typefaces are not always used in other types of legal documents. Therefore, although the examples in the white pages of the *Bluebook* will be somewhat useful to you in understanding how to cite legal authority, you cannot rely on them exclusively. The instructions in Bluepages B13 explain the differences between typeface conventions for citations in law journal and other documents.

THE TABLES. The Tables appear in the white pages with blue borders at the back of the *Bluebook*. The citation rules in the Bluepages and white pages explain the general requirements for different types of citations. Most of these rules require that certain words be abbreviated. The Tables contain abbreviations necessary for proper citations.[1] For example, Table T.1 lists

---

[1]Citations in *ALWD Manual* format also require abbreviations. The *Bluebook* and the *ALWD Manual* use identical abbreviations for many words. Some abbreviations vary, however, depending on which format you use.

each jurisdiction in the United States, and under each jurisdiction, it shows the proper abbreviations for citations to that jurisdiction's cases and statutes. Whenever you have a citation that includes an abbreviation, you will need to check the appropriate Table to find the precise abbreviation required for a proper citation. You should note, however, that the type styles of some of the abbreviations in the Tables are in law journal format and may need be modified according to Bluepages B13 for the work you will produce in your first year of law school.

THE QUICK REFERENCE EXAMPLES ON THE INSIDE FRONT AND BACK COVERS. On the inside front and back covers of the *Bluebook* you will find Quick Reference examples of different types of citations. The examples on the inside front cover are in the format for law review and journal footnotes and will be of little or no use to you in your first year of law school. The examples on the inside back cover are in the proper format for the types of documents you are likely to draft in your first year.

THE TABLE OF CONTENTS AND INDEX. As noted above, the Bluepages should be your starting point for determining how to construct a citation in *Bluebook* format. If you cannot find what you need in the Bluepages, you can find individual citation rules using the Table of Contents at the beginning of the *Bluebook* or the Index at the end. The Index references in black type refer to the pages with relevant rules. Those in blue type refer to examples of citations.

All of the pieces of the *Bluebook* work together to help you determine the proper citation format for a legal authority:

1. Use the Bluepages to find citation instructions governing the authority you want to cite.
2. If the Bluepages do not contain all the information you need for the citation, use the Index or Table of Contents to find the relevant rule in the white pages.
3. Use the Tables to find abbreviations and other information necessary for a complete citation.
4. If necessary, convert the typefaces in the rule examples and Tables into the proper format for briefs and memoranda according to Bluepages B13.
5. Use the Quick Reference guide on the inside back cover for additional examples of citations.

As you read the remaining chapters in this book, you will find more specific information about citing individual legal authorities. In general, however, you will be able to figure out how to cite almost any type of authority in *Bluebook* format by following these five steps.

2. THE *ALWD* MANUAL

The first part of the *ALWD Manual* that you should review is Part 1, Introductory Material. This section explains what citations are and how to use them, how to use the *ALWD Manual,* how local citation rules can affect citation format, and how your word processor's settings may affect citations. It explains the *ALWD Manual*'s organization clearly, so it would be redundant to repeat all of that information here. Nevertheless, a few comments on the *ALWD Manual* may be useful as you begin learning about it.

Perhaps the biggest difference between the *ALWD Manual* and the *Bluebook* is that the *ALWD Manual* uses the same citation format for all documents. The *Bluebook,* by contrast, uses one format for citations in law journal footnotes and another for practice documents like briefs and memoranda. When you are using the *ALWD Manual,* you do not need to convert any of the citations into different formats for different documents.

As you will see when you review Part 1, learning to cite authority in *ALWD Manual* format requires you to become familiar with five items:

- the Table of Contents and Index
- the text of the citation rules
- the Appendices
- the "Fast Formats"
- the ALWD web site.

THE TABLE OF CONTENTS AND INDEX. To locate individual citation rules, you can use the Table of Contents at the beginning of the *ALWD Manual* or the Index at the end. Unless otherwise indicated, the references in the Index are to rule numbers, not page numbers or specific examples.

THE TEXT OF THE CITATION RULES. Most of the *ALWD Manual* is devoted to explaining the rules for citing different types of authority. The rules are divided into the following Parts:

1. Part 2 (with Rules 1 through 11) contains general rules applicable to a citation to any type of authority. For example, Rule 3 discusses spelling and capitalization.
2. Part 3 (with Rules 12 through 37) contains rules for citing various primary and secondary authorities available in print. For example, Rule 12 governs citations to court opinions, and Rule 14 governs citations to statutes.
3. Part 4 (with Rules 38 through 42) contains rules for citing authorities published in electronic format.

4. Part 5 (with Rules 43 through 46) contains rules for incorporating citations into documents.

5. Part 6 (with Rules 47 through 49) contains rules regarding quotations.

At the beginning of each citation rule in Parts 3 and 4, you will find a description of the elements necessary for a full citation, followed by an annotated example showing how all of the elements fit together to create a complete citation. You should read this part of the rule first. The remainder of the rule will explain each component in greater detail.

Within the text of each rule in the *ALWD Manual,* you will find cross-references to other citation rules and to Appendices containing additional information that you may need for a complete citation. An explanation of the Appendices appears below.

You will also find "Sidebars" in some rules. The "Sidebars" are literally asides on citation. They provide information about sources of legal authority, help you avoid common citation errors, and offer citation tips.

THE APPENDICES. The *ALWD Manual* contains eight Appendices that follow the Parts containing the citation rules. The citation rules in Parts 3 and 4 explain the general requirements for citations to different types of authority. Most of these rules require that certain words be abbreviated. Appendices 1, 3, 4, and 5 contain abbreviations necessary for proper citations. For example, Appendix 1 lists Primary Sources by Jurisdiction. It lists each jurisdiction in the United States, and under each jurisdiction, it shows the proper abbreviations for citations to that jurisdiction's cases and statutes. Whenever you have a citation that includes an abbreviation, you will need to check the appropriate Appendix to find the precise abbreviation required for a proper citation.[2]

Appendix 2 contains local court citation rules. Some courts require special citation formats for authorities cited in documents filed with those courts. The *ALWD Manual* includes these rules in Appendix 2, so you do not have to look them up in another source if you need to use them.

Appendix 6 contains an example of a memorandum with citations included. This example can help you see how citations are integrated into a document.

Appendix 7 contains information on citations to federal taxation materials, and Appendix 8 contains information on selected federal administrative publications.

---

[2]Citations in *Bluebook* format also require abbreviations. The *ALWD Manual* and the *Bluebook* use identical abbreviations for many words. Some abbreviations differ, however, depending on which format you use.

THE FAST FORMATS. Before the text of each rule for citing an individual type of authority in Parts 3 and 4, you will find a section called "Fast Formats." The "Fast Formats" provide citation examples for each rule, in addition to the examples interwoven with the text of the rule. A "Fast Formats Locator" appears on the inside front cover of the *ALWD Manual.* You can use this alphabetical list to find "Fast Formats" pages without going to the Table of Contents or Index.

THE ALWD WEB SITE. Updates to the *ALWD Manual* are posted on the Internet. The Internet address is listed in Appendix A at the end of this text, as well as in Part 1 of the *ALWD Manual.*

All of the pieces of the *ALWD Manual* work together to help you determine the proper citation format for a legal authority:

1. Use the Table of Contents or Index to find the rule governing the authority you want to cite.
2. Read the rule, beginning with the components of a full citation at the beginning of the rule.
3. Use the Appendices to find additional information necessary for a correct citation.
4. Use the "Fast Formats" preceding the rule for additional examples of citations.
5. If necessary, check the web site for any updates.

As you read the remaining chapters in this book, you will find more specific information about citing individual legal authorities. In general, however, you will be able to figure out how to cite almost any type of authority in *ALWD Manual* format by following these five steps.

E. OVERVIEW OF THIS TEXT

Because different research projects have different starting and ending points, it is not necessary that you follow the chapters in this book in order. The sequence of assignments in your legal research class will determine the order in which you need to cover the material in this book.

Although you may not cover the chapters in order, a brief overview of the organization of this text may provide useful context for the material that follows. As noted earlier, Chapter 2 discusses how to generate search terms, one of the first steps in any research project. Secondary sources are covered next in Chapter 3. Chapters 4 through 8 explain how to research different types of primary authority, and Chapter 9 discusses how to use specialized research tools to locate both secondary and primary authority in specific subject areas of the law.

Chapters 3 through 9 are organized in a similar way. They all begin with an overview of the type of authority discussed. Then you will find an explanation of the print research process, followed by a description of electronic research sources. The material on print and electronic research will include excerpts from various research tools to highlight some of their key features. After the discussion of the research process, you will find information on citation format. The next item in each of these chapters is a section of sample pages. The sample pages contain step-by-step illustrations of the research process described earlier in the chapter. As you read through the text, you may find it helpful to review both the excerpts within the chapter and the sample pages section to get a sense of the research process for each type of authority. These chapters conclude with research checklists that summarize the research process and may be helpful to you as you work in the library.

Chapter 10 discusses general techniques for electronic research. The process of using print research sources varies according to the type of authority you are researching, which is why the preceding chapters largely focus on individual types of authority. With electronic research, however, there are certain common search techniques that can be used to research many types of authority. As a consequence, the discussion of electronic research in Chapters 3 through 9 focuses on where to locate legal authority using electronic resources, leaving most of the "how" of electronic research to Chapter 10. If you are learning about print and electronic research simultaneously, you should read Chapter 10 early in your studies. If you are learning about print research first, save Chapter 10 until you begin instruction in electronic research. When you begin learning about electronic research, you may also want to review Appendix A at the end of the text, which lists a number of Internet research sites.

The final chapter, Chapter 11, discusses research strategy and explains how to create a research plan. You do not need to read all of the preceding chapters before reading Chapter 11, although you may find Chapter 11 easier to follow after you have some background on a few research sources. Learning about research involves more than simply learning how to locate individual types of authority. You must also be able to plan a research strategy that will lead to accurate research results, and you must be able to execute your research strategy efficiently and economically. Chapter 11 sets out a process that will help you achieve these goals in any research project, whether in your legal research class or in legal practice.

CHAPTER 2

GENERATING SEARCH TERMS

> A. Generating search terms based on categories of information
>
> B. Expanding the initial search

All research sources, whether print or electronic, are indexed in some way. With print resources, you might use a subject index or a table of contents to locate information. With electronic resources, you might use word searches to find documents containing particular terms. No matter where you begin your search for authority, one of the first steps in the research process is generating a list of words that are likely to lead you through each resource's indexing system. This chapter discusses how to generate a useful list of search terms.

A. GENERATING SEARCH TERMS BASED ON CATEGORIES OF INFORMATION

When presented with a set of facts, you could generate a list of search terms by constructing a random list of words that seem relevant to the issue. But a more structured approach—working from a set of categories, instead of random terms that sound relevant—will help ensure that you are covering all of your bases in conducting your research.

There are a number of ways that you could categorize the information in your research issue to create a list of search terms. Some people prefer to use the six questions journalists ask when covering a story: who, what, when, where, why, and how. Another way to generate search terms is to categorize the information presented by the facts as follows.

■ **THE *PARTIES* INVOLVED IN THE PROBLEM, DESCRIBED ACCORDING TO THEIR RELATIONSHIPS TO EACH OTHER.**
Here, you might be concerned not only with parties who are in direct conflict with each other, but also any other individuals, entities, or groups involved. These might include fact witnesses who can testify as

to what happened, expert witnesses if appropriate to the situation, other potential plaintiffs (in civil cases), or other potential defendants (in criminal or civil cases).

In describing the parties, proper names will not ordinarily be useful search terms, although if one party is a public entity or corporation, you might be able to locate other cases in which the entity or corporation was a party. Instead, you will usually want to describe the parties in terms of their legal status or relationships to each other, such as landlords and tenants, parents and children, employers and employees, or doctors and patients.

■ **THE *PLACES AND THINGS* INVOLVED IN THE PROBLEM.**
In thinking about place, both geographical locale and type of location can be important. For example, the conduct at issue might have taken place in Pennsylvania, which would help you determine which jurisdiction's law applies. It might also have taken place at a school or in a church, which could be important for determining which legal rules apply to the situation.

"Things" can involve tangible objects or intangible concepts. In a problem involving a car accident, tangible things could include automobiles or stop signs. In other types of situations, intangible "things," such as a vacation or someone's reputation, could be useful search terms.

■ **THE *POTENTIAL CLAIMS AND DEFENSES* THAT COULD BE RAISED.**
As you become more familiar with the law, you may be able to identify claims or defenses that a research problem potentially raises. The facts could indicate to you that the problem potentially involves particular claims (such as breach of contract, defamation, or bribery) or particular defenses (such as consent, assumption of the risk, or self-defense). When that is the case, you can often use claims and defenses effectively as search terms.

If you are dealing with an unfamiliar area of law, however, you might not know of any claims or defenses potentially at issue. In that situation, you can generate search terms by thinking about the conduct and mental states of the parties, as well as the injury suffered by the complaining party. Claims and defenses often flow from these considerations, and as a result, these types of terms can appear in a research tool's indexing system. When considering conduct, consider what was not done, as well as what was done. The failure to do an act might also give rise to a claim or defense.

For example, you could be asked to research a situation in which one person published an article falsely asserting that another person was guilty of tax evasion, knowing that the accusation was not true. You might recognize this as a potential claim for the tort of defamation, which occurs when one person publishes false information that is damaging to

another person's reputation. Even if you were unfamiliar with this tort, however, you could still generate search terms relevant to the claim by considering the defendant's conduct (publication) or mental state (intentional actions), or the plaintiff's injury (to reputation). These search terms would likely lead you to authority on defamation.

■ **THE *RELIEF* SOUGHT BY THE COMPLAINING PARTY.**
Indexing systems often categorize information according to the relief a party is seeking. Damages, injunction, specific performance, restitution, attorneys' fees, and other terms relating to the relief sought can lead you to pertinent information.

As an example of how you might go about using these categories to generate search terms, assume you have been asked to research the following situation: Your client recently went to Illinois on vacation. While waiting to meet a friend in the lobby of the hotel where she was staying, she decided to use the ladies' room. The lobby restrooms were unlocked and accessible to the public. Upon entering the ladies' room, she was surprised by a man who tackled her to the ground and grabbed her purse. Just then, another woman entered the ladies' room. The man ran out the door, dropping the purse as he ran. He was never caught. Your client recovered her purse after the incident but suffered a broken wrist. She wants to know if the hotel is liable for her injury.

■ **PARTIES:** hotel, guest, robber.
■ **PLACES AND THINGS:** hotel, vacation, Illinois, purse, restroom.
■ **POTENTIAL CLAIMS AND DEFENSES:** negligence, strict liability, assumption of the risk, contributory negligence. Additional terms could be generated according to conduct ("robbery" or "failure to protect"), mental state ("knowledge," regarding the hotel's awareness of criminal activity in the area), or injury ("broken wrist").
■ **RELIEF:** damages, restitution for expenses, physical pain and suffering, mental or emotional distress.

This is not an exhaustive list of search terms for this problem, but it illustrates how you can use these categories of information to develop useful search terms.

B. EXPANDING THE INITIAL SEARCH

Once you have developed an initial set of search terms for your issue, the next task is to try to expand that list. The terms you originally generated may not appear in a print index or electronic database. Therefore, once you have developed your initial set of search terms, you should try

FIGURE 2.1   EXPANDING THE BREADTH OF SEARCH TERMS

Increasing breadth with synonyms and related terms: motel ↔ hotel ↔ inn

to increase both the breadth and the depth of the list. You can increase the breadth of the list by identifying synonyms and terms related to the initial search terms, and you can increase the depth by expressing the concepts in your search terms both more abstractly and more concretely.

Increasing the breadth of your list with synonyms and related terms is essential to your research strategy. This is especially true for word searches in computer research. In a print index, if you get close to the correct term, a cross-reference might refer you to an entry with relevant information. In computer word searching, however, the computer searches only for the specific terms you identify. Therefore, to make sure you locate all of the pertinent information on your issue, you need to have a number of synonyms for the words and concepts in your search. In the research scenario described above, there are a number of synonyms and related terms for one of the initial search terms: hotel. As **Figure 2.1** illustrates, you might also search for terms such as motel or inn.

You are also more likely to find useful research material if you increase the depth of your list by varying the level of abstraction at which you express the terms you have included. For example, while the research scenario above involves a robbery, which is taking another's property by force or threat of force, you might find relevant information if you expressed the term more abstractly: theft or crime. See **Figure 2.2.** In the same vein, if you were researching a problem involving "transportation equipment," you would want to consider search terms that are more concrete: automobile, train, airplane, etc.

FIGURE 2.2   INCREASING THE DEPTH OF SEARCH TERMS

Increasing depth with varying levels of abstraction: robbery
↕
theft
↕
crime

Once you have developed a list of search terms, you are ready to begin looking for authority in print or electronic legal research tools. The chapters that follow explain the indexing tools in a variety of legal research sources. Regardless of where you begin your research, you will be able to use the techniques described in this chapter to access information using the indexing tools in each resource you use.

CHAPTER 3

SECONDARY SOURCE RESEARCH

A. INTRODUCTION TO SECONDARY SOURCES

As you read in Chapter 1, primary authority refers to sources of legal rules, such as cases, statutes, and administrative regulations. Secondary sources, by contrast, provide commentary on the law. Although they are not binding on courts and are not cited as frequently as primary sources, secondary sources are excellent research tools. Because they often summarize or collect authorities from a variety of jurisdictions, they can help you find mandatory or persuasive primary authority on a subject. They also often provide narrative explanations of complex concepts that would be difficult for a beginning researcher to grasp thoroughly simply from reading primary sources. Equipped with a solid understanding of the background of an area of law, you will be better able to locate and evaluate primary authority on your research issue.

Secondary sources will be most useful to you in the following situations:

(1) WHEN YOU ARE RESEARCHING AN AREA OF LAW WITH WHICH YOU ARE UNFAMILIAR. Secondary sources can give you the necessary background to generate search terms. They can also lead you directly to primary authorities.

(2) WHEN YOU ARE LOOKING FOR PRIMARY PERSUASIVE AUTHORITY BUT DO NOT KNOW HOW TO NARROW THE JURISDICTIONS THAT ARE LIKELY TO HAVE USEFUL INFORMATION. If you need to find primary persuasive authority on a subject, conducting a nationwide survey of the law on the topic is not likely to be an efficient research strategy. Secondary sources can help you locate persuasive authority relevant to your research issue.

(3) WHEN YOU ARE RESEARCHING AN UNDEVELOPED AREA OF THE LAW. When you are researching a question of first impression, commentators may have analyzed how courts should rule on the issue.

(4) WHEN AN INITIAL SEARCH OF PRIMARY SOURCES YIELDS EITHER NO AUTHORITY OR TOO MUCH AUTHORITY. If you are unable to find any authority at all on a topic, you may not be looking in the right places. Secondary sources can educate you on the subject in a way that may allow you to expand or refocus your research efforts. When your search yields an unmanageable amount of information, secondary sources can do two things. First, their citations to primary authority can help you identify the most important authorities pertaining to the research issue. Second, they can provide you with information that may help you narrow your search or weed out irrelevant sources.

Knowing when *not* to use secondary sources is also important. As noted above, secondary sources are not binding on courts. Therefore, you will not ordinarily cite them in briefs or memoranda. This is especially true if you use secondary sources to lead you to primary authority. It is important never to rely exclusively on a discussion of a primary authority that appears in a secondary source. If you are discussing a primary authority in a legal analysis, you must read that authority yourself and update your research to make sure it is current.

This is true for two reasons. First, a summary of a primary authority might not include all of the information necessary to your analysis. It is important to read the primary authority for yourself to make sure you represent it correctly and thoroughly in your analysis.

Second, the information in the secondary source might not be completely current. Although most secondary sources are updated on a regular basis, the law can change at any time. The source may contain incomplete information simply because of the inevitable time lag between changes to the law and the publication of a supplement. One mistake some beginning researchers make is citing a secondary source for the text of a case or statute without checking to make sure that the case has not been overturned or that the statute has not been changed. Another potential error is citing a secondary source for a proposition about the state of the law generally, such as, "Forty-two states now recognize a cause of action for invasion of privacy based on disclosure

of private facts." While statements of that nature were probably true when the secondary source was written, other states may have acted, or some of those noted may have changed their law, in the intervening time period. Accordingly, secondary sources should only be used as a starting point for locating primary authority, not an ending point.

B. RESEARCHING SECONDARY SOURCES IN PRINT

This section discusses the following commonly used secondary sources: legal encyclopedias, treatises, legal periodicals, *American Law Reports*, Restatements of the law, and uniform laws and model acts. Locating material within each of these sources generally involves three steps: (1) using an index or table of contents to find references to material on the topic you are researching; (2) locating the material in the main text of the source; and (3) updating your research.

The first step is using an index or table of contents to find out where information on a topic is located within the secondary source. As with the index or table of contents in any other book, those in a secondary source will refer you to volumes, chapters, pages, or sections where you will find text explaining the topic you are researching. Some secondary sources consist only of a single volume. In those situations, you need simply to look up the table of contents or index references within the text. Often, however, the information in a secondary source is too comprehensive to fit within a single volume. In those cases, the source will consist of a multivolume set of books, which may be organized alphabetically by topic or numerically by volume number. The references in the index or table of contents will contain sufficient information for you to identify the appropriate book within the set, as well as the page or section number specifically relating to the topic you are researching. Locating material in the main text of the source is the second step in the process.

The final step in your research is updating the information you have located. Most secondary sources are updated with pocket parts, as described in Chapter 1. The pocket part will be organized the same way as the main volume of the source. Thus, to update your research, you need to look up the same provisions in the pocket part that you read in the main text to find any additional information on the topic. If you do not find any reference to your topic in the pocket part, there is no new information to supplement the main text.

As you will see later in this chapter, there are some variations on this technique that apply to some secondary sources. For the most part, however, you will be able to use this three-step process to research a variety of secondary sources.

1. LEGAL ENCYCLOPEDIAS

Legal encyclopedias are just like the general subject encyclopedias you have used in the past, except they are limited in scope to legal subjects. Legal encyclopedias provide a general overview of the law on a variety of topics. They do not provide analysis or suggest solutions to conflicts in the law. Instead, they simply report on the general state of the law. Because encyclopedias cover the law in such a general way, you will usually use them to get background information on your research topic and, to a lesser extent, to locate citations to primary authority. You will rarely, if ever, cite a legal encyclopedia.

There are two general legal encyclopedias, *American Jurisprudence*, Second Edition (Am. Jur. 2d) and *Corpus Juris Secundum* (C.J.S.). Each is a multivolume set organized alphabetically by topic. These sources can be researched using the three-step process described above. The indices for these encyclopedias are contained in separate softcover volumes that are usually shelved at the end of the set. The index volumes are published annually, so be sure to use the most current set. You can also find information by scanning the table of contents at the beginning of each topic. Am. Jur. 2d and C.J.S. cover material in such a general way that they are useful primarily for background information. Many of the citations to primary authority are relatively old and, as a consequence, may not provide you with much useful information.

In addition to Am. Jur. 2d and C.J.S., your library may also have encyclopedias for individual states. For example, state encyclopedias are published for California, Maryland, New York, and Ohio, among other states. State encyclopedias can be researched using the same process you would use with Am. Jur. 2d or C.J.S. When you are researching a question of state law, state encyclopedias are often more helpful than the general encyclopedias for two reasons. First, the summary of the law will be tailored to the rules and court decisions within that state, and therefore is likely to be more helpful. Second, the citations to primary authority will usually be more up to date and will, of course, be from the controlling jurisdiction. Consequently, state encyclopedias can be more useful for leading you to primary sources.

The examples in **Figures 3.1** through **3.3** are taken from Am. Jur. 2d.

FIGURE 3.1   INDEX TO AM. JUR. 2d

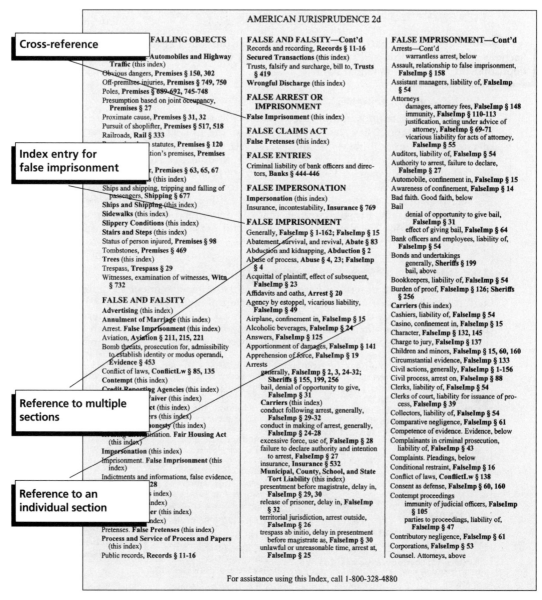

Reprinted with permission from Thomson West, *American Jurisprudence,* 2d Ed., General Index (2005), p. 226.
©2005 Thomson West.

FIGURE 3.2   AM. JUR. 2d MAIN VOLUME ENTRY UNDER FALSE IMPRISONMENT

---

§ 1   FALSE IMPRISONMENT   32 Am Jur 2d

~~tives~~ ⁶ the tort of false arrest or false imprisonment exists to protect and ~~~~dividual's interest in freedom from unwarranted interference ~~~~'s personal liberty.[7]

Sections on false imprisonment

§ 2.   False arrest; generally

False arrest, a name sometimes given to the tort more generally known as false imprisonment,[8] has also been defined as the unlawful restraint by one person of the physical liberty of another, by acting to cause a false arrest, that is, an arrest made without legal authority,[9] or without sufficient legal authority,[10] resulting in damages.[11] However, the tort of false arrest does not require a formal arrest, but rather a manifest intent to take someone into custody and subject that person to the defendant's control.[12] For false arrest, there is no requirement that the arrest be formal, that the detention be for the purpose of arraignment or that the detention continue until presentation to a judicial officer in order for the arrest to be actionable.[13]

§ 3.   Distinction between false imprisonment and false arrest

Some courts have described false arrest and false imprisonment as causes of action which are distinguishable only in terminology.[14] The two have been called virtually indistinguishable,[15] and identical.[16] However, the difference between them lies in the manner in which they arise.[17] In order to commit false imprisonment, it is not necessary either to intend to make an arrest[18] or actu-

To constitute false imprisonment, restraint must be unreasonable and unwarranted under the circumstances. Kanner v First Nat'l Bank (Fla App D3) 287 So 715.

The restraint must be "false," that is, without right or authority to do so. Tumbarella v Kroger Co., 85 Mich App 482, 271 NW2d 284.

6. Fermino v Fedco, Inc., 7 Cal 4th 701, 30 Cal Rptr 2d 18, 872 P2d 559, 59 Cal Comp Cas 296, 94 CDOS 3399, 94 Daily Journal DAR 6423, 9 BNA IER Cas 1132.

7. Phillips v District of Columbia (Dist Col App) 458 A2d 722.

8. Headrick v Wal-Mart Stores, Inc., 293 Ark 433, 738 SW2d 418.

9. Stern v Thompson & Coates, 185 Wis 2d 221, 517 NW2d 658, reconsideration den (Wis) 525 NW2d 736.

10. Limited Stores v Wilson-Robinson, 317 Ark 80, 876 SW2d 248.

11. Ting v United States (CA9 Cal) 927 F2d 1504, 91 CDOS 1794, 91 Daily Journal DAR 2996; Trenouth v United States (CA9 Cal) 764 F2d 1305, 119 BNA LRRM 3615.

12. Cooper v Dyke (CA4 Md) 814 F2d 941.

13. Day v Wells Fargo Guard Service Co. (Mo) 711 SW2d 503.

14. Johnson v Weiner, 155 Fla 169, 19 So 2d 699; Fox v McCurnin, 205 Iowa 752, 218 NW 499; Holland v Lutz, 194 Kan 712, 401 P2d 1015.

Although the distinctions are not always clearly set out by the authorities, false arrest, or unlawful arrest, is a species of the common-law action for false imprisonment. Bonkowski v Arlan's Dep't Store, 12 Mich App 88, 162 NW2d 347, revd on other grounds 383 Mich 90, 174 NW2d 765.

Forms: Instructions to jury defining false arrest. 10 Am Jur Pl & Pr Imprisonment, Form 4.

15. Kraft v Bettendorf (Io

16. Fermino v Fedco, Inc Cal Rptr 2d 18, 872 P2d 55 296, 94 CDOS 3399, 94 Daily Journal DAR 6423, 9 BNA IER Cas 1132.

17. Harrer v Montgomery Ward & Co., 124 Mont 295, 221 P2d 428; Houghtaling v State, 11 Misc 2d 1049, 175 NYS2d 659; Alter v Paul (Franklin Co) 101 Ohio App 139, 1 Ohio Ops 2d 80, 72 Ohio L Abs 332, 135 NE2d 73; Alsup v Skaggs Drug Center, 203 Okla 525, 223 P2d 530; Bender v Seattle, 99 Wash 2d 582, 664 P2d 492, 9 Media L R 2101.

18. Harrer v Montgomery Ward & Co., 124 Mont 295, 221 P2d 428; Hepworth v Covey Bros. Amusement Co., 97 Utah 205, 91 P2d 507.

References to primary authority from multiple jurisdictions

46

Reprinted with permission from Thomson West, *American Jurisprudence,* 2d Ed., Vol. 32 (1995), p. 46.
©1995 Thomson West.

FIGURE 3.3 AM. JUR. 2d POCKET PART ENTRY FOR FALSE IMPRISONMENT

FALSE IMPRISONMENT

KeyCite®: Cases and other legal materials listed in KeyCite Scope can be researched through West's KeyCite service on Westlaw®. Use KeyCite to check citations for form, parallel references, prior and later history, and comprehensive citator information, including citations to other decisions and secondary materials.

I. CIVIL ACTIONS [§§ 1–156]

A. IN GENERAL [§§ 1–7]

§ 1 Definition of false imprisonment

New research reference for § 2

Research References

Instruction to jury—False imprisonment defined. 10A Am. Jur. Pleading and Practice Forms, False Imprisonment § 14.

§ 2 False arrest; generally

Research References

Proof of Qualified Immunity Defense in 42 U.S.C.A. § 1983 or Bivens Actions Against Law Enforcement Officers, 59 Am. Jur. Proof of Facts 3d 291.

§ 3 Distinction between false imprisonment and false arrest

Research References

Instruction to jury—False arrest defined. 10A Am. Jur. Pleading and Practice Forms, False Imprisonment § 15.

Proof of Qualified Immunity Defense in 42 U.S.C.A. § 1983 or Bivens Actions Against Law Enforcement Officers, 59 Am. Jur. Proof of Facts 3d 291.

§ 4 Related torts distinguished—abuse of process

§ 5 — Malicious prosecution

Research References

Wrongful Confinement to a Mental Health or Developmental Disabilities Facility, 44 Am. Jur. Proof of Facts 3d 217.

§ 7 — Negligence

Research References

Negligent false imprisonment—Scope for re-emergence? 61 Modern LR 4:573 (1999).

B. ELEMENTS [§§ 8–34]

1. In General [§§ 8–10]

§ 8 Generally

Research References

Instruction to jury—Elements of false imprisonment. 10A Am. Jur. Pleading and Practice Forms, False Imprisonment § 193.

§ 9 Malice or motive; good faith

Research References

Instruction to jury—Good faith no justification. 10A Am. Jur. Pleading and Practice Forms, False Imprisonment § 18.

§ 10 Absence of probable cause

Cases

Arresting officers had probable cause to arrest suspected grease thief, and thus, suspect could not maintain false imprisonment or false arrest claim, where arresting police officers had authority to detain her without a warrant based on fact that their observations and exchanged information gave rise to a reasonable belief that a theft had been committed. CCP art 14.01(b); PC § 31.03(b)(1). Villegas v. Griffin Industries, 975 S.W.2d 745 (Tex. App. Corpus Christi 1998).

2. Detention or Restraint [§§ 11–20]

§ 11 Generally

Cases

Detentions and searches of vehicles of customers who entered lumber yard to load items for which they had paid did not fall withIn reasonable ground protections of statute creating immunity from false imprisonment claim for conducting search or detention based on reasonable belief that person had concealed property, where customers were selected at random for detentions and searches. I.C.A. § 808.12, subd. 3. Zohn v. Menard, Inc., 598 N.W.2d 323 (Iowa Ct. App. 1999).

Organization's president, who called police for assistance in removing nonmember from executive committee meeting, could not be liable for false imprisonment, as president merely invoked legal process and did not attempt to remove nonmember himself. Holland v. Sebunya, 2000 ME 160, 759 A.2d 205 (Me. 2000).

§ 18 Use of force; threats

Research References

Complaint, petition, or declaration—False imprisonment imposed by private individual—Attempted extortion by means of threats of violence. 10A Am. Jur. Pleading and Practice Forms, False Imprisonment § 34.

Complaint, petition, or declaration—Allega-

Reprinted with permission from Thomson West, *American Jurisprudence*, 2d Ed., Vol. 32 Cumulative Supplement (2004), p. 5. ©2004 Thomson West.

2. TREATISES

Treatises have a narrower focus than legal encyclopedias. Where legal encyclopedias provide a general overview of a broad range of topics, treatises generally provide in-depth treatment of a single subject, such as torts or constitutional law. A treatise may consist of a single volume.[1] Many, however, consist of multiple volumes. Most treatises provide both an overview of the topic and some analysis or commentary. They also usually contain citations to many primary and secondary authorities. If a treatise is widely respected and considered a definitive source in an area of law, you might cite the treatise in a brief or memorandum. Ordinarily, however, you will use treatises for research purposes and will not cite them in your written analysis.

Using a treatise once you have located it ordinarily is not difficult. With most treatises, you can use the three-step process described at the beginning of this section. The more difficult aspect of using treatises is finding one on your research topic. The on-line catalog in your library is the first place to look. Treatises will be listed there by call number with all other library holdings. Because treatises do not usually have titles identifying them as treatises, however, sometimes it can be difficult figuring out which listings refer to treatises. The reference librarians in your library are a great asset in this area; they should be able to recommend treatises on your subject.

Figure 3.4 is an example from a treatise on torts.

3. LEGAL PERIODICALS

Articles in legal periodicals can be very useful research tools. You may hear periodical articles referred to as "law review" or "journal" articles. Many law schools publish periodicals known as law reviews or journals that collect articles on a wide range of topics. Many other types of legal periodicals also exist, however, including commercially published journals, legal newspapers, and magazines.

Articles published in law reviews or journals are thorough, thoughtful treatments of legal issues by law professors, practitioners, judges, and even students. The articles are usually focused fairly narrowly on specific issues, although they often include background or introductory sections that provide a general overview of the topic. They are generally well researched and contain citations to many primary and secondary authorities. In addition, they often address undeveloped areas in the law

---

[1]One type of single-volume source with which you may already be familiar is a "hornbook." A hornbook provides a clear and straightforward statement of the law on a topic. Because a hornbook is a single volume, however, it usually is not an exhaustive source of information.

FIGURE 3.4 TREATISE MAIN VOLUME ENTRY FOR FALSE IMPRISONMENT

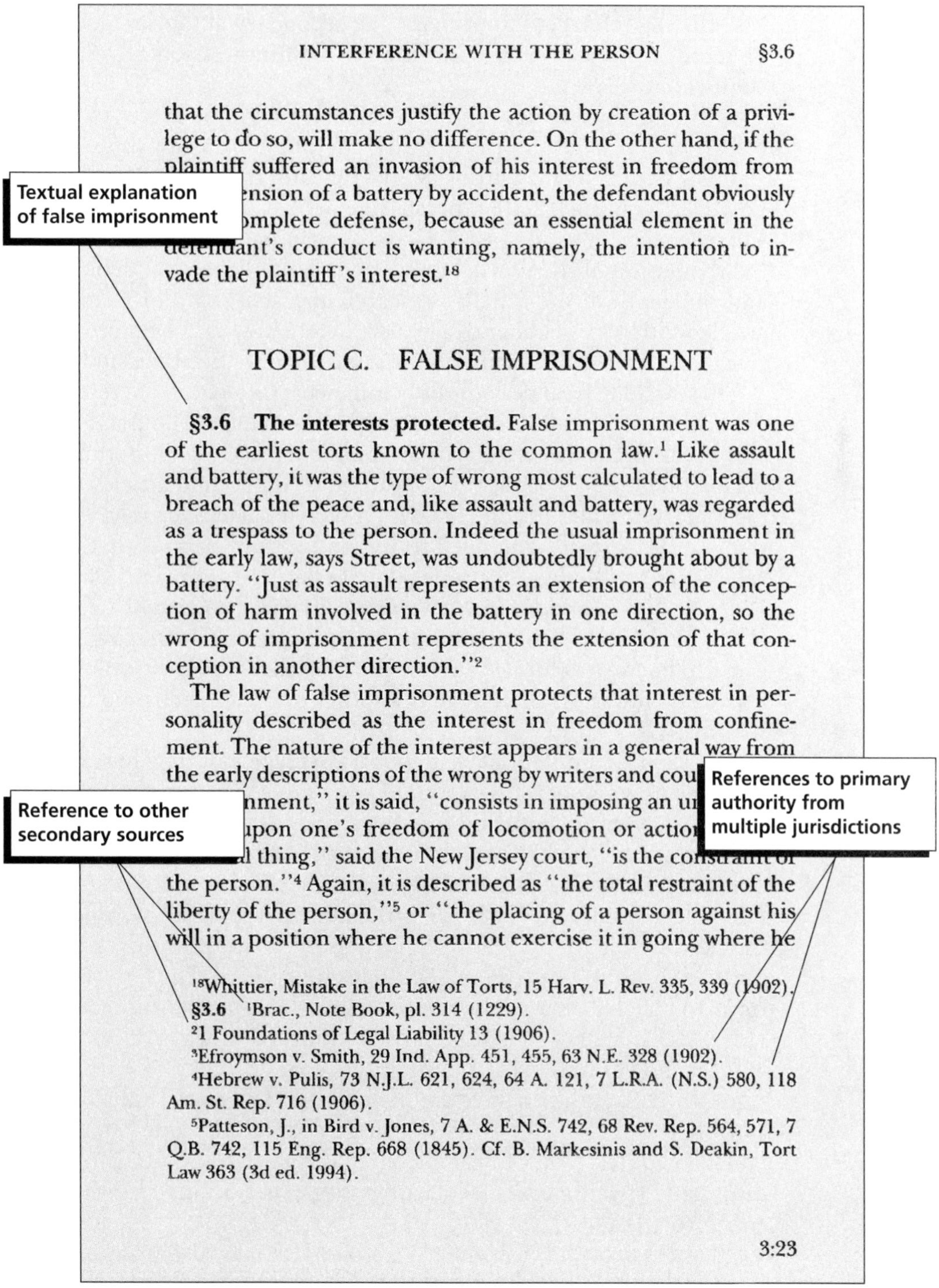

INTERFERENCE WITH THE PERSON §3.6

that the circumstances justify the action by creation of a privilege to do so, will make no difference. On the other hand, if the plaintiff suffered an invasion of his interest in freedom from [Textual explanation of false imprisonment] ension of a battery by accident, the defendant obviously omplete defense, because an essential element in the defendant's conduct is wanting, namely, the intention to invade the plaintiff's interest.[18]

TOPIC C.   FALSE IMPRISONMENT

§3.6   The interests protected. False imprisonment was one of the earliest torts known to the common law.[1] Like assault and battery, it was the type of wrong most calculated to lead to a breach of the peace and, like assault and battery, was regarded as a trespass to the person. Indeed the usual imprisonment in the early law, says Street, was undoubtedly brought about by a battery. "Just as assault represents an extension of the conception of harm involved in the battery in one direction, so the wrong of imprisonment represents the extension of that conception in another direction."[2]

The law of false imprisonment protects that interest in personality described as the interest in freedom from confinement. The nature of the interest appears in a general way from the early descriptions of the wrong by writers and cou [References to primary authority from multiple jurisdictions] nment," it is said, "consists in imposing an u [Reference to other secondary sources] pon one's freedom of locomotion or action d thing," said the New Jersey court, "is the constraint of the person."[4] Again, it is described as "the total restraint of the liberty of the person,"[5] or "the placing of a person against his will in a position where he cannot exercise it in going where he

[18]Whittier, Mistake in the Law of Torts, 15 Harv. L. Rev. 335, 339 (1902).
§3.6 [1]Brac., Note Book, pl. 314 (1229).
[2]1 Foundations of Legal Liability 13 (1906).
[3]Efroymson v. Smith, 29 Ind. App. 451, 455, 63 N.E. 328 (1902).
[4]Hebrew v. Pulis, 73 N.J.L. 621, 624, 64 A. 121, 7 L.R.A. (N.S.) 580, 118 Am. St. Rep. 716 (1906).
[5]Patteson, J., in Bird v. Jones, 7 A. & E.N.S. 742, 68 Rev. Rep. 564, 571, 7 Q.B. 742, 115 Eng. Rep. 668 (1845). Cf. B. Markesinis and S. Deakin, Tort Law 363 (3d ed. 1994).

3:23

and propose solutions for resolving problems in the law. As a result, periodical articles can be useful for obtaining an overview of an area of law, finding references to primary and secondary authority, and developing ideas for analyzing a question of first impression or resolving a conflict in the law.

Although law review and journal articles will be useful to you for research, you would not ordinarily cite one if you can support your analysis with primary authority. If you cannot find primary support, however, you might cite a persuasive article. An article's persuasive value depends on a number of factors, including the author's expertise, the reputation of the journal in which it is published, the article's age, and the depth of the article's research and analysis. For example, an article written by a recognized expert in a field would be more persuasive than a note or comment on the same topic written by a student.

Researching legal periodicals is somewhat different from researching the other secondary sources discussed in this chapter. Thousands of articles in hundreds of periodicals are published each year. Because each periodical is an independent publication, trying to find articles through the indices or tables of contents within individual publications would be impossible. Instead, you need to use an indexing service that collects references to a wide range of legal periodicals. Two print indices, the *Index to Legal Periodicals and Books* (ILP) and the *Current Law Index* (CLI), will lead you to periodical articles. Electronic indexing services can also be used to locate articles. ILP is available in electronic form at many law libraries. LegalTrac is another popular electronic indexing service.

ILP and CLI do not have identical coverage, but they index largely the same universe of publications. They both consist of noncumulative volumes covering specific periods of time. Because the volumes are noncumulative, they are not updated with pocket parts. Instead, subsequent volumes cover later time periods. This means that you must use multiple volumes to look for articles over a period of time. Both indices publish annual hardbound volumes and monthly softcover updates. Both indices organize articles by subject. Thus, to find citations to articles on a subject, you simply look up the subject within ILP or CLI. You can also find articles indexed in ways other than by subject. For example, CLI contains a separate index of authors and titles. In ILP, author names are included in the general subject index. Both ILP and CLI also contain features called the table of cases and table of statutes. You can use these tables to locate citations to articles discussing specific cases or statutes. **Figure 3.5** illustrates an index entry from ILP.

LegalTrac or the electronic version of ILP may also be available on your library's computer network. These services allow you to search for legal periodicals in a variety of ways, including by keyword and by

FIGURE 3.5   ILP INDEX ENTRY

Index entry for false imprisonment

Article on false imprisonment

SUBJECT AND AUTHOR INDEX   269

...ran J.
...f strength or source of weakness?: A critique
...."source-of-strength" doctrine in banking reform.
66 *N.Y.U. L. Rev.* 1344-403 N '91

Fallon, Richard H., Jr.
Claims Court at the crossroads. 40 *Cath. U. L. Rev.*
517-32 Spr '91
Common law court or council of revision? 101 *Yale
L.J.* 949-68 Ja '92
Reflections on Dworkin and the two faces of law. 67
Notre Dame L. Rev. 553-85 '92

False imprisonment
Detention in a police station and false imprisonment.
J. Mackenzie. 142 *New L.J.* 534-6 Ap 17 '92
He who controls the mind controls the body: false
imprisonment, religious cults, and the destruction of
volitional capacity. 25 *Val. U. L. Rev.* 407-54 Spr
'91

Falvey, Joseph L., Jr.
Health care professionals and rights warning requirements.
...*rmy Law.* 21-31 O '91
...re professionals and rights warnings. 40 *Naval
.* 173-91 '92
...rts
also
...enile courts

Family law *See* Domestic relations
Family planning *See* Birth control
Family violence *See* Domestic violence
Fanter, William F.
Attacking safety belt limitations: unconstitutional restraint
of defendants; by W. F. Fanter, B. A. Hering. 42
Fed'n Ins. & Corp. Couns. Q. 181-90 Wint '92

Farber, Daniel A.
Economic analysis and just compensation. 12 *Int'l Rev.
L. & Econ.* 125-38 Je '92
Free speech without romance: public choice and the
first amendment. 105 *Harv. L. Rev.* 554-83 D '91
The inevitability of practical reason: statutes, formalism,
and the rule of law. 45 *Vand. L. Rev.* 533-59 Ap
'92
The jurisprudential cab ride: a Socratic dialogue. 1992
B.Y.U. L. Rev. 363-70 '92
Risk regulation in perspective: Reserve Mining [Reserve
Mining Co. v. EPA, 514 F.2d 492] revisited. 21 *Envtl.
L.* 1321-57 '91
"Terminator 2 ?": the Constitution in an alternate world.
9 *Const. Commentary* 59-73 Wint '92

Farina, Cynthia R.
Getting from here to there. 1991 *Duke L.J.* 689-710
Je '91

Farley, E. Milton, III
Experts are everywhere! 12 *E. Min. L. Inst.* 5.1-.82
'91

Farley, John J., III
The new kid on the block of veterans' law: the United
States Court of Veterans Appeals. 38 *Fed. B. News
& J.* 488-92 N/D '91
Robin Hood jurisprudence: the triumph of equity in
American tort law. 65 *St. John's L. Rev.* 997-1021
Aut '91

Farm bankruptcy
Recent developments in Chapter 12 bankruptcy. S. A.
Schneider. 24 *Ind. L. Rev.* 1357-78 '91
The search for the proper interest rate under Chapter
12 (Family Farmer Bankruptcy Act). T. O. Deppersch-
midt, N. H. Kratzke. 67 *N.D. L. Rev.* 455-68 '91
Selected issues of federal farm program payments in
bankruptcy. C. R. Kelley, S. A. Schneider. 14 *J. Agric.
Tax'n & L.* 99-139 Summ '92

Farm tenancy
The mystical art of valuing agricultural tenancies. 1991
Brit. Tax Rev. 181-7 '91

Farmer, Larry
Feminist theory, professional ethics, and gender-related
distinctions in attorney negotiating styles; by L. Burton,
L. Farmer, E. D. Gee, L. Johnson, G. R. Williams.
1991 *J. Disp. Resol.* 199-257 '91

Farmer, Lindsay
'The genius of our law...': criminal law and the Scottish
legal tradition. 55 *Mod. L. Rev.* 25-43 Ja '92

Farmer, Susan Beth
Market power and the National Association of Attorneys
General Horizontal Merger Guidelines. 60 *Antitrust
L.J.* 839-48 '91/'92

Farming *See* Agriculture
Farnham, David
The marital privilege. 18 *Litig.* 34-7 Wint '92

Farnsworth, E. Allan (Edward Allan), 1928-
Comments on Professor Waddams' "Precontractual duties
of disclosure". 19 *Can. Bus. L.J.* 351-6 '91
Punitive damages in arbitration. 20 *Stetson L. Rev.*
395-418 Spr '91

Farnsworth, Edward Allan *See* Farnsworth, E. Allan (Edward
Allan), 1928-

Farrar, John H.
Cross frontier mergers. 4 *Canterbury L. Rev.* 429-46
'91

Farrell, L. M.
Financial guidelines for investing in motion picture
limited partnerships. 12 *Loy. L.A. Ent. L.J.* 127-51
'92

Farrier, David
Vegetation conservation: the planning system as a vehicle
for the regulation of broadacre agricultural land clearing.
18 *Melb. U. L. Rev.* 26-59 Je '91

Farrington, David P.
Advancing knowledge about co-offending: results from
a prospective longitudinal survey of London males;
by A. J. Reiss, Jr., D. P. Farrington. 82 *J. Crim.
L. & Criminology* 360-95 Summ '91

Farris, Juli E.
Grassroots impact litigation: mass filing of small claims;
by A. D. Freeman, J. E. Farris. 26 *U.S.F. L. Rev.*
261-81 Wint '92

Farris, Martin T.
Antitrust irrelevance in air transportation and the re-
defining of price discrimination; by L. E. Gesell, M.
T. Farris. 57 *J. Air L. & Com.* 173-97 Fall '91

Fatum, Stephen M.
A review of the Illinois Health Care Surrogate Act;
by S. M. Fatum, R. J. Kane, T. R. LeBlang. 80
Ill. B.J. 124-9+ Mr '92

Faulk, Richard O.
Epidemiology in the courtroom: a problem of statistical
significance. 59 *Def. Couns. J.* 25-30 Ja '92

Faulkner, Ellen
Lesbian abuse: the social and legal realities. 16 *Queen's
L.J.* 261-86 Summ '91

Faulkner, James
Mens rea in rape: Morgan [R. v. Morgan, [1976] A.C.
182] and the inadequacy of subjectivism or why no
should not mean yes in the eyes of the law. 18 *Melb.
U. L. Rev.* 60-82 Je '91

Faull, Jonathan
The enforcement of competition policy in the European
Community: a mature system. 15 *Fordham Int'l L.J.*
219-47 '91/'92

Faure, Michael
Self-regulation of the professions in Belgium; by R. Van
Den Bergh, M. Faure. 11 *Int'l Rev. L. & Econ.* 165-82
S '91

Faust, Richard
The great writ in action: empirical light on the federal
habeas corpus debate; by R. Faust, T. J. Rubenstein,
L. W. Yackle. 18 *N.Y.U. Rev. L. & Soc. Change*
637-710 '90/'91

Fauteux, Paul
Sources d'énergie nucléaire dans l'espace: Bilan réglemen-
taire et incertitudes américaines. 16 *Annals Air &
Space L.* 267-306 '91

Favoreu, Louis
The principle of equality in the jurisprudence of the
Conseil constitutionnel. 21 *Cap. U. L. Rev.* 165-97
Wint '92

Fawcett, James
The interrelationships of jurisdiction and choice of law
in private international law. 44 *Current Legal Probs.*
39-62 '91

FIGURE 3.6   ILP ELECTRONIC CITATION LIST

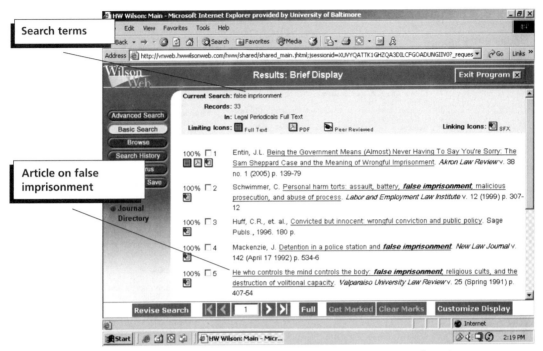

From The H.W. Wilson Co., WilsonWeb, *Index to Legal Periodicals.* © The 2005 H.W. Wilson Co.

author. When you execute the search, you will retrieve a list of citations to articles that fit the specifications of your search. You can then print a list of citations and locate the articles on the shelves in your library. **Figures 3.6** and **3.7** show portions of the results of subject searches for false imprisonment in the electronic version of ILP and LegalTrac, respectively.

Equipped with a list of citations, you are ready to head to the shelves. The citations in ILP, CLI, and LegalTrac will contain the name of the periodical (which may be abbreviated), the number of the volume containing the article, and the starting page of the article, e.g., 25 Val. U. L. Rev. 407. This citation tells you to locate the *Valparaiso University Law Review* on the shelves, locate volume 25, and turn to page 407. You can locate the periodical on the shelves by checking the on-line catalog for the call number of the publication. The electronic indexing services also provide the full text of some articles.

With most legal research tools, the next step in the process would be to update your research. Periodical articles are one exception to this rule. As noted above, ILP and CLI are updated with new, noncumulative volumes published periodically. There is no way to update an individual periodical article, however, short of locating later articles that add to or

FIGURE 3.7   LEGALTRAC CITATION LIST

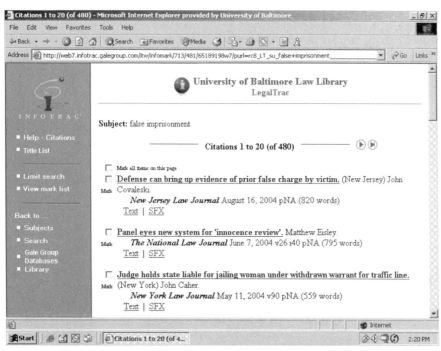

From *LegalTrac* by Gale Group. Reprinted by permission of the Gale Group.

criticize an earlier article. As a consequence, it is important to note the date of any periodical article you use. If the article is more than a few years old, you may want to supplement your research with more current material. In addition, as noted earlier, if you use the article to lead you to primary authority, you will need to update your research using the updating tools available for those primary sources to make sure your research is completely current.

4. AMERICAN LAW REPORTS

American Law Reports, or A.L.R., contains articles called "Annotations." Annotations collect summaries of cases from a variety of jurisdictions to provide an overview of the law on a topic. A.L.R. combines the breadth of topic coverage found in an encyclopedia with the depth of discussion in a treatise or legal periodical. Nevertheless, A.L.R. is different from these other secondary sources in significant ways. Because A.L.R. Annotations provide summaries of individual cases, they are more detailed than encyclopedias. Unlike treatises or legal periodicals, however, they mostly report the results of the cases without much analysis or commentary. A.L.R. Annotations are especially helpful at the beginning of your

research to give you an overview of a topic. Because Annotations collect summaries of cases from many jurisdictions, they can also be helpful in directing you toward mandatory or persuasive primary authority. More recent Annotations also contain references to other research sources, such as other secondary sources and tools for conducting additional case research. Although A.L.R. is a useful research tool, you will rarely, if ever, cite an A.L.R. Annotation.

There are eight series of A.L.R.: A.L.R., A.L.R.2d, A.L.R.3d, A.L.R.4th, A.L.R.5th, A.L.R.6th, A.L.R. Fed., and A.L.R. Fed. 2d. Each series contains multiple volumes organized by volume number. A.L.R. Fed. and Fed. 2d cover issues of federal law. The remaining series usually cover issues of state law, although they do bring in federal law as appropriate to the topic. A.L.R. and A.L.R.2d are, for the most part, out of date and will not be useful to you. They are also updated using special tools not applicable to any of the other A.L.R. series. Generally, you will find A.L.R.3d, 4th, 5th, 6th, Fed., and Fed. 2d to be the most useful.

A.L.R. Annotations can be researched using the three-step process described earlier in this chapter. Annotations can be located using the A.L.R. Index.[2] The A.L.R. Index is a separate set of index volumes usually shelved near the A.L.R. sets. It contains references to Annotations in A.L.R.2d, 3d, 4th, 5th, 6th, Fed., and Fed. 2d. The A.L.R. Index and the individual volumes in A.L.R.3d, 4th, 5th, 6th, Fed. and Fed. 2d are updated with pocket parts.

Figures 3.8 and **3.9** illustrate some of the features of an A.L.R. Annotation.

5. RESTATEMENTS

The American Law Institute publishes what are called Restatements of the law in a variety of fields. You may already be familiar with the Restatements for contracts or torts from your other classes. Restatements essentially "restate" the common-law rules on a subject. Restatements have been published in the following fields:

- Agency
- Conflicts of Laws
- Contracts
- Foreign Relations Law of the United States
- Judgments
- Law Governing Lawyers

- Property
- Restitution
- Security
- Suretyship and Guaranty
- Torts
- Trusts
- Unfair Competition

---

[2]A.L.R. also publishes "digests," which are separate finding tools from the A.L.R. Index. You do not need to use the A.L.R. digests to locate Annotations. Annotations can be located directly from the A.L.R. Index.

FIGURE 3.8 STARTING PAGE OF AN A.L.R. ANNOTATION

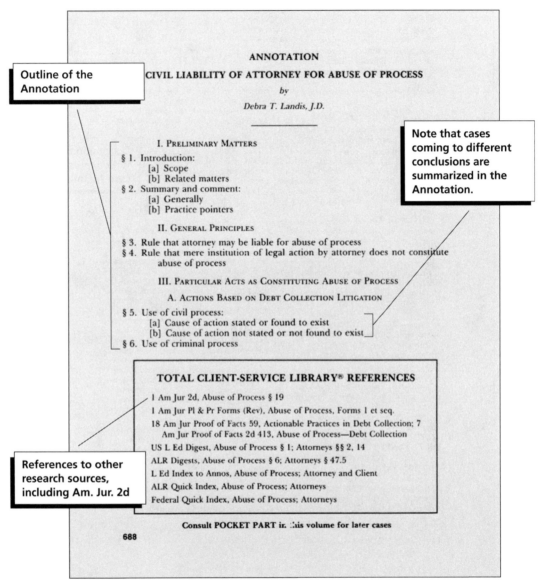

Outline of the Annotation

Note that cases coming to different conclusions are summarized in the Annotation.

References to other research sources, including Am. Jur. 2d

ANNOTATION
CIVIL LIABILITY OF ATTORNEY FOR ABUSE OF PROCESS
by
Debra T. Landis, J.D.

I. Preliminary Matters
§ 1. Introduction:
    [a] Scope
    [b] Related matters
§ 2. Summary and comment:
    [a] Generally
    [b] Practice pointers

II. General Principles
§ 3. Rule that attorney may be liable for abuse of process
§ 4. Rule that mere institution of legal action by attorney does not constitute abuse of process

III. Particular Acts as Constituting Abuse of Process

A. Actions Based on Debt Collection Litigation

§ 5. Use of civil process:
    [a] Cause of action stated or found to exist
    [b] Cause of action not stated or not found to exist
§ 6. Use of criminal process

TOTAL CLIENT-SERVICE LIBRARY® REFERENCES

1 Am Jur 2d, Abuse of Process § 19

1 Am Jur Pl & Pr Forms (Rev), Abuse of Process, Forms 1 et seq.

18 Am Jur Proof of Facts 59, Actionable Practices in Debt Collection; 7 Am Jur Proof of Facts 2d 413, Abuse of Process—Debt Collection

US L Ed Digest, Abuse of Process § 1; Attorneys §§ 2, 14

ALR Digests, Abuse of Process § 6; Attorneys § 47.5

L Ed Index to Annos, Abuse of Process; Attorney and Client

ALR Quick Index, Abuse of Process; Attorneys

Federal Quick Index, Abuse of Process; Attorneys

Consult POCKET PART in this volume for later cases

688

FIGURE 3.9   LATER PAGE OF AN A.L.R. ANNOTATION

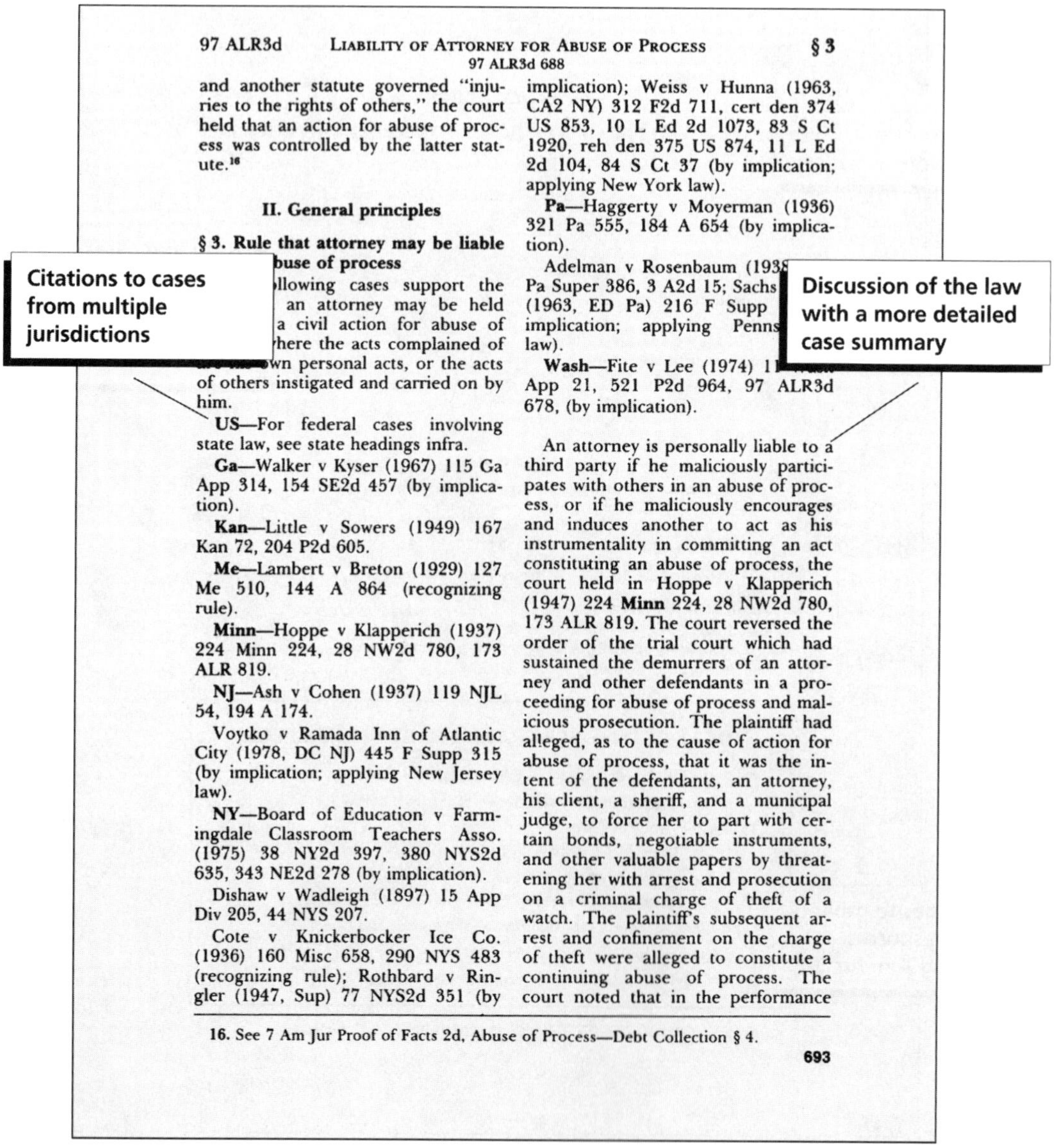

97 ALR3d   LIABILITY OF ATTORNEY FOR ABUSE OF PROCESS   § 3
97 ALR3d 688

and another statute governed "injuries to the rights of others," the court held that an action for abuse of process was controlled by the latter statute.[16]

II. General principles

§ 3. Rule that attorney may be liable

Citations to cases from multiple jurisdictions

...ollowing cases support the ... an attorney may be held ... a civil action for abuse of ...here the acts complained of ...wn personal acts, or the acts of others instigated and carried on by him.

US—For federal cases involving state law, see state headings infra.

Ga—Walker v Kyser (1967) 115 Ga App 314, 154 SE2d 457 (by implication).

Kan—Little v Sowers (1949) 167 Kan 72, 204 P2d 605.

Me—Lambert v Breton (1929) 127 Me 510, 144 A 864 (recognizing rule).

Minn—Hoppe v Klapperich (1937) 224 Minn 224, 28 NW2d 780, 173 ALR 819.

NJ—Ash v Cohen (1937) 119 NJL 54, 194 A 174.

Voytko v Ramada Inn of Atlantic City (1978, DC NJ) 445 F Supp 315 (by implication; applying New Jersey law).

NY—Board of Education v Farmingdale Classroom Teachers Asso. (1975) 38 NY2d 397, 380 NYS2d 635, 343 NE2d 278 (by implication).

Dishaw v Wadleigh (1897) 15 App Div 205, 44 NYS 207.

Cote v Knickerbocker Ice Co. (1936) 160 Misc 658, 290 NYS 483 (recognizing rule); Rothbard v Ringler (1947, Sup) 77 NYS2d 351 (by

implication); Weiss v Hunna (1963, CA2 NY) 312 F2d 711, cert den 374 US 853, 10 L Ed 2d 1073, 83 S Ct 1920, reh den 375 US 874, 11 L Ed 2d 104, 84 S Ct 37 (by implication; applying New York law).

Pa—Haggerty v Moyerman (1936) 321 Pa 555, 184 A 654 (by implication).

Adelman v Rosenbaum (193... Pa Super 386, 3 A2d 15; Sachs... (1963, ED Pa) 216 F Supp ... implication; applying Penns... law).

Discussion of the law with a more detailed case summary

Wash—Fite v Lee (1974) 1... App 21, 521 P2d 964, 97 ALR3d 678, (by implication).

An attorney is personally liable to a third party if he maliciously participates with others in an abuse of process, or if he maliciously encourages and induces another to act as his instrumentality in committing an act constituting an abuse of process, the court held in Hoppe v Klapperich (1947) 224 **Minn** 224, 28 NW2d 780, 173 ALR 819. The court reversed the order of the trial court which had sustained the demurrers of an attorney and other defendants in a proceeding for abuse of process and malicious prosecution. The plaintiff had alleged, as to the cause of action for abuse of process, that it was the intent of the defendants, an attorney, his client, a sheriff, and a municipal judge, to force her to part with certain bonds, negotiable instruments, and other valuable papers by threatening her with arrest and prosecution on a criminal charge of theft of a watch. The plaintiff's subsequent arrest and confinement on the charge of theft were alleged to constitute a continuing abuse of process. The court noted that in the performance

16. See 7 Am Jur Proof of Facts 2d, Abuse of Process—Debt Collection § 4.

693

In determining what the common-law rules are, the Restatements often look to the rules in the majority of United States jurisdictions. Sometimes, however, the Restatements will also state emerging rules where the rules seem to be changing, or proposed rules in areas where the authors believe a change in the law would be appropriate. Although the Restatements are limited to common-law doctrines, the rules in the Restatements are set out almost like statutes, breaking different doctrines down into their component parts. In addition to setting out the common-law rules for a subject, the Restatements also provide commentary on the proper interpretations of the rules, illustrations demonstrating how the rules should apply in certain situations, and summaries of cases applying and interpreting the Restatement.

Although a Restatement is a secondary source, it is one with substantial weight. Courts can decide to adopt a Restatement's view of an issue, which then makes the comments and illustrations especially persuasive in that jurisdiction. If you are researching the law of a jurisdiction that has adopted a Restatement, you can use the Restatement volumes effectively to locate persuasive authority from other Restatement jurisdictions. As a result, a Restatement is an especially valuable secondary source.

Figures 3.10 and **3.11** show some of the features of one Restatement, the *Restatement (Second) of Torts.* There are two components to the *Restatement (Second) of Torts:* the Restatement volumes, which contain the Restatement rules, comments, and illustrations; and the Appendix volumes, which contain case summaries. To research the *Restatement (Second) of Torts,* you must follow two steps: (1) find relevant sections of the Restatement in the Restatement volumes; and (2) find case summaries interpreting the Restatement in the Appendix volumes.

In the first step, the subject index or table of contents in the Restatement volumes will direct you to individual rules within the Restatement. After the formal statement of the rule, the comments and illustrations will follow. **Figure 3.10** shows the text of § 35 of the *Restatement (Second) of Torts* on false imprisonment.

In the second step, you need to go to the separate Appendix volumes. The Appendix volumes are organized numerically by Restatement section number. By looking up the appropriate section number, you will find cases from a variety of jurisdictions interpreting that section. The Appendix volumes are not cumulative; each volume covers only a specific period of time. Therefore, to find all of the cases interpreting a section, you would need to look it up in each Appendix volume. The latest Appendix volume will have a pocket part with the most recent references.

Figure 3.11 shows the Appendix entry under § 35, which lists several cases discussing this section of the Restatement.

FIGURE 3.10   SECTION 35 OF THE *RESTATEMENT (SECOND) OF TORTS*

§ 35   TORTS, SECOND   Ch. 2

TOPIC 4.   THE INTEREST IN FREEDOM FROM
CONFINEMENT

§ **35.** False Imprisonment

Rule from the Restatement

(1) An actor is subject to liability to another for false imprisonment if

(a) he acts intending to confine the other or a third person within boundaries fixed by the actor, and

(b) his act directly or indirectly results in such a confinement of the other, and

(c) the other is conscious of the confinement or is harmed by it.

(2) An act which is not done with the intention stated in Subsection (1, a) does not make the actor liable to the other for a merely transitory or otherwise harmless confinement, although the act involves an unreasonable risk of imposing it and therefore would be negligent or reckless if the risk threatened bodily harm.

See Reporter's Notes.

Caveat:

The Institute expresses no opinion as to whether the actor may not be subject to liability for conduct which involves an unreasonable risk of causing a confinement of such duration or character as to make the other's loss of freedom a matter of material value.

Comment

Comment on Subsection (1):

a.   Common-law action of trespass for false imprisonment. At common law, the appropriate form of action for imposing a confinement was trespass for false imprisonment except where the confinement was by arrest under a valid process issued by a court having jurisdiction, in which case the damages for the confinement were recoverable, if at all, as part of the damages in an action of trespass on the case for malicious prosecution or abuse of process. Therefore, an act which makes the actor liable under this Section for a confinement otherwise than by arrest under a valid process is customarily called a false imprisonment.

b.   As to the meaning of the words "subject to liability," see § 5.

See Appendix for Reporter's Notes, Court Citations, and Cross References

52

FIGURE 3.11 ENTRY UNDER § 35 IN THE APPENDIX TO THE *RESTATEMENT (SECOND) OF TORTS*

Ch. 2   CITATIONS TO RESTATEMENT SECOND   § 35

TOPIC 4. THE INTEREST IN FREEDOM FROM CONFINEMENT

C.A.1, 1995. §§ 35–45A, constituting all of Ch. 2, Topic 4, cit. in sup. and adopted. Puerto Rican resident was arrested by federal agents who mistakenly believed that she was the subject of a 1975 arrest warrant; following the dismissal of all proceedings against her, she sued the United States for false arrest. Affirming the district court's grant of summary judgment for the United States, this court held that the United States was not liable for the false arrest of plaintiff, since the name in the warrant, together with information contained in the arrest packet, provided ample basis for the arresting agents to form an objectively reasonable belief that plaintiff was the person named in the warrant. The court also held that the conduct of the federal agent responsible for instigating the errant arrest was conditionally privileged, since the arrestee was sufficiently named in the warrant and the agent reasonably believed that plaintiff was the subject of the warrant. Rodriguez v. U.S., 54 F.3d 41, 45.

§ 35. False Imprisonment

C.A.1, 1995. Cit. in ftn. Two men who were arrested and acquitted of selling cocaine sued police officers of Puerto Rico and their confidential informants for constitutional violations, alleging that defendants falsely identified them as sellers. District court held that the false-arrest claims were barred by the one-year statute of limitations and that the malicious-prosecution claims were not actionable under 42 U.S.C. § 1983. This court vacated and remanded, holding that, for purposes of determining the appropriate accrual rule, both the Fourth and Fourteenth Amendment claims more closely resembled the common law tort of malicious prosecution. Consequently, plaintiffs' § 1983 claims did not accrue until their respective criminal prosecutions ended in acquittals. Calero–Colon v. Betancourt–Lebron, 68 F.3d 1, 3.

C.A.1, 2000. Cit. in headnote, quot. in disc. After being detained by store employees who accused them of shoplifting on a prior occasion, two children and their mother sued the store for false imprisonment. District court entered judgment on jury verdict awarding plaintiffs damages. This court affirmed, holding, inter alia, that plaintiffs stated a viable false-imprisonment claim, because a reasonable jury could conclude that the store's employees intended to confine plaintiffs within boundaries fixed by the store, that the store's acts resulted in such confinement, and that plaintiffs were conscious of the confinement. Employees' direction to plaintiffs, their reference to the police, and their continued presence were enough to induce reasonable people to believe either that they would be restrained physically if they sought to leave, or that the store was claiming lawful authority to confine them until the police arrived, or both. McCann v. Wal–Mart Stores, Inc., 210 F.3d 51, 51, 53.

C.A.7, 2003. Quot. in sup. African–American store employee who was fired for allegedly stealing from a coemployee sued store for federal civil-rights violations and false imprisonment under Indiana law, alleging that store representatives locked her in her manager's office for several minutes while they investigated the theft charges. District court granted store summary judgment. This court affirmed, holding, inter alia, that plaintiff did not establish a claim of false imprisonment under Indiana law, because her several-minute confinement was accidental, and store established justification for the brief detention. No one told plaintiff that she could not leave, and store provided a reasonable explanation for having left her alone in the office: so that she could draft her written statement without distraction. Adams v. Wal–Mart Stores, Inc., 324 F.3d 935, 941.

C.A.9, 2003. Com. (a) quot. in sup. California resident who had been director of Australian corporation was extradited to Australia for criminal trial. After Australian government dropped fraud charges and jury acquitted extraditee on other charge, he sued two instrumentalities and two employees of Australian government for malicious prosecution, abuse of process, and false imprisonment. District court granted motion to dismiss for employees, but denied motion as to instrumentalities. This court reversed in part, holding that plaintiff's claims of malicious prosecution and abuse of process were barred by Foreign Sovereign Immunities Act, since plaintiff could not overcome sovereign immu-

Cit.–cited; fol.–followed; quot.–quoted; sup.–support.
A complete list of abbreviations precedes page 1.

119

Cases interpreting § 35

6. Uniform Laws and Model Acts

Uniform laws and model acts are proposed statutes that can be adopted by legislatures. Two examples with which you may already be familiar are the Uniform Commercial Code and the Model Penal Code. Uniform laws and model acts are similar to Restatements in that they set out proposed rules, followed by commentary, research notes, and summaries of cases interpreting the rules. Unlike Restatements, which are limited to common-law doctrines, uniform laws and model acts exist in areas governed by statutory law.

Although uniform laws and model acts look like statutes, they are secondary sources. Their provisions do not take on the force of law unless they are adopted by a legislature. When that happens, however, the commentary, research references, and case summaries become very useful research tools. They can help you interpret the law and direct you to persuasive authority from other jurisdictions that have adopted the law.

One of the best ways to locate uniform laws and model acts is through a publication entitled *Uniform Laws Annotated, Master Edition* (ULA). This is a multivolume set of books containing the text of a number of uniform laws and model acts. You can locate it through the on-line catalog in your library.

Once you have located the ULA set, you have several research options. To determine the best research option for your project, you should review the *Directory of Uniform Acts and Codes: Tables and Index*. This softcover booklet is published annually and explains the finding tools available in this resource. You can research uniform laws and model acts by subject, by the name of the law, or by adopting jurisdiction. Once you have located relevant information in the main volumes of the ULA set, use the pocket part to update your research.

You are most likely to research uniform laws and model acts when your project involves research into state statutes, and generally speaking, researching in the ULA set is similar to statutory research. As a consequence, if you decide to use this resource, you may also want to review Chapter 6, which discusses statutory research.

Figure 3.12 shows a uniform law as it appears in the ULA set.

C. RESEARCHING SECONDARY SOURCES ELECTRONICALLY

1. LexisNexis and Westlaw

LexisNexis and Westlaw can be useful in locating secondary sources, especially if you are looking for material that is not available in print in your law library. As of this writing, Am. Jur. 2d is available in both LexisNexis and Westlaw, and C.J.S. is available in Westlaw. Annotations

FIGURE 3.12   ULA ENTRY FOR THE UNIFORM SINGLE PUBLICATION ACT

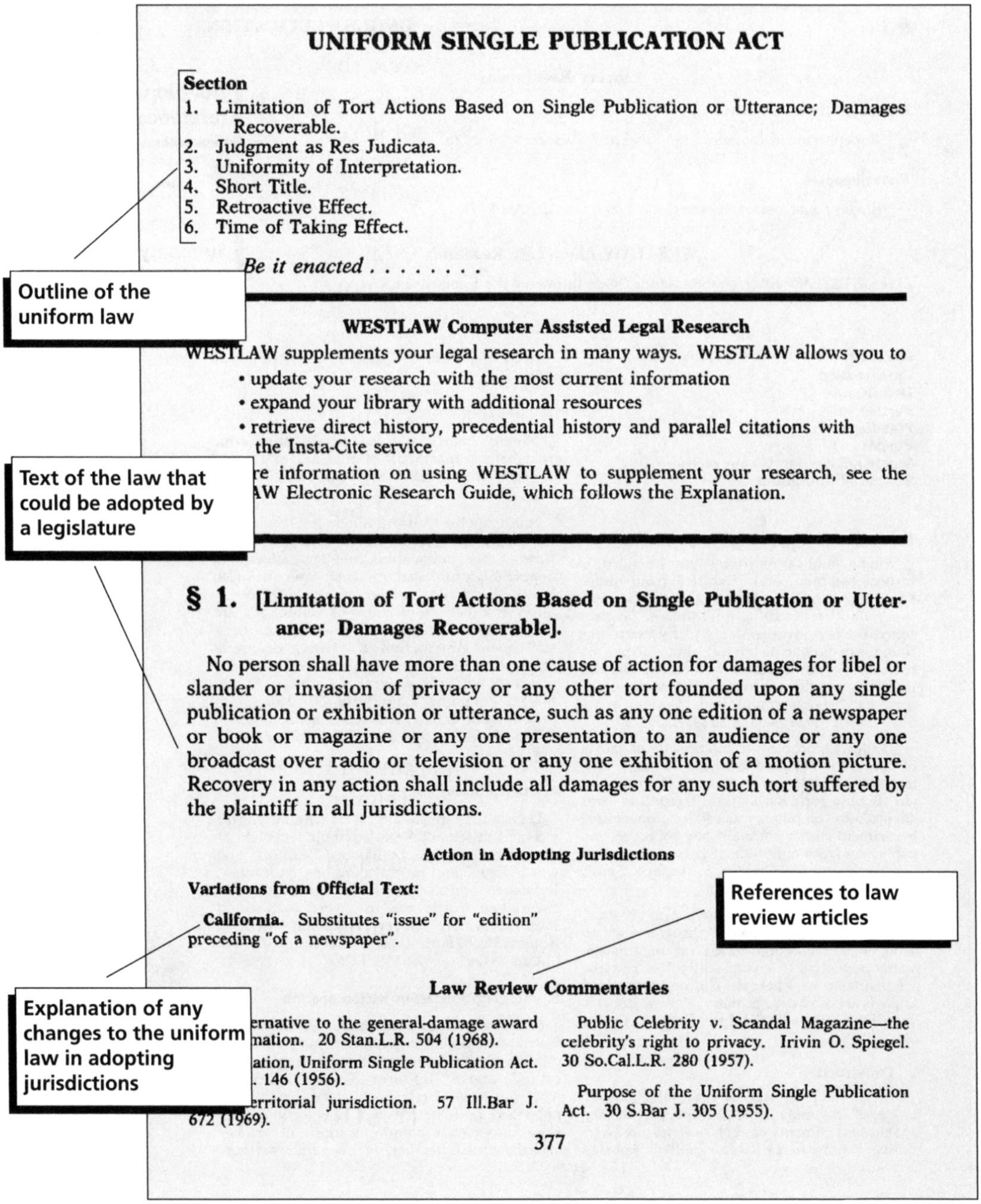

UNIFORM SINGLE PUBLICATION ACT

Section
1. Limitation of Tort Actions Based on Single Publication or Utterance; Damages Recoverable.
2. Judgment as Res Judicata.
3. Uniformity of Interpretation.
4. Short Title.
5. Retroactive Effect.
6. Time of Taking Effect.

Be it enacted . . . .

Outline of the uniform law

WESTLAW Computer Assisted Legal Research

WESTLAW supplements your legal research in many ways. WESTLAW allows you to
- update your research with the most current information
- expand your library with additional resources
- retrieve direct history, precedential history and parallel citations with the Insta-Cite service

...re information on using WESTLAW to supplement your research, see the ...AW Electronic Research Guide, which follows the Explanation.

Text of the law that could be adopted by a legislature

§ 1.   [Limitation of Tort Actions Based on Single Publication or Utterance; Damages Recoverable].

No person shall have more than one cause of action for damages for libel or slander or invasion of privacy or any other tort founded upon any single publication or exhibition or utterance, such as any one edition of a newspaper or book or magazine or any one presentation to an audience or any one broadcast over radio or television or any one exhibition of a motion picture. Recovery in any action shall include all damages for any such tort suffered by the plaintiff in all jurisdictions.

Action in Adopting Jurisdictions

Variations from Official Text:

California. Substitutes "issue" for "edition" preceding "of a newspaper".

References to law review articles

Law Review Commentaries

Explanation of any changes to the uniform law in adopting jurisdictions

...ernative to the general-damage award ...nation. 20 Stan.L.R. 504 (1968).

...ation, Uniform Single Publication Act. ... 146 (1956).

...erritorial jurisdiction. 57 Ill.Bar J. 672 (1969).

Public Celebrity v. Scandal Magazine—the celebrity's right to privacy. Irivin O. Spiegel. 30 So.Cal.L.R. 280 (1957).

Purpose of the Uniform Single Publication Act. 30 S.Bar J. 305 (1955).

377

FIGURE 3.12   ULA ENTRY FOR THE UNIFORM SINGLE PUBLICATION ACT *(Continued)*

---

§ 1   **SINGLE PUBLICATION**

Library References

Additional research references

American Digest System

Repetition of defamation, see Libel and Slander ☞26 to 28.

Encyclopedias

Single publication rule, see C.J.S. Libel and Slander § 53.

WESTLAW Electronic Research

See WESTLAW Electronic Research Guide following the Explanation.

Summary of a case interpreting the uniform law

Notes of Decisions

Generally   3
Construction   2
Definitions   4
Parties   6
Pleadings   7
Purpose   1
Single publication within section   5
Statute of limitations   8

1. Purpose

"Single publication rule" was intended to protect communication industry from undue harassment and unjust punishment by preventing plaintiff from filing multitude of lawsuits based on one tortious act, and by restricting time for commencing lawsuits, but rule permitted recovery for damages suffered by plaintiff in all communities in which defamatory statement had been communicated. Graham v. Today's Spirit, 1983, 468 A.2d 454, 503 Pa. 52.

To alleviate problem of multiplicity of causes of action for defamation under common law, legislature passed predecessor of "Uniform Single Publication Act"; this legislation was adopted to eliminate successive, oppressive harassment under common law by protecting publishers from multitude of lawsuits based on one tortious act. Graham v. Today's Spirit, 1983, 468 A.2d 454, 503 Pa. 52.

Legislature, in passing West's Ann.Civ.Proc. § 3425.1 et seq., intended to abrogate right to bring separate action based on defamatory matter appearing in several editions of newspaper or magazine where all editions comprised single issue of particular date. Belli v. Roberts Bros. Furs, 1966, 49 Cal.Rptr. 625, 240 C.A.2d 284.

2. Construction

District Court of Appeal may take judicial notice of assembly final history and senate journal and contents of each to determine legislative history of this Act. Belli v. Roberts

Bros. Furs, 1966, 49 Cal.Rptr. 625, 240 C.A.2d 284.

3. Generally

Illinois courts adopted single publication rule before enactment of this Act in Illinois. Wheeler v. Dell Pub. Co., C.A.Ill.1962, 300 F.2d 372.

Rationale for Uniform Single Publication Act is that cause of action for libel is complete at time of first publication, and any subsequent appearances or distributions of copies of original publication are of no consequence to creation or existence of cause of action, but are only relevant in computing damages; thus, subsequent distribution of existing copies of original publication neither creates fresh cause of action nor tolls applicable statute of limitations. Founding Church of Scientology of Washington, D.C. v. American Medical Ass'n, 1978, 18 Ill.Dec. 5, 377 N.E.2d 158, 60 Ill. App.3d 586.

4. Definitions

Legislature, in passing West's Ann.Civ.Proc. § 3425.1 et seq., chose to attribute technical or special meaning to both word "edition" and word "issue" and in replacing one with other, legislative body intended to discriminate between two words and use word that would most accurately convey its intent. Belli v. Roberts Bros. Furs, 1966, 49 Cal.Rptr. 625, 240 C.A.2d 284.

5. Single publication within section

Fact that allegedly defamatory articles published in separate newspapers were identical did not mean that there had been "single publication" under "Uniform Single Publication Act," and it was irrelevant that same publisher published both newspapers, for tortious acts were in separate communications of article, and thus plaintiffs had two separate actions.

378

---

from A.L.R.2d, 3d, 4th, 5th, and Fed. are available in both services, but those in the first series of A.L.R., A.L.R.6th, and A.L.R. Fed. 2d are available only in Westlaw. Westlaw also contains electronic annotations ("e-annos") that are not available in print or LexisNexis. E-annos are identified by year and number, e.g., 2005 A.L.R.6th 1. A number of uniform laws, model acts, and most Restatements of the law are available in both services. Many legal periodicals are available, but not all of them. Of those publications that are available, LexisNexis and Westlaw may not list every issue or every article in every issue, and the holdings go back only until the early 1980s. In addition, only a limited number of treatises can be accessed through these services. Thus, while LexisNexis and Westlaw are very good sources of secondary material, they are not exhaustive. You may find that computer searches do not yield all of the information you need and must be supplemented with book research.

In general, if you know which type of secondary authority you want to research, you can execute a word search in the database for that type of authority, e.g., the database for A.L.R. Annotations. LexisNexis and Westlaw also offer combined databases containing multiple secondary sources. Furthermore, you can limit your research to secondary sources covering a particular jurisdiction or subject area by searching in jurisdictional or subject area databases.

You can also view the table of contents for some secondary sources electronically. This will allow you to retrieve sections of the publication by selecting them from the table of contents without having to execute a word search. In Westlaw, click on the Table of Contents link near the top of the screen to review the publications for which tables of contents are available. In LexisNexis, if you select a source for which the table of contents is available, you will have a choice of accessing the table of contents or continuing with a word search.

The process of researching in LexisNexis and Westlaw is explained in more detail in Chapter 10.

2. HEINONLINE

HeinOnline is a service that provides electronic access to legal periodicals, among other types of authority. Many law libraries subscribe to this service. Because it is a subscription service, users generally access it through the library network.

You can search for legal periodical articles in HeinOnline in several ways. You can retrieve an article from its citation, search by title or author, or conduct word searches in the full text of the articles in HeinOnline's database. You can also browse the table of contents of individual publications.

HeinOnline is different from LexisNexis and Westlaw in two ways. First, its holdings go back further in time than those in LexisNexis and

FIGURE 3.13   HEINONLINE DISPLAY OF A LEGAL PERIODICAL ARTICLE

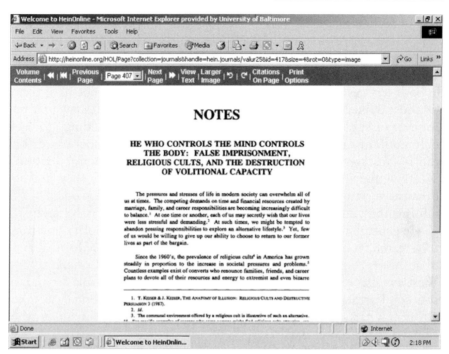

From HeinOnline. © 2005 HeinOnline.

Westlaw, often dating back to the inception of the periodicals in its database. Second, HeinOnline displays articles in .pdf format, which allows you to view an image of the printed page. The .pdf version of an article obtained through HeinOnline is often easier to read than the computer formatted versions available in LexisNexis and Westlaw.

Figure 3.13 shows the HeinOnline display of a legal periodical article.

3. INTERNET SOURCES

Although most secondary sources are not available via the Internet, some legal periodicals are. An increasing number of law reviews, journals, and other legal periodicals are beginning to publish their articles on the Internet.

To locate periodical articles on the Internet,[3] you must first identify publications that have made their contents available on the web. General legal research web sites will often contain links to legal periodicals. You can also go to individual law school web sites to see if their publications

---

[3]This is different from using LegalTrac or the electronic version of ILP on the Internet. They are commercial services available only to subscribers. The search methods described here allow you to retrieve the full text of a periodical article from a publicly available Internet site.

FIGURE 3.14 RULES FOR CITING SECONDARY SOURCES

SECONDARY SOURCE	ALWD MANUAL	BLUEBOOK
Legal encyclopedias	Rule 26	Bluepages B8
Treatises	Rule 22	Bluepages B8
Legal periodicals	Rule 23	Bluepages B9
A.L.R. Annotations	Rule 24	Rule 16.6.6
Restatements	Rule 27	Bluepages B6.1.3
Uniform laws & Model acts	Rule 27	Uniform laws—Bluepages B6.1.3; see also Rule 12.8.4 Model acts—Rule 12.8.5

are accessible on the Internet. Appendix A lists a number of Internet sites that may be useful in locating periodical articles. Some of these sites will allow you to execute word or subject searches. Others will list the tables of contents for periodicals available electronically.

If you have the citation or title of an article available on the Internet, this can be a quick and economical way to obtain it. Nevertheless, the number of periodicals accessible on the Internet is still small relative to the total number of publications available, and limitations on searching capabilities can make it difficult to locate pertinent material. Although this will no doubt change over time, at this point you would not want to rely on the Internet as the sole or starting point for periodical research. Moreover, it is important to remember that any person with a message and the appropriate equipment can publish material on the Internet. Therefore, you must evaluate the source of any secondary information you find this way. The Internet version of an established periodical is likely to be authoritative, but other sources may not be.

D. CITING SECONDARY SOURCES

The chart in **Figure 3.14** lists the rules in the *ALWD Manual* and the *Bluebook* governing citations to secondary sources. Citations to each of these sources are discussed in turn.

1. LEGAL ENCYCLOPEDIAS

Citations to legal encyclopedias are covered in *ALWD Manual* Rule 26 and *Bluebook* Bluepages B8 and are the same using either format. The

citation consists of five elements: (1) the volume number; (2) the abbreviated name of the encyclopedia; (3) the name of the topic, underlined or italicized; (4) the section cited (with a space between the section symbol (§) and the section number); and (5) a parenthetical containing the date of the book, including, if appropriate, the date of the pocket part or supplement. Here is an example:

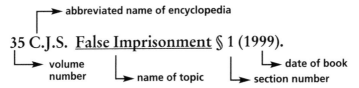

Sometimes determining which date or dates to include in the parenthetical can be confusing. The answer is always a function of where a reader would have to look to find all of the text and footnote information on the section you are citing. If all of the information appears in the main volume of the encyclopedia, the date in the parenthetical should refer only to the main volume. If the section is a new section that appears only in the pocket part, the date should refer only to the pocket part. If the reader must refer both to the main volume and to the pocket part, the parenthetical should list both dates. Here are several examples:

35 C.J.S. <u>False Imprisonment</u> § 1 (1999).

In this example, the reference is only to the main volume.

35 C.J.S. <u>False Imprisonment</u> § 1 (1999 & Supp. 2006).

In this example, the reference is both to the main volume and to the pocket part.

32 Am. Jur. 2d <u>False Imprisonment</u> § 1 (Supp. 2006).

In this example, the reference is only to the pocket part.

2. TREATISES

Citations to treatises contain roughly the same elements in both *ALWD Manual* and *Bluebook* formats. There are a few differences between them, however, and the order of the elements varies in minor respects.

In the *ALWD Manual*, citations to treatises are covered in Rule 22 and consist of four elements: (1) the author's full name (if the treatise has more than two authors, you may list the first, followed by et al.); (2) the title of the treatise, underlined or italicized; (3) a pinpoint reference containing the volume of the treatise (in a multivolume treatise), the section cited (with a space between the section symbol (§) and the

section number), and the specific page or pages cited; and (4) a parenthetical containing the edition (if more than one edition has been published), the publisher, and the date, including, if appropriate, the date of the pocket part. Here is an example in *ALWD Manual* format:

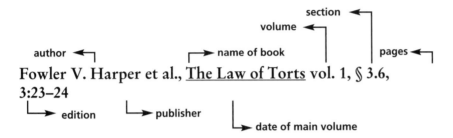

In the *Bluebook*, citations to treatises are covered in Bluepages B8 and consist of five elements: (1) the volume number of the treatise (in a multivolume set); (2) the author's full name (if the treatise has more than two authors, list the first, followed by et al.); (3) the title of the treatise, underlined or italicized; (4) the section cited (with a space between the section symbol (§) and the section number); and (5) a parenthetical containing the edition (if more than one edition has been published) and the date, including, if appropriate, the date of the pocket part. Here is an example in *Bluebook* format:

volume ← ┐   ┌→ author   ┌→ name of book   ┌→ section
    **1 Fowler V. Harper et al., <u>The Law of Torts</u> § 3.6
    (3d ed. 1996).**
edition ←┘   └→ date of main volume

Note that in both citation formats, a comma separates the part of the citation identifying the author or authors from the title of the treatise. No other commas appear in a *Bluebook* citation. In an *ALWD Manual* citation, commas also separate the components of the pinpoint reference, as well as the edition and publisher's name in the parenthetical.

Both the *ALWD Manual* and the *Bluebook* have additional requirements for books with editors or translators.

3. LEGAL PERIODICALS

Legal periodicals are published in two formats. Some publications begin the first issue within each volume with page one and continue numbering the pages of subsequent issues within that volume consecutively. These are called consecutively paginated publications. Most law reviews and journals are consecutively paginated. Other publications, such as monthly magazines, begin each new issue with page one, regardless of

where the issue falls within the volume. These are called nonconsecutively paginated publications.

There are some differences in the citations to articles published in consecutively and nonconsecutively paginated periodicals. The explanation in this section focuses on citations to articles published in consecutively paginated law reviews, which are covered in *ALWD Manual* Rule 23 and *Bluebook* Bluepages B9.

A citation to a law review article in both *ALWD Manual* and *Bluebook* formats consists of seven elements: (1) the author's full name; (2) the title of the article, underlined or italicized; (3) the volume number of the publication; (4) the abbreviated name of the publication; (5) the starting page of the article; (6) the pinpoint citation to the specific page or pages cited; and (7) a parenthetical containing the date of the publication. Here is an example:

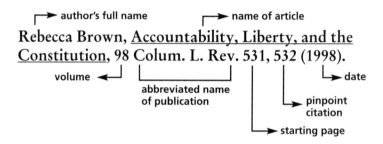

Note that the author's name, the name of the article, and the starting page of the article are followed by commas. The comma following the name of the article is not underlined or italicized.

Publication abbreviations can be found in *ALWD Manual* Appendix 5 and *Bluebook* Table T.13. Notice that the periodical abbreviations in *Bluebook* Table T.13 appear in large and small capital letters. According to Bluepages B13, however, you should not use large and small capitals when citing authority in a brief or memorandum. Use ordinary roman type for the publication's name. Both the *ALWD Manual* and the *Bluebook* have additional rules for citing articles appearing in nonconsecutively paginated publications, articles written by students, and articles with more than one author.

4. A.L.R. ANNOTATIONS

Citations to A.L.R. Annotations are covered in *ALWD Manual* Rule 24 and *Bluebook* Rule 16.6.6. They are almost identical in both formats, with only one minor difference between them. A citation to an A.L.R. Annotation consists of seven elements: (1) the author's full name (in a *Bluebook* citation, the author's name is followed by the notation

"Annotation"); (2) the title of the Annotation, underlined or italicized; (3) the volume number; (4) the A.L.R. series; (5) the starting page of the Annotation; (6) the pinpoint citation to the specific page or pages cited; and (7) a parenthetical containing the date, including, if appropriate, the date of the pocket part. Here is an example in *ALWD Manual* format:

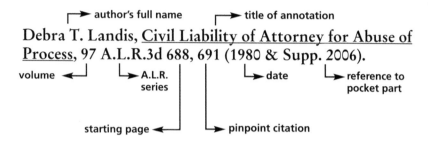

Here is an example in *Bluebook* format:

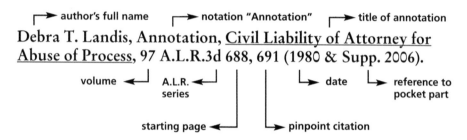

Although the example in *Bluebook* Rule 16.6.6 shows A.L.R. Fed. in large and small capital letters, use ordinary roman type pursuant to Bluepages B13 for a citation in a memorandum or brief.

5. RESTATEMENTS

Citations to Restatements are covered in *ALWD Manual* Rule 27 and *Bluebook* Bluepages B6.1.3. They contain three elements using either format: (1) the name of the Restatement; (2) the section cited (with a space between the section symbol (§) and the section number); and (3) a parenthetical containing the date. The only difference is that the name of the Restatement is underlined or italicized in *ALWD Manual* format, but not in *Bluebook* format. Here is an example in *ALWD Manual* format:

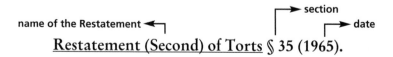

Here is an example in *Bluebook* format:

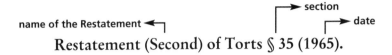

Restatement (Second) of Torts § 35 (1965).

6. UNIFORM LAWS AND MODEL ACTS

The citation format for a uniform law depends on whether the law has been adopted by a jurisdiction. If a jurisdiction adopts a uniform law, the law will be published with all of the other statutes for that jurisdiction. In that situation, cite directly to the jurisdiction's statute. The requirements for statutory citations are explained in Chapter 6.

Citations to uniform laws published in the ULA set are governed by *ALWD Manual* Rule 27. In the *Bluebook,* Bluepages B6.1.3 gives an example of a citation to a uniform law; additional information on citing laws published in the ULA set appears in Rule 12.8.4. The citation is the same using either format and consists of six elements: (1) the abbreviated title of the act; (2) the section cited (with a space between the section symbol (§) and section number); (3) the ULA volume number; (4) the abbreviation "U.L.A."; (5) the page of the ULA on which the section appears; and (6) a parenthetical containing the date of the ULA volume, including, if appropriate, the date of the pocket part. Here is an example:

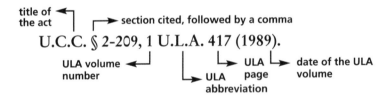

U.C.C. § 2-209, 1 U.L.A. 417 (1989).

Citations to model acts are covered in *ALWD Manual* Rule 27 and *Bluebook* Rule 12.8.5. Model act citations are almost identical in both formats, with only one minor difference between them. The citation consists of three elements: (1) the name of the act; (2) the section cited (with a space between the section symbol (§) and the section number); and (3) a parenthetical.

In *ALWD Manual* citations, the parenthetical contains the name of the organization that issued the act, abbreviated according to Appendix 3, and the date. Here is an example in *ALWD Manual* format:

name of the act ◄┐   section ◄┐   ┌► date
Model Penal Code § 5.03 (ALI 1985).
organization that issued the act ◄──┘

The *Bluebook* requires that the parenthetical include the name of the organization that issued the act for some model acts, but not others. In all model act citations, however, the *Bluebook* requires the date in the parenthetical. Here is an example in *Bluebook* format:

name of the act ◄┐ section ◄┐

Model Penal Code § 5.03 (1985).

date ◄┘

The examples of citations to uniform laws and model acts in Rules 12.8.4 and 12.8.5 show the names of the laws in large and small capital letters. According to Bluepages B13, however, you should use ordinary roman type to cite these authorities in a memorandum or brief.

E. SAMPLE PAGES FOR PRINT SECONDARY SOURCE RESEARCH

Beginning on the next page, **Figures 3.15** through **3.23** are sample pages from A.L.R. and the *Restatement (Second) of Torts* showing what you would see in the books if you had researched false imprisonment and the related topic of abuse of process.

To locate an A.L.R. Annotation, begin by looking up your subject in the A.L.R. Index. The A.L.R. Index will refer you directly to applicable Annotations. The reference will tell you the volume number, series, and starting page of the Annotation.

FIGURE 3.15   A.L.R. INDEX

ALR INDEX

FALLS AND FALLING OBJECTS —Cont'd
Swimming facility—Cont'd
  occasioned thereby, **64 ALR5th 1**
  products liability, swimming pools and accessories, **65 ALR5th 105, § 7[b], 8[b], 12, 13, 14[b], 22, 23[a]**
Taxicab, liability of taxicab carrier to passenger injured while alighting from taxi, **98 ALR3d 822**
Theaters, lighting, liability of theater owner or operator for injury to or death of patron resulting from lighting conditions on premises, **19 ALR4th 1110**
Torso or trunk, excessiveness or adequacy of damages awarded for injuries to trunk or torso, or internal injuries, **48 ALR5th 129**
Trailer park, liability of owner or operator of trailer camp or park for injury or death from condition of premises, **41 ALR3d 546**
Trees and shrubbery
  abutting landowner, liability of private owner or occupant of land abutting highway for injuries or damage resulting from tree or limb falling onto highway, **94 ALR3d 1160**
  governmental liability, liability of governmental unit for injuries or damage resulting from tree or limb falling onto highway from abutting land, **95 ALR3d 778**
Warnings, grocery store operator's liability to invitee slipping on spilled liquid or semi-liquid substance, **24 ALR4th 696**
Water, contributory negligence and assumption of risk in action against owner of store, office, or similar place of business by invitee falling on tracked-in water or snow, **20 ALR4th 517**
Window washer, tort liability for window washer's injury or death, **69 ALR4th 207**
Workers' compensation
  misrepresentation, eligibility for workers' compensation as affected by claimant's misrepresentation of health or physical condition at time of hiring, **12 ALR5th 658**
  presumption or inference that

FALLS AND FALLING OBJECTS —Cont'd
Workers' compensation—Cont'd
  accidental death of employee engaged in occupation of manufacturing or processing arose out of and in course of employment, **47 ALR5th 801**
  receipts, injuries incurred while traveling to or from work with employer's receipts, **63 ALR4th 253**

FALSE ALARMS
Alarm systems, liability of person furnishing, installing, or servicing burglary or fire alarm system for burglary or fire loss, **37 ALR4th 47**
Penalties, validity and construction of statutes or ordinances imposing civil or criminal penalties on alarm system users, installers, or servicers for false alarms, **17 ALR5th 825**

FALSE CLAIMS ACT
Jurisdictional bars, construction and application of "public disclosure" and "original source" jurisdictional bars under 31 U.S.C.A. § 3730(e)(4) (civil actions for false claims), **117 ALR Fed 263**

FALSE IMPRISONMENT AND ARREST
Abduction and kidnapping
  authority of parent or one in loco parentis, taking under, **20 ALR4th 823**
  included offense within charge of kidnapping, **68 ALR3d 828**
  prison official, seizure by inmates as kidnapping, **59 ALR3d 1306**
  separate offense, seizure or detention for purpose of committing rape, robbery, or other offense as constituting separate crime of kidnapping, **39 ALR5th 283**
Abuse of process
  attorney, civil liability of attorney for abuse of process, **97 ALR3d 688**
  private citizen calling on police for assistance after disturbance or

> Index entry for false imprisonment

> Reference to an annotation

Consult POCKET PART for Later Annotations

350

The Annotation will begin with an outline and references to related research sources. After the outline, an alphabetical index of topics within the Annotation will appear.

FIGURE 3.16   A.L.R. ANNOTATION

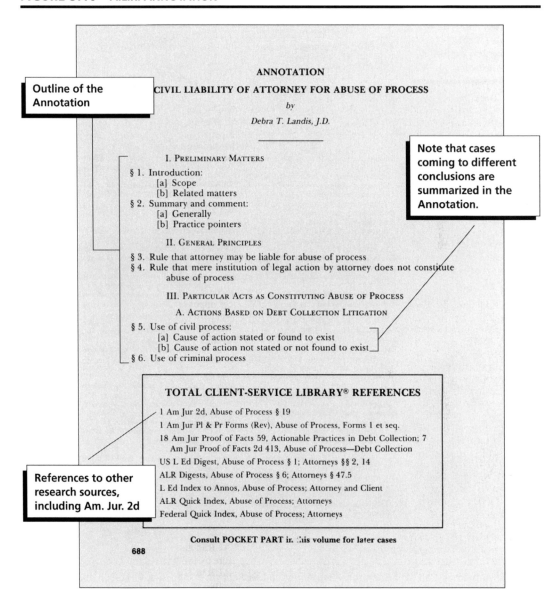

ANNOTATION

Outline of the Annotation

CIVIL LIABILITY OF ATTORNEY FOR ABUSE OF PROCESS

by

Debra T. Landis, J.D.

Note that cases coming to different conclusions are summarized in the Annotation.

I. PRELIMINARY MATTERS

§ 1. Introduction:
 [a] Scope
 [b] Related matters
§ 2. Summary and comment:
 [a] Generally
 [b] Practice pointers

II. GENERAL PRINCIPLES

§ 3. Rule that attorney may be liable for abuse of process
§ 4. Rule that mere institution of legal action by attorney does not constitute abuse of process

III. PARTICULAR ACTS AS CONSTITUTING ABUSE OF PROCESS

A. ACTIONS BASED ON DEBT COLLECTION LITIGATION

§ 5. Use of civil process:
 [a] Cause of action stated or found to exist
 [b] Cause of action not stated or not found to exist
§ 6. Use of criminal process

TOTAL CLIENT-SERVICE LIBRARY® REFERENCES

1 Am Jur 2d, Abuse of Process § 19

1 Am Jur Pl & Pr Forms (Rev), Abuse of Process, Forms 1 et seq.

18 Am Jur Proof of Facts 59, Actionable Practices in Debt Collection; 7 Am Jur Proof of Facts 2d 413, Abuse of Process—Debt Collection

US L Ed Digest, Abuse of Process § 1; Attorneys §§ 2, 14

ALR Digests, Abuse of Process § 6; Attorneys § 47.5

L Ed Index to Annos, Abuse of Process; Attorney and Client

ALR Quick Index, Abuse of Process; Attorneys

Federal Quick Index, Abuse of Process; Attorneys

References to other research sources, including Am. Jur. 2d

Consult POCKET PART in this volume for later cases

688

FIGURE 3.16 A.L.R. ANNOTATION *(Continued)*

After the outline, each Annotation has its own subject index to help you locate information within the Annotation.

97 ALR3d   Liability of Attorney for Abuse of Process
97 ALR3d 688

B. Other Actions

§ 7. Filing of action alone or together with initial process or pleading:
   [a] At law for tort
   [b] In equity
   [c] For unspecified relief
§ 8. Use of subpoena
§ 9. Use of other process

INDEX

Affidavit, making oath to as abuse of process, § 5[a]

Alimony, attempt to force payment of by arrest and imprisonment, § 6

Arrest, matters concerning, §§ 4, 6

Attempted extortion, allegation of, § 5

Bank account, garnishment of, § 5[b]

Body process, necessity for in abuse of process action, § 7[a]

Bonds, attempt by attorney to force client to part with, §§ 3, 9

Chose in action, withholding of, § 5[b]

Civil process based on debt collection litigation as constituting abuse of process, § 5

Comment and summary, § 2

Conspiracy, allegations as to, §§ 3, 5[b], 7[a]

Criminal process based on debt collection litigation as constituting abuse of process, §§ 4, 6, 7[a]

Debt collection litigation, actions based on as abuse of process, §§ 3, 5, 6

Default judgment, entering of, § 5[b]

Disorderly persons charge, attempt to collect hotel bill by, § 6

Elements necessary to establish cause of action for abuse of process, § 4

Equitable proceedings, institution of as constituting abuse of process, § 7[b]

Equity, filing of action alone or together with initial process or pleading as abuse of process, § 7[b]

Execution sale of judgment debtors' assets, § 5[b]

Extortion of money, allegation of attempt, § 5

Filing of action alone or together with initial process or pleading, as abuse of process, § 7

Forgery of signature, request for admissions related to alleged forgery as abuse, § 9

Garnishment procedure, institution of, § 5

Harassment, issuance of process for purposes of as abuse, § 7[a]

Hotel bill, prosecution for failure to pay as abuse, § 6

Imprisonment, attempt to collect debt by as abuse, § 6

Income tax refund check, request for admissions related to cashing of as abuse, § 9

Institution of legal action by attorney as not constituting abuse of process, § 4

Interrogation at police station, issuance of grand jury subpoena for purposes of as abuse, § 8

Introduction, § 1

Judgment by confession, securing of, § 5[b]

Judgment debt, use of writ of execution to sell, § 5[b]

Lien as constituting abuse of process, §§ 5[a], 7[a]

Malice, disclosure of as affecting abuse of process action, § 5[a]

Medical malpractice suit, filing of against physician as abuse of process, § 7[a]

Money, alleged attempt to extort, § 5

Negotiable instruments, attempt by attorney to force plaintiff to part with as abuse, §§ 3, 9

Other actions constituting abuse of process, §§ 7-9

Other process as constituting abuse of process, § 9

Particular acts as constituting abuse of process, §§ 5-9

Physician, effect of filing medical malprac-

689

Following the subject index, you will see a list of the jurisdictions from which authority is cited within the Annotation. The first part of the Annotation will set out the scope of coverage, list Annotations on related subjects, and summarize the law on the topic.

FIGURE 3.17 A.L.R. ANNOTATION

§ 1[a]   LIABILITY OF ATTORNEY FOR ABUSE OF PROCESS   97 ALR3d
97 ALR3d 688

tice suit against that resulted in no cause of action, § 7[a]
Power of attorney, use of against client's interest as abuse, § 7[b]
Practice pointers, § 2[b]
Preliminary matters, §§ 1, 2
Related matters, § 1[b]
Rent, filing suit for return of, § 5[b]
Scope of annotation, § 1[a]
Security deposit, filing suit for return of, § 5[b]
Seizure of property, necessity for in abuse of process action, § 4
Subpoena, use of as constituting abuse of process, § 8
Summary and comment, § 2
Teachers, issuance of subpoenas to force attendance at hearing as abuse, § 8

Temporary injunction, use of to delay delivery for monetary gain as abuse, § 7[b]
Theft, prosecution for to force plaintiff to part with bonds as abuse, §§ 3, 9
Tort, filing of action alone or together with initial process or pleading at law for, § 7[a]
Unspecified relief, filing of action alone or together with initial process or pleading for, § 7[c]
Void orders, procurance of as constituting abuse of process, § 5[a]
Writ, use of as constituting abuse of process, §§ 5, 6, 7[a]
Wrong parties, knowingly proceeding against as constituting abuse of process, § 5[a]

Jurisdictions from which authority is cited

TABLE OF JURISDICTIONS REPRESENTED
Consult POCKET PART in this volume for later cases

US: §§ 3, 6, 7[b]	**Mass:** §§ 5[b]
Cal: §§ 9	**Mich:** §§ 4, 7[a]
DC: §§ 5[b]	**Minn:** §§ 3, 9
Ga: §§ 3, 5[a]	**NJ:** §§ 3, 6
Ill: §§ 4, 5[b], 7[a]	**NY:** §§ 3, 4, 5[b], 6, 7[a-c], 8, 9
Kan: §§ 3, 5[a]	**Pa:** §§ 3, 5[a, b]
Me: §§ 3	**Wash:** §§ 3, 4, 5[b]

I. Preliminary matters

§ 1. Introduction

[a] Scope

This annotation collects and analyzes those state and federal cases in which the courts have decided or discussed the question of the civil liability of an attorney for an abuse of civil or criminal process.

For the purposes of this annotation, the term "attorney," refers to the person being sued for an abuse of process arising out of, or apparently out of, an attorney-client relationship.

Therefore, cases in which the person being sued for an abuse of process happens to be an attorney but in which there is no indication that an attorney-client relationship was involved are beyond the scope of this annotation. Also beyond the scope of this annotation are cases involving the civil liability of a prosecuting attorney for an alleged abuse of process resulting from acts done in an official capacity.[1]

The cases considered herein are those which clearly specify that the cause of action is founded on abuse

Introduction to the Annotation

1. As to the civil liability of a prosecuting attorney for acts done in an official
690

capacity, see 63 Am Jur 2d, Prosecuting Attorneys § 34.

FIGURE 3.17   A.L.R. ANNOTATION (Continued)

Summary of the law on this topic

Related A.L.R. Annotations

97 ALR3d   LIABILITY OF ATTORNEY FOR ABUSE OF PROCESS
97 ALR3d 688

of process, as distinguished from those which, although involving alleged wrongful conduct similar to that found in an action for abuse of process, do not state that the action is based on that tort.

s, beyond the scope of this ation is the liability of an attor-r wrongful execution or attach-of property unless the cause of action is specified to be that for an abuse of process.[2]

[b] Related matters

Institution of confessed judgment proceedings as ground of action for abuse of process or malicious prosecution. 87 ALR3d 554.

Action for breach of contract as basis of action for malicious prosecution or abuse of process. 87 ALR3d 580.

Civil liability of judicial officer for malicious prosecution or abuse of process. 64 ALR3d 1251.

What constitutes malice sufficient to justify an award of punitive damages in action for wrongful attachment or garnishment. 61 ALR3d 984.

Liability of attorney acting for client, for false imprisonment or malicious prosecution of third party. 27 ALR3d 1113.

Use of criminal process to collect debt as abuse of process. 27 ALR3d 1202.

What statute of limitations governs action for malicious use of process or abuse of process, in the absence of an express provision for such tort. 10 ALR3d 533.

When statute of limitations begins to run against action for abuse of process. 1 ALR3d 953.

§ 2. Summary and comment

[a] Generally

It has been generally stated that an abuse of legal process consists of the malicious misuse or misapplication of regularly issued civil or criminal process to accomplish some purpose not warranted or commanded by the writ.[3] The Restatement of Torts 2d § 682 similarly provides that one who uses legal process, either civil or criminal, against another person primarily to accomplish a purpose for which it was not designed is liable to the other for harm caused by the abuse of process.

The question whether an attorney, by virtue of the attorney-client relationship, enjoys exemption from civil liability for abuse of process, similar to that of a judicial officer, has arisen in some cases, and it has been held that an attorney may be held liable in an action for damages for abuse of process where the acts complained of are his own personal acts, or the acts of others wholly instigated and carried on by him.[4] However, courts have held that the mere institution of a legal action by an attorney does not constitute an abuse of process, absent other circumstances.[5]

Turning to particular allegations against attorneys in actions for abuse of process, courts have reached opposite results, under varying factual circumstances, in determining whether a cause of action was stated or existed

2. As to the liability of an attorney for wrongful attachment or execution, see 7 Am Jur 2d, Attorneys at Law § 197.

3. 1 Am Jur 2d, Abuse of Process § 1.
As to the distinction between an abuse of process and an action for malicious

prosecution, malicious use of process, or false imprisonment, see generally 1 Am Jur 2d, Abuse of Process §§ 2, 3.

4. § 3, infra.

5. § 4, infra.

691

FIGURE 3.17 A.L.R. ANNOTATION (Continued)

§ 2[a] LIABILITY OF ATTORNEY FOR ABUSE OF PROCESS 97 ALR3d
97 ALR3d 688

against an attorney by virtue of the use of civil process to collect a debt for a client.[6] Some courts have also held that where it was alleged that an attorney used criminal process as a means of collecting a debt due a client, a cause of action against the attorney for abuse of process was stated.[7]

In cases involving the filing of a tort action by an attorney, where no acts were alleged against the attorney involving the improper use of process, it has been held that a cause of action against the attorney was not stated.[8] Likewise, in a case in which no facts were stated in a complaint for abuse of process against an attorney showing that he was the active and procuring cause of the institution by his client of civil actions, whose nature was not specified in the court's opinion, or showing interference with the plaintiff's personal property, the court held that no cause of action for abuse of process was stated.[9] However, where a complaint alleged that an attorney did not act in a bona fide effort to protect the interest of a client in filing equitable actions, but rather acted in the interest of other clients to prevent the plaintiff from delivering shares of stock before a contractual deadline, the court held that a cause of action for abuse of process against the attorney was stated.[10]

It has been held or recognized that a cause of action was stated or found to exist against an attorney where the attorney was alleged to have used subpoenas for other than their legitimate purpose.[11] However, in cases involving the use of other types of process, the courts, under the particular facts, found that the complaints failed to state a cause of action against the attorney.[12]

[b] Practice pointers

Counsel representing a plaintiff in an action for abuse of process against an attorney should be aware that the same facts which give rise to the action may also establish an action for malicious prosecution, false arrest, or false imprisonment, and that the causes may be joined in the same action, but not in the same count.[13] The attorney should, however, keep in mind that an action for abuse of process is based on the improper use of the process after it has been issued, while malicious prosecution is based on the wrongful intent or malice that caused the process to be issued initially.[14]

Counsel should note that an action for abuse of process has generally been held to accrue, and the statute of limitations to commence to run, from the termination of the acts which constitute the abuse complained of and not from the completion of the action in which the process issued.[15] Actions for abuse of process are generally governed by the statute of limitations applicable to actions for injury to the person. However, in a jurisdiction in which one statute governed injury to the person

---

6. § 5[a], [b], infra.

7. § 6, infra.

8. § 7[a], infra.

9. § 7[c], infra.

10. § 7[b], infra.

11. § 8, infra.

692

12. § 9, infra.

13. As to pleading in actions for abuse of process, see generally 1 Am Jur 2d, Abuse of Process § 21.

14. 1 Am Jur 2d, Abuse of Process § 2.

15. 1 Am Jur 2d, Abuse of Process § 24.

Practice pointers

After the introductory material, the Annotation will explain the law on the topic in greater detail, summarize key cases, and provide citations to additional cases on the topic.

FIGURE 3.18   A.L.R. ANNOTATION

97 ALR3d   LIABILITY OF ATTORNEY FOR ABUSE OF PROCESS   § 3
97 ALR3d 688

and another statute governed "injuries to the rights of others," the court held that an action for abuse of process was controlled by the latter statute.[16]

II. General principles

§ 3. Rule that attorney may be liable for abuse of process

llowing cases support the an attorney may be held a civil action for abuse of here the acts complained of n personal acts, or the acts of others instigated and carried on by him.

US—For federal cases involving state law, see state headings infra.

Ga—Walker v Kyser (1967) 115 Ga App 314, 154 SE2d 457 (by implication).

Kan—Little v Sowers (1949) 167 Kan 72, 204 P2d 605.

Me—Lambert v Breton (1929) 127 Me 510, 144 A 864 (recognizing rule).

Minn—Hoppe v Klapperich (1937) 224 Minn 224, 28 NW2d 780, 173 ALR 819.

NJ—Ash v Cohen (1937) 119 NJL 54, 194 A 174.

Voytko v Ramada Inn of Atlantic City (1978, DC NJ) 445 F Supp 315 (by implication; applying New Jersey law).

NY—Board of Education v Farmingdale Classroom Teachers Asso. (1975) 38 NY2d 397, 380 NYS2d 635, 343 NE2d 278 (by implication).

Dishaw v Wadleigh (1897) 15 App Div 205, 44 NYS 207.

Cote v Knickerbocker Ice Co. (1936) 160 Misc 658, 290 NYS 483 (recognizing rule); Rothbard v Ringler (1947, Sup) 77 NYS2d 351 (by

implication); Weiss v Hunna (1963, CA2 NY) 312 F2d 711, cert den 374 US 853, 10 L Ed 2d 1073, 83 S Ct 1920, reh den 375 US 874, 11 L Ed 2d 104, 84 S Ct 37 (by implication; applying New York law).

Pa—Haggerty v Moyerman (1936) 321 Pa 555, 184 A 654 (by implication).

Adelman v Rosenbaum (1938) 133 Pa Super 386, 3 A2d 15; Sachs (1963, ED Pa) 216 F Supp implication; applying Pennsy law).

Wash—Fite v Lee (1974) 11 App 21, 521 P2d 964, 97 ALR3d 678, (by implication).

An attorney is personally liable to a third party if he maliciously participates with others in an abuse of process, or if he maliciously encourages and induces another to act as his instrumentality in committing an act constituting an abuse of process, the court held in Hoppe v Klapperich (1947) 224 **Minn** 224, 28 NW2d 780, 173 ALR 819. The court reversed the order of the trial court which had sustained the demurrers of an attorney and other defendants in a proceeding for abuse of process and malicious prosecution. The plaintiff had alleged, as to the cause of action for abuse of process, that it was the intent of the defendants, an attorney, his client, a sheriff, and a municipal judge, to force her to part with certain bonds, negotiable instruments, and other valuable papers by threatening her with arrest and prosecution on a criminal charge of theft of a watch. The plaintiff's subsequent arrest and confinement on the charge of theft were alleged to constitute a continuing abuse of process. The court noted that in the performance

16. See 7 Am Jur Proof of Facts 2d, Abuse of Process—Debt Collection § 4.

693

Reprinted with permission from Thomson West, *American Law Reports,* 3d Ser., Vol. 97 (1980), p. 693. © 1980 Thomson West.

To update, check the pocket part. The pocket part is organized by the page numbers of the Annotations, not by their titles.

FIGURE 3.19   POCKET PART ACCOMPANYING AN A.L.R. VOLUME

97 ALR3d 627-677   ALR3d

se was properly denied; since the purpose of such regulations was not to protect persons such as the plaintiff from loss of helicopters in crashes, but rather, was to ensure safety of persons both in the aircraft and on the ground. Erickson Air-Crane Co. v United Technologies Corp. (1987) 87 **Or App** 577, 743 P2d 747, review den 304 Or 680, 748 P2d 142.

Summary judgment was granted in favor of airline in strict liability and negligence action that was brought by passenger who, upon standing up from her seat to deplane American Airlines Boeing 727-200 operated by airline, hit her head on overhead bin compartment located over her seat and allegedly herniated several intervertebral discs. Civil engineer was not qualified to give expert testimony on behalf of plaintiff with regard to design of aircraft's overhead bin compartments, where civil engineer had no prior experience in design, manufacturing, or operation of aircraft and had never before analyzed ergonomics of seating and overhead compartment arrangements in aircraft interiors. Even if witness were qualified, his testimony that aircraft's overhead bin compartments were defectively designed because they were too rigid and that passengers sitting in seat located in emergency exit aisle, where plaintiff sat, have false sense of spaciousness such that airline should have warned passengers about low ceiling under bins was without scientific basis and was inadmissible. Former airline flight attendant was not qualified to render expert opinion as to whether airline should have warned passengers about existence of overhead bin compartments, even though flight attendant may have been qualified to state lay opinions, where flight attendant had no experience in design, manufacturing, or operation of aircraft that would have allowed him to determine what, if any, warning practices would have been appropriate. Flight attendant's testimony that placement of padding in overhead bin compartments would have minimized danger of serious injury thus amounted to simple speculation and was not admissible. Given fact that there was no competent scientific evidence of compartment or seating arrangement in question nor of how coach cabins and overhead bin compartments should be designed and that hazard posed to plaintiff by overhead bin compartment was apparent and obvious, plaintiff's case was insufficient to survive airline's motion for summary judgment as to plaintiff's design defect and failure to warn claims. Silva v American Airlines, Inc. (1997, **DC Puerto Rico**) 960 F Supp 528 (applying Puerto Rico law).

In action brought by and on behalf of survivors of Army pilot who was killed in crash of Army Cobra AH-1 helicopter, in which it was alleged that civilian company which had at one time been responsible for maintenance of helicopter was negligent in using improper grease, using improper maintenance procedure, and failing to supply adequate information to Army of swashplate (bearing container) malfunction that occurred in helicopter prior to swashplate malfunction that occurred when helicopter crashed, judgment on jury verdict in favor of maintenance company was affirmed on appeal. Appellate court noted that Army report of accident made no final conclusions or recommendations regarding accident. Court further noted that in addition to developing evidence to rebut allegations of negligence, maintenance company presented evidence that product defect, and not improper main[tenance] caused accident. Court stated that [review of all evidence presented at [trial] could not find that verdict was so co[ntrary to] overwhelming weight of evidence [as to be] clearly wrong and unjust. Beavers v Northrop Worldwide Aircraft Services, Inc. (1991, **Tex App Amarillo**) 821 SW2d 669.

> The pocket part is organized by page numbers

97 ALR3d 688-705

Research References

Physicians' countersuits, 35 Am Jur Trials 225

Restatement (Third) of the Law Governing Lawyers § 6 (2000), Judicial Remedies Available to a Client or Nonclient for Lawyer Wrongs.

Restatement (Third) of the Law Governing Lawyers § 56 (2000), Liability to a Client or Nonclient Under General Law.

§ 1. Introduction

[b] Related matters

Necessity and permissibility of raising claim for abuse of process by reply or counterclaim in same proceeding in which abuse occurred—state cases. 82 ALR4th 1115.

Attorney's liability, to one other than immediate client, for negligence in connection with legal duties. 61 ALR4th 615.

Liability of attorney, acting for client, for malicious prosecution. 46 ALR4th 249.

Initiating, or threatening to initiate, criminal prosecution as ground for disciplining counsel. 42 ALR4th 1000.

Abuse of process action based on misuse of discovery or deposition procedures after commencement of civil action without seizure of person or property. 33 ALR4th 650.

94

For latest cases, call the toll free number appearing on the cover of this supplement.

FIGURE 3.19 POCKET PART ACCOMPANYING AN A.L.R. VOLUME *(Continued)*

SUPPLEMENT   **97 ALR3d 688-705**

Authority of United States District Court, under 28 U.S.C.A. § 1651(a), to enjoin, sua sponte, a party from filing further papers in support of frivolous claim. 53 ALR Fed 651.

§ 2. Summary and comment
[a] Generally

Allegations that attorneys obtained default judgment based on error, and demanded payment of fee for services rendered prior to agreeing to enter satisfaction of judgment to correct error, did not state cause of action for abuse of process. Varela v Investors Ins. Holding Corp. (1992, 2d Dept) 185 App Div 2d 309, 586 **NYS2d** 272.

§ 3. Rule that attorney may be liable for abuse of process

See Mozzochi v Beck (1987) 204 **Conn** 490, ~~1, § 7[a].~~

~~ards v Auty (1989) 232 **NJ Super**~~
~~2d 1030, § 5[a].~~

~~Attorney~~ is liable if he or she causes irregular process to be issued which occasions loss to party against whom it is enforced. ERA Realty Co. v RBS Properties (1992, 2d Dept) 185 App Div 2d 871, 586 **NYS2d** 831.

Under New York law, claim for abuse of process can be stated against attorney who prepares or causes abused process to be issued in bad faith and for purpose of gaining collateral advantage. Reisner v. Stoller, 51 F. Supp. 2d 430, R.I.C.O. Bus. Disp. Guide (CCH) ¶ 9760 (**S.D.N.Y.** 1999).

Under New York law, elements for claim of abuse of process are (1) regularly issued process (civil or criminal), (2) an intent to do harm without excuse or justification, and (3) use of the process in a perverted manner to obtain a collateral objective. 3H Enterprises, Inc. v. Dwyre, 182 F. Supp. 2d 249 (**N.D. N.Y.** 2001).

Attorney who knowingly prosecutes a groundless action to accomplish a malicious purpose may be held accountable under the Dragonetti Act. 42 Pa. C.S.A. § 8351. Electronic Laboratory Supply Co. v. Cullen, 712 A.2d 304 (**Pa. Super. Ct.** 1998).

§ 4. Rule that mere institution of legal action by attorney does not constitute abuse of process

Ala—Shoney's, Inc. v. Barnett, 773 So. 2d 1015 (Ala. Civ. App. 1999), cert. denied, (Aug. 27, 1999).

Abuse of process contemplates some overt act done in addition to the initiating of the suit; thus, the mere filing or maintenance of a lawsuit, even for an improper purpose, is not ~

proper basis for an abuse of process action. Meidinger v. Koniag, Inc., 31 P.3d 77 (**Alaska** 2001).

See Tedards v Auty (1989) 232 **NJ Super** 541, 557 A2d 1030, § 5[a].

Trial court erred in denying summary judgment motion of defendant law firm in abuse of process action by former husband of firm's dissolution client, where fact that firm chose legally insufficient method of recovering fees ordered to be paid by husband (for technical reason that submitted order did not expressly compel clerk to enter judgment on interim fee award) did not support conclusion that firm knowingly used legal process for forbidden collateral purpose. Lieberman v Pobiner, London, Bashian & Buonamici (1993, 2d Dept) 190 App Div 2d 716, 593 **NYS2d** 321.

§ 5. Use of civil process
[a] Cause of action stated or found to exist

In abuse of process action by former husband against former wife's attorney regarding writ of ne exeat obtained by defendant and used to arrest and incarcerate plaintiff overnight until he posted bond sufficient to cover full amount of wife's demand and attorney fees, where attorney did not deny that he used writ to extort settlement that included payment of his fee, court found: (1) trial court improperly granted summary judgment in favor of defendant, (2) action for abuse of process would lie against one who used writ after its issuance solely to coerce or injure party, (3) husband could maintain cause of action for abuse of process against wife's former attorney, despite his prior questionable financial dealings with wife, which would entitle her to capias ad respondum which would have produced same result as writ ne exeat, and (4) husband's conduct was not deciding factor in case, but rather whether process had been abused after its issuance for ulterior purpose and acts were committed to secure this purpose. Tedards v Auty (1989) 232 **NJ Super** 541, 557 A2d 1030.

Electronic supply company could bring wrongful use of civil process claim against attorneys who procured ex parte seizure order on behalf of scrap metal seller, separate and apart from negotiated settlement of underlying federal case involving seller. 42 Pa. C.S.A. § 8351. Electronic Laboratory Supply Co. v. Cullen, 712 A.2d 304 (**Pa. Super. Ct.** 1998).

[b] Cause of action not stated or not found to exist

In abuse of process action by judgment

95

For latest cases, call the toll free number appearing on the cover of this supplement.

[annotation callout:] Newer cases are summarized

To research in the *Restatement (Second) of Torts,* the first step is locating pertinent Restatement sections using either the subject index or the table of contents. This example shows a portion of the table of contents.

FIGURE 3.20   TABLE OF CONTENTS, *RESTATEMENT (SECOND) OF TORTS*

TABLE OF CONTENTS

Section

17. Bodily harm caused otherwise than by contact
[Omitted. See § 46.]

TOPIC 2. THE INTEREST IN FREEDOM FROM OFFENSIVE BODILY CONTACT

18. Battery: offensive contact
19. What constitutes offensive contact
20. Character of intent necessary

TOPIC 3. THE INTEREST IN FREEDOM FROM APPREHENSION OF A HARMFUL OR OFFENSIVE CONTACT

21. Assault
22. Attempt unknown to other
23. Termination of attempt after other's knowledge
24. What constitutes apprehension
25. Source of danger
26. Person threatened by actor's conduct
27. Unreasonable character of apprehension
28. Apprehension of unintended bodily contact
29. Apprehension of imminent and future contact
30. Conditional threat
31. Threat by words
32. Character of intent necessary
33. Ability to carry out threat
34. Personal hostility

Table of contents entry for false imprisonment

TOPIC 4. THE INTEREST IN FREEDOM FROM CONFINEMENT

35. False imprisonment
36. What constitutes confinement
37. Confinement: how caused
38. Confinement by physical barriers
39. Confinement by physical force
40. Confinement by threats of physical force
40 A. Confinement by other duress
41. Confinement by asserted legal authority
42. Knowledge of confinement
43. Act intended to affect third parties
44. Malice
45. Refusal to release or to aid in escape
45 A. Instigating or participating in false imprisonment

TOPIC 5. THE INTEREST IN FREEDOM FROM EMOTIONAL DISTRESS

46. Outrageous conduct causing severe emotional distress

XII

The Restatement sections are organized numerically. Comments follow the Restatement section. If Illustrations are provided, they will follow the appropriate Comment. The Illustrations demonstrate how the Restatement section is intended to apply to hypothetical situations.

FIGURE 3.21   *RESTATEMENT (SECOND) OF TORTS § 35*

§ **35**   TORTS, SECOND   Ch. 2

TOPIC 4.   THE INTEREST IN FREEDOM FROM
CONFINEMENT

§ **35.** False Imprisonment

Rule from the Restatement

(1) An actor is subject to liability to another for false imprisonment if

(a) he acts intending to confine the other or a third person within boundaries fixed by the actor, and

(b) his act directly or indirectly results in such a confinement of the other, and

(c) the other is conscious of the confinement or is harmed by it.

(2) An act which is not done with the intention stated in Subsection (1, a) does not make the actor liable to the other for a merely transitory or otherwise harmless confinement, although the act involves an unreasonable risk of imposing it and therefore would be negligent or reckless if the risk threatened bodily harm.

See Reporter's Notes.

Caveat:

The Institute expresses no opinion as to whether the actor may not be subject to liability for conduct which involves an unreasonable risk of causing a confinement of such duration or character as to make the other's loss of freedom a matter of material value.

Comment

Comment on Subsection (1):

a. Common-law action of trespass for false imprisonment. At common law, the appropriate form of action for imposing a confinement was trespass for false imprisonment except where the confinement was by arrest under a valid process issued by a court having jurisdiction, in which case the damages for the confinement were recoverable, if at all, as part of the damages in an action of trespass on the case for malicious prosecution or abuse of process. Therefore, an act which makes the actor liable under this Section for a confinement otherwise than by arrest under a valid process is customarily called a false imprisonment.

b. As to the meaning of the words "subject to liability," see § 5.

See Appendix for Reporter's Notes, Court Citations, and Cross References

52

FIGURE 3.21   *RESTATEMENT (SECOND) OF TORTS § 35 (Continued)*

Ch. 2   FALSE IMPRISONMENT   **§ 35**

    c. As to confinement caused indirectly by the institution of criminal proceedings against another, see § 37, Comment *b.*

Comment on Clause (a) of Subsection (1):

    d. The actor is liable under this Section if his act was done for the purpose of imposing confinement upon the other or with knowledge that such confinement would, to a substantial certainty, result from it. As to the effect of an intention to confine a third party, see § 43.

Illustration:

    1. A, knowing that B, a customer, is in his shop, locks its only door in order to prevent a third person from entering. This is a confinement of B, and A is subject to liability to him unless, under the circumstances, he is privileged.

    e. As to the necessity for the other's knowledge of his confinement, see § 42.

    f. As to what constitutes consent to a confinement, see §§ 892–892 D.

    g. As to the circumstances which create a privilege to confine another irrespective of the other's consent, see §§ 63–156.

Comment on Subsection (2):

    h. Extent of protection of interest in freedom from confinement. Under this Section the actor is not liable unless his act is done for the purpose of imposing confinement upon the other, or with knowledge that such a confinement will, to a substantial certainty, result from it. It is not enough that the actor realizes or should realize that his actions involve a risk of causing a confinement, so long as the likelihood that it will do so falls short of a substantial certainty.

    The mere dignitary interest in feeling free to choose one's own location and, therefore, in freedom from the realization that one's will to choose one's location is subordinated to the will of another is given legal protection only against invasion by acts done with the intention stated in Subsection (1, a). It is not protected against acts which threaten to cause such an invasion even though the likelihood is so great that if a more perfectly protected interest, such as that in bodily security, were imperiled, the actor's conduct would be negligent or even reckless.

See Appendix for Reporter's Notes, Court Citations, and Cross References

53

Illustration containing a hypothetical situation [annotation pointing to Illustration]

To locate cases interpreting the Restatement section, use the Appendix volume or volumes. Each volume is organized by section number and covers a specific period of time.

FIGURE 3.22   APPENDIX VOLUME, *RESTATEMENT (SECOND) OF TORTS*

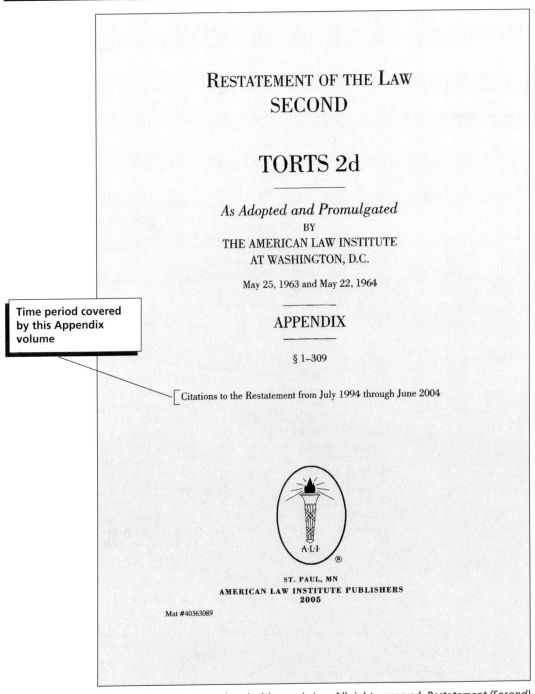

Time period covered by this Appendix volume

RESTATEMENT OF THE LAW
SECOND

TORTS 2d

As Adopted and Promulgated
BY
THE AMERICAN LAW INSTITUTE
AT WASHINGTON, D.C.

May 25, 1963 and May 22, 1964

APPENDIX

§ 1–309

Citations to the Restatement from July 1994 through June 2004

ST. PAUL, MN
AMERICAN LAW INSTITUTE PUBLISHERS
2005

Mat #40363089

The Appendix will list cases interpreting the Restatement section. The latest volume of the Appendix is updated with a pocket part containing references to the most current cases.

FIGURE 3.23　　APPENDIX VOLUME, *RESTATEMENT (SECOND) OF TORTS*

Ch. 2　　　　CITATIONS TO RESTATEMENT SECOND　　§ 35

TOPIC 4.　THE INTEREST IN FREEDOM FROM CONFINEMENT

C.A.1, 1995. §§ 35–45A, constituting all of Ch. 2, Topic 4, cit. in sup. and adopted. Puerto Rican resident was arrested by federal agents who mistakenly believed that she was the subject of a 1975 arrest warrant; following the dismissal of all proceedings against her, she sued the United States for false arrest. Affirming the district court's grant of summary judgment for the United States, this court held that the United States was not liable for the false arrest of plaintiff, since the name in the warrant, together with information contained in the arrest packet, provided ample basis for the arresting agents to form an objectively reasonable belief that plaintiff was the person named in the warrant. The court also held that the conduct of the federal agent responsible for instigating the errant arrest was conditionally privileged, since the arrestee was sufficiently named in the warrant and the agent reasonably believed that plaintiff was the subject of the warrant. Rodriguez v. U.S., 54 F.3d 41, 45.

Cases interpreting § 35

§ 35.　**False Imprisonment**

C.A.1, 1995. Cit. in ftn. Two men who were arrested and acquitted of selling cocaine sued police officers of Puerto Rico and their confidential informants for constitutional violations, alleging that defendants falsely identified them as sellers. District court held that the false-arrest claims were barred by the one-year statute of limitations and that the malicious-prosecution claims were not actionable under 42 U.S.C. § 1983. This court vacated and remanded, holding that, for purposes of determining the appropriate accrual rule, both the Fourth and Fourteenth Amendment claims more closely resembled the common law tort of malicious prosecution. Consequently, plaintiffs' § 1983 claims did not accrue until their respective criminal prosecutions ended in acquittals. Calero–Colon v. Betancourt–Lebron, 68 F.3d 1, 3.

C.A.1, 2000. Cit. in headnote, quot. in disc. After being detained by store employees who accused them of shoplifting on a prior occasion, two children and their mother sued the store for false imprisonment. District court entered judgment on jury verdict awarding plaintiffs damages. This court affirmed, holding, inter alia, that plaintiffs stated a viable false-imprisonment claim, because a reasonable jury could conclude that the store's employees intended to confine plaintiffs within boundaries fixed by the store, that the store's acts resulted in such confinement, and that plaintiffs were conscious of the confinement. Employees' direction to plaintiffs, their reference to the police, and their continued presence were enough to induce reasonable people to believe either that they would be restrained physically if they sought to leave, or that the store was claiming lawful authority to confine them until the police arrived, or both. McCann v. Wal–Mart Stores, Inc., 210 F.3d 51, 51, 53.

C.A.7, 2003. Quot. in sup. African–American store employee who was fired for allegedly stealing from a coemployee sued store for federal civil-rights violations and false imprisonment under Indiana law, alleging that store representatives locked her in her manager's office for several minutes while they investigated the theft charges. District court granted store summary judgment. This court affirmed, holding, inter alia, that plaintiff did not establish a claim of false imprisonment under Indiana law, because her several-minute confinement was accidental, and store established justification for the brief detention. No one told plaintiff that she could not leave, and store provided a reasonable explanation for having left her alone in the office: so that she could draft her written statement without distraction. Adams v. Wal–Mart Stores, Inc., 324 F.3d 935, 941.

C.A.9, 2003. Com. (a) quot. in sup. California resident who had been director of Australian corporation was extradited to Australia for criminal trial. After Australian government dropped fraud charges and jury acquitted extraditee on other charge, he sued two instrumentalities and two employees of Australian government for malicious prosecution, abuse of process, and false imprisonment. District court granted motion to dismiss for employees, but denied motion as to instrumentalities. This court reversed in part, holding that plaintiff's claims of malicious prosecution and abuse of process were barred by Foreign Sovereign Immunities Act, since plaintiff could not overcome sovereign immu-

Cit.–cited; fol.–followed; quot.–quoted; sup.–support.
A complete list of abbreviations precedes page 1.

119

F. CHECKLIST FOR SECONDARY SOURCE RESEARCH

1. LEGAL ENCYCLOPEDIAS

❐ Use legal encyclopedias for very general background information and limited citations to primary authority, but not for in-depth analysis of a topic.

❐ Use Am. Jur. 2d or C.J.S. for a general overview; look for a state encyclopedia for an overview of the law in an individual state.

❐ Locate material in a print encyclopedia by (1) using the subject index or table of contents; (2) locating relevant sections in the main subject volumes; and (3) updating with the pocket part.

❐ Locate material in legal encyclopedias in LexisNexis and Westlaw by searching in the databases for individual publications or multiple secondary sources or by viewing the table of contents.

2. TREATISES

❐ Use treatises for an in-depth discussion and some analysis of an area of law and for citations to primary authority.

❐ Locate treatises in print through the on-line catalog or by asking a reference librarian for a recommendation; locate material within a treatise by (1) using the subject index or table of contents; (2) locating relevant sections within the main text; and (3) updating with the pocket part.

❐ Locate material in treatises in LexisNexis and Westlaw by executing word searches in the databases for individual publications, multiple secondary sources, specific subject areas, or individual jurisdictions. View the table of contents for individual publications if available.

3. LEGAL PERIODICALS

❐ Use legal periodicals for background information, citations to primary authority, in-depth analysis of a narrow topic, or information on a conflict in the law or an undeveloped area of the law.

❐ Locate citations to periodical articles using print resources with the *Index to Legal Periodicals and Books* (ILP) or the *Current Law Index* (CLI); check as many noncumulative volumes as necessary to locate relevant citations.

❐ Locate citations to periodical articles electronically with the electronic version of ILP or LegalTrac; execute a search to obtain a list of citations.

❐ Locate citations to, or the full text of, legal periodicals in LexisNexis and Westlaw by searching in the databases for multiple or individual publications.

❐ Locate the full text of legal periodicals in .pdf format using HeinOnline.

❐ Selected periodicals may be available on the Internet.

4. *AMERICAN LAW REPORTS*

❐ Use A.L.R. Annotations for an overview of an area of law and citations to primary authority (especially to locate persuasive authority from other jurisdictions), but not for in-depth analysis of a topic.

❐ Use A.L.R.3d, A.L.R.4th, A.L.R.5th, A.L.R.6th, A.L.R. Fed., and A.L.R. Fed. 2d; avoid A.L.R. and A.L.R.2d as generally out-of-date sources.

❐ Locate material within A.L.R. in print by (1) using the A.L.R. Index; (2) locating relevant Annotations in the main volumes; and (3) updating with the pocket part.

❐ Locate A.L.R. Annotations in LexisNexis and Westlaw by searching in the databases for A.L.R. or multiple secondary sources.

5. RESTATEMENTS

❐ Use Restatements for research into common-law subjects and to locate mandatory and persuasive authority from jurisdictions that have adopted a Restatement.

❐ Locate Restatements in print through the on-line catalog.

❐ Locate information within a print Restatement by (1) using the subject index or table of contents to identify relevant sections within the Restatement volumes; (2) using the noncumulative Appendix volumes to find pertinent case summaries; and (3) using the pocket part in the latest Appendix volume to locate the most recent cases.

❐ Locate selected Restatements in LexisNexis and Westlaw.

6. UNIFORM LAWS AND MODEL ACTS

❐ Use uniform laws and model acts to interpret a law adopted by a legislature and to locate persuasive authority from other jurisdictions that have adopted the law.

❐ Locate uniform laws and model acts in print using *Uniform Laws Annotated, Master Edition* (ULA).

❏ Locate information in the ULA set by (1) using the *Directory of Uniform Acts and Codes: Tables and Index* to search by subject, by the name of the law, or by adopting jurisdiction; (2) locating relevant provisions in the main volumes; and (3) updating with the pocket part.

❏ Locate selected uniform laws and model acts in LexisNexis and Westlaw.

CHAPTER 4

CASE RESEARCH

A. Introduction to cases

B. Researching cases in print

C. Researching cases electronically

D. Citing cases

E. Sample pages for researching cases using a print digest

F. Checklist for case research

A. INTRODUCTION TO CASES

1. THE STRUCTURE OF THE COURT SYSTEM

The United States has more than fifty separate court systems, including the federal system, the fifty state systems, and the District of Columbia system. You may recall from Chapter 1 that there are three levels of courts in the federal system: the United States District Courts (the trial courts), the United States Courts of Appeals (the intermediate appellate courts), and the United States Supreme Court (the court of last resort). Most state court systems are structured the same way as the federal court system.

Judges from any of these courts can issue written decisions, and their decisions are one source of legal rules. This chapter focuses on where these decisions are published and how they are indexed.

2. CASE REPORTERS

Court opinions, or cases, are published in books called reporters. Reporters are sets of books collecting cases in chronological order. Many sets of reporters are limited to opinions from a single jurisdiction or level of court. Thus, for example, federal reporters contain opinions from federal courts, and state reporters contain opinions from state

courts. In addition, each set of reporters may be subdivided into different series covering different time periods.

A reporter published under government authority is known as an official reporter.[1] Reporters published by commercial publishers are called unofficial reporters. Because these two types of reporters exist, the same opinion may be published in more than one reporter. The text of the opinion should be exactly the same in an official and an unofficial reporter; the only difference is that the former is published by the government, and the latter is not. When a case appears in more than one reporter, it is described as having parallel citations. This is because each set of reporters will have its own citation for the case.

The only federal court opinions published by the government are those of the United States Supreme Court; these are published in a reporter called *United States Reports.* State governments usually publish the decisions of their highest courts, and most also publish decisions from some of their lower courts.

Perhaps the largest commercial publisher of cases is Thomson West, formerly West Publishing Company. West has created a network of unofficial reporters called the *National Reporter System,* which comprises reporters with decisions from almost every United States jurisdiction.

West publishes United States Supreme Court decisions in the *Supreme Court Reporter.* Decisions from the United States Courts of Appeals are published in the *Federal Reporter,* and those from United States District Courts are published in the *Federal Supplement.* West also publishes some specialized reporters that contain decisions from the federal courts. For example, *Federal Rules Decisions* (F.R.D.) contains federal district court decisions interpreting the Federal Rules of Civil and Criminal Procedure, and *Federal Appendix* (F. Appx.) contains nonprecedential decisions from some of the federal courts of appeals. (Non-precedential decisions are discussed in more detail below.)

West publishes state court decisions in what are called regional reporters. West has divided the country into seven regions. The reporter for each region collects state court decisions from all of the states within that region.

Because West publishes reporters for almost every jurisdiction in a common format with common indexing features, this chapter will focus on research using West publications. The chart in **Figure 4.1** shows where cases from the various state and federal courts can be found.

---

[1]The government may publish the reporter itself, or it may arrange for the reporter to be published by a commercial publisher. As long as the government arranges for the publication, the reporter is official, even if it is physically produced by a commercial publisher.

FIGURE 4.1 REPORTERS

COURT OR JURISDICTION	REPORTER (followed by reporter abbreviation; multiple abbreviations denote multiple series)
United States Supreme Court	*United States Reports* (U.S.)* *Supreme Court Reporter* (S. Ct.) *United States Supreme Court Reports, Lawyer's Edition* (L. Ed., L. Ed. 2d)
United States Courts of Appeals	*Federal Reporter* (F., F.2d, F.3d) *Federal Appendix* (F. Appx.)
United States District Courts	*Federal Supplement* (F. Supp., F. Supp. 2d) *Federal Rules Decisions* (F.R.D.)
Atlantic Region States (Connecticut, Delaware, District of Columbia, Maine, Maryland, New Hampshire, New Jersey, Pennsylvania, Rhode Island, Vermont)	*Atlantic Reporter* (A., A.2d)
North Eastern Region States (Illinois, Indiana, Massachusetts, New York, Ohio)	*North Eastern Reporter* (N.E., N.E.2d) New York: *New York Supplement* (N.Y.S., N.Y.S.2d) Illinois: *Illinois Decisions* (Ill. Dec.)
South Eastern Region States (Georgia, North Carolina, South Carolina, Virginia, West Virginia)	*South Eastern Reporter* (S.E., S.E.2d)
Southern Region States (Alabama, Florida, Louisiana, Mississippi)	*Southern Reporter* (So., So. 2d)
South Western Region States (Arkansas, Kentucky, Missouri, Tennessee, Texas)	*South Western Reporter* (S.W., S.W.2d, S.W.3d)
North Western Region States (Iowa, Michigan, Minnesota, Nebraska, North Dakota, South Dakota, Wisconsin)	*North Western Reporter* (N.W., N.W.2d)
Pacific Region States (Alaska, Arizona, California, Colorado, Hawaii, Idaho, Kansas, Montana, Nevada, New Mexico, Oklahoma, Oregon, Utah, Washington, Wyoming)	*Pacific Reporter* (P., P.2d, P.3d) California: *California Reporter* (Cal. Rptr., Cal. Rptr. 2d, Cal. Rptr. 3d)

*Official reporter published by the federal government.

Decisions for most states can be found in the state's official reporter, as well as in the reporters listed in **Figure 4.1**[2]

3. The Anatomy of a Published Case

A case published in a West reporter has five components:

1. The heading containing the parallel citation (if any) to an official reporter, the case name, the court that rendered the decision, and the date of the decision.
2. A synopsis of the decision written by case editors, not by the court.
3. One or more paragraphs summarizing the key points within the decision. These summary paragraphs are called headnotes, and they are written by case editors, not by the court.
4. The names of the attorneys who represented the parties and the judge or judges who decided the case.
5. The opinion of the court. If the decision has any concurring or dissenting opinions, these will follow immediately after the majority or plurality opinion.

Only the fifth item on this list, the opinion of the court, constitutes legal authority. All of the remaining items are editorial enhancements. These editorial enhancements are very useful for locating cases, but they are not part of the court's opinion. Therefore, you should never rely on any part of a case other than the text of the opinion itself.[3]

Figure 4.2 shows an excerpt from a case published in a West reporter.

4. Unpublished, or Non-precedential, Opinions

Not all court decisions are published; only those designated by the courts for publication appear in print reporters. The decisions not designated for publication are called unpublished decisions. In the past, the only ways to obtain copies of unpublished decisions were from the parties to

---

[2]West also publishes separate unofficial state reporters for New York, California, and Illinois. Thus, New York, California, and Illinois cases may appear in three places: (1) an official state reporter; (2) a West regional reporter; and (3) a West unofficial state reporter. Some lower court opinions published in West's New York and California reporters are not published in the regional reporters covering those states. By contrast, all of the cases in *West's Illinois Decisions* are included in the regional reporter covering Illinois.

[3]There are limited exceptions to this rule. For example, in Ohio, the text of the opinion is preceded by a "syllabus," or summary of the opinion, which is written by the court and which contains the holding of the decision. Ordinarily, however, everything other than the opinion itself is an editorial enhancement. Unless you see a notation indicating otherwise, you should assume that only the text of the opinion is authoritative.

FIGURE 4.2 EXCERPT FROM *POPKIN v. NEW YORK STATE*

Case name

Headnote

Court

Attorneys

Editorial summary

Judges

The court's opinion

18   547 FEDERAL REPORTER, 2d SERIES

Mildred POPKIN, Plaintiff-Appellant,

v.

NEW YORK STATE HEALTH AND MENTAL HYGIENE FACILITIES IMPROVEMENT CORPORATION, Defendant-Appellee.

No. 80, Docket 76–7167.

United States Court of Appeals, Second Circuit.

Argued Oct. 20, 1976.

Decided Dec. 15, 1976.

Former employee of corporation which was created to provide improved state facilities for the care of the mentally disabled brought civil rights action charging sex discrimination in her discharge. The United States District Court for the Southern District of New York, Lloyd F. MacMahon, J., 409 F.Supp. 430, granted a defense motion to dismiss for failure to state a claim on which relief could be granted, and plaintiff appealed. The Court of Appeals, J. Joseph Smith, Circuit Judge, held that although the aforesaid corporation was classified under New York law as a public benefit corporation, not as a political subdivision, the corporation was nevertheless excluded before 1972 from coverage under Title VII of the Civil Rights Act of 1964.

Affirmed.

s ⚙⟶41

Although corporation, which was created by state to provide improved state facilities for the care of the mentally disabled, was classified under New York law as a public benefit corporation, not as a political subdivision, the corporation was nevertheless excluded before 1972 from coverage under Title VII of the Civil Rights Act of 1964, §§ 701(b), led 42 U.S.C.A. §§ 2000e(b), 2000e–7, McK.Unconsol.Laws N.Y. §§ 4402, 4404.

2. States ⚙⟶4.1

In the absence of a plain indication to the contrary by Congress, the application of a federal act is not dependent on state law.

3. Civil Rights ⚙⟶41

The Equal Employment Opportunity Act of 1972 was designed to broaden jurisdictional coverage of Title VII of the Civil Rights Act of 1964 by deleting the existing exemptions of state and local government employees and of certain employees of educational institutions. Civil Rights Act of 1964, §§ 701 et seq., 701(b) as amended 42 U.S.C.A. §§ 2000e et seq., 2000e(b).

4. Civil Rights ⚙⟶2

The 1972 Amendments to Title VII of the Civil Rights Act of 1964 have no retroactive effect where they create new substantive rights. Civil Rights §§ 701 et seq., 701(b) as am C.A. §§ 2000e et seq., 2000e(b).

Floyd S. Weil, New York City (Milton Kean, New York City, of counsel), for plaintiff-appellant.

Joan P. Scannell, Deputy Asst. Atty. Gen., New York City (Louis J. Lefkowitz, Atty. Gen., State of New York, Samuel A. Hirshowitz, First Asst. Atty. Gen., New York City, of counsel), for defendant-appellee.

Before SMITH, OAKES and TIMBERS, Circuit Judges.

J. JOSEPH SMITH, Circuit Judge:

Mildred Popkin appeals from an order of the United States District Court for the Southern District of New York, Lloyd F. MacMahon, *Judge*, dismissing her complaint, brought under Title VII of the Civil Rights Act of 1964, 42 U.S.C. § 2000e, *et seq.*, for failure to state a claim upon which relief can be granted, pursuant to Rule 12(b)(6) of the Federal Rules of Civil Procedure. We affirm.

Appellant was employed as an architect by the New York State Health and Mental Hygiene Facilities Improvement Corporation ("the Corporation"). In November,

FIGURE 4.2   EXCERPT FROM *POPKIN v. NEW YORK STATE* (Continued)

POPKIN v. N. Y. ST. HEALTH & MENTAL HYGIENE, ETC.   **19**
Cite as 547 F.2d 18 (1976)

1970 she was notified that her employment would be terminated as of January 15, 1971. Appellant instituted this action under Title VII alleging that the termination was an act of discrimination based on her sex. Jur~~is~~~~diction~~ was based on 42 U.S.C. § 2000e *et* ~~seq.~~ ~~an~~d 28 U.S.C. § 1332. The district ~~court~~ dismissed the complaint on the ~~ground~~ that the Corporation was a "politi~~cal sub~~division" of New York State and was ~~therefo~~re excluded from coverage of 42 ~~U.S.C.~~ § 2000e *et seq.* prior to March 24, ~~1972.~~ The 1972 amendments to Title VII, extending coverage of the Act to political subdivisions, were held by the district court not to have retroactive effect.

[1, 2] The Corporation was created by the Health and Mental Hygiene Facilities Improvement Act as a "corporate governmental agency constituting a public benefit corporation." McKinney's Unconsol.Laws §§ 4402, 4404. Appellant contends that because under New York law her employer is classified as a public benefit corporation and not as a political subdivision, the Corporation was not excluded from Title VII coverage before 1972 under 42 U.S.C. § 2000e(b). We disagree. Title VII does not provide that the terms of the federal statute are to be construed according to state law. Title 42 U.S.C. § 2000e–7 merely provides that state laws prohibiting employment discrimination will remain in effect. In the absence of a plain indication to the contrary by Congress, the application of a federal act is not dependent on state law. *Jerome v. United States*, 318 U.S. 101, 104,

63 S.Ct. 483, 87 L.Ed. 640 (1943). Congressional intent concerning coverage of Title VII and the actual nature of appellee's relationship to the state determine whether or not the Corporation was covered by Title VII before 1972.

[3] The Equal Employment Opportunity Act of 1972 was designed to broaden jurisdictional coverage of Title VII by deleting the existing exemptions of state and local government employees and of certain employees of educational institutions. The bill amended the Civil Rights Act of 1964 to include state and local governments, governmental agencies, and political subdivisions within the definition of "employer" in 42 U.S.C. § 2000e(b). H.R.Rep.No.92–238, 92nd Cong., 2d Sess., *reprinted in* 1972 U.S. Code Cong. & Ad.News 2137, 2152. The conference report of the Senate Amendment to H.R. 1746, which was adopted by the conference, stated explicitly that the Senate Amendment "expanded coverage to include: (1) State and local governments, governmental agencies, political subdivisions . . . ." *Id.* at 2180. The 1964 House Report on the Civil Rights Act of 1964, on the other hand, refers to the exclusion from the term "employer" of "all Federal, State, and local government agencies. . . . " 1964 U.S.Code Cong. & Ad. News 2402. Until 1972, state agencies as well as political subdivisions were exempt from Title VII. Under the terms of the Mental Hygiene Facilities Development Corporation Act, "state agencies" include public benefit corporations.[2]

1. Section 701(b) of Title VII, the Civil Rights Act of 1964, P.L. 88–352 as enacted provided in relevant part:

(b) The term "employer" means a person engaged in an industry affecting commerce who has twenty-five or more employees for each working day in each of twenty or more calendar weeks in the current or preceding calendar year, and any agent of such a person, but such term does not include (1) the United States, a corporation wholly owned by the Government of the United States, an Indian tribe, or a State or political subdivision thereof. . . .

In 1972 § 701(b), 42 U.S.C. § 2000e(b) was amended as follows:

(b) The term "employer" means a person engaged in an industry affecting commerce who has fifteen or more employees for each working day in each of twenty or more calendar weeks in the current or preceding calendar year, and any agent of such a person, but such term does not include (1) the United States, a corporation wholly owned by the Government of the United States, an Indian tribe, or any department or agency of the District of Columbia subject by statute to procedures of the competitive service (as defined in section 2102 of Title 5). . . .

2. McKinney's Unconsol.Laws § 4403(17) contains the following definition:

"State agency" means any officer, department, board, commission, bureau division,

> Bracketed numbers indicate the place in the opinion where material summarized in the headnotes appears.

the case or from the clerk's office at the courthouse. This is still true today for some unpublished decisions, especially those issued by state courts. Many unpublished decisions, however, are available through electronic research services and on the Internet. The federal courts of appeals are in the process of making all their decisions, both published and unpublished, available on their web sites. In addition, many of the unpublished decisions issued by the federal courts of appeals since 2001 are now available in print in the *Federal Appendix*, a West reporter.

Because these decisions are increasingly available electronically and in print, the term "unpublished" opinion has become a misnomer. A more accurate term is "non-precedential" opinion. Non-precedential decisions are often subject to special court rules. For example, unlike decisions published in the *Federal Reporter*, those appearing in the *Federal Appendix* are not treated as binding precedent by the courts, which is why they are described as "non-precedential" decisions. The federal courts of appeals also often limit the circumstances under which non-precedential decisions can be cited in documents filed with the court. Thus, many decisions in the *Federal Appendix* contain notations indicating that they are not binding precedent and cautioning readers to check court rules before citing the opinions. Non-precedential decisions by other courts may also be subject to special rules.

Although courts have issued non-precedential opinions for many years, the practice is not without controversy. The authoritative value of non-precedential decisions is a subject of ongoing debate in the legal community. Regardless of the controversy, non-precedential decisions can be valuable research tools. Therefore, you should not disregard them when you are conducting case research.

B. RESEARCHING CASES IN PRINT

1. LOCATING CASES USING A DIGEST

a. What Is a Digest?

Reporters are published in chronological order; they are not organized by subject. Trying to research cases in chronological order would be impossible. The research tool that organizes cases by subject is called a digest, and that is the finding tool you will ordinarily use to locate cases by topic.

The term "digest" literally means to arrange and summarize, and that is exactly what a digest does. In a digest, the law is arranged into different subject categories such as torts, contracts, or criminal law. Then, within each category, the digest provides summaries of cases that discuss the law on that subject. You can use the summaries to decide which cases you should read to find the answer to your research question.

The digest system created by West is the most commonly used digest in legal research. West has divided the law into more than 400 subject categories called topics. Under each topic, West provides summaries of cases relevant to the subject. Each topic is listed alphabetically in the digest. Because there are so many topics, a digest actually consists of a multivolume set of books. This is similar to a set of encyclopedias with multiple volumes covering topics in alphabetical order.

The West topics are quite broad. Subject areas such as torts or contracts generate thousands of cases. Therefore, the topics have been further subdivided into smaller categories. Each subdivision within a topic is assigned a number that West calls a key number. Thus, the case summaries within a West digest will appear under the relevant key number. Instead of requiring you to read summaries of all the cases on a very broad topic, the key number subdivisions allow you to focus more specifically on the precise issue you are researching.

The topic, key number, and case summary that you find in a West digest will correspond exactly to one of the headnotes at the beginning of an opinion published in a West reporter.

The following examples illustrate some of the features of a West digest. **Figure 4.3** shows the beginning of the West topic for Innkeepers, including the outline of subtopics covered in each key number. **Figure 4.4** shows a summary of a case under key number 10.2.

Digests, like many other research tools, are updated with pocket parts, which are explained in Chapter 1. If the pocket part gets too big to fit in the back of the book, you may find a separate softcover pamphlet on the shelf next to the hardcover volume. Whenever you use any hardcover book in digest research, it is especially important to check the pocket part for new information because hardcover digest volumes are not reprinted frequently.

b. The Digest Research Process

The digest research process consists of four steps:

1. locating the correct digest set for the type of research you are doing
2. locating relevant topics and key numbers within the digest
3. reading the case summaries under the topics and key numbers
4. updating your research to make sure you find summaries of the most recent cases.

(1) Locating the correct digest set

Reporters and digests are similar in several ways. Just as there are different reporters containing cases from different jurisdictions, there are also different sets of digests for finding cases from these various jurisdictions.

FIGURE 4.3 BEGINNING OF THE WEST TOPIC FOR "INNKEEPERS"

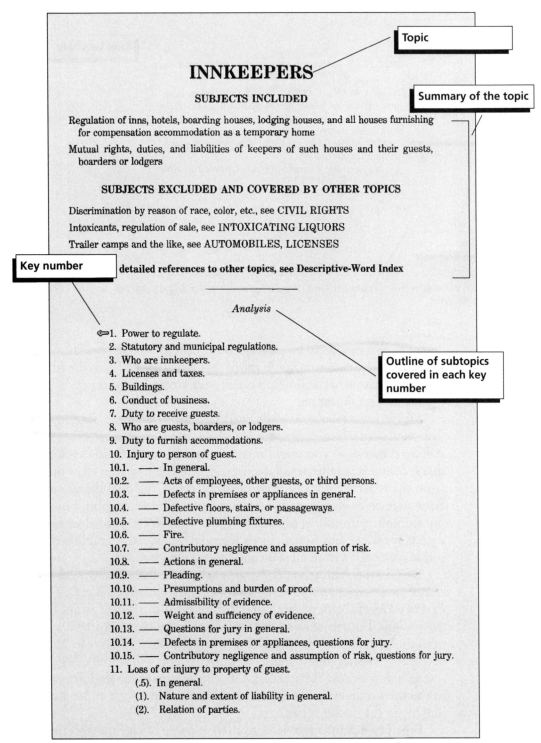

INNKEEPERS

SUBJECTS INCLUDED

Regulation of inns, hotels, boarding houses, lodging houses, and all houses furnishing for compensation accommodation as a temporary home

Mutual rights, duties, and liabilities of keepers of such houses and their guests, boarders or lodgers

SUBJECTS EXCLUDED AND COVERED BY OTHER TOPICS

Discrimination by reason of race, color, etc., see CIVIL RIGHTS

Intoxicants, regulation of sale, see INTOXICATING LIQUORS

Trailer camps and the like, see AUTOMOBILES, LICENSES

For detailed references to other topics, see Descriptive-Word Index

Analysis

1. Power to regulate.
2. Statutory and municipal regulations.
3. Who are innkeepers.
4. Licenses and taxes.
5. Buildings.
6. Conduct of business.
7. Duty to receive guests.
8. Who are guests, boarders, or lodgers.
9. Duty to furnish accommodations.
10. Injury to person of guest.
   10.1. —— In general.
   10.2. —— Acts of employees, other guests, or third persons.
   10.3. —— Defects in premises or appliances in general.
   10.4. —— Defective floors, stairs, or passageways.
   10.5. —— Defective plumbing fixtures.
   10.6. —— Fire.
   10.7. —— Contributory negligence and assumption of risk.
   10.8. —— Actions in general.
   10.9. —— Pleading.
   10.10. —— Presumptions and burden of proof.
   10.11. —— Admissibility of evidence.
   10.12. —— Weight and sufficiency of evidence.
   10.13. —— Questions for jury in general.
   10.14. —— Defects in premises or appliances, questions for jury.
   10.15. —— Contributory negligence and assumption of risk, questions for jury.
11. Loss of or injury to property of guest.
      (.5). In general.
      (1). Nature and extent of liability in general.
      (2). Relation of parties.

Labels in figure: Topic; Summary of the topic; Key number; Outline of subtopics covered in each key number

Reprinted with permission from Thomson West, *West's Federal Practice Digest*, 4th Ser., Vol. 63 (1998), p. 1. © 1998 Thomson West.

FIGURE 4.4   CASE SUMMARY UNDER THE "INNKEEPERS" TOPIC, KEY NUMBER 10.2

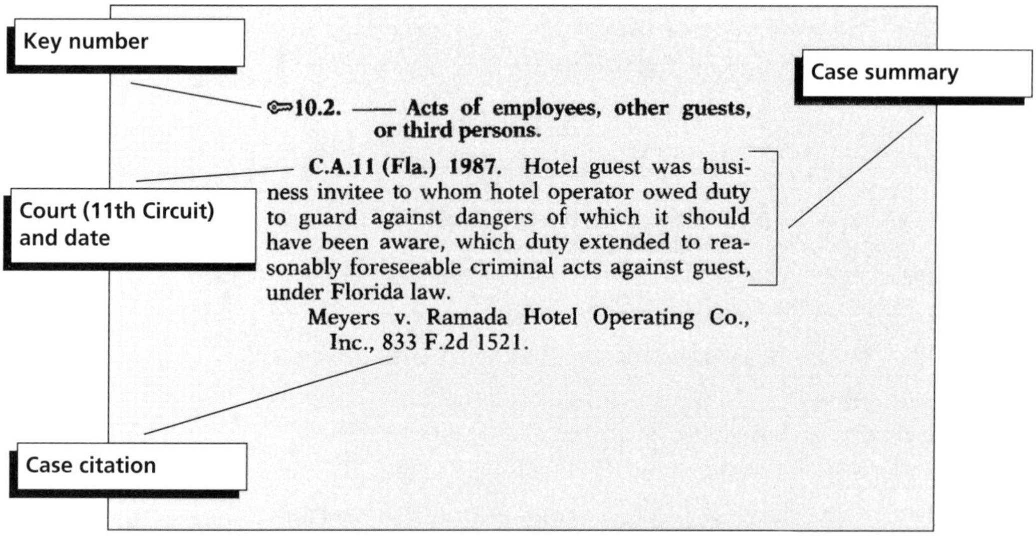

Key number

Case summary

Court (11th Circuit) and date

Case citation

🔑**10.2.** —— **Acts of employees, other guests, or third persons.**

   C.A.11 (Fla.) 1987. Hotel guest was business invitee to whom hotel operator owed duty to guard against dangers of which it should have been aware, which duty extended to reasonably foreseeable criminal acts against guest, under Florida law.

   Meyers v. Ramada Hotel Operating Co., Inc., 833 F.2d 1521.

Reprinted with permission from Thomson West, *West's Federal Practice Digest*, 4th Ser., Vol. 63 (1998), p. 8. © 1998 Thomson West.

And just as a case may be published in more than one reporter, so also could a case be summarized in more than one digest. Thus, the first step in finding cases that will help you answer a research question is choosing the correct digest set.

Digest sets are organized by jurisdiction and by date. The four jurisdictional categories for digests are federal, state, regional, and combined. A federal digest, as you might imagine, summarizes federal cases. A state digest contains summaries of decisions from that state as well as opinions from the federal courts located in that state. A regional digest summarizes state court decisions from the states within the region, but it does not contain summaries of any federal cases. West publishes regional digests for some, but not all, of its regional reporters. A combined digest summarizes cases from all state and federal jurisdictions.

Within each category, the digest set may be divided into different series covering different time periods. For example, *West's Federal Practice Digest,* one of the federal digests, is currently in its Fourth Series. The Fourth Series contains cases from the early 1980s to the present. Earlier cases, from 1975 through the early 1980s, can be found in the Third Series of the digest. Ordinarily, you will want to begin your research in the most current series. If you are unable to find information in the most current series, however, you could locate older cases by looking in the earlier series.

Figures 4.5 through **4.7** summarize some of the characteristics of West digests.

FIGURE 4.5 FEDERAL DIGESTS

DESCRIPTION	*WEST'S FEDERAL PRACTICE DIGEST, FOURTH SERIES*	WEST'S *UNITED STATES SUPREME COURT DIGEST*
What is included	Summaries of cases from all federal courts	Summaries of cases from the United States Supreme Court
What is excluded	Summaries of state cases	Summaries of cases from lower federal courts and all state courts
Coverage	Includes summaries of cases from the early 1980s–present. Older cases are summarized in prior series of this set (e.g., *West's Federal Practice Digest*, Third Series).	Includes summaries of all United States Supreme Court cases

FIGURE 4.6 STATE AND REGIONAL DIGESTS

DESCRIPTION	STATE DIGESTS	REGIONAL DIGESTS
What is included	Summaries of cases from the state's courts and the federal courts within the state	Summaries of cases from the state courts within the region
What is excluded	Summaries of state and federal cases from courts outside the state	Summaries of state cases from states outside the region and all federal cases
Coverage	West publishes state digests for all states except Delaware, Nevada, and Utah. The *Virginia Digest* summarizes cases from both Virginia and West Virginia. The *Dakota Digest* summarizes cases from both North and South Dakota. Some state digests have multiple series.	West publishes Atlantic, North Western, Pacific, and South Eastern Digests. West *does not* publish North Eastern, Southern, or South Western Digests. All of the regional digests have multiple series.

FIGURE 4.7   COMBINED DIGESTS

DESCRIPTION	COMBINED DIGESTS
What is included	Summaries of state and federal cases from all jurisdictions across the United States
What is excluded	Nothing
Coverage	The combined digests are divided into the *General, Decennial,* and *Century Digests,* covering the following dates:

General Digest, 11th Series (Each volume in the *General Digest* set is noncumulative.)	2005–present
Eleventh Decennial Digest, Part 2	2001–2004
Eleventh Decennial Digest, Part 1	1996–2001
Tenth Decennial Digest, Part 2	1991–1996
Tenth Decennial Digest, Part 1	1986–1991
Ninth Decennial Digest, Part 2	1981–1986
Ninth Decennial Digest, Part 1	1976–1981
Eighth Decennial Digest	1966–1976
Seventh Decennial Digest	1956–1966
Sixth Decennial Digest	1946–1956
Fifth Decennial Digest	1936–1946
Fourth Decennial Digest	1926–1936
Third Decennial Digest	1916–1926
Second Decennial Digest	1907–1916
First Decennial Digest	1897–1906
Century Digest	1658–1896

To decide which digest is the best choice for your research, you will need to consider the nature and scope of the project. Usually, you will want to choose the narrowest digest that still has enough information for you to find relevant legal authority. Sometimes you will need to use more than one digest to find all of the cases you need.

West's Federal Practice Digest is the best place to start looking for federal cases. If you are researching case law from an individual state, the digest from that state is usually the best starting place. If you do not have access to the state digest, the regional digest is another good place to look. It is also a good place to find persuasive authority from surrounding jurisdictions. Remember, however, that regional digests summarize only state court decisions, no federal decisions. Therefore, if you also want to find cases from the federal courts located within an

individual state, you will need to supplement your regional digest research by using *West's Federal Practice Digest.*

The combined digests have the most comprehensive coverage, but they are also the most difficult to use. You would probably begin with *West's General Digest*, Eleventh Series, which covers cases from roughly the beginning of 2005 to the present. The *General Digest* volumes are noncumulative. Thus, you would need to begin by researching in each volume of the most recent series. For earlier cases, you would also need to use the *Eleventh Decennial Digest, Part 2*, and as many previous series as necessary to locate cases on your topic. Because this is a cumbersome process, the combined digests are usually only useful when you know the approximate time period you want to research or when you are conducting nationwide research.

Figure 4.8 summarizes when you might want to consider using each of these types of digests.

(2) Locating topics and key numbers

Once you have decided which set or sets of the digest to use, the next step is locating topics and key numbers relevant to your research issue. You can do this in three ways:

i.   using the headnotes in a case on point
ii. using the index to the digest
iii. going directly to topics relevant to your research.

(i) Using the headnotes in a case on point

The easiest way to find relevant topics and key numbers is to use the headnotes in a case that you have already determined is relevant to your research. If you have read other chapters in this book, you already know that the digest is not the only way to locate cases. Many other research sources, including secondary sources (covered in Chapter 3) and statutes (covered in Chapter 6), can lead you to relevant cases. Therefore, when another source has led you to a relevant case that is published in a West reporter, you can use the headnotes to direct you to digest topics and key numbers.

(ii) Using the Descriptive-Word Index

If you do not already have a case on point, you will need to use the index to find topics and key numbers in the digest. The index in a West digest is called the Descriptive-Word Index (DWI). The DWI actually consists of several volumes that may be located either at the beginning or at the end of the digest set, and it lists subjects in alphabetical order.

To use the DWI, all you need to do is look up the subjects you want to research. The subjects will be followed by abbreviations indicating the topics and key numbers relevant to each subject. A list of abbreviations

FIGURE 4.8   WHEN TO USE DIFFERENT DIGESTS

FEDERAL DIGESTS	STATE DIGESTS	REGIONAL DIGESTS	COMBINED DIGESTS
To research federal cases	To research state and federal cases from an individual state	To research state cases from an individual state within the region (may require additional research with the federal digest)	To research federal cases or cases from an individual state if you know the approximate time period you wish to research
To supplement regional digest research by locating federal cases within an individual state		To locate persuasive authority from surrounding jurisdictions	To research the law of all jurisdictions within the United States

appears at the beginning of the volume. You may also see cross-references to other index entries with additional information on the subject. An excerpt from a page in the DWI appears in **Figure 4.9**.

The DWI volumes, like all other hardcover volumes within the digest set, are updated with pocket parts. The next step in using the index is checking the pocket part. Because the hardcover DWI volumes are not reprinted frequently, many of the newer entries may be in the pocket part. Moreover, West sometimes uses information from specific cases to generate index entries. Therefore, it is important to check the pocket part for new material that may be relevant to your research. If you do not find anything listed in the pocket part, no new index entries on that subject are available.

Once you have identified relevant topics and key numbers, the next step is looking them up within the digest volumes. Remember that digest volumes are organized alphabetically. Therefore, you will need to look on the spines of the books until you locate the volume covering your topic. When you look up the topic, you will see that the key numbers follow in numerical order.

(iii) Going directly to relevant topics
Because digest topics are arranged alphabetically, you can bypass the DWI and go directly to the topic you are interested in researching. At the beginning of each topic, West provides an overview section that lists the subjects included and excluded, as well as an outline of all the key

FIGURE 4.9 EXCERPT FROM THE DESCRIPTIVE-WORD INDEX

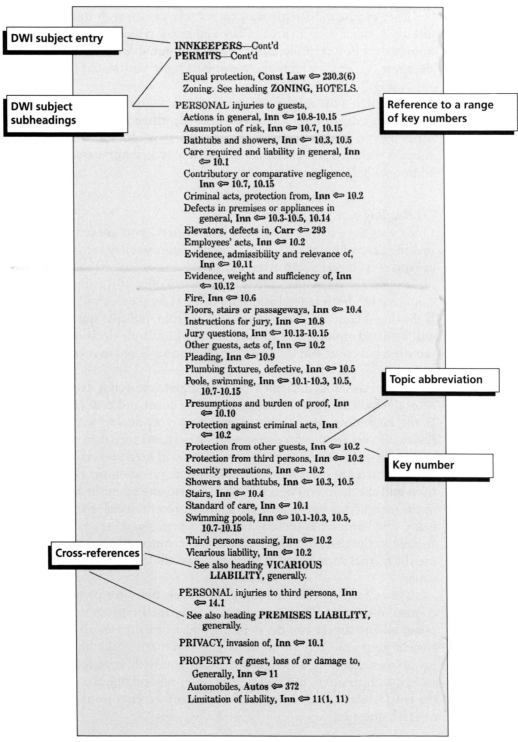

Reprinted with permission from Thomson West, *West's Federal Practice Digest,* 4th Ser., Descriptive-Word Index, Vol. 98A (2002), p. 235. © 2002 Thomson West.

numbers under the topic. Case summaries, of course, follow the overview in key number order.

This can be a difficult way to start your research unless you are already familiar with an area of law and know which topics are likely to be relevant. For example, cases regarding immigration are listed under the topic "Aliens," which might not be a topic you would have considered using.

Although you might not want to start your research by going directly to a digest topic, once you have identified useful topics through other means, you may want to review the overview section. The list of subjects included and excluded and outline of key numbers can provide additional helpful research leads.

(3) Reading case summaries

Once you have reviewed the topic overview, you are ready to begin reading case summaries. There is some inconsistency in the way West organizes its digest summaries, but in general, summaries are organized in descending order from highest to lowest court. If the digest contains summaries of both federal and state cases, federal cases will appear first. If the digest contains summaries of cases from multiple states, the states will be listed alphabetically. Summaries of multiple decisions from the same level of court and the same jurisdiction are listed in reverse chronological order.

One of the most difficult aspects of digest research is deciding which cases to read based on the summaries. The court and date abbreviations at the beginning of each entry will help you decide which cases to review. If you are using a digest with cases from more than one jurisdiction, paying attention to the abbreviations will help you stay focused on the summaries of cases from the appropriate jurisdiction. The abbreviations will also help you figure out which cases are from the highest court in the jurisdiction and which are the most recent decisions. In addition, many case summaries include not only a synopsis of the rule the court applied in the case, but also a concise description of the facts. You can use the factual summaries to narrow down the cases applicable to your issue.

Even a fact-specific summary, however, does not provide the full context of the case. Using the digest is only the first step in researching cases; all the digest can do is point you toward cases that may help answer your research question. Digest summaries, like headnotes, are editorial enhancements designed to assist you with your research. They are not authoritative, and you should never rely on one as a statement of the law. Always read the case in full before relying on it to answer a research question.

(4) Updating digest research

The final step in digest research is updating. The updating process involves three steps:

i.   checking the pocket part for the subject volume covering your topic
ii. checking a separate set of interim pamphlets at the end of the digest set
iii. updating beyond the digest set for cases published after the supplements were printed.

It is very important to update your research for new cases. Newer cases may reflect a change in the law, or cases more factually relevant to your problem may have been decided since the hardcover books were published. Obviously, in legal practice you must find these cases for your research to be complete. In law school, professors love to assign research problems for which the best material is in the updating sources. Therefore, you should get in the habit now of updating your research thoroughly.

(i) Pocket parts

Each subject volume should have either a pocket part or a separate supplement on the shelf next to the hardcover book. This is the first place to look to update your research.

The pocket part is organized the same way as the main volume. The topics are arranged alphabetically, and the key numbers are arranged in numerical order within each topic. There are two pieces of information you will find in the pocket part. First, if any cases under the key number were decided after the main volume was published, you will find summaries of those cases in the pocket part. These case summaries will be organized in the same order as those in the main volume. If no reference to your topic and key number appears in the pocket part, no new decisions have been issued during the time period covered by the pocket part.

Second, you may find that West has created new key numbers or divided the key numbers from the main volume into a series of subsections. If that is the case, you will find a short outline of the new subsections at the beginning of the original key number, along with summaries of any cases categorized under the new subsections.

(ii) Interim pamphlets

The pocket part is not the only supplement you should check. Pocket parts are generally published only once a year. For some digest sets, West also publishes interim pamphlets to update for cases decided since the pocket part was published. These pamphlets are ordinarily softcover booklets, although occasionally you will see hardcover supplements. They are usually shelved at the end of the digest set. The pamphlets

contain summaries of new decisions under all of the topics and key numbers within the digest set. Just as with pocket parts, the topics in the interim pamphlets are arranged alphabetically. And as with pocket parts, if no entry appears under your topic and key number, no new cases have been decided during the time period covered by the interim pamphlet.

Some interim pamphlets are cumulative, meaning you only need to look in the one book to update your research. Others, however, are noncumulative. If the pamphlets you are using are noncumulative, each one covers a specific time period, and you must check each one to update your research completely. To determine the dates covered by an interim pamphlet, check the dates on the spine or cover of the book.

(iii) Closing tables
Once you have checked the interim pamphlets accompanying the digest, you have updated your research as far as the digest will take you. The final step in the process is checking for cases decided after the last interim pamphlet was published.

To do this, you will need to refer to the chart on the inside front cover of the latest interim pamphlet. This chart is called a closing table. **Figure 4.10** contains an example of a closing table. If the digest set you are using does not have interim pamphlets, you should check the closing table on the inside front cover of the pocket part for the subject volume.

The closing table lists the names of all of the reporters whose decisions are summarized within the digest set. For each of those reporters, the table lists the last volume with decisions summarized in the interim

FIGURE 4.10   INTERIM PAMPHLET CLOSING TABLE

Closing with Cases Reported in	
Supreme Court Reporter	125 S.Ct. 376
Federal Reporter, Third Series	386 F.3d 1147
Federal Appendix	110 Fed.Appx. 129
Federal Supplement, Second Series	337 F.Supp.2d
Federal Rules Decisions	224 F.R.D. 197
Bankruptcy Reporter	316 B.R. 100
Federal Claims Reporter	62 Fed.Cl. 473
Military Justice Reporter — U.S.Armed Forces	60 M.J. 305
Military Justice Reporter — A.F.Ct.Crim.App.	60 M.J. 726
Veterans Appeals Reporter	18 Vet.App. 431

Reprinted with permission from Thomson West, *West's Federal Practice Digest,* 4th Ser., December 2004, Pamphlet (2004), inside cover. © 2004 Thomson West.

pamphlet. For example, the closing table in **Figure 4.10** lists the *Federal Supplement*, Second Series, closing with volume 337. That means that decisions through volume 337 of F. Supp. 2d are summarized within the interim pamphlet. Any cases reported in volume 338 and beyond came out too late to be included in the interim pamphlet.

To find out if any relevant cases are reported after volume 337, therefore, you will need to check the reporters on the shelves. Within each reporter, you will find a mini-digest in the back of the book. The mini-digest summarizes all of the decisions within that volume. You need to look up your topic and key number in each of the reporter volumes after volume 337 through the end of the set to make sure no new relevant decisions were issued after the interim pamphlet was published. Again, if nothing is listed under the topic and key number, no new decisions were issued, and your updating is complete.

Students often ask whether this last updating step is truly necessary. The answer largely depends on the progress of your research. If you have not been able to locate a sufficient amount of authority, you might want to use the closing table and mini-digests to expand your research results. This is especially true if the digest set does not have interim pamphlets and a number of months have passed since the pocket part was printed. If you are satisfied that you have located the pertinent cases on your issue and only need to verify that they still state the law accurately, the closing table and mini-digests are not the best tools for you to use. Chapter 5 discusses resources you can use to verify case research. These resources will allow you to check your research more efficiently than the closing table and mini-digests. As Chapter 5 explains, they can also be used to expand your research results, although you may still find the case summaries in the mini-digests helpful.

2. ADDITIONAL FEATURES OF DIGESTS

In addition to collecting case summaries under subject matter topics, digests have two other features you can use to locate cases: the Table of Cases and the Words and Phrases feature. All West digest sets have a Table of Cases, but not all have the Words and Phrases feature.

a. Table of Cases

The Table of Cases lists cases alphabetically by the name of both the plaintiff and the defendant.[4] Thus, if you know either party's name, you

---

[4]West used to divide the Table of Cases into two tables: the Table of Cases, which listed cases by the plaintiff's name, and the Defendant-Plaintiff Table, which listed cases by the defendant's name. West now consolidates these two tables into one, called the Table of Cases. In some older digest sets, however, you may still find a separate Defendant-Plaintiff Table.

FIGURE 4.11   **EXCERPT FROM THE TABLE OF CASES**

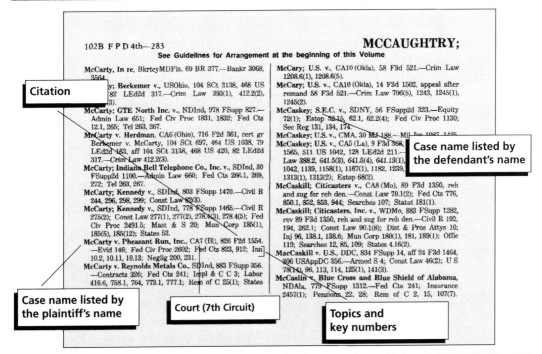

Reprinted with permission from Thomson West, *West's Federal Practice Digest*, 4th Ser., Vol. 102B (2000), p. 283. © 2005 Thomson West.

can find the case in the Table of Cases. In the Table of Cases, you will find the following items of information:

1. the full name of the case
2. the court that decided the case
3. the complete citation to the case, including the parallel citation (if any) to an official reporter
4. a list of the topics and key numbers appearing in the headnotes to the case.

Figure 4.11 is an excerpt from the Table of Cases.

The Table of Cases usually appears at the end of the digest set. Often, it is contained in a separate volume or set of volumes, but in smaller digest sets, it may be included in a volume containing other material.

The Table of Cases is updated the same way as the subject volumes. The volumes containing the Table of Cases should have pocket parts. Some older digest sets also have hardcover supplements. If the digest set has interim pamphlets, one of those pamphlets will also contain a Table of Cases listing cases decided during the time period covered by the pamphlet.

b. Words and Phrases

The Words and Phrases feature provides citations to cases that have defined legal terms or phrases. Because dictionary definitions are not legally binding on courts, Words and Phrases can help you find legally binding definitions from cases that have interpreted or construed a term. Words and Phrases is organized much like a dictionary. To determine whether the courts have defined a term, you simply look up the term alphabetically. If the term is listed, you will find citations to cases construing it. Newer volumes also contain a brief summary of each case.

Words and Phrases is usually located near the Table of Cases within the digest set and is updated the same way as that table.

Figure 4.12 illustrates the Words and Phrases feature.

C. RESEARCHING CASES ELECTRONICALLY

1. THE FORMAT OF A CASE IN WESTLAW AND LEXISNEXIS

The format of a case varies slightly in Westlaw and LexisNexis. In both systems, you will see a caption with the name of the case and other identifying information. The caption will be followed by an editorial summary of the decision.

In Westlaw, the summary will be followed by one or more numbered headnotes and then the full text of the opinion. Just as in the print version of a case, the editorial summary and headnotes, if any, are not part of the decision and are not authoritative.

No key number headnotes appear in the LexisNexis version of a case because the key number system is an editorial feature unique to West. LexisNexis has a similar editorial feature, however, called LexisNexis Headnotes. At the beginning of a case, you will find one or more summary paragraphs organized by subject and quoting passages from the case. Even though the LexisNexis Headnotes usually quote the opinion verbatim, they are not part of the decision and are not authoritative. The LexisNexis Headnotes feature is relatively new. LexisNexis has been adding headnotes to all cases decided since 1999 and is gradually adding them to the older cases in its database. As of this writing, approximately 90 percent of the cases in LexisNexis have headnotes.

Figures 4.13 and **4.14** show what a case looks like in Westlaw and LexisNexis.

2. WORD SEARCHING IN WESTLAW AND LEXISNEXIS

In both Westlaw and LexisNexis, you can locate cases by executing word searches. Word searching differs from digest searching. Because the digest organizes case summaries by subject, you are conducting a

FIGURE 4.12 WORDS AND PHRASES

INJURIES

109 F P D 4th—334

INJURIES TO THE PERSON OF THE DEBTOR

Bkrtcy.D.Minn. 1994. Chapter 7 debtor's pre-petition claims for sexual discrimination and harassment were not rights of action for "injuries to the person of the debtor" within meaning of Minnesota property exemption statute, even though debtor sought damages for pain and suffering, and other general damages. M.S.A. § 550.37, subd. 22.—In re Crawford, 208 B.R. 924.—Exemp 35.

Bkrtcy.D.Minn. 1994. Chapter 7 debtor's legal malpractice claim against attorney who had represented him in divorce case was not right of action for "injuries to the person of the debtor," and could not be claimed as exempt on that basis pursuant to Minnesota law, though attorney's supposed malpractice had allegedly resulted in finding that debtor engaged in fraud on divorce court, which finding had resulted in injury to debtor's reputation; any injury that debtor sustained was not injury to debtor's body or person, as required under Minnesota exemption statute. M.S.A. § 550.37, subd. 22.—In re Maranda, 208 B.R. 467.—Exemp 35.

INJURIOUS

C.A.5 1992. Exposure to work-related stimuli may be considered "injurious" under the Longshore and Harbor Workers' Compensation Act (LHWCA), regardless of brevity of exposure, if exposure has potential to cause disease. Longshore and Harbor Workers' Compensation Act, § 1 et seq., 33 U.S.C.A. § 901 et seq.—Avondale Industries, Inc. v. Director, Office of Workers' Compensation Programs, 977 F.2d 186.—Work Comp 521.

INJURY

U.S. 1994. Although compensable "injury" can carry a fault connotation, it need not do so. 38 U.S.C.A. § 1151.—Brown v. Gardner, 115 S.Ct. 552, 513 U.S. 115, 130 L.Ed.2d 462.—Armed S 104.1.

U.S.Pa. 1994. Term "injury," as used in FELA, includes emotional injury. Federal Employers' Liability Act, §§ 1–10, as amended, 45 U.S.C.A. §§ 51–60.—Consolidated Rail Corp. v. Gottshall, 114 S.Ct. 2396, 512 U.S. 532, 129 L.Ed.2d 427, on remand Carlisle v. Consolidated Rail Corp., 43 F.3d 1460, on remand 56 F.3d 530.—Emp Liab 173.

CMA 1987. "Injury," for purposes of statute prohibiting willful injury or attempt to injure any national-defense material, premises, or utilities included disabling of aircraft from operating in intended manner, thereby depriving government of benefit of such investment, even though injury did not involve physical damage or destruction which required replacement and aircraft was disabled for only short period of time. 18 U.S.C.A. § 2155(a).—U.S. v. Ortiz, 24 M.J. 164, on remand 25 M.J. 570.—Mil Jus 790.

C.A.D.C. 1989. Contractors' loss of opportunity to compete for contracts under Air Force's program for contractor operated civil engineer supply stores was "injury" for purposes of standing, even though contractors had no right to obtain contract under program, and even though Air Force invoked no procurement process when allowing contracts to expire; contractors were alleging that Air Force violated the law by discontinuing contracts for nonpriced materials without first conducting recompetitions for those contracts and undertaking cost comparison studies to evaluate merits of private contractors as against in-house program. U.S.C.A. Const. Art. 3, § 1 et seq.; National Defense Authorization Act for Fiscal Year 1987, § 1 et seq., 100 Stat. 3816.—CC Distributors, Inc. v. U.S., 883 F.2d 146, 280 U.S.App.D.C. 74.—U S 64.60(2).

C.A.D.C. 1989. Health organizations had standing to challenge Federal Trade Commission's decision to exempt utilitarian items such as T-shirts and other promotional products from the warning requirements imposed under Comprehensive Smokeless Tobacco Health Education Act; organizations established that exemption would directly deprive their members of valuable warnings to which Congress determined they were entitled, and deprivation of information constituted a constitutionally cognizable "injury." Comprehensive Smokeless Tobacco Health Education Act of 1986, §§ 2–9, 3(a)(1, 2), 15 U.S.C.A. §§ 4401–4408, 4402(a)(1, 2).—Public Citizen v. F.T.C., 869 F.2d 1541, 276 U.S.App.D.C. 222.—Trade Reg 764.

C.A.D.C. 1987. Allegation by nontheist philosophy professor challenging refusal of House of Representatives and Senate chaplains to invite nontheists to deliver secular remarks during period reserved for morning prayer, that professor had been prohibited from addressing each House of Congress by exclusion, satisfied "injury" requirement for Article III standing. U.S.C.A. Const. Art. 3, § 1 et seq.; Amends. 1, 5.—Kurtz v. Baker, 829 F.2d 1133, 265 U.S.App.D.C. 1, certiorari denied 108 S.Ct. 2831, 486 U.S. 1059, 100 L.Ed.2d 931.—Const Law 42.1(1).

C.A.2 1991. Former shipyard worker established "injury" under LHWCA by presenting uncontroverted evidence of pleural thickening linked to asbestos exposure, even though Benefits Review Board had found that condition had not caused worker any harm. Longshore and Harbor Workers' Compensation Act, §§ 1 et seq., 7, as amended, 33 U.S.C.A. §§ 901 et seq., 907.—Crawford v. Director, Office of Workers' Compensation Programs, U.S. Dept. of Labor, 932 F.2d 152.—Work Comp 538.

C.A.5 1993. Medical benefits are available for workers who have suffered work-related hearing loss injury even if that injury does not satisfy requirements for entitlement to disability benefits; lack of "impairment" or "injury" meeting requirements for disability benefits within meaning of Longshore and Harbor Workers Compensation Act did not mean no medical benefits. Longshore and Harbor Workers' Compensation Act, §§ 7, 8, 8(c)(13), (c)(13)(E), 33 U.S.C.A. §§ 907, 908, 908(c)(13), (c)(13)(E).—Ingalls Shipbuilding, Inc. v. Director, Office of Workers' Compensation Programs, U.S. Dept. of Labor, 991 F.2d 163.—Work Comp 966.

Entry for word defined

Summary of a case defining the word

FIGURE 4.13   EXAMPLE OF A CASE IN WESTLAW

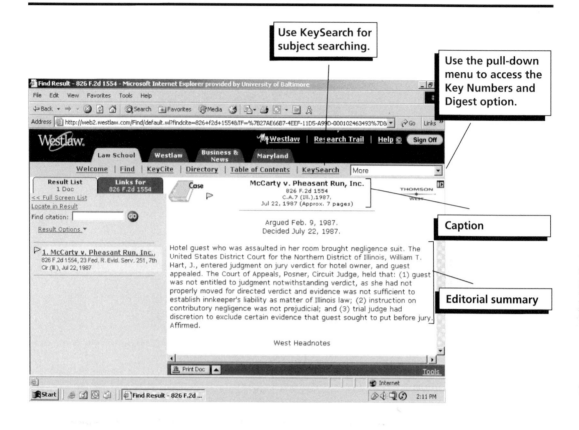

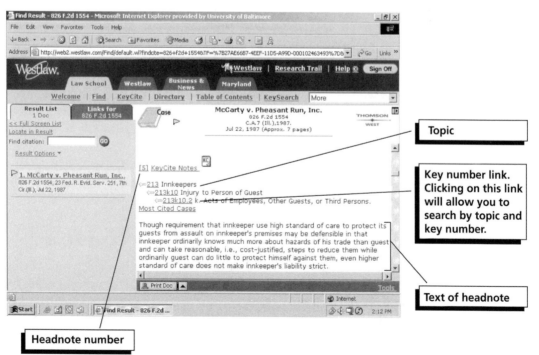

FIGURE 4.13   EXAMPLE OF A CASE IN WESTLAW *(Continued)*

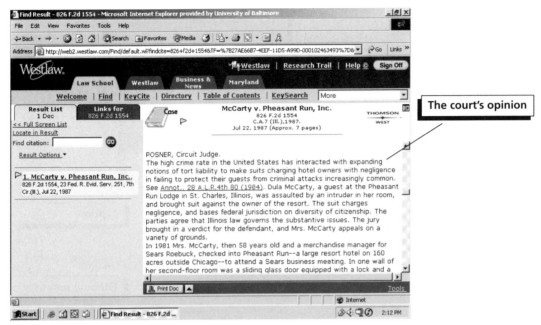

Reprinted with permission from Thomson West, from Westlaw, 826 F.2d 1554. © 2005 Thomson West.

subject search when you use a digest. Electronic word searches, by contrast, retrieve cases containing the precise terms and characteristics you specify. In a sense, this allows you to create your own "digest."

To locate cases using word searches, you must select a database in which to search. Selecting a database is similar to selecting a print digest. You should use the narrowest one that still has enough information to answer your research question. In general, both Westlaw and LexisNexis have databases with cases from federal courts or individual states, as well as combined databases with both federal and state decisions. In addition, both systems have subject-matter databases containing federal and state cases in specific subject areas such as products liability or family law.

Once you have selected a database, you are ready to construct and execute a word search. Chapter 10 contains more information on the process of word searching in Westlaw and LexisNexis.

3. SUBJECT SEARCHING IN WESTLAW AND LEXISNEXIS

Although the digests themselves are not accessible electronically in exactly the same way they are in print, you can still search for cases by subject in Westlaw and LexisNexis.

Westlaw has two functions that allow you to search by subject using the digest topics and key numbers. One is the Custom Digest function.

FIGURE 4.14 EXAMPLE OF A CASE IN LEXISNEXIS

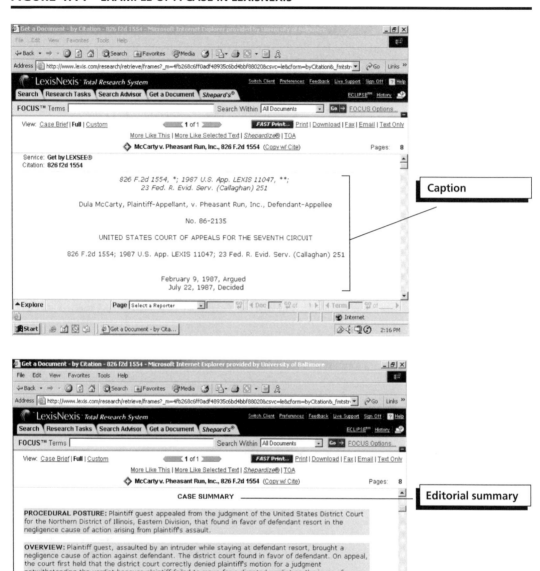

FIGURE 4.14   EXAMPLE OF A CASE IN LEXISNEXIS (*Continued*)

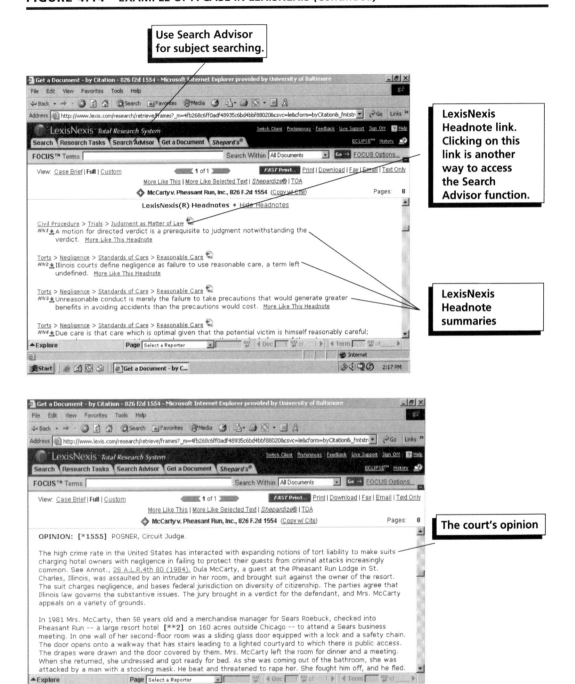

Reprinted with permission of LexisNexis, from LexisNexis, 826 F.2d 1554.

You can access the Custom Digest function by choosing the Key Numbers and Digest option from the pull-down menu in the upper right corner of the Westlaw screen. This will display a list of the digest topics. You can view individual key numbers by expanding the list under each topic, and you can select the topic(s) and key number(s) you want to search. If you locate a relevant case, you can also access the Custom Digest function by clicking on the key number link. Using either approach brings up a search screen that allows you to customize your search. For example, you can select the jurisdiction in which to execute the search and add your own terms to further refine the search.

Another way to search using the West digest topics and key numbers is with the KeySearch function. You can access this function by clicking on the KeySearch link near the top of the Westlaw screen. This brings up an alphabetical list of search topics. Each topic contains multiple subtopics, and most subtopics are further subdivided into even narrower categories. You can find a subject to search by selecting a subject and browsing the subdivisions, or you can search for a subject using the search box on the left side of the screen.

The relationship between the KeySearch function and the West digest topics is not immediately apparent. Although KeySearch lists subjects alphabetically, the subject categories are not identical to the topics in a West digest. In a KeySearch search, the query consists of a combination of various topics and key numbers, plus additional search terms that West selects. Thus, although it is largely driven by the topic and key number system, it usually will not retrieve exactly the same results that a Custom Digest search will. From the KeySearch search screen, you can further customize the search by selecting the jurisdiction and sources you wish to search, as well as by adding your own search terms.

The topic and key number system is unique to West. Therefore, you can search by topic and key number only in Westlaw. LexisNexis, however, has its own subject searching capabilities through the Search Advisor function and LexisNexis Headnotes. Clicking on the Search Advisor tab near the top of the screen brings up an alphabetical list of search topics. Each topic contains multiple subtopics, and most subtopics are further subdivided into even narrower categories. You can find a subject to search in three ways: You can select a subject you have searched before by browsing the last twenty topics you have selected. You can search for a subject using the search box. Or you can explore a general subject by clicking on it and browsing the subtopics.

After you select a search topic, LexisNexis displays a search screen. At the top of the search screen, you will see a row of tabs: cases, analytical materials, and forms. Under the cases tab, you will see a search screen you can use to locate cases relevant to the subject area you selected. The search screen contains a variety of options to allow you to customize your search. For example, you can select the jurisdiction in which to

execute the search and add search terms to further refine the search. Under the analytical materials tab you will find a directory of secondary sources. Under the forms tab you will find a directory of publications containing forms, or templates, for documents you might file in court, such as a complaint or an answer. Clicking on one of the secondary source or forms links will automatically generate a list of citations to information within the source you selected.

Search Advisor is linked to the LexisNexis Headnotes. Therefore, you can click on the link to a LexisNexis Headnote at the beginning of a case to locate additional cases with headnotes on the same subject. Clicking on the link brings up a search screen from which you can customize your search.

Search Advisor is a relatively new feature, and as noted above, not all cases in the LexisNexis database contain LexisNexis Headnotes. Therefore, although the Search Advisor and LexisNexis Headnotes searching options will search most cases in the LexisNexis database, they will not search all of them as of this writing.

4. RESEARCHING CASES ON THE INTERNET

Judicial opinions are increasingly available on the Internet. To locate cases on the Internet, you can try two approaches. The first is to review the web site for the court whose decisions you are trying to locate. Many courts and government organizations maintain web sites with the full text of court opinions. The second is to go to general legal research sites. Many of these sites either include links to sites with court opinions or index their own databases of cases. Appendix A lists the Internet addresses for a number of legal research web sites that may be useful for case research.

Once you have located a source containing cases, several searching options may be available. You may be able to search by date, docket number, case name, or key word, depending on how the web site is organized.

Because comprehensive digesting tools are not yet available on the Internet, it is not likely to be an effective resource unless you know which jurisdiction's cases you want to research. In addition, a number of databases only contain decisions going back a few years, so comprehensive research over time may not be possible. Once you have located a case, you will usually only see the text of the court's opinion. Internet sources generally lack the editorial enhancements available with commercial research services, which may hinder your research efforts.

Despite these difficulties, the Internet can be effective for locating the most recent opinions, opinions from courts that maintain up-to-date web sites, and opinions from lower courts whose decisions are not published in any print reporters. For example, United States Supreme Court decisions are available on the Internet within hours after they are issued.

Opinions of municipal courts or local agencies may only be available on the Internet. In addition, the Internet is a more cost-effective way to access cases otherwise available in LexisNexis, Westlaw, or other commercial services. Thus, although cases are not yet sufficiently accessible to make Internet research viable as your sole or beginning avenue for research, it may be a cost-effective way to supplement other research methods.

D. CITING CASES

As Chapter 1 explains, any time you report the results of your research in written form, you must cite your sources properly. This is especially important for cases because the information in the citation can help the reader assess the weight of the authority you are citing.

A case citation has three basic components:

1. the case name
2. information on the reporter in which the case is published
3. a parenthetical containing the jurisdiction, the level of court that decided the case, and the year of decision.

You can find rules for each component in the *ALWD Manual* and the *Bluebook*. Using the *ALWD Manual*, you should read Rule 12 and use Appendices 1, 3, and 4 for any necessary abbreviations. Using the *Bluebook*, you should begin with Bluepages B5 and use Tables T.1, T.6, and T.10 to find any necessary abbreviations. **Figure 4.15** directs you to the citation rules for cases.

The remainder of this section uses an example citation to illustrate each of these components. The example citation is to a fictional 1983 decision of

FIGURE 4.15   *ALWD MANUAL* AND *BLUEBOOK* RULES GOVERNING CASE CITATIONS

CITATION COMPONENT	*ALWD MANUAL,* RULE 12	*BLUEBOOK,* BLUEPAGES B5
Case name	Rule 12.2 & Appendix 3	Bluepages B5.1.1 & Tables T.6 & T.10
Reporter information	Rules 12.3–12.5 & Appendix 1	Bluepages B5.1.2, B5.1.3, & Table T.1
Parenthetical	Rules 12.6–12.7 & Appendices 1 & 4	Bluepages B5.1.3 & Table T.1

the Delaware Court of Chancery in the case of Patricia Ellis and Sam Anson versus Acme Manufacturing Company, published in volume 327 of the *Atlantic Reporter*, Second Series, beginning on page 457.

1. THE CASE NAME

The name of the case appears first and must be <u>underlined</u> or *italicized*. The case name consists of the name of the first party on either side of the "v." In other words, if more than one plaintiff or defendant is listed in the full case name, give only the name of the first named plaintiff or first named defendant. In the example citation, Sam Anson would not be listed. Do not include "et al." when a case has multiple parties; simply refer to the first named party on both sides. If a person is named as a party, use only the person's last name, but if a company or other entity is listed, use the entity's full name.

Often, the case name will be abbreviated. The abbreviation rules vary slightly in the *ALWD Manual* and the *Bluebook*. You will need to read the rules and refer to the appropriate appendix or table to determine when words should be abbreviated and what the proper abbreviations are. The case name should be followed by a comma, which is not underlined or italicized.

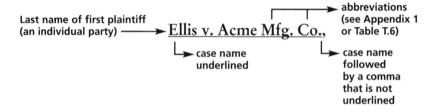

2. THE REPORTER

After the case name, the citation should list information on the reporter in which the case is published. If the case is published in more than one reporter, you will need to determine which reporter or reporters to cite, as explained in *ALWD Manual* Rule 12.4 and *Bluebook* Bluepages B5.1.3. In the citation, the name of the reporter will be abbreviated, so you must also determine the proper abbreviation. In the *ALWD Manual*, you can find this information in Appendix 1, which lists each jurisdiction in the United States alphabetically. For each jurisdiction, Appendix 1 lists reporter names and abbreviations. In the *Bluebook*, this same information appears in Table T.1.

Ordinarily, you will list the volume of the reporter, the reporter abbreviation, and the starting page of the case. If you are citing a specific page within the case, you will also usually cite to that page as well, using what is called a pinpoint citation. A comma should appear between the starting

page and the pinpoint citation, but the pinpoint citation should not be followed by a comma.

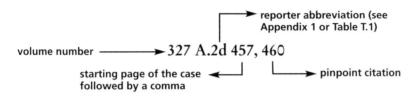

reporter abbreviation (see Appendix 1 or Table T.1)

volume number ⟶ 327 A.2d 457, 460

starting page of the case followed by a comma ← pinpoint citation

3. THE PARENTHETICAL

Following the information on the reporter, the case citation should include a parenthetical containing the abbreviated name of the jurisdiction, the abbreviated name of the level of court that decided the case, and the year the court issued its decision. This information is important because it can help the reader assess the weight of the authority you are citing.

The place to find the proper abbreviation for the jurisdiction and level of court is Appendix 1 in the *ALWD Manual* or Table T.1 in the *Bluebook*. Appendix 1 and Table T.1 list the levels of courts under each jurisdiction. Next to the name of each court, an abbreviation will appear in parentheses. This is the abbreviation for both the jurisdiction and the level of court, and this is what should appear in your parenthetical. You will notice that for the highest court in each state, the jurisdiction abbreviation is all that is necessary. This alerts the reader that the decision came from the highest court in the state; no additional court name abbreviation is necessary. Neither Appendix 1 nor Table T.1 lists the abbreviations for all courts. If you do not find the abbreviations you need in Appendix 1 in the *ALWD Manual,* consult Appendix 4, which contains court abbreviations. In the *Bluebook,* Table T.7 contains court names.

The last item to appear in the parenthetical is the year of the decision. The date when the court heard the case is not necessary in the citation; only the year of decision is required. No comma should appear before the year. After the year, the parenthetical should be closed.

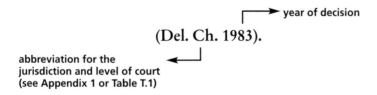

year of decision

(Del. Ch. 1983).

abbreviation for the jurisdiction and level of court (see Appendix 1 or Table T.1) ←

When all of the pieces are put together, the citation should look like this:

Ellis v. Acme Mfg. Co., 327 A.2d 457, 460 (Del. Ch. 1983).

E. SAMPLE PAGES FOR RESEARCHING CASES USING A PRINT DIGEST

On the following pages, you will find sample pages illustrating the process of print digest research. If you have read Chapter 2 on generating search terms, you may recall that the hypothetical fact pattern used in that chapter involved a guest at a hotel in Illinois who was robbed in a lobby restroom and seeks to recover from the hotel for her injuries. If you were researching this issue, you might want to see if any federal cases interpreting Illinois law were relevant. **Figures 4.16** through **4.23** show what you would see in *West's Federal Practice Digest*, Fourth Series. **Figure 4.24** shows the mini-digest in the back of an individual reporter volume. **Figure 4.25** contains sample pages from a case published in West's *Federal Reporter*, Second Series.

The first step is using the Descriptive-Word Index to lead you to relevant topics and key numbers. One search term you might have used is "Hotels." This entry directs you to another term: "Innkeepers." Because digests are organized by subject, other terms in the DWI could have referred you to "Innkeepers" as well.

FIGURE 4.16 DESCRIPTIVE-WORD INDEX

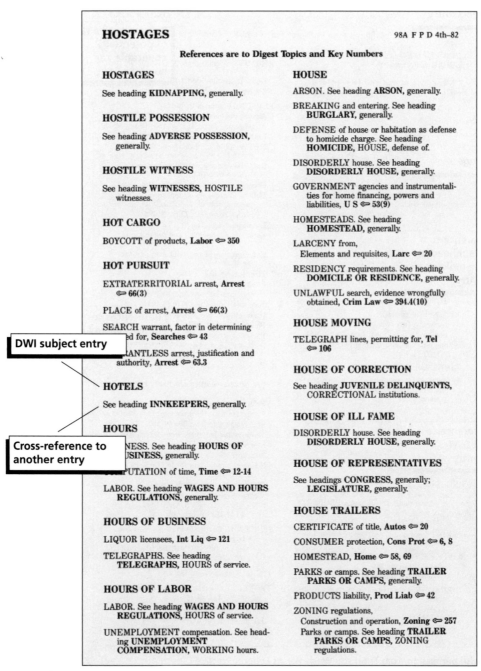

HOSTAGES   98A F P D 4th–82

References are to Digest Topics and Key Numbers

HOSTAGES

See heading **KIDNAPPING**, generally.

HOSTILE POSSESSION

See heading **ADVERSE POSSESSION**, generally.

HOSTILE WITNESS

See heading **WITNESSES**, HOSTILE witnesses.

HOT CARGO

BOYCOTT of products, **Labor** ⬩ 350

HOT PURSUIT

EXTRATERRITORIAL arrest, **Arrest** ⬩ 66(3)

PLACE of arrest, **Arrest** ⬩ 66(3)

SEARCH warrant, factor in determining ...d for, **Searches** ⬩ 43

...ANTLESS arrest, justification and authority, **Arrest** ⬩ 63.3

HOTELS

See heading **INNKEEPERS**, generally.

HOURS

...NESS. See heading **HOURS OF** ...USINESS, generally.

...PUTATION of time, **Time** ⬩ 12-14

LABOR. See heading **WAGES AND HOURS REGULATIONS**, generally.

HOURS OF BUSINESS

LIQUOR licensees, **Int Liq** ⬩ 121

TELEGRAPHS. See heading **TELEGRAPHS**, HOURS of service.

HOURS OF LABOR

LABOR. See heading **WAGES AND HOURS REGULATIONS**, HOURS of service.

UNEMPLOYMENT compensation. See heading **UNEMPLOYMENT COMPENSATION**, WORKING hours.

HOUSE

ARSON. See heading **ARSON**, generally.

BREAKING and entering. See heading **BURGLARY**, generally.

DEFENSE of house or habitation as defense to homicide charge. See heading **HOMICIDE**, HOUSE, defense of.

DISORDERLY house. See heading **DISORDERLY HOUSE**, generally.

GOVERNMENT agencies and instrumentalities for home financing, powers and liabilities, **U S** ⬩ 53(9)

HOMESTEADS. See heading **HOMESTEAD**, generally.

LARCENY from, Elements and requisites, **Larc** ⬩ 20

RESIDENCY requirements. See heading **DOMICILE OR RESIDENCE**, generally.

UNLAWFUL search, evidence wrongfully obtained, **Crim Law** ⬩ 394.4(10)

HOUSE MOVING

TELEGRAPH lines, permitting for, **Tel** ⬩ 106

HOUSE OF CORRECTION

See heading **JUVENILE DELINQUENTS**, CORRECTIONAL institutions.

HOUSE OF ILL FAME

DISORDERLY house. See heading **DISORDERLY HOUSE**, generally.

HOUSE OF REPRESENTATIVES

See headings **CONGRESS**, generally; **LEGISLATURE**, generally.

HOUSE TRAILERS

CERTIFICATE of title, **Autos** ⬩ 20

CONSUMER protection, **Cons Prot** ⬩ 6, 8

HOMESTEAD, **Home** ⬩ 58, 69

PARKS or camps. See heading **TRAILER PARKS OR CAMPS**, generally.

PRODUCTS liability, **Prod Liab** ⬩ 42

ZONING regulations, Construction and operation, **Zoning** ⬩ 257 Parks or camps. See heading **TRAILER PARKS OR CAMPS**, ZONING regulations.

DWI subject entry

Cross-reference to another entry

Reprinted with permission from Thomson West, *West's Federal Practice Digest,* 4th Ser., Vol. 98A (2002), p. 82. © 2002 Thomson West.

Under "Innkeepers," the entry for "personal injuries to guests" refers to relevant topics and key numbers. The abbreviation "Inn" refers to the "Innkeepers" topic, and the numbers refer to key numbers under that topic. Several relevant index entries refer you to key number 10.2.

FIGURE 4.17   DESCRIPTIVE-WORD INDEX

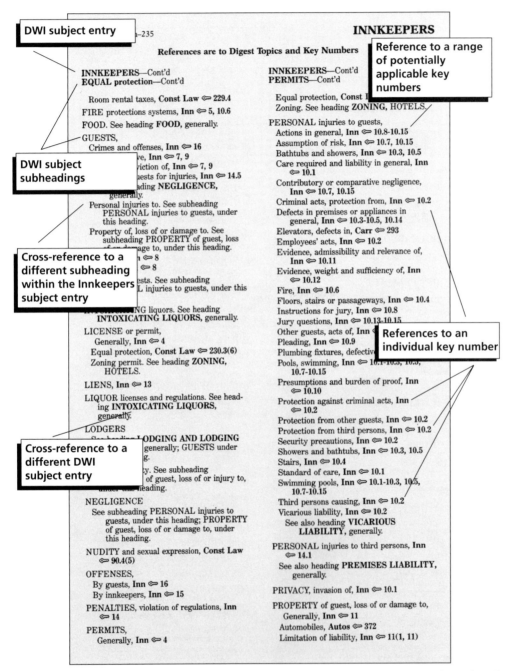

The index, as a hardcover volume, is updated with a pocket part. The pocket part entry under "Innkeepers" does not provide any additional topic and key number references relevant to this issue.

FIGURE 4.18 DESCRIPTIVE-WORD INDEX, POCKET PART

98A F P D 4th–41

INSTRUCTIONS

References are to Digest Topics and Key Numbers

INFORMED CONSENT

HEALTH, Health ☞ 906

MEDICAL treatment, Health ☞ 906

INFORMERS

DRUGS and controlled substances. See heading DRUGS AND CONTROLLED SUBSTANCES, SEARCHES and seizures, Informers.

INFRINGEMENT

TRADEMARKS and trade names,
   Domain names, internet, Trade Reg ☞ 350.1
   Internet domain names, Trade Reg ☞ 350.1

INJUNCTION

CIVIL rights,
   Federal actions, Civil R ☞ 1449
   State and local actions, Civil R ☞ 1759

EMPLOYEE pension and benefit plans. See heading EMPLOYEE PENSION AND BENEFIT PLANS, INJUNCTION.

ENVIRONMENT,
   Judicial review, Environ Law ☞ 700

HEALTH care professionals, injunction pending review, Health ☞ 159

WRONGFUL injunction,
   Damages,
      On dissolution, Inj ☞ 185.1-188

INNKEEPERS

CIVIL rights violations, public accommodations, Civil R ☞ 1046

DRUGS and controlled substances,
   Searches and seizures,
      Warrantless search, Controlled Subs ☞ 135

INQUEST

HOMICIDE. See heading HOMICIDE, INQUEST, proceedings at.

INSANITY

HOMICIDE. See heading HOMICIDE, CAPACITY to commit crime.

INSECTICIDES

AGRICULTURAL use,
   Generally, Agric ☞ 9.3
   Crop dusting, Agric ☞ 9.4
   Licenses, Agric ☞ 9.3
   Negligence, Agric ☞ 9.5
   Offenses, Agric ☞ 9.6
   Penalties, Agric ☞ 9.6

INSECTICIDES—Cont'd
AGRICULTURAL use—Cont'd
   Tort liability, Agric ☞ 9.5

ENVIRONMENTAL regulation,
   Generally, Environ Law ☞ 422, 424
   Labeling, Environ Law ☞ 423
   Registration, Environ Law ☞ 423

NEGLIGENCE, Neglig ☞ 306

PRODUCTS liability, Prod Liab ☞ 43.5

INSOLVENCY

EMPLOYEE pension and benefit plans. See heading EMPLOYEE PENSION AND BENEFIT PLANS, INSOLVENT plans.

INSPECTION

EMPLOYERS' liability. See heading EMPLOYERS' LIABILITY, INSPECTION and testing.

HEALTH, public health, fees, Health ☞ 401

MINES and minerals,
   Employees,
      Safety and health regulations, Labor & Emp ☞ 2661

PUBLIC health, fees, Health ☞ 401

INSTRUCTIONS

ASSAULT with intent to kill. See heading ASSAULT WITH INTENT TO KILL, INSTRUCTIONS.

CIVIL rights,
   Federal actions, Civil R ☞ 1433
   State and local actions, Civil R ☞ 1751

DEFENSES,
   Generally, Crim Law ☞ 772(6), 773-775, 782(13-16)

DRUGS and controlled substances. See heading DRUGS AND CONTROLLED SUBSTANCES, INSTRUCTIONS.

EMPLOYERS' liability. See heading EMPLOYERS' LIABILITY, INSTRUCTIONS to jury.

ENVIRONMENT,
   Criminal law, Environ Law ☞ 760
   Judicial review, Environ Law ☞ 693

FELLOW employees, Labor & Emp ☞ 2943

HEALTH care professionals,
   Compensation actions, Health ☞ 958
   Negligence or malpractice, Health ☞ 827

HEALTH, criminal law, Health ☞ 992

HOMICIDE. See heading HOMICIDE, INSTRUCTIONS.

INDEMNITY, Indem ☞ 103

> No new relevant entries are listed.

Reprinted with permission from Thomson West, *West's Federal Practice Digest,* 4th Ser., Cumulative Annual Pocket Part, Vol. 98A (2004), p. 41. © 2004 Thomson West.

The next step is looking up the topic "Innkeepers" in the subject volumes. The outline at the beginning of the topic identifies other key numbers that may be relevant.

FIGURE 4.19   KEY NUMBER OUTLINE, "INNKEEPERS" TOPIC

INNKEEPERS

SUBJECTS INCLUDED

Regulation of inns, hotels, boarding houses, lodging houses, and all houses furnishing for compensation accommodation as a temporary home

Mutual rights, duties, and liabilities of keepers of such houses and their guests, boarders or lodgers

SUBJECTS EXCLUDED AND COVERED BY OTHER TOPICS

Discrimination by reason of race, color, etc., see CIVIL RIGHTS

Intoxicants, regulation of sale, see INTOXICATING LIQUORS

Trailer camps and the like, see AUTOMOBILES, LICENSES

For detailed references to other topics, see Descriptive-Word Index

Analysis

&1. Power to regulate.
 2. Statutory and municipal regulations.
 3. Who are innkeepers.
 4. Licenses and taxes.
 5. Buildings.
 6. Conduct of business.
 7. Duty to receive guests.
 8. Who are guests, boarders, or lodgers.
 9. Duty to furnish accommodations.
 10. Injury to person of guest.
 10.1. —— In general.
 10.2. —— Acts of employees, other guests, or third persons.
 10.3. —— Defects in premises or appliances in general.
 10.4. —— Defective floors, stairs, or passageways.
 10.5. —— Defective plumbing fixtures.
 10.6. —— Fire.
 10.7. —— Contributory negligence and assumption of risk.
 10.8. —— Actions in general.
 10.9. —— Pleading.
 10.10. —— Presumptions and burden of proof.
 10.11. —— Admissibility of evidence.
 10.12. —— Weight and sufficiency of evidence.
 10.13. —— Questions for jury in general.
 10.14. —— Defects in premises or appliances, questions for jury.
 10.15. —— Contributory negligence and assumption of risk, questions for jury.
 11. Loss of or injury to property of guest.
   (.5). In general.
   (1). Nature and extent of liability in general.
   (2). Relation of parties.

Range of relevant key numbers

FIGURE 4.19 **KEY NUMBER OUTLINE, "INNKEEPERS" TOPIC** *(Continued)*

INNKEEPERS

63 F P D 4th—2

&11. Loss of or injury to property of guest.—Continued.
    (3). Care required of innkeeper.
    (4). Loss of or injury to property by servants.
    (5). Loss of or injuries to animals.
    (6). Property for which innkeeper is liable.
    (7). Rules and regulations.
    (8). Property transported to and from depot.
    (9). Place of leaving property.
    (10). Contributory negligence.
    (11). Statutes limiting liability.
    (12). Actions.
  12. Compensation.
  13. Lien.
  14. Penalties for violations of regulations.
  14.1. Injuries to third persons.
  14.5. Liabilities of guests for injuries.
  15. Offenses by innkeepers.
  16. Offenses by guests, boarders, or lodgers.

For detailed references to other topics, see Descriptive-Word Index

Reprinted with permission from Thomson West, *West's Federal Practice Digest,* 4th Ser., Vol. 63 (1998), pp. 1–2. © 1998 Thomson West.

The case summaries under key number 10.2 include several potentially relevant cases from the Seventh Circuit and Northern District of Illinois.

FIGURE 4.20   CASE SUMMARIES UNDER "INNKEEPERS" TOPIC

☞10.1   INNKEEPERS   63 F P D 4th—8

For later cases see same Topic and Key Number in Pocket Part

protect them against unreasonable risk of physical harm.

> Manahan v. NWA, 821 F.Supp. 1105, reconsideration denied 821 F.Supp. 1110, affirmed 995 F.2d 218.

Key number 10.2

s not insurer against all risk of ~~injury to guests~~, but is obligated only to take reasonable steps to minimize risks to its guests that are foreseeable when they are reasonably within its sphere of control.

> Manahan v. NWA, 821 F.Supp. 1105, reconsideration denied 821 F.Supp. 1110, affirmed 995 F.2d 218.

☞10.2. —— Acts of employees, other guests, or third persons.

Summaries of potentially relevant cases

C.A.11 (Fla.) 1987. Hotel guest was business invitee to whom hotel operator owed duty ~~to protect~~ against dangers of which it should ~~be~~ aware, which duty extended to reasonably foreseeable criminal acts against guest, under Florida law.

> Meyers v. Ramada Hotel Operating Co., Inc., 833 F.2d 1521.

C.A.7 (Ill.) 1989. As general rule, Illinois does not impose duty to protect others from criminal attacks by third parties; however, exception is recognized where criminal attack was reasonably foreseeable and parties had special relationship such as carrier-passenger, innkeeper-guest, business invitor-invitee, or voluntary custodian-protectee.

> Figueroa v. Evangelical Covenant Church, 879 F.2d 1427, rehearing denied.

C.A.7 (Ill.) 1989. Negligence of motel owners in connection with intruder's early-morning assault of guest in her room was at most "simple" under Illinois law, rather than "willful and wanton," in context of guest's claim that her own negligence was irrelevant; although motel was located near high-crime area and owners failed to specifically warn guest of neighborhood's dangers or of previous crimes involving guests, no rational jury could find that owners consciously disregarded high probability of serious physical harm.

> Wassell v. Adams, 865 F.2d 849.

As innkeepers, motel owners had duty to exercise high degree of care under Illinois law to protect guests from assaults on motel premises.

> Wassell v. Adams, 865 F.2d 849.

Under Illinois law, motel owners were not required to tell guest not to open her door in middle of night under any circumstances without carefully ascertaining who was trying to enter room any more than they were required to warn guests not to stick fingers into electrical outlets.

> Wassell v. Adams, 865 F.2d 849.

C.A.7 (Ill.) 1987. Though requirement that innkeeper use high standard of care to protect its guests from assault on innkeeper's premises may be defensible in that innkeeper ordinarily knows much more about hazards of his trade than guest and can take reasonable, i.e., cost-justified, steps to reduce them while ordinarily guest can do little to protect himself against them, even higher standard of care does not make innkeeper's liability strict.

> McCarty v. Pheasant Run, Inc., 826 F.2d 1554.

C.A.4 (N.C.) 1988. Evidence of prior criminal activity in the area was ~~sufficient~~

Summary of a potentially relevant case

reasonably foreseeable that "operating in the metropolitan a~~rea~~ motel where guests were rob~~bed~~ thereby giving rise to a dut~~y~~ that particular risk; evidence showed that in the two weeks just before the attack, seven motels within the general area had been victimized, the systematic nature of the attacks, their apparent perpetration by a single group and the fact that the group continued to operate even after law enforcement efforts had focused on them and area motels were alerted to their presence made it reasonably foreseeable that the attacks would continue, and the premises where the attack occurred was a motel near a major highway, making it similar to several of the previously victimized motels.

> Crinkley v. Holiday Inns, Inc., 844 F.2d 156.

Motel guests who were injured by assault on motel property were not required to show that motel's specific security deficiencies proximately caused the specific criminal assault upon them, but were required to show that the attack was foreseeable in order to recover against premises owner.

> Crinkley v. Holiday Inns, Inc., 844 F.2d 156.

C.A.1 (Puerto Rico) 1995. Under Puerto Rico law, driver of vehicle provided by hotel to furnish guests at hotel with transportation from airport to hotel was innkeeper who potentially owed duty to ensure safety of guests riding in vehicle where driver was not common carrier for hire but employee of hotel performing private service for private purpose. 31 L.P.R.A. §§ 3021, 5141.

> Coyne v. Taber Partners I, 53 F.3d 454, rehearing and suggestion for rehearing denied.

C.A.9 (Wash.) 1995. As to conditions on land, under Washington law, landowner may have duty to warn licensee of criminal conduct of third parties, but does not have that duty in absence of special relationship; special relationships include custodian and ward, innkeeper

For cited U.S.C.A. sections and legislative history, see United States Code Annotated

FIGURE 4.20 CASE SUMMARIES UNDER "INNKEEPERS" TOPIC *(Continued)*

63 F P D 4th—9   **INNKEEPERS**   ⌐10.2

For references to other topics, see Descriptive-Word Index

and guest, tavern owner and patron, and employer and employee.
> Will v. U.S., 60 F.3d 656, appeal after remand 152 F.3d 932.

D.Conn. 1996. Tour operator which booked tourist's vacation was not vicariously liable for tourist's injuries allegedly caused by negligence of hotel employees, where there was no evidence that there was common corporate structure between operator and hotel, or that tour operator owned, operated, managed, or supervised hotel.
> Passero v. DHC Hotels and Resorts, Inc., 981 F.Supp. 742.

D.Del. 1996. Under Delaware law, hotel guest who was robbed in hotel room failed to establish prima facie case of negligence on part of hotel corporation where guest failed to show that there were prior assaults on hotel guests or that hotel knew or should have known of such attacks but failed to take reasonable security precautions.
> Naghiu v. Inter-Continental Hotels Group, Inc., 165 F.R.D. 413.

N.D.Ga. 1993. Under Georgia law, there was no implied contract between hotel and guests to provide protection from criminal acts of third parties, and so guests could not recover for damages arising from robbery in hotel under theory of breach of implied contract.
> Burnett v. Stagner Hotel Courts, Inc., 821 F.Supp. 678, affirmed 42 F.3d 645.

Under Georgia law, innkeeper is not liable for injuries proximately caused by criminal actions of third parties, unless innkeeper has reasonable grounds to believe that particular criminal acts are likely to occur; when innkeeper is aware of unreasonable risk of particular type of criminal attack, he has duty to exercise ordinary care to protect his guests against that risk. O.C.G.A. § 51–3–1.
> Burnett v. Stagner Hotel Courts, Inc., 821 F.Supp. 678, affirmed 42 F.3d 645.

In action to recover for injuries inflicted by criminal acts of third party under Georgia law, guest has burden of proving that host was placed on notice of danger by prior substantially similar incidents.
> Burnett v. Stagner Hotel Courts, Inc., 821 F.Supp. 678, affirmed 42 F.3d 645.

Prior crimes allegedly occurring at hotel were not so substantially similar to litigated incident, in which guests were robbed by armed men in their room, to attract innkeeper's attention to alleged dangerous condition which resulted in armed robbery of guests, where most of prior crimes involved theft by stealth or trickery rather than direct confrontation and the two prior robberies involving direct confrontation occurred nearly three years before

and over four years before litigated robbery. O.C.G.A. § 51–3–1.
> Burnett v. Stagner Hotel Courts, Inc., 821 F.Supp. 678, affirmed 42 F.3d 645.

Even if guests had succeeded in showing that hotel had duty to protect them from armed robbery in their room, hotel was not liable under negligence theory, since guests failed to provide any evidence showing that security measures taken by hotel were not reasonable; mere citation of additional security measures hotel could have taken was not sufficient.
> Burnett v. Stagner Hotel Courts, Inc., 821 F.Supp. 678, affirmed 42 F.3d 645.

Hotel was not liable under negligence law for damages resulting [from] robbery of guests in their room, [where] sudden and unprovoked criminal a[ct] evidence showed was independent [and] perpetrated unexpectedly and with[out warning] by third parties, where guests fail[ed to show] that hotel could have prevented incident by exercise of ordinary care.
> Burnett v. Stagner Hotel Courts, Inc., 821 F.Supp. 678, affirmed 42 F.3d 645.

Summaries of federal district court cases follow summaries of circuit court cases.

N.D.Ill. 1996. In terms of hotel-guest relationship under Illinois law, whether or not defendant has duty to protect plaintiff from independent, intervening criminal acts of third persons depends upon whether such acts are foreseeable; more specifically, where assault upon guest by third party is involved, hotel is held to high degree of care.
> DeMyrick v. Guest Quarters Suite Hotels, 944 F.Supp. 661.

Under Illinois Human Rights Act, absence of arrest record was not a bona fide occupational qualification for attendant who parked cars for hotel guests; therefore, employer of attendants could not be held liable under negligent hiring theory based on its failure to discover arrest records of off-duty attendants who were involved in shooting at hotel. S.H.A. 775 ILCS 5/2–104(A)(1).
> DeMyrick v. Guest Quarters Suite Hotels, 944 F.Supp. 661.

Under Illinois law, even if employer of hotel parking attendants could have obtained conviction information regarding one attendant, its failure to do so was not a proximate cause of fatal shooting of hotel guest occurring after two off-duty attendants and one nonattendant gained access to guest floors of hotel; it was not attendant with criminal record who actually shot and killed guest, but attendant who worked at entirely different location and who did not have any record, and attendant actually in-

For cited U.S.C.A. sections and legislative history, see United States Code Annotated

The next step is checking the pocket part for this volume. The entry under key number 10.2 in the pocket part includes two potentially relevant cases from the Seventh Circuit and Northern District of Illinois.

FIGURE 4.21   DIGEST VOLUME, POCKET PART

☞10.1 INNKEEPERS

63 F P D 4th—2

C.A.7 (Ill.) 1999. Under Illinois law, as predicted by the Court of Appeals, defense of contributory negligence, as recognized under law of Mexico, was not so repugnant to public policy of Illinois that Illinois court would choose not to enforce that defense, even if it would apply the rest of Mexico's tort law, in negligence action brought by Illinois resident against owner of Mexican hotel.—Spinozzi v. ITT Sheraton Corp., 174 F.3d 842.

N.D.Ga. 2003. Complaint which alleged that motel and its manager breached legal duties imposed by Georgia statutes prohibiting discrimination in public places based on utilization of service animal and requiring innkeepers to provide accommodations to guests of good character when they prohibited legally blind individual and his service dog from staying at their hotel and that plaintiff allegedly suffered injury, including humiliation, embarrassment, and emotional distress, as direct and proximate result of defendants' actions stated all elements necessary for recovery under the Georgia theory of negligence per se and Georgia general tort statute. West's Ga:Code Ann. §§ 30–4–2, 43–21–3, 51–1–6.—Amick v. BM & KM, Inc., 275 F.Supp.2d 1378.

D.Hawai'i 1999. Hotel facing beach but separated from ocean by both road and county-operated beach park did not "front" beach within meaning of Hawaii statute limiting hotelkeeper's duty to warn against hazardous beach or ocean conditions; contiguity with beach was required for statute to apply. HRS § 486K–5.5.—Rygg v. County of Maui, 98 F.Supp.2d 1129.

Hawaii statute limiting beachfront hotelkeeper's duty to warn against hazardous beach or ocean conditions did not abrogate non-beachfront hotelkeeper's common-law duty to warn invitees of dangers known or obvious to hotelkeeper but unknown to guests, possibly including dangers of nearby beach and ocean; rather, purpose of statute was to preclude beachfront hotelkeeper's liability for injuries incurred by casual passersby having no nexus to hotel. HRS § 486K–5.5.—Id.

Under Hawaii law, hotelkeeper's duty to warn extends to such places in or about hotel's premises as hotel's guests may be reasonably expected to go during their visit.—Id.

D.Me. 2002. Under Maine law, innkeepers are not required to meet heightened standard of care by virtue of that status alone.—Smith v. Otis Elevator Co., 217 F.Supp.2d 105.

E.D.Mich. 2001. Under Michigan law, patron of restaurant located in hotel was invitee entitled to highest standard of care by hotel through which patron passed to reach restaurant; hotel held open its business for commercial purposes, and patron visited the premises for that reason.—Vella v. Hyatt Corp., 166 F.Supp.2d 1193.

D.Minn. 1998. Under Minnesota law, generally, a special relationship giving rise to a duty to warn is only found on the part of common carriers, innkeepers, possessors of land who hold it open to the public, and persons who have custody of another person under circumstances in which that other person is deprived of normal opportunities of self-protection.—Grozdanich v. Leisure Hills Health Center, Inc., 25 F.Supp.2d 953, reconsideration denied 48 F.Supp.2d 885.

D.R.I. 2001. Under Massachusetts and Rhode Island law, charter tour operator's involvement in management and operation of hotel was not sufficient to impose duty on it as innkeeper or owner to ensure safety of hotel premises, and thus was not liable for injuries sustained by

participant when chair collapsed at hotel, even though tour operator described hotel as "dependable," had employee visit hotel daily, provided assistance at airport, hotel transfers and check-in assistance, orientation sessions, bulletin board in hotel lobby, and various activities for tour participants, absent evidence that tour operator owned, operated, or controlled hotel.—McElheny v. Trans Nat. Travel, Inc., 165 F.Supp.2d 190.

W.D.Tex. 2000. In Texas, motel owners owe a duty to use ordinary care to protect the safety of their guests and invitees; this duty is grounded in Texas law, not contract principles and would apply whether or not the guest was in direct privity of contract to the motel owner.—Paredes v. City of Odessa, 128 F.Supp.2d 1009.

D.Virgin Islands 2002. Concession agreement between National Park Service and operators of campground that did not give operators control over swimming area, access to beach, or beach itself, did not bring site of injury within operators' sphere of control sufficient to support claim of vacationer who was injured while body surfing within campground boundaries against operators for breaching their innkeepers' duty to protect their guests from unreasonable risks of harm under Virgin Islands law; concession agreement gave operators no sphere of control over beach or designated swimming area where vacationer suffered his injuries.—Fabend v. Rosewood Hotels and Resorts, L.L.C., 181 F.Supp.2d 439.

Water-related activities of operators of campground in National Park did not bring site of injury within operators' sphere of control sufficient to support claim of vacationer who was injured while body surfing within campground boundaries against operators for breaching their innkeepers' duty to protect their guests from unreasonable risks of harm under Virgin Islands law; only National Park Service had authority to designate area of water in which vacationer was injured for swimming, and vacationer was not using or wearing anything purchased or rented from operators at time of his accident. 36 C.F.R. § 1.5(a)(2); 12 V.I.C. § 402.—Id.

E.D.Wis. 1999. Under Wisconsin law, hotelkeeper's duty depends on foreseeability of the injury; hotelkeeper's duty is established when it can be said that it was foreseeable that his omission to act may cause harm to some H.K. Mallak, Inc. v. Fairfield FMC Co F.Supp.2d 748, reversed 209 F.3d 960, re en banc denied.

Under Wisconsin law, there is no duty on the part of a hotelkeeper to guard against abnormal or unusual events or things that with reasonable care, skill, and foresight could not have been anticipated, discovered, or prevented; its duty is to protect only against those risks that it could have discovered in the exercise of ordinary care.—Id.

Under Wisconsin law, once negligence of hotelkeeper is established, hotelkeeper is liable for unforeseeable consequences as well as foreseeable ones.—Id.

☞10.2. —— **Acts of employees, other guests, or third persons.**

C.A.7 (Ill.) 2003. Hotel chain district manager was acting within the scope of his employment in refusing hotel manager's recommendation to close the hotel while every room was sprayed by exterminator to treat bedbug infestation, and thus, the hotel chain's liability, to hotel guests who were subsequently bitten by bedbugs, for compensatory damages as the district ma

† This Case was not selected for publication in the National Reporter System

[Callout: Pocket part entry for key number 10.2]

[Callout: Summary of a potentially relevant case]

FIGURE 4.21 **DIGEST VOLUME, POCKET PART** *(Continued)*

63 F P D 4th—3

INNKEEPERS ☞10.8

employer, was automatic on the basis of the principle of respondeat superior.—Mathias v. Accor Economy Lodging, Inc., 347 F.3d 672.

C.A.5 (La.) 2001. Under Louisiana law, finding that motel owner was eighty percent at fault for assault and battery of guest was supported by evidence that area was unsafe, that only access to guest rooms was through lobby occupied by single desk clerk, and that no security guard was on duty on night unidentified intruders robbed guest in his room.—McAvey v. Lee, 260 F.3d 359, rehearing and rehearing denied 273 F.3d 1105.

† **C.A.4 (N.C.) 2001.** Armed robbery of motel patrons in motel parking lot was not reasonably foreseeable, and thus, motel proprietors were not liable in negligence to patrons based on alleged failure to take steps to prevent robbery.—Dettlaff v. Holiday Inns, Inc., 10 Fed.Appx. 100.

† **C.A.10 (Okla.) 2001.** If independent contractor's security guard had knowledge that two men he saw in the hotel which contracted with his employer were about to commit a criminal act, that knowledge would be imputed to the hotel, under Oklahoma law.—Ring v. Lexington Apartments & Motor Inns-Oklahoma, 3 Fed.Appx. 847.

N.D.Ill. 2001. Illinois law does not impose a duty to protect another from a criminal attack by a third person unless the attack was reasonably foreseeable and the parties were common carrier and passenger, innkeeper and guest, business invitor and invitee, or voluntary custodian and protectee.—Ryan v. U.S., 156 F.Supp.2d 900.

N.D.Ind. 1999. Under Indiana law, it was not foreseeable that underage hotel guest would assault another guest at private party in room, and ~~hotel did not have duty to protect guest from~~ criminal act, even if hotel was aware that ~~teenage drinking was taking place in hotel,~~ ~~absent evidence of prior violent acts in hotel.—~~ ~~Foster v. Walker, 79 F.Supp.2d 965.~~

~~Under Indiana law, hotel did not undertake~~ ~~to protect invitees from unforeseeable as-~~ ~~sault by another invitee during private party in~~ ~~room during graduation week of local school due~~ to fact that it hired additional security personnel to protect hotel property during graduation weekend.—Id.

E.D.La. 1998. Under Louisiana law, innkeeper may be liable if he fails to exercise reasonable care to provide adequate security to deter type of criminal activity that results in guest's injury.—McAvey v. Lee, 58 F.Supp.2d 724.

E.D.N.Y. 2002. In New York, innkeepers have a duty to protect guests and patrons from reasonably foreseeable criminal attacks.—Sawyer v. Wight, 196 F.Supp.2d 220.

Criminal attacks may be reasonably foreseeable, for purposes of determining whether hotel or inn had duty to protect patrons from such attacks, when the hotel or inn where the attack occurred was plagued by ambient crime; however, attacks may not be reasonably foreseeable when the hotel provided adequate security or when the attack was directed specifically at the victim because of his own remarks.—Id.

For purposes of hotel patron's personal injury action, arising out of hotel's alleged failure to maintain order in lobby, hotel owed patron a duty to protect him from the foreseeable criminal activities of third persons, under New York law.—Id.

E.D.Wis. 1999. Under Wisconsin law, hotel has a duty to exercise ordinary care to provide adequate protection for its guests and their property from assaultive and other types of criminal activity.—H.K. Mallak, Inc. v. Fairfield FMC

Corp., 33 F.Supp.2d 748, reversed 209 F.3d 960, rehearing en banc denied.

Under Wisconsin law, hotelkeeper must provide security commensurate with the facts and circumstances that are or should be apparent to the ordinarily prudent person; the standard of care may vary according to the particular circumstances and location of the hotel.—Id.

Under Wisconsin law, relevant factors in deciding whether a hotel has exercised ordinary care in providing adequate security are: industry standards, the community's crime rate, the extent of assaultive or criminal activity in the area or in similar business enterprises, the presence of suspicious persons, and the peculiar security problems posed by the hotel's design.—Id.

☞10.3. —— **Defects in premises or appliances in general.**

E.D.Mich. 2001. Under Michigan law, district court was required as a threshold matter to determine whether alleged dangerous condition on premises was "open and obvious" in patron's negligence action against hotel, to identify whether special aspects of condition made it unreasonably dangerous so as to impose a duty where one would otherwise not exist.—Vella v. Hyatt Corp., 166 F.Supp.2d 1193.

☞10.4. —— **Defective floors, stairs, or passageways.**

E.D.Mich. 2001. Patron was not required to demonstrate that hotel had actual or constructive knowledge of slippery floors, in patron's slip and fall action against hotel, where defendant cleaned and/or polished floors on nightly basis and knew that material from which its floors were made was of a type with a low coefficient of friction.—Vella v. Hyatt Corp., 166 F.Supp.2d 1193.

☞10.5. —— **Defective plumbing fixtures.**

† **C.A.7 (Ill.) 2003.** Under Illinois law, evidence that hotel took precautions against falls in hotel bathrooms by installing mats in bathtubs, requiring room attendants to check daily, and regularly replacing mats was insufficient to establish that hotel's precautions were inadequate to protect guest from slip and fall on mat, which allegedly was inadequately secured.—Galarnyk v. Hostmark Management, Inc., 55 Fed.Appx. 763.

☞10.7. —— **Contributory negligence and assumption of risk.**

C.A.7 (Ill.) 1999. Under Illinois law, as predicted by the Court of Appeals, defense of contributory negligence, as recognized under law of Mexico, was not so repugnant to public policy of Illinois that Illinois court would choose not to enforce that defense, even if it would apply the rest of Mexico's tort law, in negligence action brought by Illinois resident against owner of Mexican hotel.—Spinozzi v. ITT Sheraton Corp., 174 F.3d 842.

E.D.La. 1998. Under Louisiana law, fault was not to be apportioned between unknown intentional tortfeasors who assaulted guest on hotel premises and innkeeper that breached its duty to exercise reasonable care to provide adequate security. LSA–C.C. art. 2323.—McAvey v. Lee, 58 F.Supp.2d 724.

☞10.8. —— **Actions in general.**

C.A.7 (Ill.) 1999. Under Illinois' conflict of law principles, law of Mexico, under which hotel guest's contributory negligence was complete defense to negligence liability, governed negligence action brought against owner of Mexican hotel by guest, who was Illinois resident and was injured

† **This Case was not selected for publication in the National Reporter System**

Summaries of federal district court cases follow those of circuit court cases.

At the end of *West's Federal Practice Digest,* Fourth Series, are a series of noncumulative interim pamphlets with cases decided after the pocket part was published. Under the topic "Innkeepers" in this example, one case from the Seventh Circuit is summarized, but it appears under key number 13.

FIGURE 4.22   NONCUMULATIVE INTERIM PAMPHLET

Interim pamphlet entry for Innkeepers

The only entry is under key number 13.

INNKEEPERS   882

INNKEEPERS

⚷▷13. Lien.
C.A.7 (Ill.) 2004. Circumstances or services recognized at Illinois common law as giving rise to entitlement to a possessory lien include the following: (1) a bailee who at the request of the bailor does work upon or adds materials to a chattel, [which] does not necessarily require the chattel's value to increase, (2) transportation of a [chattel b]y a common carrier, (3) a hotelkeeper, (4) [repair] of a chattel provided by a warehouseman, [storing] a chattel for which a specific reward is offered, (6) sale of a chattel, if the seller is in possession, (7) advancing money or incurring liability by an agent on behalf of his principal in respect of a chattel in his possession, (8) a landlord who enters and seizes chattels in the tenant's possession after a default on rent, and (9) a possessor of land who seizes a thing doing damage on the land. Restatement of Security § 61.—In re Midway Airlines, Inc., 383 F.3d 663.

INSURANCE

I. IN GENERAL; NATURE OF INSURANCE.

⚷▷1011. —— Life.
† **C.A.5 (La.) 2004.** Under Louisiana law, as predicted by Court of Appeals, insurance policy was form of health and accident insurance, rather than life insurance policy, given that focus of policy's provisions was to insure against certain forms of bodily injury, disablement, or death by accident or accidental means, policy contained provisions generally tracking those required by state law to be included in all health and accident insurance policies, but omitted some provisions required to be in all life insurance policies, and policy was titled as "accidental death and loss of sight or limbs policy." LSA–R.S. 22:6(1), (2)(a), 22:170(a), 22:213(A).—Washington v. Western & Southern Life Ins. Co., 107 Fed.Appx. 433.

⚷▷1012. —— Health and accident.
† **C.A.5 (La.) 2004.** Under Louisiana law, as predicted by Court of Appeals, insurance policy was form of health and accident insurance, rather than life insurance policy, given that focus of policy's provisions was to insure against certain forms of bodily injury, disablement, or death by accident or accidental means, policy contained provisions generally tracking those required by state law to be included in all health and accident insurance policies, but omitted some provisions required to be in all life insurance policies, and policy was titled as "accidental death and loss of sight or limbs policy." LSA–R.S. 22:6(1), (2)(a), 22:170(a), 22:213(A).—Washington v. Western & Southern Life Ins. Co., 107 Fed.Appx. 433.

II. REGULATION IN GENERAL.

(C) STATE AGENCIES AND REGULATION.

⚷▷1022. In general.
C.A.5 2004. Under Texas insurance law, insurance company employee who in course of his employment engages in business of insurance is "person" regulated by state insurance code's Unfair Competition and Unfair Practices statute; however, employee cannot be liable under statute absent evidence that employee himself, as opposed to insurer, committed statutory violation. V.A.T.S. Insurance Code, art. 21.21.—Hornbuckle v. State Farm Lloyds, 385 F.3d 538.

III. WHAT LAW GOVERNS.

(A) CHOICE OF LAW.

⚷▷1088. —— Place of contracting or performance.
W.D.Ark. 2004. Under Arkansas law, law of the state where the contract was made—the lex loci contractus rule—governs insurance contract disputes.—Hicks v. American Heritage Life Ins. Co., 332 F.Supp.2d 1193.

⚷▷1091(4). —— In general.
S.D.N.Y. 2004. Under New York's choice-of-law rules, law of New York, where binders and policies were negotiated and issued by authorized New York insurance company for properties in that state, governed liability policies; New York had most significant relationship to transaction and parties.—In re September 11th Liability Ins. Coverage Cases, 333 F.Supp.2d 111.

⚷▷1091(7). Life insurance.
W.D.Ark. 2004. Under Arkansas choice-of-law rule, law of Missouri, where life insurance contract was made, applied in resolving insurance policy dispute.—Hicks v. American Heritage Life Ins. Co., 332 F.Supp.2d 1193.

⚷▷1097. —— Construction.
† **C.A.6 (Ohio) 2004.** Choice-of-law provision in arbitration clause of insurance contract applied only to arbitration between insurer and insureds, and thus did not govern choice-of-law issue in declaratory judgment action brought by insurer to determine its duty to defend and indemnify insureds.—Illinois Union Ins. Co. v. Shefchuk, 108 Fed.Appx. 294.

(B) PREEMPTION; APPLICATION OF STATE OR FEDERAL LAW.

⚷▷1100. In general.
C.A.6 (Tenn.) 2004. Reverse preemption under McCarran–Ferguson Act, which precludes application of federal statute to invalidate or impair state law enacted to regulate insurance, depends upon the policies that undergird state law, and when state law protects state insurance-policyholders, it is a law enacted for the purpose of regulating the business of insurance within meaning of Act; however, when state law protects other interests, such as those of stockholders in insurance companies, it is not such a law within the meaning of the Act. McCarran–Ferguson Act, § 2(b), 15 U.S.C.A. § 1012(b).—AmSouth Bank v. Dale, 386 F.3d 763, 2004 Fed.App. 321P.

When assessing whether a general federal statute that creates a cause of action "impairs" the operation of a state law, within meaning of prohibition under McCarran–Ferguson Act against application of federal statute to invalidate or impair state law enacted to regulate the business of insurance, proper inquiry is whether the particular suit being brought would impair state law. McCarran–Ferguson Act, § 2(b), 15 U.S.C.A. § 1012(b).—Id.

⚷▷1101. The "business of insurance" in general.
C.A.6 (Tenn.) 2004. Reverse preemption under McCarran–Ferguson Act, which precludes application of federal statute to invalidate or impair state law enacted to regulate insurance, depends upon the policies that undergird state law, and when state law protects state insurance-policyholders, it is a law enacted for the purpose of regulating the business of insurance within meaning of Act; how-

† This Case was not selected for publication in the National Reporter System

On the inside front cover of the December 2004 pamphlet is the closing table indicating the last volumes of the reporters with cases summarized in this pamphlet. The *Federal Supplement,* Second Series, closes with volume 337.

FIGURE 4.23 NONCUMULATIVE INTERIM PAMPHLET, CLOSING TABLE

Closing with Cases Reported in

Supreme Court Reporter ———————————————— 125 S.Ct. 376
Federal Reporter, Third Series ————————————— 386 F.3d 1147
Federal Appendix ——————————————————— 110 Fed.Appx. 129
Federal Supplement, Second Series ————————— 337 F.Supp.2d
Federal Rules Decisions ——————————————— 224 F.R.D. 197
Bankruptcy Reporter ————————————————— 316 B.R. 100
Federal Claims Reporter —————————————— 62 Fed.Cl. 473
Military Justice Reporter — U.S.Armed Forces ————— 60 M.J. 305
Military Justice Reporter — A.F.Ct.Crim.App. ————— 60 M.J. 726
Veterans Appeals Reporter —————————————— 18 Vet.App. 431

COPYRIGHT © 2004
By
West, a Thomson business

The above symbol, KeyCite, WESTLAW®, WEST's and Federal Practice Digest are registered trademarks. Registered in the U.S. Patent and Trademark Office.

West, a Thomson business, has created this publication to provide you with accurate and authoritative information concerning the subject matter covered. However, this publication was not necessarily prepared by persons licensed to practice law in a particular jurisdiction. West is not engaged in rendering legal or other professional advice, and this publication is not a substitute for the advice of an attorney. If you require legal or other expert advice, you should seek the services of a competent attorney or other professional.

Reprinted with permission from Thomson West, *West's Federal Practice Digest,* 4th Ser., December 2004 Pamphlet (2004), inside cover. © 2004 Thomson West.

To find cases decided after the interim pamphlet closed, the next step is checking the mini-digest in the back of each individual volume of F. Supp. 2d after volume 337. Most of them do not include any entries under "Innkeepers." The example below comes from 343 F. Supp. 2d, which lists one case under key number 10.2.

FIGURE 4.24   343 F. Supp. 2d, MINI-DIGEST

☞68.5 INFANTS

INFANTS

VI. CRIMES.

☞68.5. —— Jurisdiction of adult or juvenile court; necessity for juvenile court waiver.
W.D.N.Y. 2004. Plaintiff's alleged prosecution and sentencing as an adult at time he was actually a juvenile did not violate plaintiff's constitutional rights, as required to support claim under § 1983 against individuals involved in his prosecution, where plaintiff was unaware of his actual birthdate until after his release from prison and believed he was an adult at the time, and there was no indication that anyone involved in his criminal prosecution knew otherwise. 42 U.S.C.A. § 1983.—Jordan v. New York, 343 F.Supp.2d 199.

INJUNCTION

IV. PRELIMINARY AND INTERLOCUTORY INJUNCTIONS.

(A) GROUNDS AND PROCEEDINGS TO PROCURE.

1. IN GENERAL.

☞132. Nature and scope of provisional remedy.
S.D.Miss. 2004. Injunctive relief is an extraordinary and drastic remedy, not to be granted routinely, but only when the movant, by a clear showing, carries the burden of persuasion.—Cox v. City of Jackson, 343 F.Supp.2d 546.

4. PROCEEDINGS.

☞147. Counter affidavits and other evidence.
C.D.Cal. 2004. District court has discretion to consider otherwise inadmissible evidence in ruling on merits of application for preliminary injunction.—Rosen Entertainment Systems, LP v. Eiger Vision, 343 F.Supp.2d 908.
Moving party bears burden of establishing that preliminary injunction should issue.—Id.
S.D.Miss. 2004. Injunctive relief is an extraordinary and drastic remedy, not to be granted routinely, but only when the movant, by a clear showing, carries the burden of persuasion.—Cox v. City of Jackson, 343 F.Supp.2d 546.

INNKEEPERS

☞10.2. —— Acts of employees, other guests, or third persons.
D.Kan. 2004. Under Virgin Islands law, innkeeper is liable to guests for negligent acts or omissions of its contractors.—Clayman v. Starwood Hotels & Resorts Worldwide, 343 F.Supp.2d 1037.

☞10.3. —— Defects in premises or appliances in general.
D.Kan. 2004. Under Virgin Islands law, hotel had duty to take reasonable action to protect guest against unreasonable risk of physical harm while using exercise facility in hotel.—Clayman v. Starwood Hotels & Resorts Worldwide, 343 F.Supp.2d 1037.

☞10.7. —— Contributory negligence and assumption of risk.
D.Kan. 2004. Under Virgin Islands law, express assumption of risk was not permissible defense in
(58)

guest's action against innkeeper to recover for personal injuries sustained in facility's exercise room, even if guest signed release and waiver prior to beginning his workout. Restatement (Second) of Torts § 496B.—Clayman v. Starwood Hotels & Resorts Worldwide, 343 F.Supp.2d 1037.
Under Virgin Islands law, hotel guest was not comparatively negligent as result of his alleged misuse of cable cross-over machine in hotel's exercise room to perform lateral pull-down exercise, and thus guest was not thereby barred from recovering from hotel for personal injuries sustained when cable broke, absent explanation as to how guest's alleged breach caused his injury. 5 V.I.C. § 1451.—Id.
Under Virgin Islands law, innkeeper could not reduce any judgment in guest's personal injury action by affirmative defense of comparative negligence among tortfeasors, where alleged tortfeasors were not parties to action.—Id.

INSURANCE

III. WHAT LAW GOVERNS.

(A) CHOICE OF LAW.

☞1091(4). —— In general.
D.Kan. 2004. Under Kansas choice of law rule of lex loci contractus, Kansas law governed interpretation of commercial general liability (CGL) insurance policy that was made in Kansas when it was issued to insured.—Lone Star Steakhouse and Saloon, Inc. v. Liberty Mut. Ins. Group, 343 F.Supp.2d 989.

(B) PREEMPTION; APPLICATION OF STATE OR FEDERAL LAW.

☞1117(4). Disability benefits.
N.D.Ga. 2004. Action brought by insured against long-term disability insurer seeking to recover benefits due under policy was governed by the Employee Retirement Income Security Act (ERISA) and thus ERISA preempted any breach of contract claims sought to be asserted by insured; although insured had resigned her employment herself, the insurance policy was originally obtained in connection with an ERISA plan and paid for by the employer and, upon employee's resignation, there was no conversion or creation of a new relationship with the insurer. Employee Retirement Income Security Act of 1974, § 3, 29 U.S.C.A. § 1002.—Griggers v. Equitable Life Assur. Society of U.S., 343 F.Supp.2d 1190.
N.D.Miss. 2004. Beneficiary's breach of contract claims against long term disability insurer and employer, which was acting as the agent for insurer with respect to policy, were preempted by ERISA, but beneficiary's claims for fraudulently misrepresenting scope of benefits were not preempted; breach of contract claim involved the interpretation of ERISA policy, but fraudulent misrepresentation claims only indirectly related to ERISA plan. Employee Retirement Income Security Act of 1974, § 514(a), 29 U.S.C.A. § 1144(a).—Moore v. Yellow Book USA, Inc., 343 F.Supp.2d 539.

XIII. CONTRACTS AND POLICIES.

(G) RULES OF CONSTRUCTION.

☞1812. —— In general.
D.Kan. 2004. Under Kansas law, an insurance policy is to be interpreted in a way that will give

Mini-digest entry for key number 10.2

Case summary

Reprinted with permission from Thomson West, West's *Federal Supplement,* 2d Ser., Vol. 343 (2004), p. 58 (key number digest). © 2004 Thomson West.

This is the opinion in *McCarty v. Pheasant Run, Inc.,* a case summarized in the main subject volume of the digest. You would want to review this case, as well as the others identified in the main digest volume and pocket part, in conducting your research.

FIGURE 4.25 *McCARTY v. PHEASANT RUN, INC.,* 826 F.2d 1554 (7th CIR. 1987)

1554   826 FEDERAL REPORTER, 2d SERIES

Dula McCARTY, Plaintiff-Appellant,

v.

PHEASANT RUN, INC.,
Defendant-Appellee.

No. 86–2135.

United States Court of Appeals,
Seventh Circuit.

Argued Feb. 9, 1987.

Decided July 22, 1987.

Hotel guest who was assaulted in her room brought negligence suit. The United States District Court for the Northern District of Illinois, William T. Hart, J., entered judgment on jury verdict for hotel owner, and guest appealed. The Court of Appeals, Posner, Circuit Judge, held that: (1) guest was not entitled to judgment notwithstanding verdict, as she had not properly moved for directed verdict and evidence was not sufficient to establish innkeeper's liability as matter of Illinois law; (2) instruction on contributory negligence was not prejudicial; and (3) trial judge had discretion to exclude certain evidence that guest sought to put before jury.

Affirmed.

1. Federal Civil Procedure ⟶2602

Modern rationale for rule that motion for directed verdict is prerequisite to judgment n.o.v. is that opposing party should have chance to rectify, or at least seek court's leave to rectify, deficiencies in his evidence before it is too late, i.e., before case goes to jury. Fed.Rules Civ.Proc.Rule 50(b), 28 U.S.C.A.

2. Federal Civil Procedure ⟶2602

Plaintiff's motion for directed verdict on issue of contributory negligence and defendant's motion for directed verdict on issue of negligence could not substitute for motion by plaintiff for directed verdict on issue of negligence, which was prerequisite to judgment notwithstanding verdict for defendant on that issue. Fed.Rules Civ. Proc.Rule 50(b), 28 U.S.C.A.

3. Negligence ⟶1

Analytically, though not necessarily operationally, most precise formulation of negligence standard is "Hand Formula," which involves determining whether burden of precaution is less than magnitude of accident if it occurs, multiplied by probability of accident's occurrence; if burden is less, then precaution should be taken.

See publication Words and Phrases for other judicial constructions and definitions.

4. Negligence ⟶4

Due care is that care which is optimal given that potential victim is himself reasonably careful; careless person cannot by his carelessness raise standard of care of those he encounters.

5. Innkeepers ⟶10.2

Though requirement that innkeeper use high standard of care to protect its guests from assault on innkeeper's premises may be defensible in that innkeeper ordinarily knows much more about hazards of his trade than guest and can take reasonable, i.e., cost-justified, steps to reduce them while ordinarily guest can do little to protect himself against them, even higher standard of care does not make innkeeper's liability strict.

6. Innkeepers ⟶10.13

Under Illinois law, evidence of hotel owner's negligence did not establish its liability as matter of law to guest who was assaulted in her hotel room; guest did not attempt to show that mishap could have been prevented by precautions of reasonable cost and efficacy and guest might have failed to take elementary precaution of locking sliding door before she left room.

7. Federal Courts ⟶912

Even if instruction on contributory negligence was not supported by evidence, giving of that instruction was not prejudicial in negligence action where jury returned verdict for defendant rather than verdict for plaintiff with truncated damages.

FIGURE 4.25   *McCARTY v. PHEASANT RUN, INC.*, 826 F.2d 1554 (7th CIR. 1987)
(*Continued*)

McCARTY v. PHEASANT RUN, INC.   **1555**
Cite as 826 F.2d 1554 (7th Cir. 1987)

8. Evidence ⟸146

Federal Courts ⟸823

Trial judge has broad discretion in excluding relevant evidence if its probative significance is substantially outweighed by its prejudicial, confusing, or cumulative effect, and where judge explains reasoning process behind those exclusions they will rarely be overturned. Fed.Rules Evid.Rule 403, 28 U.S.C.A.

9. Innkeepers ⟸10.11

In negligence action by hotel guest whose assailant entered room through unlocked sliding glass door, evidence of proper key-control procedures, of previous criminal activity that did not involve breaking into room in that manner, of advertisements for locks that were more effective than that on door in foiling intruders, and of hotel's inadequate maintenance of doors could be excluded by trial court. Fed. Rules Evid.Rule 403, 28 U.S.C.A.

Arthur L. Klein, Arnstein, Gluck, Lehr, Barron & Milligan, Chicago, Ill., for plaintiff-appellant.

Byron D. Knight, Judge & Knight, Ltd., Park Ridge, Ill., for defendant-appellee.

Before BAUER, Chief Judge, and CUDAHY and POSNER, Circuit Judges.

POSNER, Circuit Judge.

The high crime rate in the United States has interacted with expanding notions of tort liability to make suits charging hotel owners with negligence in failing to protect their guests from criminal attacks increasingly common. See Annot., 28 A.L.R.4th 80 (1984). Dula McCarty, a guest at the Pheasant Run Lodge in St. Charles, Illinois, was assaulted by an intruder in her room, and brought suit against the owner of the resort. The suit charges negligence, and bases federal jurisdiction on diversity of citizenship. The parties agree that Illinois law governs the substantive issues. The jury brought in a verdict for the defendant, and Mrs. McCarty appeals on a variety of grounds.

In 1981 Mrs. McCarty, then 58 years old and a merchandise manager for Sears Roebuck, checked into Pheasant Run—a large resort hotel on 160 acres outside Chicago—to attend a Sears business meeting. In one wall of her second-floor room was a sliding glass door equipped with a lock and a safety chain. The door opens onto a walkway that has stairs leading to a lighted courtyard to which there is public access. The drapes were drawn and the door covered by them. Mrs. McCarty left the room for dinner and a meeting. When she returned, she undressed and got ready for bed. As she was coming out of the bathroom, she was attacked by a man with a stocking mask. He beat and threatened to rape her. She fought him off, and he fled. He has never been caught. Although Mrs. McCarty's physical injuries were not serious, she claims that the incident caused prolonged emotional distress which, among other things, led her to take early retirement from Sears.

Investigation of the incident by the police revealed that the sliding glass door had been closed but not locked, that it had been pried open from the outside, and that the security chain had been broken. The intruder must have entered Mrs. McCarty's room by opening the door to the extent permitted by the chain, breaking the chain, and sliding the door open the rest of the way. Then he concealed himself somewhere in the room until she returned and entered the bathroom.

[1, 2] Mrs. McCarty argues that the judge should have granted her motion for judgment notwithstanding the jury's verdict for the defendant. But she failed to move for a directed verdict on the issue of the defendant's negligence, and that is a prerequisite to judgment n.o.v. Fed.R. Civ.P. 50(b). It is true that she made a motion for a directed verdict on the issue of her contributory negligence, which was denied, and that the defendant made a motion for a directed verdict on the issue of its negligence, which was also denied, but these motions were not equivalent to the motion she failed to make. Even if she had been innocent of contributory negligence as

FIGURE 4.25 *McCARTY v. PHEASANT RUN, INC.,* 826 F.2d 1554 (7th CIR. 1987) *(Continued)*

1556   826 **FEDERAL REPORTER, 2d SERIES**

a matter of law, this would not have made the defendant guilty of negligence as a matter of law; in many accidents, neither injurer nor victim is at fault, and then there is no liability. Similarly, all that the denial of the defendant's motion for a directed verdict showed was that the defendant was not innocent of negligence as a matter of law; it could of course be guilty of negligence as a matter of law. Thus, neither motion for directed verdict presented the question whether the issue of the defendant's negligence should be withdrawn from the jury and resolved in the plaintiff's favor. She could not present that issue for the first time in her motion for judgment n.o.v.

The modern rationale for the rule that a motion for directed verdict is a prerequisite to judgment n.o.v. is that the opposing party should have a chance to rectify (or at least seek the court's leave to rectify) deficiencies in his evidence before it is too late, that is, before the case goes to the jury. *McKinnon v. City of Berwyn,* 750 F.2d 1383, 1388 (7th Cir.1984); see also *Benson v. Allphin,* 786 F.2d 268, 273–74 (7th Cir. 1986). That rationale is applicable to this case. After both motions for directed verdict (the plaintiff's on contributory negligence, and the defendant's on negligence) were denied, the defendant had no reason to think it hadn't put in enough evidence to get to the jury on the issue of liability. If the plaintiff thought otherwise she had to move for a directed verdict on that issue.

As an alternative ground for denying the motion for judgment n.o.v., the district judge correctly pointed out that the case was not so one-sided in the plaintiff's favor that the grant of a directed verdict or judgment n.o.v. in her favor would be proper. Her theories of negligence are that the defendant should have made sure the door was locked when she was first shown to her room; should have warned her to keep the sliding glass door locked; should have equipped the door with a better lock; should have had more security guards (only two were on duty, and the hotel has more than 500 rooms), cf. *Nordmann v. National Hotel Co.,* 425 F.2d 1103, 1107 (5th Cir. 1970); should have made the walkway on

which the door opened inaccessible from ground level; should have adopted better procedures for preventing unauthorized persons from getting hold of keys to guests' rooms; or should have done some combination of these things. The suggestion that the defendant should have had better procedures for keeping keys away from unauthorized persons is irrelevant, for it is extremely unlikely that the intruder entered the room through the front door. Compare *Danile v. Oak Park Arms Hotel, Inc.,* 55 Ill.App.2d 2, 203 N.E.2d 706 (1964). The other theories were for the jury to accept or reject, and its rejection of them was not unreasonable. Cf. *Courtney v. Remler,* 566 F.Supp. 1225, 1233–34 (D.S. C.1983).

[3] There are various ways in which courts formulate the negligence standard. The analytically (not necessarily the operationally) most precise is that it involves determining whether the burden of precaution is less than the magnitude of the accident, if it occurs, multiplied by the probability of occurrence. (The product of this multiplication, or "discounting," is what economists call an expected accident cost.) If the burden is less, the precaution should be taken. This is the famous "Hand Formula" announced in *United States v. Carroll Towing Co.,* 159 F.2d 169, 173 (2d Cir.1947) (L. Hand, J.), an admiralty case, and since applied in a variety of cases not limited to admiralty. See, e.g., *United States Fidelity & Guaranty Co. v. Jadranska Slobodna Plovidba,* 683 F.2d 1022, 1026 (7th Cir.1982); *Maryland Cas. Co. v. City of Jackson,* 493 So.2d 955, 960 n. 3 (Miss.1986) (dictum); *People Express Airlines, Inc. v. Consolidated Rail Corp.,* 100 N.J. 246, 266–67, 495 A.2d 107, 117–18 (1985); *Micallef v. Miehle Co.,* 39 N.Y.2d 376, 386, 384 N.Y.S.2d 115, 348 N.E.2d 571, 577–78 (1976); *Phillips v. Croy,* 173 Ind.App. 401, 404–05, 363 N.E.2d 1283, 1285 (1977); *Benlehr v. Shell Oil Co.,* 62 Ohio App.2d 1, 9 and n. 5, 402 N.E.2d 1203, 1208 and n. 5 (1978); *Golden v. McCurry,* 392 So.2d 815, 819 (Ala.1980) (separate opinion); 3 Harper, James & Gray, The Law of Torts § 16.9, at pp. 467–

FIGURE 4.25   *McCARTY v. PHEASANT RUN, INC.*, 826 F.2d 1554 (7th CIR. 1987)
(Continued)

McCARTY v. PHEASANT RUN, INC.   **1557**
Cite as 826 F.2d 1554 (7th Cir. 1987)

68 (2d ed. 1986); Prosser and Keeton on the Law of Torts § 31, at p. 173 (5th ed. 1984); cf. *East River S.S. Corp. v. Transamerica Delaval, Inc.*, 476 U.S. 858, 106 S.Ct. 2295, 2302, 90 L.Ed.2d 865 (1986); *Prentis v. Yale Mfg. Co.*, 421 Mich. 670, 687, 365 N.W.2d 176, 184 (1984).

We are not authorized to change the common law of Illinois, however, and Illinois courts do not cite the Hand Formula but instead define negligence as failure to use reasonable care, a term left undefined. See, e.g., *Hardware State Bank v. Cotner*, 55 Ill.2d 240, 247–48, 302 N.E.2d 257, 262 (1973); *Denniston v. Skelly Oil Co.*, 47 Ill.App.3d 1054, 1067, 6 Ill.Dec. 77, 87, 362 N.E.2d 712, 722 (1977). But as this is a distinction without a substantive difference, we have not hesitated to use the Hand Formula in cases governed by Illinois law. See *EVRA Corp. v. Swiss Bank Corp.*, 673 F.2d 951, 958 (7th Cir.1982); *Davis v. Consolidated Rail Corp.*, 788 F.2d 1260, 1263–64 (7th Cir.1986). The formula translates into economic terms the conventional legal test for negligence. This can be seen by considering the factors that the Illinois courts take into account in negligence cases: the same factors, and in the same relation, as in the Hand Formula. See *Hendricks v. Peabody Coal Co.*, 115 Ill.App.2d 35, 45–46, 253 N.E.2d 56, 61 (1969); *Bezark v. Kostner Manor, Inc.*, 29 Ill.App.2d 106, 111–12, 172 N.E.2d 424, 426–27 (1961). Unreasonable conduct is merely the failure to take precautions that would generate greater benefits in avoiding accidents than the precautions would cost.

Ordinarily, and here, the parties do not give the jury the information required to quantify the variables that the Hand Formula picks out as relevant. That is why the formula has greater analytic than operational significance. Conceptual as well as practical difficulties in monetizing personal injuries may continue to frustrate efforts to measure expected accident costs with the precision that is possible, in principle at least, in measuring the other side of the equation—the cost or burden of precaution. Cf. *Conway v. O'Brien*, 111 F.2d 611, 612 (2d Cir.1940) (L. Hand, J.), rev'd on other

826 F.2d—36

grounds, 312 U.S. 492, 61 S.Ct. 634, 85 L.Ed. 969 (1941). For many years to come juries may be forced to make rough judgments of reasonableness, intuiting rather than measuring the factors in the Hand Formula; and so long as their judgment is reasonable, the trial judge has no right to set it aside, let alone substitute his own judgment.

[4–6] Having failed to make much effort to show that the mishap could have been prevented by precautions of reasonable cost and efficacy, Mrs. McCarty is in a weak position to complain about the jury verdict. No effort was made to inform the jury what it would have cost to equip every room in the Pheasant Run Lodge with a new lock, and whether the lock would have been jimmy-proof. The excluded exhibits (of which more later) were advertisements for locks, and Mrs. McCarty's lawyer expressed no interest in testing the claims made in them, or in calculating the expense of installing new locks in every room in the resort. And since the door to Mrs. McCarty's room was unlocked, what good would a better lock have done? No effort was made, either, to specify an optimal security force for a resort the size of Pheasant Run. No one considered the fire or other hazards that a second-floor walkway not accessible from ground level would create. A notice in every room telling guests to lock all doors would be cheap, but since most people know better than to leave the door to a hotel room unlocked when they leave the room—and the sliding glass door gave on a walkway, not a balcony—the jury might have thought that the incremental benefits from the notice would be slight. Mrs. McCarty testified that she didn't know there was a door behind the closed drapes, but the jury wasn't required to believe this. Most people on checking into a hotel room, especially at a resort, are curious about the view; and it was still light when Mrs. McCarty checked in at 6:00 p.m. on an October evening.

It is a bedrock principle of negligence law that due care is that care which is optimal given that the potential victim is himself reasonably careful; a careless per-

FIGURE 4.25 *McCARTY v. PHEASANT RUN, INC.,* 826 F.2d 1554 (7th CIR. 1987) (Continued)

1558   **826 FEDERAL REPORTER, 2d SERIES**

son cannot by his carelessness raise the standard of care of those he encounters. *Davis v. Consolidated Rail Corp., supra,* 788 F.2d at 1265. The jury may have thought it was the hotel's responsibility to provide a working lock but the guest's responsibility to use it. See *Brewer v. Roosevelt Motor Lodge,* 295 A.2d 647, 652 (Me.1972). We do not want to press too hard on this point. A possible explanation for the condition of the door as revealed by the police investigation is that Mrs. McCarty on leaving the room for the evening left the door unlocked but with the safety chain fastened, and she might have been reasonable in thinking this a sufficient precaution. But it would not follow that the hotel was negligent, unless it is negligence to have sliding doors accessible to the public, a suggestion the jury was not required to buy. We doubt whether a boilerplate notice about the dangers of unlocked doors would have altered the behavior of the average guest; in any event this too was an issue for the jury. Cf. *Rosier v. Gainsville Inns Associates, Ltd.,* 347 So.2d 1100, 1102 (Fla.App.1977); *Otwell v. Motel 6, Inc.,* 755 F.2d 665, 667 (8th Cir.1985) (per curiam).

Now it is true that in Illinois an innkeeper, which in contemplation of law this defendant is, is required to use a high (not merely the ordinary) standard of care to protect its guests from assaults on the innkeeper's premises. *Mrzlak v. Ettinger,* 25 Ill.App.3d 706, 712–13, 323 N.E.2d 796, 800 (1975); *Danile v. Oak Park Arms Hotel, Inc., supra,* 55 Ill.App.2d at 8–9, 203 N.E.2d at 709. This is not the general rule, see, e.g., *Kveragas v. Scottish Inns, Inc.,* 733 F.2d 409, 413 (6th Cir.1984); *Peters v. Holiday Inns, Inc.,* 89 Wis.2d 115, 123–24, 278 N.W.2d 208, 212 (1979); *Phillips Petroleum Co. v. Dorn,* 292 So.2d 429, 431–32 (Fla.App.1974), though it has some ambiguous support in Louisiana, see *Kraaz v. La Quinta Motor Inns, Inc.,* 410 So.2d 1048 (La.1982)—ambiguous because while the court said that "a guest is entitled to a *high* degree of care and protection," it promptly added that "the innkeeper has a duty to take *reasonable* precautions against criminals" (*id.* at 1053, emphasis

added). Conceivably, as suggested in *Dorn,* it is no longer the rule in Illinois either, though *Yamada v. Hilton Hotel Corp.,* 60 Ill.App.3d 101, 112, 17 Ill.Dec. 228, 237, 376 N.E.2d 227, 236 (1977), decided after *Dorn,* suggests it is. The rule may simply be an inadvertent extrapolation from the principle (see Restatement (Second) of Torts, § 314A and comment e (1965); *Kveragas v. Scottish Inns, Inc., supra,* 733 F.2d at 412) that an innkeeper, like a common carrier but unlike a mere bystander, has a duty to prevent (or rescue from) dangers created by third parties. See *Fortney v. Hotel Rancroft, Inc.,* 5 Ill.App.2d 327, 331, 125 N.E.2d 544, 546 (1955), seeming to equate these distinct propositions.

The rule, if it is a rule, may be defensible however; and whether it is or is not defensible is relevant to whether it is a genuine rule or a mere inadvertence. Ordinarily the innkeeper knows much more about the hazards of his trade than the guest, and can take reasonable (=cost-justified) steps to reduce them, while ordinarily the guest can do little to protect himself against them. See *Banks v. Hyatt Corp.,* 722 F.2d 214, 226–27 (5th Cir.1984). Pheasant Run, Inc. knows more about the danger of break-ins to guest rooms at its lodge than the guests do, and more about the alternative methods for preventing such break-ins, as well. Maybe this asymmetry in the parties' position should make the defendant's standard of care higher than it would be in, say, an ordinary collision case. See *Danile v. Oak Park Arms Hotel, Inc., supra,* 55 Ill.App.2d at 6–8, 203 N.E.2d at 708–09. But it does not make the defendant's liability strict. In this case there was evidence of negligence but not so much as to establish liability as a matter of law or (the plaintiff's alternative argument) to require a new trial. And the rule, based as it seems to be on an asymmetry in the parties' abilities to prevent mishaps, has a certain hollowness in a case such as this, where the victim may have failed to take an elementary precaution—locking the sliding door before leaving the room.

FIGURE 4.25 *McCARTY v. PHEASANT RUN, INC.*, 826 F.2d 1554 (7th CIR. 1987) (Continued)

McCARTY v. PHEASANT RUN, INC. **1559**
Cite as 826 F.2d 1554 (7th Cir. 1987)

[7] The next issue that Mrs. McCarty seeks to raise is whether the judge should have instructed the jury to decide whether she had been contributorily negligent. She argues that there was no evidence of her contributory negligence. Pheasant Run is not in the middle of a large city and it might not occur to a guest that a safety chain on a sliding door to the outside was an inadequate protection against nocturnal marauders. On the other hand Mrs. McCarty was an experienced business traveler, so maybe she should have known better; and most people don't consider a safety chain an adequate substitute for a lock. But even if there was no evidence of contributory negligence, there was no prejudicial error in giving an instruction on it. The jury was clearly and correctly instructed that contributory negligence in Illinois is not a complete defense; it just cuts down the amount of damages that the plaintiff would otherwise be entitled to. This is the principle of comparative negligence, and at the time of the trial of this case it existed in Illinois in its pure form, meaning that the plaintiff is entitled to some damages even if he was more negligent than the defendant. See *Alvis v. Ribar*, 85 Ill.2d 1, 25–28, 52 Ill.Dec. 23, 421 N.E.2d 886, 897–98 (1981). (The rule has since been modified. See Ill.Rev.Stat. ch. 110, ¶¶ 2–1107.1, 2–1116; *Davis v. United States*, 824 F.2d 549, 551 (7th Cir.1987).) Since the jury returned a verdict for the defendant, rather than a verdict for the plaintiff with truncated damages, it probably thought that the defendant had not been negligent at all or that its negligence had not caused the mishap; in either case the plaintiff's contributory negligence or lack thereof would be moot. It is unlikely that the mere giving of the instruction somehow signaled to the jury the judge's belief that the verdict should be for the defendant.

[8, 9] The remaining questions concern the judge's exclusion of evidence that the plaintiff sought to put before the jury. The exclusion of evidence about proper key-control procedures was proper for a reason we have already indicated: such evidence was not relevant to any plausible theory of the defendant's negligence. Also

proper or at least defensible was the judge's decision to exclude evidence of previous criminal activity at Pheasant Run that did not involve breaking into a room through the sliding glass door. The judge admitted evidence of the nine previous break-ins that did. The principal evidence in the previous-crimes category that he excluded was of two alleged sexual assaults and eleven alleged thefts from rooms. This evidence was of limited relevance, at best. One of the so-called assaults involved a complaint from a man who said that he saw a man and woman having intercourse in a hallway and that he sprained his ankle pursuing the man; it is entirely unclear whether the intercourse was coerced or what the relationship of the complainant to the couple was. The circumstances of the other alleged assault are equally shadowy. Neither involved an intrusion into a room. The eleven reports of theft appear to include cases where a guest lost or mislaid an item as well as cases of genuine theft, but in any event are remote from the issues in this case; among other things, none involved forcing the sliding glass door.

A trial judge has broad discretion in administering Rule 403 of the Federal Rules of Evidence, which authorizes him to exclude relevant evidence if its probative significance is substantially outweighed by its prejudicial, confusing, or cumulative effect. Where as here the judge explains the reasoning process behind his exclusions, they will rarely be overturned. See *United States v. Beasley*, 809 F.2d 1273, 1278–79 (7th Cir.1987). Pheasant Run is a large place, and it is not to be supposed that it would be free of criminal activity no matter how careful (within the bounds of reason) the management was. There is no indication that its experience with criminal activity was abnormal or indicative of a need to take additional precautions. Maybe the jury should have been allowed to figure this out for itself, but a jury's ability to digest statistical evidence is limited, especially when no comparison was attempted by the plaintiff's counsel between the frequency of criminal activity at Pheasant

FIGURE 4.25 *McCARTY v. PHEASANT RUN, INC.*, 826 F.2d 1554 (7th CIR. 1987) (Continued)

1560   826 FEDERAL REPORTER, 2d SERIES

Run and at comparable resort hotels, cf. *Anderson v. Malloy*, 700 F.2d 1208, 1211–12 (8th Cir.1983), and no effort was made to show that precautions which would have averted crimes not involving the forcing of the sliding glass doors would also have averted the attack on Mrs. McCarty.

She also complains about the exclusion from evidence of advertisements for locks for sliding glass doors. These locks are designed to foil intruders, as the advertisements make clear, and Mrs. McCarty argues with some show of reason that the advertised locks appear to be more effective than the locks on the sliding glass doors at Pheasant Run. The problem is the absence of a causal relationship between the failure to have fancy locks and the attack on Mrs. McCarty. There is no evidence that Mrs. McCarty's assailant jimmied the *lock*. The door was unlocked. The world's fanciest lock—a lock to foil a Houdini—would thus have done her no good, and the failure to install a precaution that would not have avoided *this* accident (the accident that is the basis of the suit) is not actionable. *Kveragas v. Scottish Inns, Inc.*, *supra*, 733 F.2d at 415. Her complaint about the exclusion of evidence of inadequate maintenance by the defendant of its sliding glass doors fails for the same reason; there is no indication that her failure to lock the door was due to improper maintenance. Finally, it is merely speculation that if the door had been equipped with a lock that locked automatically when the door was slid closed, the door would not have been left open with merely the safety chain fastened.

AFFIRMED.

GREYCAS, INC., Plaintiff-Appellee,

v.

Theodore S. PROUD, Defendant-Appellant.

No. 86–2340.

United States Court of Appeals, Seventh Circuit.

Argued Feb. 17, 1987.

Decided Aug. 3, 1987.

Rehearing Denied Aug. 17, 1987.

Finance company sued attorney for negligent misrepresentation in connection with loan made to attorney's brother-in-law. The United States District Court for the Southern District of Illinois, William L. Beatty, J., entered judgment against attorney, who appealed. The Court of Appeals, Posner, Circuit Judge, held that under Illinois law, attorney who in practice of his profession falsely represents that he has conducted search revealing absence of prior liens on property pledged as collateral breaches duty of due care and is liable for negligent misrepresentation where lender detrimentally relies on that representation by making loan.

Affirmed.

Bauer, Chief Judge, concurred and filed opinion.

1. Fraud ⬤⊃36
   Negligence ⬤⊃97
   There is no defense of contributory or comparative negligence to deliberate tort, such as fraud.

2. Attorney and Client ⬤⊃105
   Tort of malpractice normally refers to lawyer's careless or otherwise wrongful conduct toward his own client, though Illinois has discarded common-law requirement of privity of contract for professional malpractice.

3. Attorney and Client ⬤⊃109
   Under Illinois law of negligent misrepresentation, attorney who in practice of his

F. CHECKLIST FOR CASE RESEARCH

1. SELECT A PRINT DIGEST

❏ Use *West's Federal Practice Digest* to locate all federal cases.
❏ Use a state digest to locate state and federal cases from an individual state.
❏ Use a regional digest to locate state cases only within the region.
❏ Use a combined digest to locate state and federal cases from all United States jurisdictions.

2. LOCATE TOPICS AND KEY NUMBERS IN A PRINT DIGEST

❏ From a case on point, use the headnotes at the beginning of the decision to identify relevant topics and key numbers.
❏ From the Descriptive-Word Index, look up relevant subjects, check the pocket part for new index headings, and look up the topics and key numbers in the subject volumes.
❏ From a topic entry, review subjects included and excluded and the outline of key numbers.

3. READ THE CASE SUMMARIES IN THE PRINT DIGEST

❏ Use the court and date abbreviations to target appropriate cases.

4. UPDATE PRINT DIGEST RESEARCH

❏ Check the pocket part for the subject volume.
❏ Check any cumulative or noncumulative interim pamphlets at the end of the digest set.
❏ Check the closing table on the inside front cover of the most recent interim pamphlet (if there is no interim pamphlet, check the closing table on the inside front cover of the pocket part).
❏ If necessary, check the mini-digests in the back of each reporter volume published after the latest volume listed in the closing table.

5. ELECTRONIC CASE RESEARCH

❏ In Westlaw and LexisNexis, execute word searches for cases using federal, state, or combined databases.
❏ In Westlaw, use the Custom Digest function to search by digest topic and key number or the KeySearch function to search by subject.
❏ In LexisNexis, use the Search Advisor function to search by subject.
❏ Selected cases may be available on the Internet.

Research with Shepard's Citations and Other Citators

A. INTRODUCTION TO CITATORS

1. THE PURPOSE OF A CITATOR

Virtually all cases contain citations to legal authorities, including other cases, secondary sources, statutes, and regulations. These decisions can affect the continued validity of the authorities they cite. For example, earlier cases can be reversed or overruled, or statutes can be held unconstitutional. Even if an authority remains valid, the discussion of the authority in later cases can be helpful in your research. As a consequence, when you find an authority that helps you answer a research question, you will often want to know whether the authority has been cited elsewhere, and if so, what has been said about it.

The tool that helps you do this is called a citator. Citators catalog cases and secondary sources, analyzing what they say about the authorities they cite. Some citators also track the status of statutes and regulations, indicating, for example, whether a statute has been amended or repealed. Citators will help you determine whether an authority is still "good law," meaning it has not been changed or invalidated since it was

published. They will also help you locate additional authorities that pertain to your research question. The print citator most commonly used in legal research is Shepard's Citations. Shepard's is also available electronically in LexisNexis, and Westlaw has its own citator service called KeyCite.

Using Shepard's to check legal authority is such an integral part of the research process that the term "to Shepardize" is a well-known term in the legal lexicon. At first, Shepardizing may seem like a daunting process because Shepard's uses many symbols and abbreviations that can appear undecipherable to someone unfamiliar with the service. Once you understand how the material is organized, however, you will see that Shepardizing is a fairly mechanical process that is not especially difficult.

Citators can be used in researching many types of authority, including cases, statutes, regulations, and some secondary sources. Section C discusses the scope of the citators available in LexisNexis and Westlaw, and Section D outlines some of the types of authority for which Shepard's is available in print. In addition, later chapters in this book discuss the use of Shepard's in researching different types of authority. The process of using a citator, however, is the same for almost any type of authority. Accordingly, for purposes of introducing you to this process, this chapter focuses on the use of citators in case research.

2. WHEN TO USE A CITATOR IN CASE RESEARCH

You must check every case on which you rely to answer a legal question to make sure it is still good law. In general, you will want to use Shepard's or another citator early in your research, after you have identified what appear to be a few key cases, to make sure you do not build your analysis on authority that is no longer valid. Using a citator at this stage will also help direct you to other relevant authorities. You should also check every case you cite before handing in your work to make sure each one continues to be authoritative. Citing bad authority is every attorney's nightmare, and failing to check your citations can constitute professional malpractice. As a consequence, now is the time to get in the habit of updating your case research carefully.

B. USING SHEPARD'S CITATIONS IN PRINT FOR CASE RESEARCH

Shepardizing cases in print requires four steps:

- locating the correct set of books to Shepardize the citation
- locating the correct volumes within the set of Shepard's

- locating the entry for the case within each volume
- interpreting the entries.

This section uses the case of *Kenney v.Scientific, Inc.*, 497 A.2d 1310 (N.J. Super. L. Div. 1985), to illustrate the Sheypardizing process. *Kenney* will be referred to as the original case. The later authorities that cite *Kenney* will be referred to as citing sources.

1. LOCATING THE CORRECT SET OF BOOKS

The first step in Sheypardizing cases is locating the correct set of Shepard's books. Shepard's publishes different sets of books that correspond to various sets of reporters. **Figure 5.1** identifies some of Shepard's case citators.

If you are Sheypardizing a federal case, you will probably use either *Shepard's United States Citations* or *Shepard's Federal Citations*, depending on which court decided the case. Shepard's for state court decisions is a little more complex. A state set of Shepard's usually covers two sets of reporters: the state's official reporter and West's regional reporter. Thus, you can use the state books to Sheypardize an original case that has been published in either type of reporter. The regional set of Shepard's,

FIGURE 5.1 SHEPARD'S® CITATORS FOR CASES

IF YOUR CITATION IS FROM . . .	YOU CAN USE THIS SET OF SHEPARD'S
United States Supreme Court	*Shepard's United States Citations*
Any United States District Court or Court of Appeals	*Shepard's Federal Citations*
Any state court	Shepard's publishes a separate set for each state. An original case from a state court published in either an official reporter or a West regional reporter can be Sheypardized in that state's set of Shepard's.
	Shepard's publishes regional sets for each of West's regional reporters. Only original cases published in West regional reporters can be Sheypardized in a regional set of Shepard's.

however, covers only decisions published in the regional reporter. Therefore, you will not be able to use a regional set of Shepard's unless you have a regional reporter citation for the original case. The information provided in the two sets of Shepard's also varies slightly. Although either set will give you information to determine whether the original case is still good law, you will usually find more research references in the regional set than in the state set.

In our example, *Kenney* was decided by the New Jersey Superior Court, and the case was published in the *Atlantic Reporter,* Second Series. Therefore, it can be Shepardized either in *Shepard's New Jersey Citations* or *Shepard's Atlantic Reporter Citations.*

2. LOCATING THE CORRECT VOLUMES

Each set of Shepard's books contains multiple volumes. Therefore, once you have located the correct set, the next step is figuring out which of the volumes you need to use to Shepardize the original case thoroughly. Unlike digests, Shepard's is not updated with pocket parts. Instead, each Shepard's volume covers a specific period of time. To update a case from the date it was decided until the present, therefore, you need to look up the citation in a series of noncumulative volumes.

In addition to publishing a series of hardbound volumes, Shepard's also publishes supplements in the form of softcover booklets and pamphlets. The most recent booklet or pamphlet on the shelf is the starting point for determining which volumes you need to check. On the front cover of the supplement, you will see a section entitled "What Your Library Should Contain." It explains which Shepard's volumes you need to use. **Figure 5.2** illustrates the "What Your Library Should Contain" section. As **Figure 5.2** indicates, to Shepardize *Kenney,* you would need to look in two volumes of *Shepard's Atlantic Reporter Citations:* the 2005 Bound Volume and the May 2005 Cumulative Supplement.

3. LOCATING THE ENTRY FOR THE CASE WITHIN EACH VOLUME

Now that you have gathered all the books you need, you are ready to begin looking up the citation to the original case. The entries in a Shepard's volume are organized numerically, first by reporter volume number and then by the starting page number of each case, as shown in **Figure 5.3**.

Remember that some Shepard's sets cover more than one reporter. For example, *Shepard's New Jersey Citations* will contain references both to New Jersey's official reporter (*New Jersey Superior Court Reports*) and West's *Atlantic Reporter.* If you are using a Shepard's set covering

FIGURE 5.2   "WHAT YOUR LIBRARY SHOULD CONTAIN"

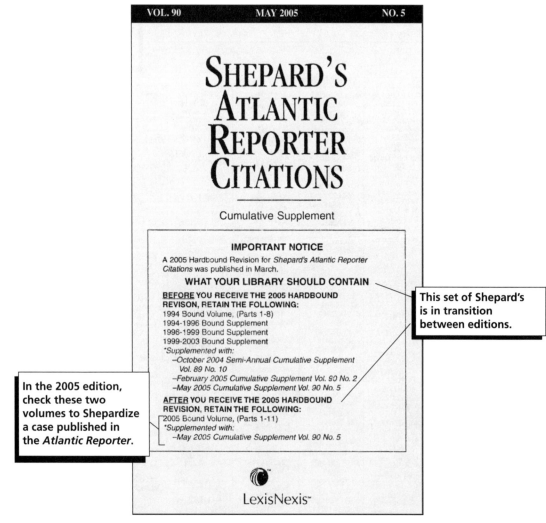

VOL. 90   MAY 2005   NO. 5

SHEPARD'S ATLANTIC REPORTER CITATIONS

Cumulative Supplement

IMPORTANT NOTICE

A 2005 Hardbound Revision for *Shepard's Atlantic Reporter Citations* was published in March.

WHAT YOUR LIBRARY SHOULD CONTAIN

BEFORE YOU RECEIVE THE 2005 HARDBOUND REVISON, RETAIN THE FOLLOWING:
1994 Bound Volume, (Parts 1-8)
1994-1996 Bound Supplement
1996-1999 Bound Supplement
1999-2003 Bound Supplement
*Supplemented with:
    –October 2004 Semi-Annual Cumulative Supplement
    Vol. 89 No. 10
    –February 2005 Cumulative Supplement Vol. 90 No. 2
    –May 2005 Cumulative Supplement Vol. 90 No. 5

AFTER YOU RECEIVE THE 2005 HARDBOUND REVISION, RETAIN THE FOLLOWING:
2005 Bound Volume, (Parts 1-11)
*Supplemented with:
    –May 2005 Cumulative Supplement Vol. 90 No. 5

This set of Shepard's is in transition between editions.

In the 2005 edition, check these two volumes to Shepardize a case published in the *Atlantic Reporter*.

LexisNexis™

Reproduced by permission of LexisNexis. Further reproduction of any kind is strictly prohibited. From *Shepard's Atlantic Reporter Citations,* Vol. 90, No. 5 (May 2005), cover page.

multiple reporters, be sure to look in the section of the Shepard's volume covering the correct reporter for your citation.

Because Shepard's is not cumulative, you must repeat this process in each book you collected. Each volume covers only a specific time period, so it is important to check each one for references to the original case.

4. INTERPRETING THE ENTRIES

Once you have located an entry for the original case, you will need to decipher the list of numbers and letters that you find. The entry for the original

FIGURE 5.3   **EXCERPT FROM *SHEPARD'S ATLANTIC REPORTER CITATIONS***

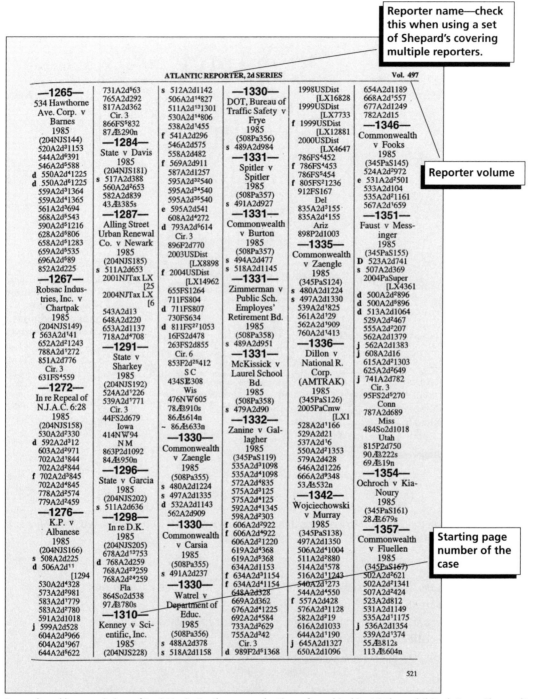

Reporter name—check this when using a set of Shepard's covering multiple reporters.

Reporter volume

Starting page number of the case

FIGURE 5.4   SHEPARD'S ENTRY FOR *KENNEY v. SCIENTIFIC, INC.*

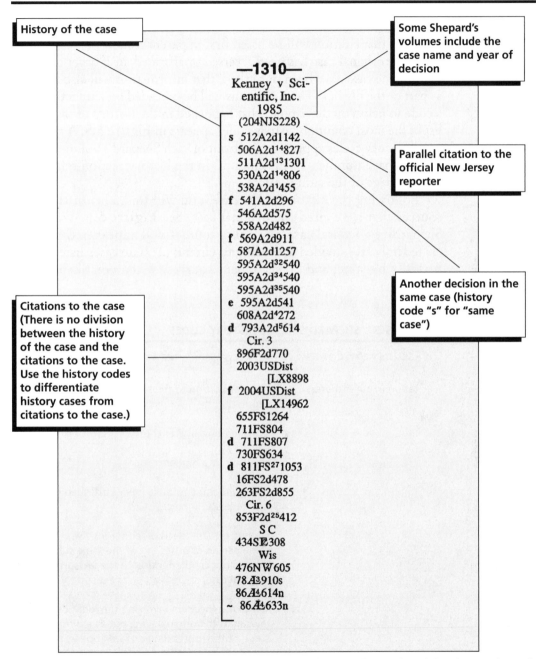

Reproduced by permission of LexisNexis. Further reproduction of any kind is strictly prohibited. From *Shepard's Atlantic Reporter Citations,* 2005 Bound Volume, Part 8, p. 521.

case will contain a list of abbreviated citations to the citing sources (the other cases and secondary sources that have cited the original case). As shown in **Figure 5.4**, this information can be divided into two categories: the history of the case and the citations to the case.

The section of the entry containing the history of the original case will give you citations to decisions emanating from the same lawsuit. For example, if the original case has a parallel citation in another reporter, that citation will be listed first in parentheses.

If the original case has been reversed or affirmed, or if other decisions in the same case have been published, that information will also be listed as part of the history. These citations will be preceded by letters that form a code to help you determine what happened in the history of the case. A list of the most common history codes appears in **Figure 5.5.** A complete list of history codes appears in the front of each Shepard's volume.

The page numbers of the citations in the history section refer to the starting page of the citing source.

Following the history of the case, you will find a list of the citing sources that have cited the original case. See **Figure 5.6.** When you Shepardize a federal case, the citing sources will appear in this order: (1) federal cases divided according to circuit; (2) state cases listed alphabetically by state; and (3) secondary sources. When you Shepardize a

FIGURE 5.5   SHEPARD'S® CASE HISTORY CODES

CASE HISTORY CODES	MEANING
(citation in parentheses)	parallel citation to the same decision in another reporter
a	affirmed by a higher court
r	reversed by a higher court
m	ruling modified (usually means affirmed in part and reversed in part)
cc	connected case (decision either involves the same parties or arises out of the same subject matter, but is not identical to the lawsuit in the original case)
s	same case (decision involving the identical lawsuit as the original case, but at a different stage of the proceedings; often appears in the history of an appellate case to identify the trial court's decision)
v	vacated (the opinion has been rendered void and no longer has any precedential value)
US Cert. Den.	United States Supreme Court denied certiorari

FIGURE 5.6   SHEPARD'S® ENTRY FOR *KENNEY v. SCIENTIFIC, INC.*

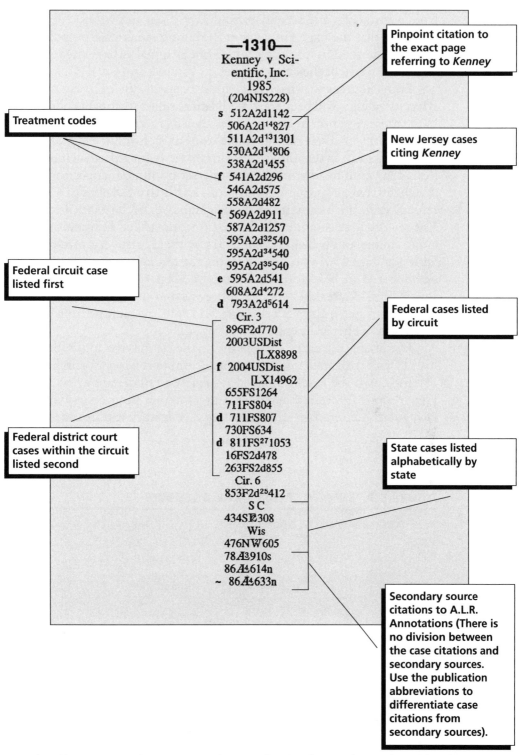

Reproduced by permission of LexisNexis. Further reproduction of any kind is strictly prohibited. From *Shepard's Atlantic Reporter Citations,* 2005 Bound Volume, Part 8, p. 521.

state case, the list of citing sources will begin with cases from the same state as the original case. Then you will see federal cases by circuit, cases from other states, and secondary sources.

Note that the page numbers in the citations here are pinpoint citations to the specific pages on which the original case is cited, not the beginning pages of the citing sources.

Citing sources that have treated the original case in a way that may affect its validity will be marked with letters called treatment codes. A list of the more common treatment codes appears in **Figure 5.7.** A complete list of treatment codes appears in the front of each volume of Shepard's.

Citing sources that discuss the original case for a particular proposition of law will be identified by a superscript number appearing immediately after the reporter abbreviation, as **Figure 5.8** shows. These are references to the headnotes in the original case. In the example citation, *Kenney* discusses a point of law that is summarized in headnote 13. A citing source, published in volume 511 of the *Atlantic Reporter*, Second Series, at page 1301, has cited *Kenney* for the same proposition of law summarized in headnote 13. Thus, the Shepard's entry includes the superscript 13 after the reporter abbreviation for the citing source. The illustrations in **Figures 5.9** through **5.11** trace a headnote from an original case to a Shepard's entry to a citing source.

The Shepard's entry for the original case may be quite long. The history and treatment codes and the headnote references will help you narrow down the cases you need to review to update your research. If you are only interested in determining whether your case is still good law, you should look primarily for negative history and treatment codes

FIGURE 5.7   SHEPARD'S® CASE TREATMENT CODES

CASE TREATMENT CODES	MEANING
c	criticized
d	distinguished
e	explained
f	followed
j	cited in a dissenting opinion
o	overruled
q	questioned

FIGURE 5.8 SHEPARD'S® ENTRY FOR *KENNEY v. SCIENTIFIC, INC.*

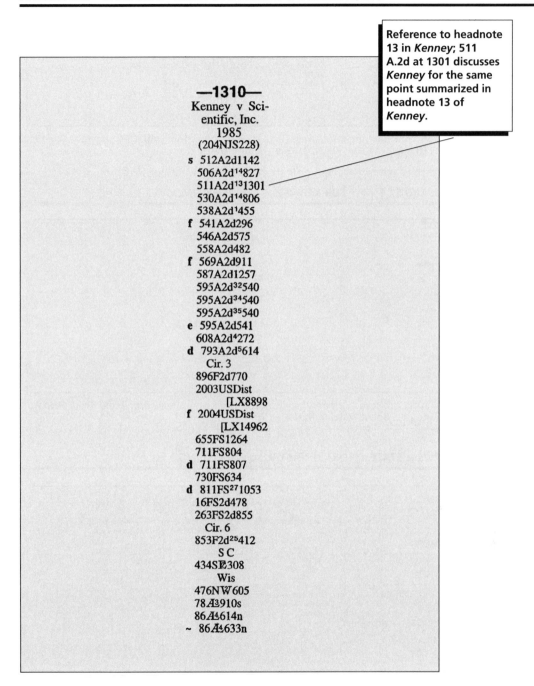

Reference to headnote 13 in *Kenney*; 511 A.2d at 1301 discusses *Kenney* for the same point summarized in headnote 13 of *Kenney*.

—1310—
Kenney v Scientific, Inc.
1985
(204NJS228)
s 512A2d1142
506A2d¹⁴827
511A2d¹³1301
530A2d¹⁴806
538A2d¹455
f 541A2d296
546A2d575
558A2d482
f 569A2d911
587A2d1257
595A2d³²540
595A2d³⁴540
595A2d³⁵540
e 595A2d541
608A2d⁴272
d 793A2d⁵614
Cir. 3
896F2d770
2003USDist
[LX8898
f 2004USDist
[LX14962
655FS1264
711FS804
d 711FS807
730FS634
d 811FS²⁷1053
16FS2d478
263FS2d855
Cir. 6
853F2d²⁵412
S C
434SE2308
Wis
476NW605
78A3910s
86A4614n
~ 86A4633n

Reproduced by permission of LexisNexis. Further reproduction of any kind is strictly prohibited. From *Shepard's Atlantic Reporter Citations,* 2005 Bound Volume, Part 8, p. 521.

FIGURE 5.9   HEADNOTE 13 FROM THE ORIGINAL CASE, *KENNEY v. SCIENTIFIC, INC.*

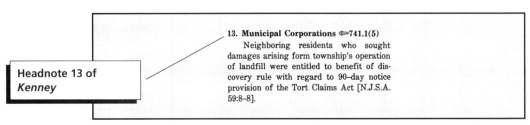

Reprinted with permission from Thomson West, West's *Atlantic Reporter,* 2d Ser., Vol. 497, *Kenney v. Scientific, Inc.,* 497 A.2d 1310, 1311 (N.J. Super. L. Div. 1985). © 1985 Thomson West.

FIGURE 5.10   SHEPARD'S® ENTRY FOR *KENNEY v. SCIENTIFIC, INC.*

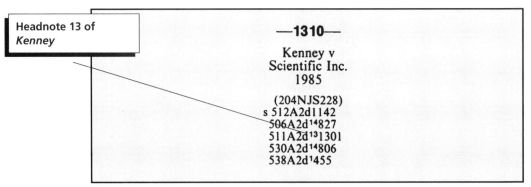

Reproduced by permission of LexisNexis. Further reproduction of any kind is strictly prohibited. From *Shepard's Atlantic Reporter Citations,* 2005 Bound Volume, Part 8, p. 521.

FIGURE 5.11   *SERVIS v. STATE,* CITING *KENNEY v. SCIENTIFIC, INC.*

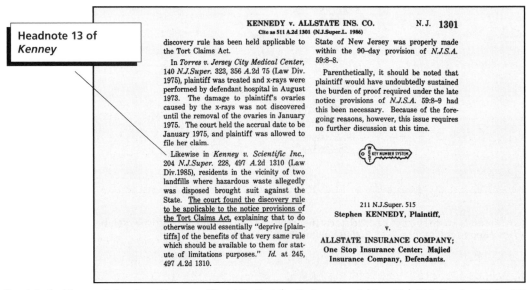

Reprinted with permission from Thomson West, West's *Atlantic Reporter,* 2d Ser., Vol. 511, *Servis v. State,* 511 A.2d 1299, 1301 (N.J. Super. L. Div. 1986). © 1986 Thomson West.

that might cause you to question whether the case continues to be authoritative. If you are looking for additional authority, favorable treatment codes and headnote references will help you identify the cases most likely to be relevant to your research.

If you look in a volume of Shepard's and do not find any entry for the original case, this means the original case was not cited during the time period covered by that volume. Before you conclude that the original case is still good law, however, you may want to check that you have the correct citation and that you are looking in the section of the Shepard's volume that covers the correct reporter.

C. CHECKING CITATIONS ELECTRONICALLY

Shepard's is available electronically in LexisNexis, but not in Westlaw. Westlaw has its own citator service called KeyCite. Each of these services is discussed in turn.

1. USING SHEPARD'S IN LEXISNEXIS

A variety of authorities can be Shepardized electronically in LexisNexis, including cases, statutes, and administrative materials. Shepard's in LexisNexis contains the same types of information you would find in the print version. The electronic entries are also organized the same way the print entries are. Case history appears first. Citing sources organized by jurisdiction appear next, followed by secondary sources.

There are some differences between Shepard's in LexisNexis and Shepard's in print. Shepard's in LexisNexis is current within twenty-four hours, so it is more up to date than print versions of Shepard's. In addition, LexisNexis allows you to view the complete Shepard's entry or a restricted entry with limited information. For cases, Shepard's in LexisNexis automatically shows LexisNexis Headnote references. You can also locate official reporter and West headnote references using the FOCUS – Restrict By function.

Shepard's is linked with other services in LexisNexis. For example, if you retrieve a case from LexisNexis, a notation at the beginning will indicate whether Shepard's contains an entry for it and, if so, what type of treatment the case has received. These notations are called Shepard's Signals. The Shepard's Signal will also appear at the beginning of the Shepard's entry for the case. The definitions of these signals appear in **Figure 5.12**.

It is often difficult to reduce the history of a case to a single notation. Determining the continued validity of a decision often requires study of the later cases. For example, a case with a negative Shepard's Signal such as a red stop sign may no longer be good law for one of its

FIGURE 5.12 SHEPARD'S® SIGNALS

SIGNAL	MEANS
Red stop sign	Warning: Negative treatment is indicated. This signal is used when the case has been reversed, overruled, or otherwise given very negative treatment.
Orange square surrounding the letter Q	Questioned: Validity questioned by citing references. This signal is used when the authoritative value of the case has been questioned, but it has not expressly been reversed or overruled.
Yellow triangle	Caution: Possible negative treatment. This signal is used when the case has received treatment that could be negative, such as being distinguished.
Green diamond surrounding a plus sign	Positive treatment is indicated. This signal is used when the case has received positive treatment, such as being affirmed or followed.
Blue circle surrounding the letter A	Citing references with analysis available. This signal is used when the case has received treatment that is neither positive nor negative, such as being explained.
Blue circle surrounding the letter I	Citation information available. This signal is used when the case has been cited, but no history or treatment codes have been assigned to the citing sources.

points, but it may continue to be authoritative on other points. If you were to rely on the red stop sign without further inquiry, you might miss a case that is important for the issue you are researching. As a consequence, although Shepard's Signals can be helpful research tools, you should not rely on them in deciding whether a case is valid. Always research the Shepard's entry and review the citing sources carefully to satisfy yourself about the status of a case.

Figure 5.13 shows part of a Shepard's entry in LexisNexis.

2. USING KEYCITE IN WESTLAW

Westlaw provides its own citator service called KeyCite. KeyCite is available for cases, statutes, and administrative materials. It is similar

FIGURE 5.13 SHEPARD'S® ENTRY EXCERPT IN LEXISNEXIS FOR 552 A.2d 258

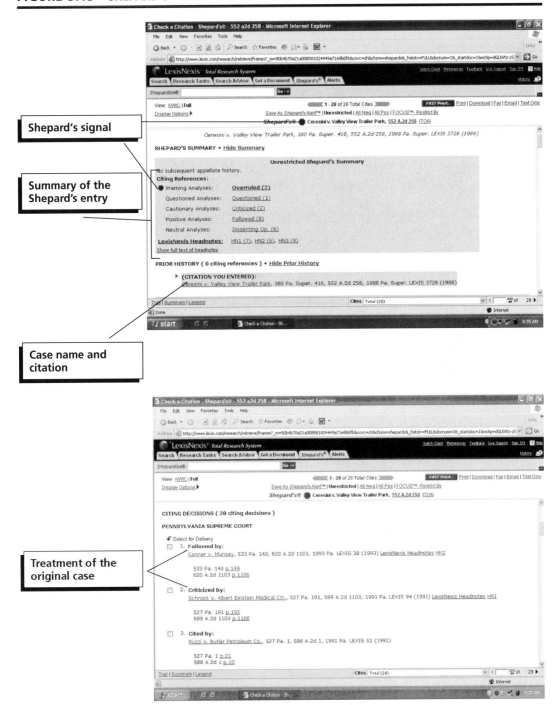

Reprinted with permission of LexisNexis. SHEPARD'S® entry for 552 A.2d 258.

to Shepard's in the information it provides, although it is more up to date than Shepard's in print because as soon as an authority is added to Westlaw's databases, KeyCite is updated to reflect the new information.

A KeyCite entry for a case begins with the full citation to the case and its complete direct history. After the direct history, any negative indirect history is listed. If the original case has negative indirect history, you may notice that some of the negative citations are followed by one or more stars. The star categories indicate how much discussion of the original case you will find in the citing case. There are four star categories: (a) examined (four stars); (b) discussed (three stars); (c) cited (two stars); and (d) mentioned (one star). **Figure 5.14** delineates how West defines these terms.

In addition to case history, KeyCite provides a variety of research references to the original case. To locate research references, you may want to review a segment of the KeyCite entry called Citing References, which contains citations to the case. Negative cases are listed first, followed by positive cases, secondary sources, and court documents. Positive and negative cases are organized by depth of treatment and then by jurisdiction within the depth of treatment category. In addition, if the original case has been quoted, quotation marks will appear after the entry. You can go directly to the quoted language by clicking on the quotation marks. Headnote references follow the case citations.

FIGURE 5.14   DEFINITIONS OF KEYCITE STAR CATEGORIES

NUMBER OF STARS	MEANING	DEFINED
Four stars	Examined	Contains an extended discussion of the original case, usually more than a printed page of text
Three stars	Discussed	Contains a substantial discussion of the original case, usually more than one paragraph but less than a printed page
Two stars	Cited	Contains some discussion of the original case, usually less than a paragraph
One star	Mentioned	Contains a brief reference to the original case, usually in a string citation

KeyCite is linked with cases in Westlaw's databases with a notation system similar to Shepard's Signals in LexisNexis. If a case has a KeyCite entry, a notation called a "status flag" will appear at the beginning of both the case and the KeyCite entry to give you some indication of the case's treatment in KeyCite. West's definitions of the status flags are explained in **Figure 5.15.**

Like Shepard's Signals, KeyCite status flags are useful research tools, but cannot substitute for your own assessment of the continued validity of a case. You should always research the KeyCite entry and review the citing sources carefully to satisfy yourself about the status of a case.

Figure 5.16 shows an excerpt from a KeyCite entry in textual form.

You can also view the history of a case in chart format using Graphical KeyCite. **Figure 5.17** shows a Graphical KeyCite display. Graphical KeyCite is useful when you are checking the validity of a case with complex history because it allows you to see a snapshot of any prior or subsequent history. Graphical KeyCite uses bands of color to identify the level of the court that issued each decision in a case's history, working from lowest to highest level. The KeyCited case is marked to make it easily identifiable on the screen. You can view the entire history of the case in thumbnail view on a single screen, or you can use the zoom in and out feature to focus on specific aspects of the case's history. If you are viewing the entire case history in thumbnail view, you can focus on the information in each chart box by moving the cursor to an individual block. Placing the cursor over a block brings up a pop-up box displaying the information in the block, including links both to the case described in the box and any relevant history cases. Graphical KeyCite shows only direct history. Therefore, you need to switch back to the textual format to view any indirect history or citing references.

FIGURE 5.15   WESTLAW STATUS FLAGS INDICATING KEYCITE HISTORY

NOTATION	MEANS
Red flag	The case is no longer good law for at least one of the points it contains.
Yellow flag	The case has some negative history, but has not been reversed or overruled.
Blue H	The case has some history that is not known to be negative.
Green C	The case has citing references, but no direct or negative indirect history.

FIGURE 5.16   KEYCITE ENTRY EXCERPT FOR 552 A.2d 258

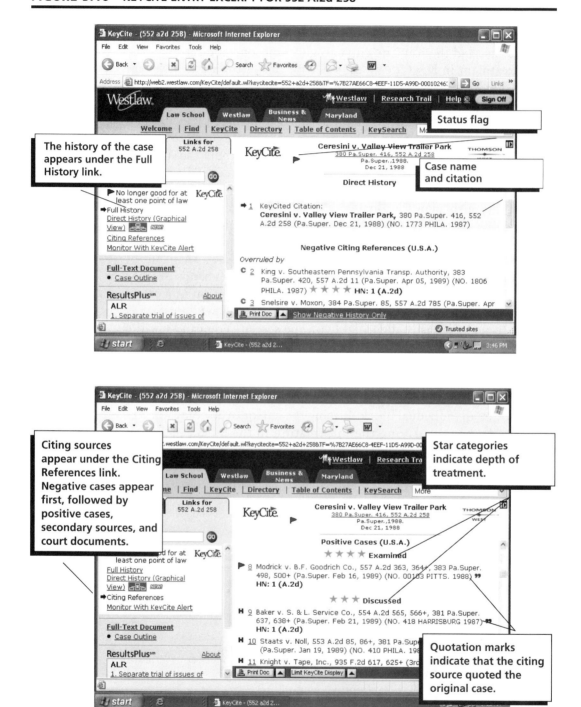

Reprinted with permission from Thomson West, from Westlaw, KeyCite entry for 552 A.2d 258. © 2005 Thomson West.

FIGURE 5.17   GRAPHICAL KEYCITE DISPLAY FOR 125 S. CT. 2764

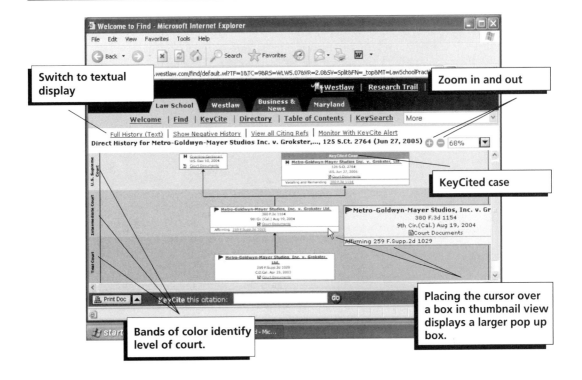

Reprinted with permission from Thomson West, from Westlaw, Graphical KeyCite display for 125 S. Ct. 2764.
© 2005 Thomson West.

D. SHEPARD'S FOR ADDITIONAL TYPES OF AUTHORITY

So far, this chapter has been devoted to the process of Shepardizing cases. Shepard's publishes a wide variety of citators, however, for almost every legal resource. **Figure 5.18** lists some examples of the types of Shepard's citators available.

In general, whenever you learn to use a new research tool, you should find out whether there is a corresponding set of Shepard's. If so, Shepard's will help you locate additional authority and may help you determine the validity of the authority you have already located.

The process of Shepardizing other forms of authority is the same as that for Shepardizing cases. The entries you find within the Shepard's volumes, however, will vary depending on the source. For example, Shepard's statutory citators do not contain a code for reversal because statutes cannot be "reversed." Instead, the codes for statutes indicate, for example, whether the statute has been repealed or held unconstitutional. You can always find a sample Shepard's entry and a list of abbreviations

FIGURE 5.18   SHEPARD'S® CITATORS

SHEPARD'S SET	ALLOWS YOU TO SHEPARDIZE . . .
Shepard's for individual states	State statutes (and sometimes administrative materials) in addition to state cases
Shepard's Federal Statute Citations	Federal statutes
Shepard's Code of Federal Regulations Citations	Federal administrative regulations
Shepard's Restatement of the Law Citations	Sections of the Restatement
Shepard's Law Review Citations	Law review and journal articles that are cited in court opinions
Shepard's Citations for Annotations	A.L.R. Annotations that are cited in court opinions
Shepard's for specific subject areas	Citations specific to the subject area. For example, in Shepard's Environmental Law Citations, you can Shepardize citations to federal decisions on environmental law, federal environmental statutes, and administrative regulations and executive orders on environmental law.

at the beginning of each Shepard's volume to help you interpret the entries for the set you are using.

E. SAMPLE PAGES FOR SHEPARDIZING A CASE IN PRINT

Beginning on the next page, **Figures 5.19** through **5.21** contain sample pages illustrating the process of Shepardizing a case in print. The case in this example is *Commonwealth v. Chopak*, 615 A.2d 696 (Pa. 1992). The first step in the process would be identifying the correct set of Shepard's for this citation. Because this case is published in the *Atlantic Reporter*, Second Series, you could use *Shepard's Atlantic Reporter Citations*. The sample pages show the entries for this case in *Shepard's Atlantic Reporter Citations*.

Once you locate *Shepard's Atlantic Reporter Citations,* you need to find the most recent supplement, which in this example is a pamphlet dated May 2005. Use the "What Your Library Should Contain" section on the front cover to identify the necessary volumes of Shepard's. This section says to use the 2005 Bound Volume and the May 2005 Cumulative Supplement to Shepardize this citation.

FIGURE 5.19 "WHAT YOUR LIBRARY SHOULD CONTAIN"

Reproduced by permission of LexisNexis. Further reproduction of any kind is strictly prohibited. From *Shepard's®* *Atlantic Reporter Citations,* Vol. 90, No. 5 (May 2005), cover page.

Within the May 2005 Cumulative Supplement, turn to the section with references to volume 615 of the *Atlantic Reporter,* Second Series, and look for a reference to starting page 696. In this example, you find one reference to the original case.

FIGURE 5.20   MAY 2005 CUMULATIVE SUPPLEMENT ENTRY FOR 615 A.2d 696

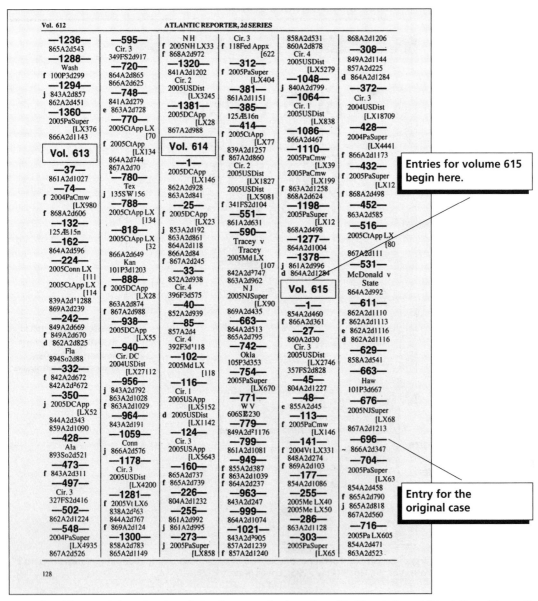

Reproduced by permission of LexisNexis. Further reproduction of any kind is strictly prohibited. From *Shepard's Atlantic Reporter Citations,* Vol. 90, No. 5 (May 2005), p. 128.

The next step is looking up the citation in the 2005 Bound Volume. In the listing for volume 615, page 696, a number of references to the case appear. At this point, you have finished Shepardizing the citation and are ready to read any cases listed in Shepard's necessary for your research. You can use the headnote references, history codes, and treatment codes to focus on the most important cases.

FIGURE 5.21   2005 BOUND VOLUME ENTRY FOR 615 A.2d 696

The 2005 Bound Volume includes the case name and year of decision.

Reproduced by permission of LexisNexis. Further reproduction of any kind is strictly prohibited. From *Shepard's Atlantic Reporter Citations,* 2005 Bound Volume, Part 9, p. 1230.

F. CHECKLIST FOR CASE RESEARCH WITH SHEPARD'S CITATIONS AND OTHER CITATORS

1. LOCATE THE CORRECT SET OF SHEPARD'S IN PRINT

❐ Use a state or regional set of Shepard's to Shepardize a state case, keeping in mind that the regional set will usually contain the most complete research references.

❐ Use *Shepard's Federal Citations* or *Shepard's United States Citations* to Shepardize federal cases.

2. LOCATE THE CORRECT VOLUMES WITHIN THE PRINT SET

❐ Check the most recent supplement (softcover booklet or pamphlet) for the section "What Your Library Should Contain."

3. LOCATE THE ENTRIES FOR THE CASE WITHIN EACH VOLUME LOCATED IN STEP 2

❐ Check each noncumulative Shepard's volume for entries on the case.

❐ If the Shepard's set covers more than one reporter, check the section covering the reporter for your citation.

❐ If there is no entry for the citation within a Shepard's volume, the case was not cited during that time period.

4. INTERPRET THE ENTRIES

❐ Case history appears first. Parallel citations appear in parentheses. History codes signal the action taken in the history cases.

❐ Citing sources appear second. Look for authorities in this order:

■ For state cases only, cases from the same state as the original case.

■ Federal cases by circuit (within each circuit, appellate cases first, followed by district court cases).

■ Cases from state courts listed alphabetically by state.

■ Secondary sources.

❐ Treatment codes signal how the citing sources treated the original case.

❐ Headnote references signal the proposition for which a citing source refers to the original case.

5. CHECK CASE CITATIONS ELECTRONICALLY

❐ To Shepardize a case in LexisNexis, enter the citation in Shepard's and choose whether to view the complete or restricted entry. Interpret the entries as in Step 4.

❐ In Westlaw, use KeyCite by entering the citation.

- Review direct and negative indirect history to determine whether the case is still good law.
- Review Citing References for both positive and negative research references.
- Use star categories and quotation marks to identify key sources.
- Use Graphical KeyCite to view the direct history in chart form.

CHAPTER 6

STATUTORY RESEARCH

A. INTRODUCTION TO STATUTORY LAW

1. THE PUBLICATION OF STATUTORY LAW

Statutes enacted by a legislature are organized by subject matter into what is called a "code. " Codes are published by jurisdiction; each jurisdiction that enacts statutes collects them in its own code. Thus, the federal government publishes the federal code, which contains all federal statutes. Statutes for each state are published in individual state codes. Most codes contain too many statutes to be included in a single volume. Instead, a code usually consists of a multivolume set of books containing all of the statutes passed within a jurisdiction. The federal code also includes the text of the United States Constitution. Most state codes contain the text of the state constitution, and many include the text of the United States Constitution as well.

When a federal law is enacted, it is published in three steps: (1) it is published as a separate document; (2) it is included in a chronological listing of all statutes passed within a session of Congress; and (3) it is reorganized by subject matter and placed within the code. In the first step of the process, every law passed by Congress is assigned a public law number. The public law number indicates the session of Congress in which the law was passed and the order in which it was passed. Thus, Public Law 103-416 was the 416th law passed during the 103d session

of Congress. Each public law is published in a separate booklet or pamphlet containing the full text of the law as it was passed by Congress. This booklet is known as a slip law and is identified by its public law number.

In the second step of the process, slip laws for a session of Congress are compiled together in chronological order. Laws organized within this chronological compilation are called session laws because they are organized according to the session of Congress during which they were enacted. Session laws are compiled in a publication called *United States Statutes at Large*. A citation to *Statutes at Large* will tell you the volume of *Statutes at Large* containing the law and the page number on which the text of the law begins. Thus, a citation to 108 Stat. 4305 tells you that this law can be located in volume 108 of *Statutes at Large*, beginning on page 4305. Both the slip law and session law versions of a statute should be identical. The only difference is the form of publication.

The third step in the process is the codification of the law. When Congress enacts a law, it enacts a block of legislation that may cover a wide range of topics. A single bill can contain provisions applicable to many different parts of the government. For example, a drug abuse prevention law could contain provisions applicable to subject areas such as food and drugs, crimes, and public health. If federal laws remained organized chronologically by the date of passage, it would be virtually impossible to research the law by subject. Laws relating to individual subjects could have been passed at so many different times that it would be extremely difficult to find all of the relevant provisions.

In the third step of the process, therefore, the pieces of the bill are reorganized according to the different subjects they cover, and they are placed by subject, or codified, within the federal code. Once legislation is codified, it is much easier to locate because it can be indexed by subject much the way cases are indexed by subject in a digest.

Figure 6.1 illustrates the publication process.

Figure 6.2 contains an example of a statute that has been codified within the federal code.

2. TITLE AND SUBJECT-MATTER ORGANIZATION OF CODES

Although all codes are organized by subject, not all codes are numbered the same way. The federal code is organized into what are called "Titles." There are fifty Titles in the federal code, and each Title covers a different subject area. Title 18, for instance, contains the laws pertaining to federal crimes, and Title 35 contains the laws pertaining to patents. Each Title is subdivided into chapters, and each chapter is further subdivided into sections. To locate a provision of the federal code, you would

FIGURE 6.1 PUBLICATION PROCESS FOR A FEDERAL STATUTE

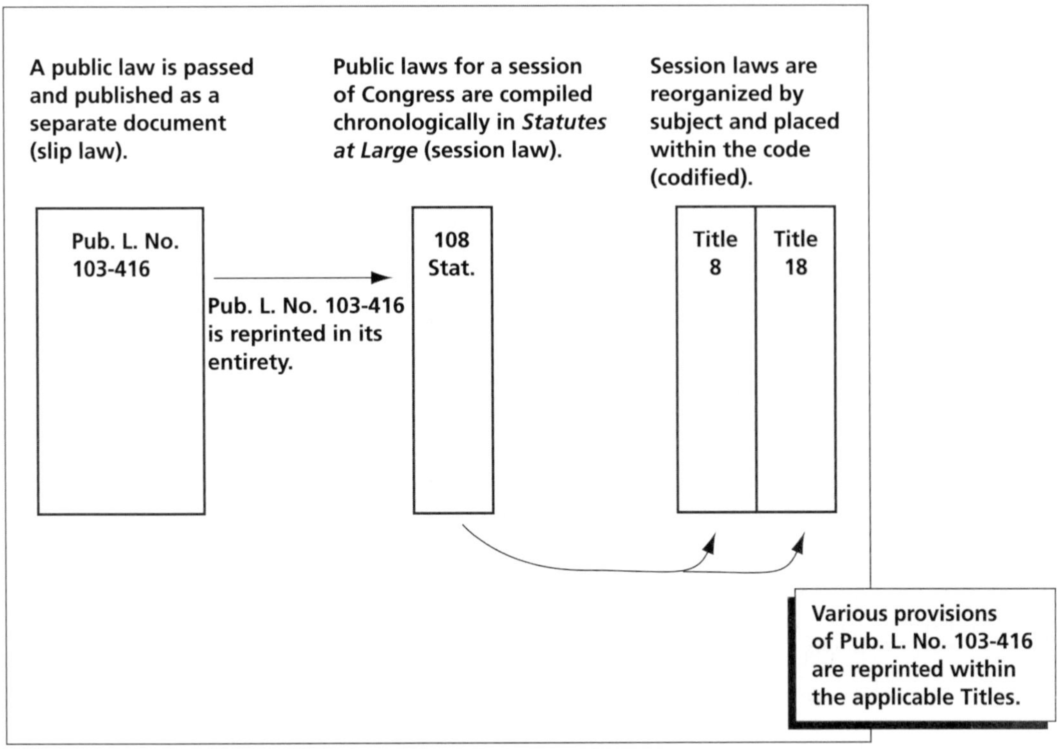

| A public law is passed and published as a separate document (slip law). | Public laws for a session of Congress are compiled chronologically in *Statutes at Large* (session law). | Session laws are reorganized by subject and placed within the code (codified). |

Pub. L. No. 103-416

Pub. L. No. 103-416 is reprinted in its entirety.

108 Stat.

Title 8 Title 18

Various provisions of Pub. L. No. 103-416 are reprinted within the applicable Titles.

need to know the Title and the section number assigned to it. For example, the provision of the federal code prohibiting bank robbery is located in Title 18, section 2113.

Not all codes are organized this way. Some states organize their codes by subject name, rather than Title number. Within each subject name, the code is then usually subdivided into chapters and sections. To find a provision of the code, you would need to know the subject area and the section number assigned to that provision. For example, the provision of New York law that prohibits issuing a bad check is located in the subject volume of the New York code containing the Penal Law, section 190.05.

3. OFFICIAL VS. UNOFFICIAL CODES AND ANNOTATED VS. UNANNOTATED CODES

Although there is only one "code " for each jurisdiction, in the sense that each jurisdiction has only one set of statutes in force, the text of the laws may be published in more than one set of books. Sometimes

FIGURE 6.2   8 U.S.C.A. § 1431

8 § 1430   ALIENS AND NATIONALITY   Ch. 12
Note 30

chapter 11 of this title at time he applied for citizenship, notwithstanding letter written by alien to Bureau of Internal Revenue involving controversy concerning income tax in which he mentioned abandoning his residence. Petition of Herschmann, C.C.A.7 (Ill.) 1947, 163 F.2d 865.

In a proceeding to obtain naturalization on ground of marriage to a United States citizen, applicant must establish validity of marriage by satisfactory evidence, notwithstanding statute to effect that legality of a regularly solemnized marriage is presumed and burden of proof is upon him who seeks to attack such marriage. Petition of Lujan, D.C.Guam 1956, 144 F.Supp. 150.

Where petitioners for naturalization, although entitled to a presumption of lawful entry for purpose of permanent residence because of entry into Virgin Islands before July 1, 1938, notwithstanding that there was no record made of entry, later received certificates of arrival, which were required to be attached to petitions for naturalization, on basis of re-entries which were made less than requisite period before filing petitions,

petitions were denied for want of proof of lawful entry a sufficient time prior to the filing thereof, since the presumption was unavailable for naturalization purposes. In re Simmiolkjier, D.C.Virgin Islands 1947, 71 F.Supp. 553.

An applicant for naturalization must show by satisfactory evidence that he has the specified qualifications. Petition of Sam Hoo, N.D.Cal.1945, 63 F.Supp. 439.

Mere proof of ceremonial marriage to American citizen by one previously married in China and affidavits concerning deaths of prior wives and renunciation of marriage to applicant by one of them and remarriage of such prior wife were insufficient to show valid marriage to American citizen so as to entitle applicant to naturalization. Petition of Sam Hoo, N.D.Cal.1945, 63 F.Supp. 439.

31. Collateral attack

Proceedings on petition for naturalization of alien whose naturalization depended upon wife's citizenship would not be used as basis for collateral attack on wife's citizenship. Petition of Pellegrini, S.D.N.Y.1954, 126 F.Supp. 742.

> **Name of the section**

> **Section number**

§ 1431. **Children born outside United States of one alien and one citizen parent; conditions for automatic citizenship**

> **Text of the statute**

(a) A child born outside of the United States, one of whose parents at the time of the child's birth was an alien and the other of whose parents then was and never thereafter ceased to be a citizen of the United States, shall, if such alien parent is naturalized, become a citizen of the United States, when—

(1) such naturalization takes place while such child is under the age of eighteen years; and

(2) such child is residing in the United States pursuant to a lawful admission for permanent residence at the time of naturalization or thereafter and begins to reside permanently in the United States while under the age of eighteen years.

(b) Subsection (a) of this section shall apply to an adopted child only if the child is residing in the United States at the time of naturalization of such adoptive parent, in the custody of his adoptive parents, pursuant to a lawful admission for permanent residence.

(June 27, 1952, c. 477, Title III, ch. 2, § 320, 66 Stat. 245; Oct. 5, 1978, Pub.L. 95–417, § 4, 92 Stat. 917; Dec. 29, 1981, Pub.L. 97–116, § 18(m), 95 Stat. 1620; Nov. 14, 1986, Pub.L. 99–653, § 14, 100 Stat. 3657; Oct. 24, 1988, Pub.L. 100–525, §§ 8(*l*), 9(w), 102 Stat. 2618, 2621.)

326

FIGURE 6.3   CHARACTERISTICS OF OFFICIAL AND UNOFFICIAL CODES

OFFICIAL CODES	UNOFFICIAL CODES
Published under government authority (e.g., U.S.C.)	Published by a commercial publisher without government authorization (e.g., U.S.C.A. and U.S.C.S.)
May or may not contain research references (annotations). U.S.C. is not an annotated code.	Usually contain research references (annotations). Both U.S.C.A. and U.S.C.S. are annotated codes.

a government arranges for the publication of its laws; this is known as an "official" code.[1] Sometimes a commercial publisher will publish the laws for a jurisdiction without government authorization; this is known as an "unofficial" code. Some jurisdictions have both official and unofficial codes, but in other jurisdictions, only one or the other type of code will be available. If both official and unofficial codes are published for a jurisdiction, they will usually be organized and numbered identically (e.g., all sets will be organized by subject or by Title). For federal laws, the government publishes an official code, *United States Code* or U.S.C. Two other sets of the federal code are also available through commercial publishers, *United States Code Annotated* (U.S.C.A.) and *United States Code Service* (U.S.C.S.).

In addition, a published code can come in one of two formats: annotated or unannotated. An annotated code contains the text of the law, as well as different types of research references. The research references may include summaries of cases or citations to secondary sources discussing a statute. An unannotated code contains only the text of the law. It may have a few references to the statutes' original public law numbers, but other than that, it will not contain research references. Most unofficial codes are annotated codes. Official codes may or may not be annotated. As you might imagine, an annotated code is much more useful as a research tool than an unannotated code.

In the federal code, U.S.C. (the official code) is an unannotated code. The two unofficial codes, U.S.C.A. and U.S.C.S., are annotated codes. See **Figure 6.3** for a summary of the characteristics of official and unofficial codes.

---

[1]The government may publish the code itself, or it may arrange for a commercial publisher to publish the code. As long as the government arranges for the publication, the code is an official code, even if it is physically produced by a commercial publisher.

B. RESEARCHING STATUTES IN PRINT

The process of researching statutes is fairly uniform for state and federal codes. This section illustrates the process of researching federal statutes in detail using U.S.C.A. You should be able to adapt this process to almost any kind of statutory research. After the detailed discussion of U.S.C.A., this section discusses two additional sources for federal statutory research, U.S.C. and U.S.C.S., as well as state statutes, rules of procedure, and uniform codes and model acts. This section concludes with an explanation of how to use Shepard's Citations in statutory research.

1. RESEARCHING FEDERAL STATUTES

a. Researching Federal Statutes in *United States Code Annotated*

You can research federal statutes in U.S.C.A. in several ways. The most common way to locate statutes is to search by subject using the General Index. You can also use tables accompanying the code to search by the popular name of the law or public law number.

(1) Researching in U.S.C.A. by subject

Researching federal statutes by subject in U.S.C.A. is a four-step process:

   i. Look up the topics you want to research in the General Index.
  ii. Locate the relevant code section(s) in the main volumes of U.S.C.A. and evaluate the material in the accompanying annotations.
 iii. Update your research using the pocket part.
  iv. Update your research using the supplementary pamphlets at the end of the code.

Because U.S.C.A. contains the United States Constitution, you can locate federal constitutional provisions by subject the same way you would locate any federal statute.

(i) Using the general index

The General Index to U.S.C.A. is an ordinary subject index that consists of a series of softcover books. It is published annually, so be sure to check the most recent set of index books.

Using the General Index is just like using any other subject index. Topics are listed alphabetically. Next to each topic are references to the Title and section number(s) of the statutory provisions relevant to that topic. The abbreviation "et seq." means that the index is referring to a series of sections beginning with the section listed; often, this will be a reference

to an entire Chapter within the Title. The index also contains cross-references to other subjects relevant to the topic. An example of an index page appears in **Figure 6.4.**

(ii) Locating statutes and reading the annotations
Once you have located relevant Title and section numbers in the General Index, the next step is finding the statute within the books. The books are organized numerically by Title, although some Titles span more than one volume. Using the Title number, you should be able to locate the correct volume. The sections within the Title will be listed in numerical order within the volume.[2] At the beginning of each chapter, you will find an outline of the code sections within the chapter.

Following the text of the code section, you may find a series of annotations with additional information about the statute. **Figure 6.5** describes some of the types of information you can find in the annotations in U.S.C.A.

Not all statutes have annotations. Those that do may not contain all of the information in **Figure 6.5** or may have additional information. The information provided depends on the research references that are appropriate for that statute. If a statute has any annotations, they will always follow after the text of the code section. **Figure 6.6** shows the annotations accompanying 8 U.S.C.A. § 1431.

(iii) Updating statutory research using pocket parts
Like other hardcover books used in legal research, U.S.C.A. volumes are updated with pocket parts. If the pocket part gets too big to fit in the back of the book, you should find a separate softcover pamphlet on the shelf next to the hardcover volume.

The pocket part is organized in the same way as the main volume. Therefore, to update your research, you need only look up the section numbers you located in the main volume. The pocket part will show any revisions to the statute, as well as additional annotations if, for example, new cases interpreting the section have been decided. If the pocket part shows new statutory language, the text in the pocket part supersedes the text in the main volume. If no reference to the section appears in the pocket part, the statute has not been amended, and no new research references are available. **Figure 6.7** shows a portion of the pocket part update to 8 U.S.C.A. § 1431.

---

[2]If the statute was enacted after the main volume was published, you will not find it in the hardcover book. More recent statutes will appear in the pocket part or noncumulative supplements, which are explained in the next section.

FIGURE 6.4   EXCERPT FROM THE U.S.C.A. GENERAL INDEX

Index entry

Reference to Title 8, section 1431 and beyond: Indicates multiple sections may apply.

Reference to an individual code section pertaining to the citizenship of a child born outside the U.S.

117

CITIZENS

CITIZENS AND CITIZENSHIP—Cont'd
Canal Zone,
  American parentage, 8 § 1403
  Certificate of citizenship, 8 § 1452
Certificates and certification, 8 § 1451 et seq.
  Application, 8 § 1452
  Cancellation, 8 §§ 1451, 1453
  Certified copies, 8 § 1454
  Children born outside U.S., 8 § 1433
  Derivative citizenship, 8 § 1444
  Illegal procurement, cancellation, 8 § 1451
  New certificate, lost, mutilated or destroyed certificate, 8 § 1454
  Noncitizen national status, 8 § 1452
  Printing, safety paper, 8 § 1443
  Validity, 8 § 1101 nt
Certified copies, certificate of citizenship, 8 § 1454
Children and minors, 8 § 1431 et seq.
  Born outside U.S.,
    Canal Zone or Panama Republic, American parents, 8 § 1403
    Certificate of citizenship, 8 § 1433
    Citizen parents, 8 § 1401
    Wedlock, 8 § 1409
  Canal Zone or Panama Republic, American parents, 8 § 1403
  Certificate of citizenship, child born outside U.S., 8 § 1433
  Definitions, 8 § 1101
  Physical presence abroad as dependent, 8 § 1401
  Revocation, naturalization of parent, 8 § 1451
  Unknown parentage, 8 § 1401
Citizenship and Immigration Services Bureau, generally, this index
Civil Rights, generally, this index
Civil service, standards for competitive examinations, 5 § 3301 nt, EON 10577
Colonial National Historical Park, 16 § 81h
Committees, National Conference, 36 § 150705
Communications, Government agencies, Immigration and Naturalization Service, 8 § 1373
Compensation and salaries, death, foreign countries, real estate, 22 § 2715c
Constitution of the United States, this index
Contracts, National Conference, 36 § 150706
Corporation for Public Broadcasting, 47 § 396
Counterfeiting, naturalization, books and papers, 18 § 1426
Crimes and offenses, 18 § 1421 et seq.
Damages, National Conference, 36 § 150712
Day, 36 § 106
Death, foreign countries,
  Notice, 22 § 2715b
  Personal property, 22 § 2715c
Debtors and creditors, death, foreign countries, 22 § 2715c
Declaration of intention, 8 § 1445
  Officers and employees of U.S. Government, compensation paid out of appropriations, 5 § 3101 nt

CITIZENS AND CITIZENSHIP—Cont'd
Decorations, medals, and badges, National Conference, 36 §§ 150706, 150707
Defense Department, noncitizens, 10 § 1584, 1584 nt
Definitions, U.S. Const. Am. XIV
  Merchant Marine Act of 1936, 46 App. § 1244
  Antarctica, notice, 16 § 2406
Delegate to Congress, eligibility for office, Guam and Virgin Islands, 48 § 1713
Departures, war, national emergency, 8 § 1185
Derivative citizenship, 8 § 1444
Desert land entries, requirement as to patentee, 43 § 329
Deserters, Armed Forces, 8 § 1425
Directors, National Conference, 36 § 150705
Disabled American veterans, 36 § 50303
Discrimination, workforce investment, 29 § 2938
Dissolution, National Conference, 36 § 150713
Dividends, National Conference, 36 § 150708
Documentation, 22 § 2705
Draft evaders, 8 § 1425
Due process of law, U.S. Const. Am. XIV
Elections, U.S. Const. Am. XV
  Absentee voting, overseas, 42 § 1973ff et seq.
  Discrimination, U.S. Const. Am. XV
  Fraud, 42 § 15544
  National Conference, 36 § 150703 et seq.
Employee Retirement Income Security Program, officers and employees, 29 § 1111
Engineers, vessels, license, requirement, 46 § 7102
Entry into U.S., war, national emergency, 8 § 1185
Equal protection of the laws, U.S. Const. Am. XIV
Eskimos, birth, 8 § 1401
Estate Tax, this index
Ethical conduct, principles for Government officers and employees, 5 § 7301 nt, EON 12674
False impersonation, Foreign Service, special agents, 22 § 2709
False representation, fines, penalties and forfeitures, 18 § 911
Farm Credit Administration Board, qualification for membership, 12 § 2242
Federal employees, pay, prevailing rate employees, requirements concerning, 5 § 5342
Federal employment, requirements for, 5 § 3301 nt, EON 10577, 11935
Federal Housing Finance Board directors, requirement, 12 § 1422a
Federal officers and employees, ethical conduct, principles of, 5 § 7301 nt, EON 12674
Fees, demanding or receiving additional fees, fines, penalties and forfeitures, 18 § 1422
Female genital mutilation, information, Immigration and Naturalization Service, 8 § 1374

Reprinted with permission from Thomson West, *United States Code Annotated*, 2004 General Index C, p. 117. © 2004 Thomson West.

FIGURE 6.5 INFORMATION CONTAINED IN U.S.C.A. ANNOTATIONS

CATEGORIES OF INFORMATION IN ANNOTATIONS	CONTENTS
Historical Note Sometimes this section is called Historical and Statutory Notes.	Contains the history of the section, including summaries of amendments and the public law numbers and *Statutes at Large* citations for the laws containing the revisions. This section can also refer to the legislative history of the statute (for more discussion of legislative history, see Chapter 7).
Cross-References	Contains cross-references to related provisions of the code.
Library References Sometimes this section is subdivided into categories for Administrative Law, American Digest System, Encyclopedias, Law Reviews, Texts and Treatises, and Forms.	Contains references to related topics and key numbers in the West digest system, as well as references to legal encyclopedia sections with information on the subject (see Chapter 4 for more discussion of the digest system and Chapter 3 for more discussion of legal encyclopedias).
Code of Federal Regulations Sometimes this appears as a separate section, and sometimes it is included with Library References, under the Administrative Law category.	Contains references to administrative agency regulations implementing the statute (for more discussion of administrative regulations, see Chapter 8).
Law Review Articles Sometimes this appears as a separate section, and sometimes it is included with Library References, under the Law Reviews category.	Contains references to relevant law review articles (for more discussion of law reviews and other legal periodicals, see Chapter 3).
Notes of Decisions	Contains summaries of cases interpreting the statute. If the statute has been discussed in a large number of cases, the Notes of Decisions will be divided into subject categories, and each category will be assigned a number. Cases on each subject will be listed under the appropriate number. *Note that these subject and number categories do not correspond to the topics and key numbers within the West digest system.*

FIGURE 6.6 ANNOTATIONS ACCOMPANYING U.S.C.A. § 1431

Information on the enactment of and later amendments to the statute

IMMIGRATION AND NATIONALITY **8 § 1431**

HISTORICAL AND STATUTORY NOTES

Revision Notes and Legislative Reports
1952 Acts. House Report No. 1365 and Conference Report No. 2096, see 1952 U.S. Code Cong. and Adm. News, p. 1653.

1978 Acts. House Report No. 95–1301, see 1978 U.S. Code Cong. and Adm. News, p. 2301.

1981 Acts. House Report No. 97–264, see 1981 U.S. Code Cong. and Adm. News, p. 2577.

1986 Acts. House Report No. 99–916, see 1986 U.S. Code Cong. and Adm. News, p. 6182.

Codifications
Section 14 of Pub.L. 99–653, set out in the credit to this section, was repealed by Pub.L. 100–525, § 8(*l*), Oct. 24, 1988, 102 Stat. 2618.

Amendments
1988 Amendments. Subsec. (a)(1). Pub.L. 100–525, § 8(*l*), struck out "unmarried and" following "such child is".

Subsec. (b). Pub.L. 100–525, § 9(w), expanded restrictions on applicability of provisions of subsec. (a), which restrictions formerly had applied only to subsec. (a)(1), to cover subsec. (a) in its entirety.

Amendments. Subsec. (a)(1). 653 added "unmarried and" such child is".

1981 Amendments. Subsec. (b). Pub.L. 97–116 substituted "an adopted child only if the child" for "a child adopted while under the age of sixteen years who".

1978 Amendments. Subsec. (a). Pub.L. 95–417 substituted in pars. (1) and (2) "eighteen years" for "sixteen years".

Subsec. (b). Pub.L. 95–417 substituted provisions making subsec. (a)(1) of this section applicable to adopted children for provisions making subsec. (a) of this section inapplicable to adopted children.

Effective Dates
1988 Acts. Section 8(*l*) of Pub.L. 100–525 effective as if included in the enactment of Pub.L. 99–653, see section 309(b)(15) of Pub.L. 102–232, set out as a note under section 1101 of this title.

1981 Acts. Amendment by Pub.L. 97–116 effective on Dec. 29, 1981, see section 21(a) of Pub.L. 97–116, set out as a note under section 1101 of this title.

Repeal
Pub.L. 99–653, § 14, Nov. 14, 1986, 100 Stat. 3658, set out in the credit of this section, was repealed by Pub.L. 100–525, § 8(*l*), Oct. 24, 1988, 102 Stat. 2618. The repeal served to strike out the words "unmarried and" after "while such child is" in subsec. (a)(1) of this section.

Cross references to related statutes

CROSS REFERENCES

Definition of the term—
Alien, see 8 USCA § 1101(a)(3).
Child, as used in subchapters I and II of this chapter, see 8 USCA § 1101(b)(1).
Child, as used in this subchapter, see 8 USCA § 1101(c)(1).
Lawfully admitted for permanent residence, see 8 USCA § 1101(a)(20).
Naturalization, see 8 USCA § 1101(a)(23).
Parent, as used in subchapters I and II of this chapter, see 8 USCA § 1101(b)(2).
Parent, as used in this subchapter, see 8 USCA § 1101(c)(2).
sidence, see 8 USCA § 1101(a)(33).
ited States, see 8 USCA § 1101(a)(38).

Digest topic and key number

References to secondary sources

LIBRARY REFERENCES

Administrative Law
Children not requiring naturalization, see West's Federal Practice Manual § 6637.
Naturalized citizens, evidence, see West's Federal Practice Manual § 6519.

American Digest System
Citizens ⬉9.

327

Reprinted with permission from Thomson West, *United States Code Annotated*, Title 8 (1999), p. 327. © 1999 Thomson West.

FIGURE 6.7 POCKET PART UPDATE FOR 8 U.S.C.A. § 1431

ALIENS AND NATIONALITY

8 § 1431

Immigration Law Service § 30:104, Regular Employment Abroad.

Immigration Law Service § 30:105, Military Personnel; Proof.

Immigration Law Service § 30:106, Intention to Reside Abroad With Spouse.

Immigration Law Service § 30:107, Effect of Government Restrictions.

Immigration Law Service § 30:108, Residence and Physical Presence Requirements.

Immigration Law Service § 30:109, Other Naturalization Requirements.

Immigration Law Service § 30:110, Basic Requirements; Residence and Physical Presence.

Immigration Law Service § 30:111, Other Requirements.

Immigration Law Service § 30:154, Naturalization Requirements; Proof.

Immigration Law Service § 30:155, Effect of Eligibility Under Other Provisions.

Immigration Law Service § 30:188, Employees of Nonprofit Communications Organizations Residence and Physical Presence Requirements.

Immigration Law Service § 30:189, Other Requirements.

Immigration Law Service § 30:196, Seamen Eligibility.

Immigration Law Service § 30:205, Nationals of United States.

Immigration Law Service § 30:219, When to Apply.

Immigration Law Service § 30:228, Supplementary Information Required of Certain Applicants.

Immigration Law Service § 30:259, Limitation to Persons Residing Within Jurisdiction (Venue).

Immigration Law Service § 36:220, Time as Cr Counts Towards Naturalization.

Immigration Law Service PSD INA § 334, § 334 (8 U.S.C.A. § 1445). Application for Naturalization; Declaration of Intention.

Steel on Immigration Law, 2d § 15:10, Residence Requirements.

Steel on Immigration Law, 2d § 15:11, Special Classes.

U.S. Citizenship and Naturalization Handbook § 6:2, Structure of Ina.

U.S. Citizenship and Naturalization Handbook § 11:1, Overview.

U.S. Citizenship and Naturalization Handbook § 11:2, Overview.

U.S. Citizenship and Naturalization Handbook § 11:3, Requirements.

U.S. Citizenship and Naturalization Handbook § 11:5, in General.

U.S. Citizenship and Naturalization Handbook § 11:6, Requirements.

U.S. Citizenship and Naturalization Handbook § 9:20, Other Bases for Eligibility.

U.S. Citizenship and Naturalization Handbook § 9:59, Jurisdiction to Administer Oath; Generally.

U.S. Citizenship and Naturalization Handbook § 11:10, in General.

U.S. Citizenship and Naturalization Handbook § 11:22, Physical and Legal Custody Requirements.

U.S. Citizenship and Naturalization Handbook § 11:25, in General.

U.S. Citizenship and Naturalization Handbook § 11:26, in General.

Notes of Decisions

9. Continuance of marital relationship

Immigration and Naturalization Service (INS) could not deny a naturalization application based on status as spouse of citizen solely because applicant ceased to reside in marital union with her citizen spouse prior to naturalization but after filing the application; fact that applicant no longer resided with her husband did not change her legal status as "spouse" of a citizen. Ali v. Smith, W.D.Wash.1999, 39 F.Supp.2d 1254. Aliens ⟨⇒ 62(1)

§ 1431. **Children born outside the United States and residing permanently in the United States; conditions under which citizenship automatically acquired**

(a) A child born outside of the United States automatically becomes a citizen of the United States when all of the following conditions have been fulfilled:

(1) At least one parent of the child is a citizen of the United States, whether by birth or naturalization.

(2) The child is under the age of eighteen years.

(3) The child is residing in the United States in the legal and physical custody of the citizen parent pursuant to a lawful admission for permanent residence.

(b) Subsection (a) of this section shall apply to a child adopted by a United States citizen parent if the child satisfies the requirements applicable to adopted children under section 1101(b)(1) of this title.

(June 27, 1952, c. 477, Title III, ch. 2, § 320, 66 Stat. 245; Oct. 5, 1978, Pub.L. 95–417, § 4, 92 Stat. 917; Dec. 29, 1981, Pub.L. 97–116, § 18(m), 95 Stat. 1620; Nov. 14, 1986, Pub.L. 99–653, § 14, 100 Stat. 3657; Oct. 24, 1988, Pub.L. 100–525, §§ 8(l), 9(w), 102 Stat. 2618, 2621; Oct. 30, 2000, Pub.L. 106–395, Title I, § 101(a), 114 Stat. 1631.)

HISTORICAL AND STATUTORY NOTES

Revision Notes and Legislative Reports

2000 Acts. House Report No. 106–852, see 2000 U.S. Code Cong. and Adm. News, p. 1499.

Amendments

2000 Amendments. Pub.L. 106–395, § 101(a), rewrote the section, which formerly read:

47

> **New statutory language supersedes the language in the main volume.**

> **New annotations follow the text of the statute.**

Reprinted with permission from Thomson West, *United States Code Annotated*, 2004 Cumulative Pocket Part, Title 8, p. 47. © 2004 Thomson West.

(iv) Updating statutory research using supplementary pamphlets

The pocket part for each volume is published only once a year. Congress may change a statute after the pocket part is printed, however, and cases interpreting a statute can be published at any time. Therefore, to update your research, you need to check an additional source.

At the end of the U.S.C.A. set, you should find a series of softcover pamphlets. These are supplements that are published after the pocket part. They are noncumulative, meaning that each pamphlet covers a specific time period. To update your research thoroughly, you must look for your code section in each pamphlet published since the pocket part.[3] The dates of coverage of each pamphlet should appear on the cover.

The noncumulative pamphlets are organized the same way as the rest of the code: by Title and section number. Therefore, you need to look up the Title and section number of the statute you are researching. The pamphlet, like the pocket part, will list any changes to the statute, as well as additional annotations. If no reference to the section appears in the noncumulative pamphlet, then there is no additional information for you to research. **Figure 6.8** is an excerpt from a page in a noncumulative pamphlet updating 8 U.S.C.A. § 1431. Notice in this example that the statutory language has not changed, but there are additional Notes of Decisions.

(2) The popular name and conversion tables

Research using a subject-matter index is appropriate when you know the subject you want to research but do not know the exact statute you need to find. Sometimes, however, you will know which statute you need to find. In that situation, the easiest way to find the citation may be through the popular name table or the conversion tables. In U.S.C.A., the popular name table is published as a separate volume accompanying the General Index. The conversion tables appear in separate softcover "Tables" volumes.

The popular name table allows you to locate statutes according to their popular names. For example, if you wanted to research the Freedom of Access to Clinic Entrances Act (FACE Act) but did not know its citation, you could look up a variety of topics in the General Index until you found it. An easier way to do this would be to look up the FACE Act according to its popular name. The popular name table lists the public law number, the *Statutes at Large* citation, and the Title and section numbers where the act is codified within U.S.C.A. Remember that when a law is passed by a legislature, it may affect many

---

[3]If a change to the statute appears in an earlier pamphlet, the later pamphlets will refer back to the earlier pamphlet. Later pamphlets will not, however, refer back to additional annotations. Therefore, to locate all new annotations, you must check each supplementary pamphlet.

FIGURE 6.8   NONCUMULATIVE PAMPHLET ENTRY FOR 8 U.S.C.A. § 1431

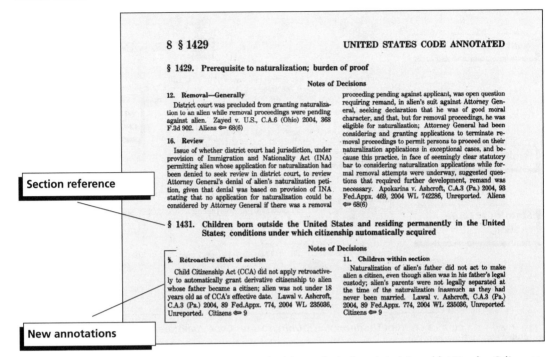

Reprinted with permission from Thomson West, *United States Code Annotated*, Pamphlet Number 3 (January 2005), p. 270. © 2005 Thomson West.

different areas of the law and, therefore, may be codified in many different places within the code. Thus, the popular name table may refer you to a number of different Titles and sections. For many well-known statutes, however, the popular name table is an efficient way to locate the law within the code. **Figure 6.9** shows the popular name table entry for the FACE Act.

Another way to locate a statute in U.S.C.A. is through the conversion tables. If you know the public law number for a statute, you can use the tables to find the *Statutes at Large* citation and the Titles and sections where the law has been codified. **Figure 6.10** is an example from the conversion table showing where the FACE Act is codified.

Because the popular name and conversion tables are published annually, there is no pocket part update for the tables. At the end of each noncumulative supplement, however, you will find updates to the tables. Therefore, if you are unable to find the material you want in the General Index or Tables, check for more recent material in the noncumulative supplements.

FIGURE 6.9 FACE ACT ENTRY, POPULAR NAME TABLE

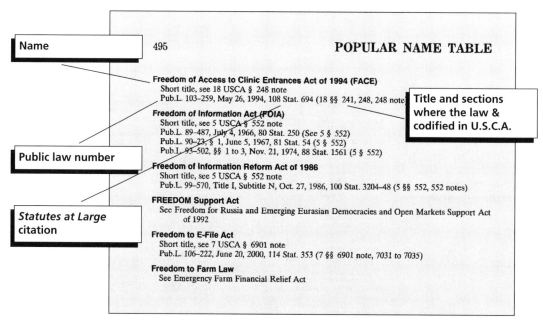

Reprinted with permission from Thomson West, *United States Code Annotated*, 2004 Popular Name Table, p. 495. © 2004 Thomson West.

b. Researching Federal Statutes in *United States Code*

The index, popular name, and conversion table methods of locating statutes are all available with U.S.C. The main difference in researching U.S.C. concerns updating. The index and main volumes of the code are published every six years. In the intervening years, U.S.C. is not updated with pocket parts. Instead, it is updated with hardcover cumulative supplements. A new supplement is issued each year until the next publication of the main set.

In theory, using the supplements should be sufficient to update your research. In practice, however, the system presents some difficulties. Laws can be changed more frequently than the supplements are published, and the government is often two or three years behind in publishing the supplements. To update completely, you would need to research session and slip laws published since the latest supplement. Therefore, U.S.C. is not usually an appropriate source for locating the most current version of a statute, and because it lacks the research references contained in the annotated federal codes, it is not the most useful statutory research tool.

FIGURE 6.10 CONVERSION TABLE ENTRY FOR PUB. L. NO. 103-259, THE FACE ACT

103–252   **1994**

§ 207	108 Stat 656	42 § 9910b
§ 208	108 Stat 657	42 § 9901 nt
§ 301(a)	108 Stat 657	42 § 8821 nt
§ 302	108 Stat 657	42 § 8621
§ 303	108 Stat 658	42 § 8621
§ 304(a)	108 Stat 658	42 § 8621
§ 304(b)	108 Stat 658	42 § 8622
§ 304(c)	108 Stat 659	42 § 8623
§ 305	108 Stat 659	42 § 8624
§ 306 to 309	108 Stat 659	42 § 8624
§ 310	108 Stat 661	42 § 8626
§ 311(a)(1)	108 Stat 661	42 § 8624
§ 311(a)(2)	108 Stat 661	42 § 8626a
§ 311(a)(3)	108 Stat 661	42 § 8628a
§ 311(b)	108 Stat 661	42 § 8624
§ 311(c)(1)	108 Stat 662	42 § 8621
§ 311(c)(2)	108 Stat 662	42 § 8622
§ 311(c)(3)	108 Stat 662	42 § 8623
§ 311(c)(4),(5)	108 Stat 662	42 § 8624
§ 311(c)(6)	108 Stat 662	42 § 8626a
§ 311(c)(7)	108 Stat 662	42 § 8629
§ 312	108 Stat 662	42 § 8626b
§ 314	108 Stat 666	42 § 8621 nt
§ 401(a)	108 Stat 666	42 § 5116
§ 401(a)	108 Stat 666	42 § 5116a .... Elim.
§ 401(a)	108 Stat 666	42 § 5116b .... Elim.
§ 401(a)	108 Stat 666	42 § 5116c .... Elim.
§ 401(a)	108 Stat 666	42 § 5116d .... Elim.
§ 401(a)	108 Stat 666	42 § 5116e .... Elim.
§ 401(a)	108 Stat 666	42 § 5116f .... Elim.
§ 401(a)	108 Stat 666	42 § 5116g .... Elim.
§ 401(b)(1)	108 Stat 672	42 § 12339 .... Rep.
§ 401(b)(2)	108 Stat 672	42 § 5106a–1 .... Rep.
§ 402(a)	108 Stat 672	42 § 12314
§ 402(b)	108 Stat 673	42 § 12340
§ 403(a)	108 Stat 673	42 § 12353
§ 403(b)	108 Stat 673	42 § 12355

May 19, 1994 103–254

§ 1	108 Stat 679	15 § 2201 nt
§ 2	108 Stat 679	15 § 2201 nt
§ 3	108 Stat 679	15 § 2221
§ 4	108 Stat 682	15 § 2220
§ 5	108 Stat 682	15 § 2228
§ 6	108 Stat 682	15 § 2227
§ 7	108 Stat 682	15 § 2216
§ 8	108 Stat 683	15 § 2216 nt

103–255 ... § 4 .... 108 Stat 686 .... 16 § 1132 nt
May 26, 1994 103–259

§ 1, 2	108 Stat 694	18 § 248 nts
§ 3	108 Stat 694	18 § 248
§ 4	108 Stat 697	18prec. 241
§ 5	108 Stat 697	18 § 248 nt
§ 6	108 Stat 697	18 § 248 nt

103–260 ... § 1 .... 108 Stat 698 .... 49 App. § 2201 nt

§ 101	108 Stat 698	49 App. § 2204 ...... Rev.T. 49
§ 102	108 Stat 698	49 App. § 2206 ...... Rev.T. 49
§ 103	108 Stat 698	49 App. § 2206 ...... Rev.T. 49
§ 104(a)	108 Stat 698	49 App. § 2206 ...... Rev.T. 49
§ 104(b)	108 Stat 699	49 App. § 2206 nt .... Elim.

Callouts:
- *Statutes at Large* citation
- Public law number
- Title and sections where the law & codified in U.S.C.A.

c. Researching Federal Statutes in *United States Code Service*

U.S.C.S. is organized much the same way as U.S.C.A. The index, popular name, and conversion table methods of locating statutes are all available with U.S.C.S. U.S.C.S. often has fewer references to court decisions than the Notes of Decisions in U.S.C.A., but the references to administrative materials are often more comprehensive than those in U.S.C.A.[4] The nature of your research project and the materials available in your library will determine whether it is more appropriate for you to use U.S.C.S. or U.S.C.A. for federal statutory research.

The process of updating U.S.C.S. research is basically the same as that for U.S.C.A. Hardcover main volumes are updated with pocket parts. In addition, at the end of U.S.C.S., you will find softcover supplements to the code as a whole called the Cumulative Later Case and Statutory Service. Unlike the supplements to U.S.C.A., the U.S.C.S. supplements are cumulative, so you only need to check the most recent one. The supplements are organized by Title and section number and will reflect both changes to the statutory language and additional annotations.

2. RESEARCHING STATE CODES, RULES OF PROCEDURE, AND UNIFORM LAWS AND MODEL ACTS

a. State Codes

State codes have many of the same features of U.S.C.A. All have subject indices that can be used to locate statutes. Some also have popular name tables. Most do not, however, have the equivalent of the conversion tables. In addition, the updating process for state statutory research can vary. Virtually all state codes are updated with pocket parts, but some have different or additional updating tools. You may want to check with a reference librarian if you have questions about updating statutory research for a particular state. Sample pages illustrating the process of state statutory research appear in Section E of this chapter.

b. Rules of Procedure

You are probably learning about rules of procedure governing cases filed in court in your Civil Procedure class. Whenever you are preparing to file a document or take some action that a court requires or permits, the court's rules of procedure will tell you how to accomplish your task. The rules of procedure for most courts are published as part of the code for the jurisdiction where the court is located. For example, the Federal Rules

---

[4]Chapter 8 explains administrative materials and administrative law research.

of Civil Procedure appear with Title 28 in the federal code. In many states, court procedural rules are published in a separate Rules volume.

If you want to locate procedural rules, therefore, one way to find them is through the applicable code. In print, you can locate them using the subject index, or you can go directly to the rules themselves if they are published in a separate volume. Many procedural rules have been interpreted in court opinions, and you need to research those opinions to understand the rules' requirements fully. If you locate rules in an annotated code, summaries of the decisions will follow the rules, just as they do any other provision of the code. You can update your research with the pocket part and any cumulative or noncumulative supplements accompanying the code.

A couple of caveats about locating rules of procedure are in order. First, understanding the rules can be challenging. As with any other type of research, you may want to locate secondary sources for commentary on the rules and citations to cases interpreting the rules to make sure you understand them. For the Federal Rules of Civil Procedure, two helpful treatises are *Moore's Federal Practice* and Wright & Miller's *Federal Practice and Procedure*. For state procedural rules, a state "deskbook," or handbook containing practical information for lawyers practicing in the jurisdiction, may contain both the text of the rules and helpful commentary on them. If you locate the rules through a secondary source, however, be sure to update your research because the rules can be amended at any time.

Second, virtually all jurisdictions have multiple types and levels of courts, and each of these courts may have its own procedural rules. Therefore, be sure you locate the rules for the appropriate court. Determining which court is the appropriate one may require separate research into the jurisdiction of the courts.

Third, many individual districts, circuits, or divisions of courts have local rules with which you must comply. Local rules cannot conflict with the rules of procedure published with the code, but they may add requirements that do not appear in the rules of procedure. Local rules usually are not published with the code, but you can obtain them from a number of sources, including the court itself, a secondary source such as a practice "deskbook," or a web site or on-line database. To be sure that your work complies with the court's rules, do not neglect any local rules that may add to the requirements spelled out in the rules of procedure.

c. Uniform Laws and Model Acts

Uniform laws and model acts, as explained in Chapter 3, are proposed statutes that can be adopted by legislatures. Technically, they are secondary sources; their provisions do not take on the force of law unless they are adopted by a legislature. If your research project involves

a statute based on a uniform law or model act, however, you may want to research these sources.

Many uniform laws and model acts are published in a multivolume set of books entitled *Uniform Laws Annotated, Master Edition* (ULA). The ULA set is organized like an annotated code. It contains the text of the uniform law or model act and annotations summarizing cases from jurisdictions that have adopted the statute. It also provides commentary that can help you interpret the statute. Chapter 3, on secondary sources, provides a more detailed explanation of how to use the ULA set.

3. SHEPARD'S CITATIONS FOR STATUTES

Chapter 5 discusses Shepard's Citations and how to use this service in conducting case research. Shepard's is also available as a research and updating tool for state and federal statutes. Sheparding statutes is useful in two situations. First, if you do not have access to an annotated code, Shepard's is a useful tool for locating cases interpreting a statute. Second, Shepard's is published more frequently than pocket parts and supplementary pamphlets are, so you may find more recent research references in Shepard's. Because Shepard's for statutes uses only letter codes to provide information about the cases listed, it does not provide as much information as the case summaries in an annotated code, and many of the cases listed in Shepard's will ultimately be summarized in an annotated code. Therefore, the utility of Sheparding a statute will depend on the type of research you are doing, the number and nature of the research references in the statutory annotations, and the research materials to which you have access.

The process of Sheparding statutes is the same as that for Sheparding cases: (1) locate the correct set of books; (2) locate the correct volumes within the set; (3) locate the entries for the statute within each volume; and (4) interpret the entries.

(1) LOCATE THE CORRECT SET OF BOOKS. *Shepard's Federal Statute Citations* contains references to federal statutes. For state statutes, the set of Shepard's for each individual state usually contains either a section or a separate volume covering state statutes.

(2) LOCATE THE CORRECT VOLUMES WITHIN THE SET. The section labeled "What Your Library Should Contain" will list the volumes to which you should refer to Shepardize the statute.

(3) LOCATE ENTRIES FOR THE STATUTE WITHIN EACH VOLUME. Shepard's for statutes will be organized the same way the code is organized. For example, *Shepard's Federal Statute Citations* is organized according to Title and section; Shepard's for state codes organized by subject matter

will generally be organized alphabetically by subject and then numerically by section within each subject.

Remember that you must look up the statute in each statutory Shepard's volume listed under "What Your Library Should Contain " to Shepardize the statute thoroughly.

(4) INTERPRET THE ENTRIES. Shepard's entries for statutes can be divided into three components: entries reflecting action taken on the statute by the legislature, references to cases citing the statute, and references to secondary sources discussing the statute. As with Shepard's for cases, the entries may be preceded by letter codes. A complete list of letter codes can be found at the beginning of each volume of Shepard's covering statutes.

In the first category of entries, you will see references to legislation affecting the statute. Each entry in this category will be accompanied by a letter code indicating the type of action taken. For example, if a federal statute has been amended, Shepard's will list the *Statutes at Large* citation for the law effecting the change, along with the letter "A" for amended. The example in **Figure 6.11** shows how the entry appears in Shepard's.

In the second category, you will see references to cases that have cited the statute. Cases that have given significant treatment to the statute will be accompanied by treatment codes. In **Figure 6.11,** the statute was held constitutional; accordingly, the reference to that decision is accompanied by the treatment code "C" for constitutional.

The third category of information available in Shepard's for statutes is citations to secondary sources discussing the statute. An example of a reference to A.L.R. Fed. is noted in **Figure 6.11.**

C. RESEARCHING STATUTES ELECTRONICALLY

Much statutory material is available electronically. The federal code, all fifty state codes, the District of Columbia code, and a variety of other statutory materials are all available in electronic format. This section discusses search options for researching statutes using Westlaw, LexisNexis, and Internet sources.

Regardless of which source you choose for conducting electronic statutory research, bear in mind the fact that statutory analysis often requires application of interrelated code provisions. Rarely will an individual code section viewed in isolation resolve your research question. More often you will need to research an entire statutory scheme encompassing multiple code sections. For example, assume you retrieved a code provision applicable to your research issue but failed to retrieve a nearby section containing definitions of terms used in the applicable

FIGURE 6.11 SHEPARD'S® ENTRY FOR A STATUTE

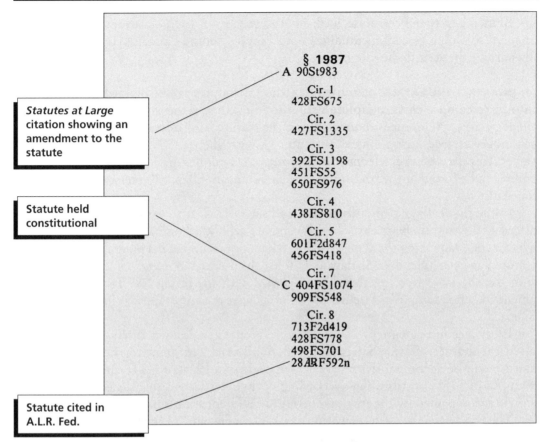

Reproduced by permission of LexisNexis. Further reproduction of any kind is strictly prohibited. From *Shepard's Federal Statute Citations*, Vol. 3, 1996, p. 240.

provision. If you relied only on the one section your initial search revealed, your research would not be accurate. In print, it is fairly easy to turn the page to see preceding and subsequent code sections. Because electronic sources often retrieve individual code sections as separate documents, it is easy to lose sight of the need to research multiple sections. When you use electronic sources for statutory research, therefore, be sure to view the entire statutory scheme to ensure that you consider all potentially applicable code sections.

1. WESTLAW

Westlaw contains annotated versions of many codes, including the federal code, all fifty state codes, and the District of Columbia code. The annotated version of the federal code in Westlaw is derived from

U.S.C.A., although U.S.C. is also available. For most jurisdictions, you will find court rules of procedure included with the code, and for some you will find local court rules as well.

The display for an individual code section begins with a heading containing, among other things, the citation for the section. The text of the statute then appears, followed by annotations like those in a print code. When you retrieve an individual code section, you have several options for viewing the complete statutory outline. You can view the table of contents for the statutory chapter and the entire code by clicking on the Table of Contents link on the left hand menu. By clicking on the links in the table of contents display, you can view the surrounding statutory material. You can also browse preceding or subsequent code sections using the Documents in Sequence function. To access that function, click on the Tools link in the lower right corner and select the option for Documents in Sequence. **Figure 6.12** shows how a federal statute appears in Westlaw.

Statutory materials in Westlaw are usually up-to-date. A notation in each document will tell you the date through which it is updated. In addition, Westlaw's KeyCite service is available for both state and federal statutes.

FIGURE 6.12   THREE SCREENS SHOWING PORTIONS OF 8 U.S.C.A. § 1431 IN WESTLAW

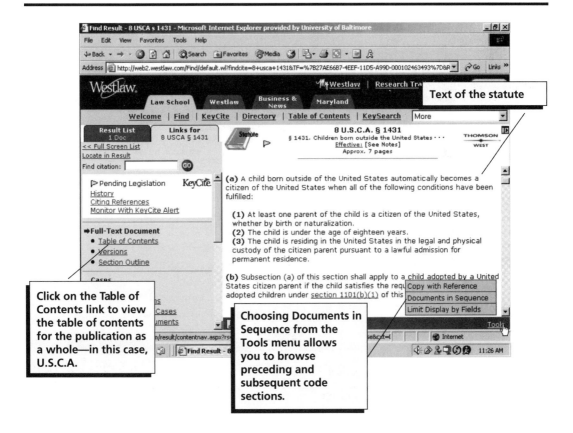

FIGURE 6.12 **THREE SCREENS SHOWING PORTIONS OF 8 U.S.C.A. § 1431 IN WESTLAW**
(Continued)

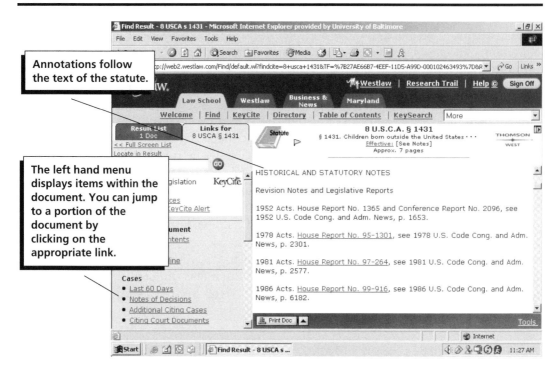

Annotations follow the text of the statute.

The left hand menu displays items within the document. You can jump to a portion of the document by clicking on the appropriate link.

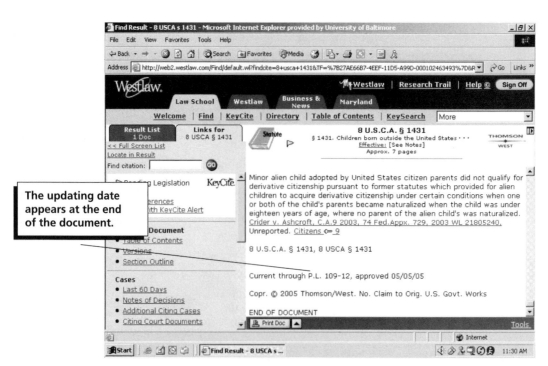

The updating date appears at the end of the document.

Reprinted with permission from Thomson West, from Westlaw, 8 U.S.C.A. § 1431. © 2005 Thomson West.

To conduct statutory research in Westlaw, the first step is selecting the statutory database you want to search. If you know the name of the database, you can enter it in the box under "Search these databases" on the Westlaw Welcome screen. If you do not know the name of the database, you can select an option from those listed on the Welcome screen. You can select from a wider range of database options by clicking on the Directory or Table of Contents link at the top of the screen and drilling down through the menu options until you locate the database you want to search. Once you have selected a database, Westlaw provides up to six search options, depending on the code you select. These are listed across the top of the screen: Standard Search, which is a word search; Find by Citation; Table of Contents; Statutes Index; Popular Name Table; 50 State Surveys. **Figure 6.13** shows the Westlaw Table of Contents search screen and the search options available for researching U.S.C.A.

Standard, or word, searching involves searching through the database for documents containing words you select. Word searching is discussed in more detail in Chapter 10, on electronic research. Note that a word search in a database containing an annotated code will search both the statutory language and the annotations. Thus, it will retrieve documents when the search terms appear in the annotations, such as in a case summary, even if they do not appear in the statutory language. Word searching is useful when you are searching for unique terms that are not likely to be included in the statutory index or table of contents.

FIGURE 6.13   WESTLAW U.S.C.A. TABLE OF CONTENTS SEARCH SCREEN

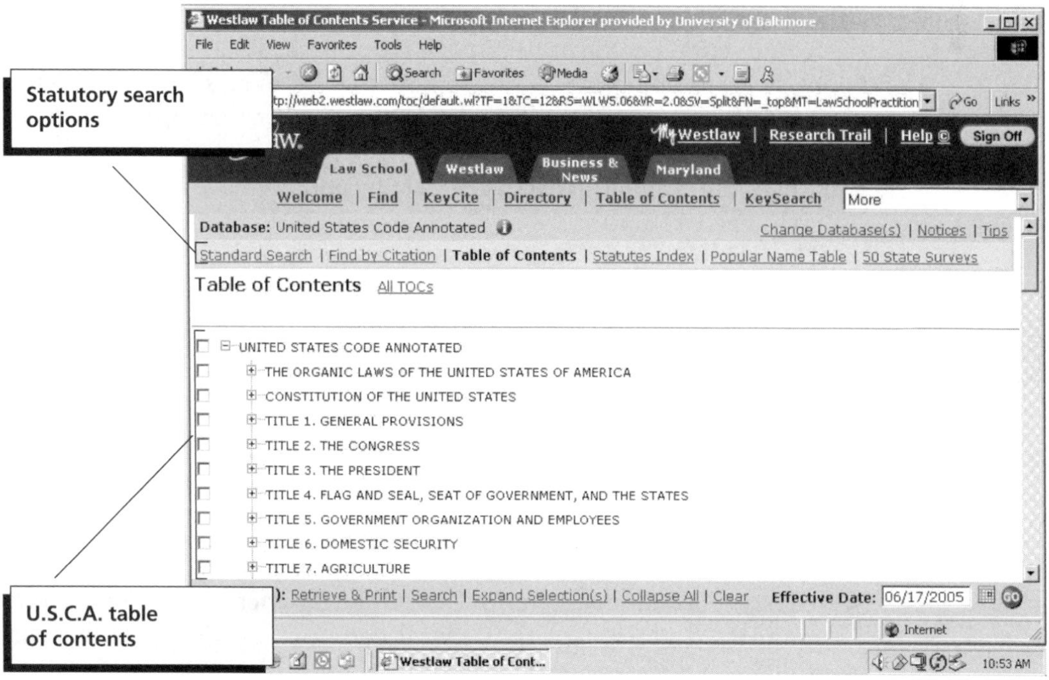

Reprinted with permission from Thomson West, from Westlaw, U.S.C.A. Table of Contents search screen. © 2005 Thomson West.

The second option, Find by Citation, involves retrieving a code section when you know its citation. Clicking on this option brings up a list of templates you can use to retrieve statutory citations. You can also retrieve a statute from its citation by clicking on the Find link at the top of the screen.

The Table of Contents option allows you to browse a code's table of contents. The table of contents will be organized by Title or subject. You can drill down from the main Title or subject headings to chapters and individual code sections. You can retrieve an individual code section by clicking on the link to it. You can also execute a word search within selected portions of the code by checking the box in the table of contents next to each item you want to search. Table of Contents searching is a good option when you are familiar enough with the code to know which subject areas are likely to contain relevant statutes but do not have specific statutory citations. It is also an excellent feature for viewing an entire statutory scheme.

The Statutes Index allows you to search the code's subject index just as you would if you were researching in print. Westlaw's statutory indices are identical to the print indices, although West reports that the electronic versions are updated more frequently than the print versions are. The index entries will refer you to statutory provisions the same way a print index would. This is a good research option when you want to search by subject because the index is organized around concepts instead of individual terms in a document and contains cross-references to related terms and concepts. Word searches, by contrast, will search only for the precise terms you specify.

The Popular Name Table lists laws by their popular names. It is the electronic version of the print popular name table. Choosing the Popular Name Table option brings up an alphabetical list of acts by their popular names. Clicking on the link to an act's popular name will retrieve an entry listing the Title(s) and section(s) where the act is codified. When you know the popular name of a statute but do not have its citation, this is a good research option.

The option for 50 State Surveys accesses a database that West describes as containing "a variety of topical surveys providing references to applicable state laws." It consists mostly of secondary material describing state law on a variety of topics and providing citations to state statutory provisions. It may be useful when you are researching the law of multiple jurisdictions.

2. LexisNexis

LexisNexis also contains annotated versions of many codes, including the federal code, all fifty state codes, and the District of Columbia code. The annotated version of the federal code in LexisNexis is derived from U.S.C.S. For most jurisdictions, you will find court rules of

procedure included with the code, and for some you will find local court rules as well.

The display for an individual code section begins with a heading containing, among other things, the citation for the section. The text of the statute then appears, followed by annotations like those in a print code. When you retrieve an individual code section, you have several options for viewing the complete statutory outline. You can view the table of contents for the statutory chapter and the entire code by clicking on the TOC link in the top left corner of the screen. By clicking on the links in the table of contents display, you can view the surrounding statutory material. You can also browse preceding or subsequent code sections using the Book Browse function. **Figure 6.14** shows how a federal statute appears in LexisNexis.

Statutory materials in LexisNexis are usually up-to-date. A notation at the beginning of each document will tell you the date through which it is updated. In addition, you can Shepardize both state and federal statutes in LexisNexis.

LexisNexis offers several statutory research options, including citation, word, table of contents, and popular name searching. You can retrieve a statute from its citation using the Get A Document function. This is the easiest way to locate a statute when you know its citation.

FIGURE 6.14   THREE SCREENS SHOWING PORTIONS OF 8 U.S.C.S. § 1431 IN LEXISNEXIS

FIGURE 6.14   **THREE SCREENS SHOWING PORTIONS OF 8 U.S.C.S. § 1431 IN LEXISNEXIS**
(Continued)

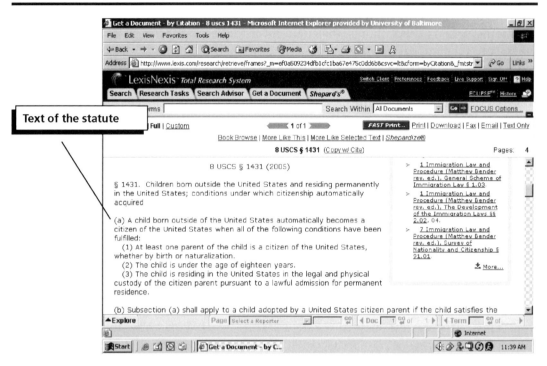

Text of the statute

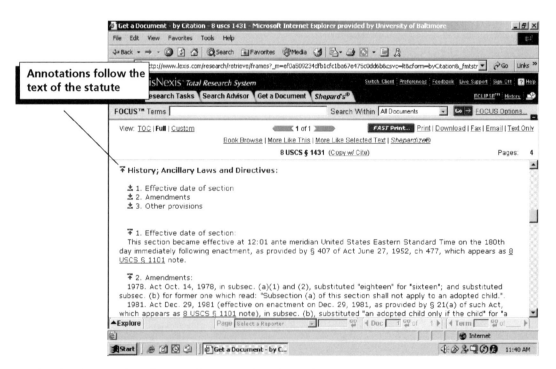

Annotations follow the text of the statute

Reprinted with permission of LexisNexis. From LexisNexis, 8 U.S.C.S. § 1431.

For word or table of contents searches, the first step is selecting a database, which LexisNexis calls a Source, in which to search. A list of Sources appears under the Search tab, Sources option. You can select one of the Sources listed or choose a general category of authority to view additional Source options. Once you have selected a statutory Source, the search screen will give you the option of executing a word search or browsing the table of contents. If you execute a word search in an annotated code, LexisNexis will look for your search terms in both the statutory language and in any annotations.

To browse the table of contents, you can drill down through the main Title or subject headings to individual code sections. You can also restrict your word search to individual Titles, chapters, or sections of the code by checking the box next to each part of the code you want to search. Again, word searching is useful if you are searching for specific statutory terms, and browsing the table of contents is useful for viewing an entire statutory scheme. The table of contents also provides a mechanism for searching statutory subject categories because LexisNexis does not offer index searching as of this writing. **Figure 6.15** shows the search screen for searching U.S.C.S.

You can also search the U.S.C.S. Popular Name Table to locate federal statutes by name. As of this writing, you can access the popular name table by following this path: Federal Legal—U.S., United States Code Service (USCS) Materials, USCS—Popular Name Table. Once

FIGURE 6.15 LEXISNEXIS U.S.C.S. SEARCH SCREEN

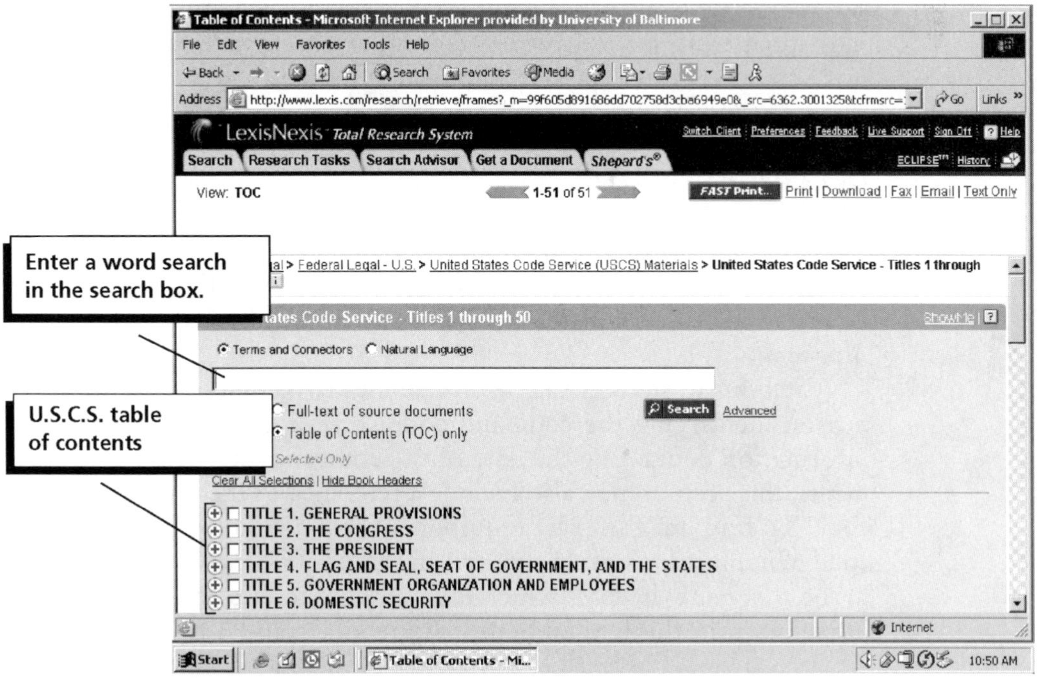

Reprinted with permission of LexisNexis. From LexisNexis, U.S.C.S. search screen.

you select this Source, you can execute a word search for the name of an act or browse the alphabetical list. Clicking on the link to an act's popular name will retrieve an entry listing the Title(s) and section(s) where the act is codified. LexisNexis does not allow you to browse state statutes by popular name. If you need to find a state statute by name, you can use the popular name as a word search to locate the act.

3. INTERNET SOURCES

The federal code, all fifty state codes, and the District of Columbia code are available on the Internet. You can locate them through government web sites, such as the web site for the House of Representatives, or general legal research web sites. Often these sites have search functions that will allow you to retrieve statutes using word, subject, or table of contents searches. Appendix A lists the Internet addresses for web sites that may be useful for statutory research. In addition, court rules of procedure, including local court rules, are often available on court web sites. If the code or rules of procedure you need to research are available and up to date on the Internet, this can be an economical alternative to LexisNexis and Westlaw research.

Three caveats, however, are important to mention. First, the codes available on the Internet are usually unannotated codes, so you will only find the statutory text, not any additional research references. Second, it is important to check the date of any statutory material you use. If the material is not up to date, you will need to update your research. Third, statutory research often requires analysis of a complete statutory scheme. As with any other statutory research, you should not rely on an individual code section retrieved from a search without conducting more comprehensive research into related statutes.

D. CITING STATUTES

The citation format for statutes is the same using either the *ALWD Manual* or the *Bluebook*. The general rules for citing statutes can be found in Rule 14 in the *ALWD Manual* and Bluepages B6 in the *Bluebook*.

Citations to statutes can be broken into two components: (a) information identifying the code and code section; and (b) parenthetical information containing the date of the code and any relevant supplements; this section may also include a reference to the publisher of the code. To find out the exact requirements for a citation to a particular code, you must look at Appendix 1 in the *ALWD Manual* or Table T.1 in the *Bluebook*, both of which tell you how to cite codes from every jurisdiction in the United States. Appendix 1 and Table T.1 include

information on which code to cite if more than one is published, how to abbreviate the name of the code, and whether the name of the publisher must be included with the date in the parenthetical.

In a citation to a Title code, you will ordinarily give the Title number, the abbreviated name of the code, the section symbol, the section number, and a parenthetical containing the date the book was published and, if necessary, the publisher.

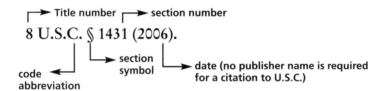

In a citation to a subject-matter code, you will ordinarily list the abbreviated name of the code, the section symbol, the section number, and a parenthetical containing the date the book was published and, if necessary, the publisher.

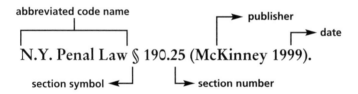

In this example, Appendix 1 and Table T.1 provide that citations to McKinney's *Consolidated Laws of New York Annotated* must include the name of the publisher in the parenthetical, which is why you see the reference to McKinney in this citation. In both examples, note that there is a space between the section symbol (§) and the section number.

Sometimes determining which date or dates to include in the parenthetical can be confusing. The answer is always a function of where a reader would have to look to find the full and up-to-date language of the statute. If the full statute is contained in the main volume of the code, the date in the parenthetical should refer only to the main volume. If the full statute is contained only in the pocket part, the date should refer only to the pocket part. If the reader must refer both to the main volume and to the pocket part, the parenthetical should list both dates. In making this determination, you should consider *only* the language of the statute itself, not the annotations. If the full text of the statute itself is in the main volume, you do not need to cite the pocket part even if it contains additional annotations. Once you have determined which date to place in the parenthetical, you should then refer to Appendix 1 or Table T.1 to determine whether the publisher must also be included. The following are

examples of citations with different date information included in the parenthetical.

N.Y. Penal Law § 190.05 (McKinney 1999).

In this example, Appendix 1 and Table T.1 require the name of the publisher, and the full text of the statute can be found in the main volume.

N.Y. Penal Law § 190.05 (McKinney Supp. 2006).

In this example, Appendix 1 and Table T.1 require the name of the publisher, and the full text of the statute can be found in the pocket part.

N.Y. Penal Law § 190.05 (McKinney 1999 & Supp. 2006).

In this example, Appendix 1 and Table T.1 require the name of the publisher, and the reader must refer both to the main volume and to the pocket part to find the full text of the statute.

In citations to a code for which no publisher is required, the only difference would be the omission of the publisher's name, as in the example below.

Haw. Rev. Stat. § 328-1 (1993).

When you look at the entries in Table T.1 of the *Bluebook*, you will notice that the names of the codes are in large and small capital letters, e.g., N.Y. PENAL LAW § 190.05 (McKinney 1999). Remember that this is the type style for law review footnotes, not for briefs and memoranda. According to Bluepages B13, large and small capitals are never used in briefs and memoranda. Therefore, in briefs and memoranda, you should use regular type when citing statutes. You should not use all capital letters, nor should you use large and small capital letters, even if you have the capability of printing in that font.

E. SAMPLE PAGES FOR PRINT STATUTORY RESEARCH

Beginning on the next page, **Figures 6.16** through **6.21** contain sample pages from U.S.C.A. showing the research process if you were researching federal statutes concerning the citizenship of a child born outside the United States. **Figures 6.22** through **6.24** contain sample pages from Vernon's *Texas Statutes and Codes Annotated* showing the research process if you were researching Texas statutes concerning assumption of the risk.

The first step in U.S.C.A. research is using the most recent General Index to locate relevant code sections. This example shows what you would find if you looked under "Citizens and Citizenship."

FIGURE 6.16   EXCERPT FROM U.S.C.A. GENERAL INDEX

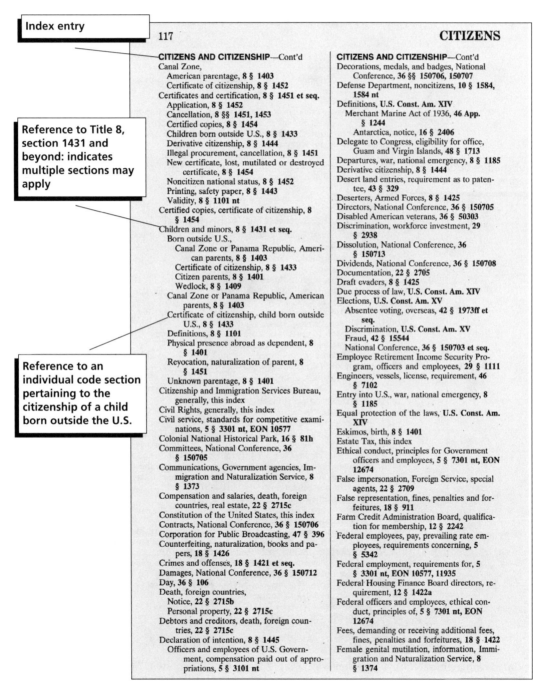

Index entry

Reference to Title 8, section 1431 and beyond: indicates multiple sections may apply

Reference to an individual code section pertaining to the citizenship of a child born outside the U.S.

117

CITIZENS AND CITIZENSHIP—Cont'd
Canal Zone,
  American parentage, **8 § 1403**
  Certificate of citizenship, **8 § 1452**
Certificates and certification, **8 § 1451 et seq.**
  Application, **8 § 1452**
  Cancellation, **8 §§ 1451, 1453**
  Certified copies, **8 § 1454**
  Children born outside U.S., **8 § 1433**
  Derivative citizenship, **8 § 1444**
  Illegal procurement, cancellation, **8 § 1451**
  New certificate, lost, mutilated or destroyed certificate, **8 § 1454**
  Noncitizen national status, **8 § 1452**
  Printing, safety paper, **8 § 1443**
  Validity, **8 § 1101 nt**
Certified copies, certificate of citizenship, 8 § 1454
Children and minors, **8 § 1431 et seq.**
  Born outside U.S.,
    Canal Zone or Panama Republic, American parents, **8 § 1403**
    Certificate of citizenship, **8 § 1433**
    Citizen parents, **8 § 1401**
    Wedlock, **8 § 1409**
  Canal Zone or Panama Republic, American parents, **8 § 1403**
  Certificate of citizenship, child born outside U.S., **8 § 1433**
  Definitions, **8 § 1101**
  Physical presence abroad as dependent, **8 § 1401**
  Revocation, naturalization of parent, **8 § 1451**
  Unknown parentage, **8 § 1401**
Citizenship and Immigration Services Bureau, generally, this index
Civil Rights, generally, this index
Civil service, standards for competitive examinations, **5 § 3301 nt, EON 10577**
Colonial National Historical Park, **16 § 81h**
Committees, National Conference, **36 § 150705**
Communications, Government agencies, Immigration and Naturalization Service, **8 § 1373**
Compensation and salaries, death, foreign countries, real estate, **22 § 2715c**
Constitution of the United States, this index
Contracts, National Conference, **36 § 150706**
Corporation for Public Broadcasting, **47 § 396**
Counterfeiting, naturalization, books and papers, **18 § 1426**
Crimes and offenses, **18 § 1421 et seq.**
Damages, National Conference, **36 § 150712**
Day, **36 § 106**
Death, foreign countries,
  Notice, **22 § 2715b**
  Personal property, **22 § 2715c**
Debtors and creditors, death, foreign countries, **22 § 2715c**
Declaration of intention, **8 § 1445**
  Officers and employees of U.S. Government, compensation paid out of appropriations, **5 § 3101 nt**

CITIZENS

CITIZENS AND CITIZENSHIP—Cont'd
Decorations, medals, and badges, National Conference, **36 §§ 150706, 150707**
Defense Department, noncitizens, **10 § 1584, 1584 nt**
Definitions, **U.S. Const. Am. XIV**
  Merchant Marine Act of 1936, **46 App. § 1244**
  Antarctica, notice, **16 § 2406**
Delegate to Congress, eligibility for office, Guam and Virgin Islands, **48 § 1713**
Departures, war, national emergency, **8 § 1185**
Derivative citizenship, **8 § 1444**
Desert land entries, requirement as to patentee, **43 § 329**
Deserters, Armed Forces, **8 § 1425**
Directors, National Conference, **36 § 150705**
Disabled American veterans, **36 § 50303**
Discrimination, workforce investment, **29 § 2938**
Dissolution, National Conference, **36 § 150713**
Dividends, National Conference, **36 § 150708**
Documentation, **22 § 2705**
Draft evaders, **8 § 1425**
Due process of law, **U.S. Const. Am. XIV**
Elections, **U.S. Const. Am. XV**
  Absentee voting, overseas, **42 § 1973ff et seq.**
  Discrimination, **U.S. Const. Am. XV**
  Fraud, **42 § 15544**
  National Conference, **36 § 150703 et seq.**
Employee Retirement Income Security Program, officers and employees, **29 § 1111**
Engineers, vessels, license, requirement, **46 § 7102**
Entry into U.S., war, national emergency, **8 § 1185**
Equal protection of the laws, **U.S. Const. Am. XIV**
Eskimos, birth, **8 § 1401**
Estate Tax, this index
Ethical conduct, principles for Government officers and employees, **5 § 7301 nt, EON 12674**
False impersonation, Foreign Service, special agents, **22 § 2709**
False representation, fines, penalties and forfeitures, **18 § 911**
Farm Credit Administration Board, qualification for membership, **12 § 2242**
Federal employees, pay, prevailing rate employees, requirements concerning, **5 § 5342**
Federal employment, requirements for, **5 § 3301 nt, EON 10577, 11935**
Federal Housing Finance Board directors, requirement, **12 § 1422a**
Federal officers and employees, ethical conduct, principles of, **5 § 7301 nt, EON 12674**
Fees, demanding or receiving additional fees, fines, penalties and forfeitures, **18 § 1422**
Female genital mutilation, information, Immigration and Naturalization Service, **8 § 1374**

The next step is looking up the statute in the main volume. Because the index indicates that several code provisions may be applicable, you might want to review the chapter outline.

FIGURE 6.17 EXCERPT FROM CHAPTER OUTLINE, TITLE 8, U.S.C.A.

Ch. 12   IMMIGRATION AND NATIONALITY

Sec.
1369. Treatment of expenses subject to emergency medical services exception.
1370. Reimbursement of States and localities for emergency ambulance services.
1371. Reports.
1372. Program to collect information relating to nonimmigrant foreign students and other exchange program participants.
1373. Communication between Government agencies and the Immigration and Naturalization Service.
1374. Information regarding female genital mutilation.
1375. Mail-order bride business.
1376. Data on nonimmigrant overstay rates.
1377. Collection of data on detained asylum seekers.
1378. Collection of data on other detained aliens.

Subchapter outline begins here.

SUBCHAPTER III—NATIONALITY AND NATURALIZATION
Part I—Nationality at Birth and Collective Naturalization
1401. Nationals and citizens of United States at birth.
1401a. Birth abroad before 1952 to service parent.
1401b. Repealed.
1402. Persons born in Puerto Rico on or after April 11, 1899.
1403. Persons born in the Canal Zone or Republic of Panama on or after February 26, 1904.
1404. Persons born in Alaska on or after March 30, 1867.
1405. Persons born in Hawaii.
1406. Persons living in and born in the Virgin Islands.
1407. Persons living in and born in Guam.
1408. Nationals but not citizens of the United States at birth.
1409. Children born out of wedlock.

Part II—Nationality Through Naturalization
1421. Naturalization authority.
1422. Eligibility for naturalization.
1423. Requirements as to understanding the English language, history, principles and form of government of the United States.
1424. Prohibition upon the naturalization of persons opposed to government or law, or who favor totalitarian forms of government.
1425. Ineligibility to naturalization of deserters from the Armed Forces.
1426. Citizenship denied alien relieved of service in Armed Forces because of alienage.
1427. Requirements of naturalization.
1428. Temporary absence of persons performing religious duties.
1429. Prerequisite to naturalization; burden of proof.
1430. Married persons and employees of certain nonprofit organizations.
1431. Children born outside United States of one alien and one citizen parent; conditions for automatic citizenship.
1432. Children born outside of United States of alien parents; conditions for automatic citizenship.
1433. Child born outside United States; application for certificate of citizenship requirements.
1434. Repealed.
1435. Former citizens regaining citizenship.

5

Reprinted with permission from Thomson West, *United States Code Annotated*, Title 8 (1999) p. 5. © 1999 Thomson West.

The individual code section sets out conditions for automatic citizenship.

FIGURE 6.18 8 U.S.C.A. § 1431

---

8 § 1430
Note 30

ALIENS AND NATIONALITY Ch. 12

chapter 11 of this title at time he applied for citizenship, notwithstanding letter written by alien to Bureau of Internal Revenue involving controversy concerning income tax in which he mentioned abandoning his residence. Petition of Herschmann, C.C.A.7 (Ill.) 1947, 163 F.2d 865.

In a proceeding to obtain naturalization on ground of marriage to a United States citizen, applicant must establish validity of marriage by satisfactory evidence, notwithstanding statute to effect that legality of a regularly solemnized marriage is presumed and burden of proof is upon him who seeks to attack such marriage. Petition of Lujan, D.C.Guam 1956, 144 F.Supp. 150.

Where petitioners for naturalization, although entitled to a presumption of lawful entry for purpose of permanent residence because of entry into Virgin Islands before July 1, 1938, notwithstanding that there was no record made of entry, later received certificates of arrival, which were required to be attached to petitions for naturalization, on basis of re-entries which were made less than requisite period before filing petitions,

petitions were denied for want of proof of lawful entry a sufficient time prior to the filing thereof, since the presumption was unavailable for naturalization purposes. In re Simmiolkjier, D.C.Virgin Islands 1947, 71 F.Supp. 553.

An applicant for naturalization must show by satisfactory evidence that he has the specified qualifications. Petition of Sam Hoo, N.D.Cal.1945, 63 F.Supp. 439.

Mere proof of ceremonial marriage to American citizen by one previously married in China and affidavits concerning deaths of prior wives and renunciation of marriage to applicant by one of them and remarriage of such prior wife were insufficient to show valid marriage to American citizen so as to entitle applicant to naturalization. Petition of Sam Hoo, N.D.Cal.1945, 63 F.Supp. 439.

31. Collateral attack

Proceedings on petition for naturalization of alien whose naturalization depended upon wife's citizenship would not be used as basis for collateral attack on wife's citizenship. Petition of Pellegrini, S.D.N.Y.1954, 126 F.Supp. 742.

[annotation: Name of the section]

[annotation: Section number]

§ 1431. **Children born outside United States of one alien and one citizen parent; conditions for automatic citizenship**

(a) A child born outside of the United States, one of whose parents at the time of the child's birth was an alien and the other of whose parents then was and never thereafter ceased to be a citizen of the United States, shall, if such alien parent is naturalized, become a citizen of the United States, when—

(1) such naturalization takes place while such child is under the age of eighteen years; and

(2) such child is residing in the United States pursuant to a lawful admission for permanent residence at the time of naturalization or thereafter and begins to reside permanently in the United States while under the age of eighteen years.

(b) Subsection (a) of this section shall apply to an adopted child only if the child is residing in the United States at the time of naturalization of such adoptive parent, in the custody of his adoptive parents, pursuant to a lawful admission for permanent residence.

[annotation: Text of the statute]

(June 27, 1952, c. 477, Title III, ch. 2, § 320, 66 Stat. 245; Oct. 5, 1978, Pub.L. 95–417, § 4, 92 Stat. 917; Dec. 29, 1981, Pub.L. 97–116, § 18(m), 95 Stat. 1620; Nov. 14, 1986, Pub.L. 99–653, § 14, 100 Stat. 3657; Oct. 24, 1988, Pub.L. 100–525, §§ 8(*l*), 9(w), 102 Stat. 2618, 2621.)

326

Reprinted with permission from Thomson West, *United States Code Annotated*, Title 8 (1999), p. 326. © 1999 Thomson West.

The annotations list a variety of research references.

FIGURE 6.19   ANNOTATIONS ACCOMPANYING 8 U.S.C.A. § 1431

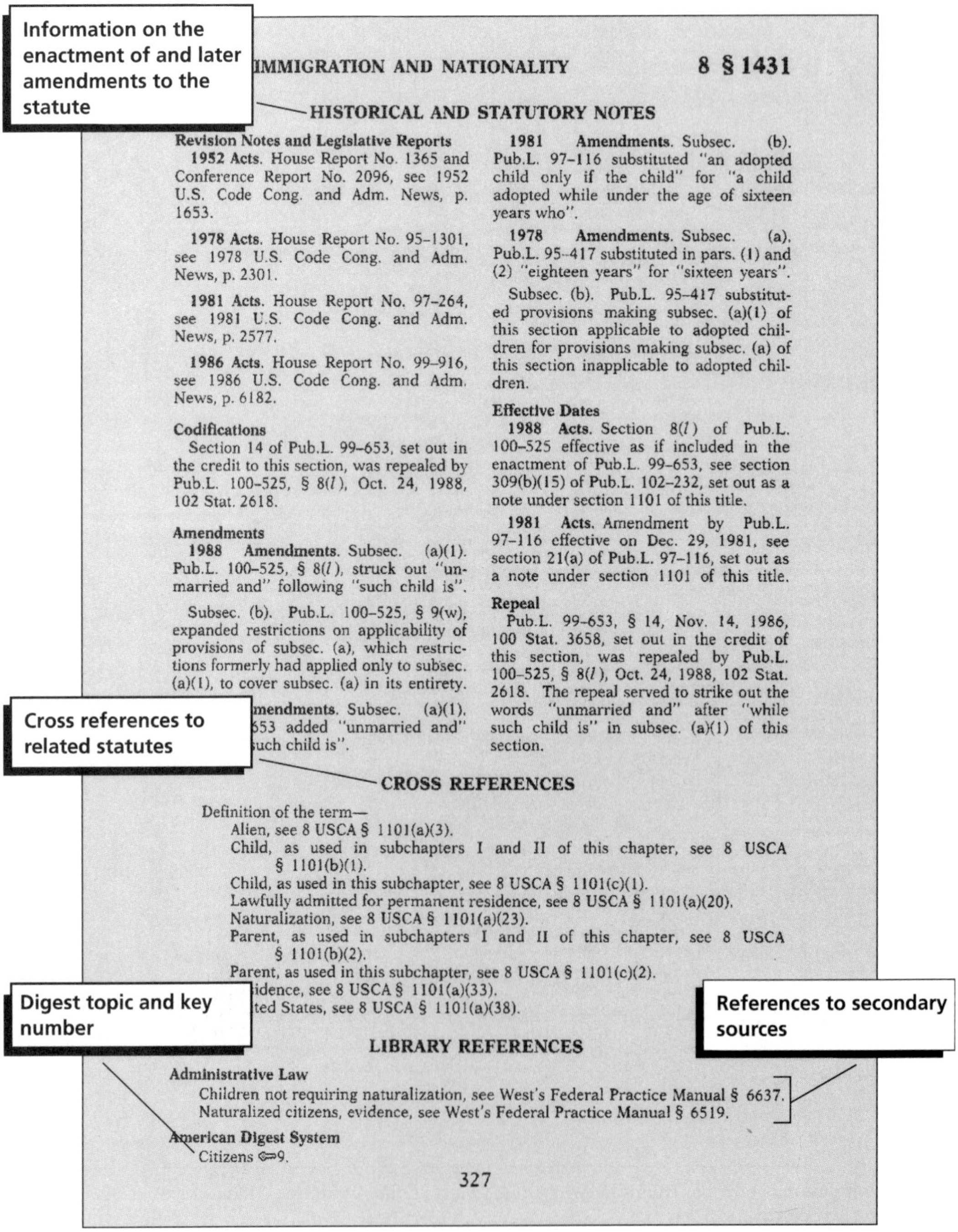

Information on the enactment of and later amendments to the statute

IMMIGRATION AND NATIONALITY   8 § 1431

HISTORICAL AND STATUTORY NOTES

Revision Notes and Legislative Reports
1952 Acts. House Report No. 1365 and Conference Report No. 2096, see 1952 U.S. Code Cong. and Adm. News, p. 1653.

1978 Acts. House Report No. 95-1301, see 1978 U.S. Code Cong. and Adm. News, p. 2301.

1981 Acts. House Report No. 97-264, see 1981 U.S. Code Cong. and Adm. News, p. 2577.

1986 Acts. House Report No. 99-916, see 1986 U.S. Code Cong. and Adm. News, p. 6182.

Codifications
Section 14 of Pub.L. 99-653, set out in the credit to this section, was repealed by Pub.L. 100-525, § 8(*l*), Oct. 24, 1988, 102 Stat. 2618.

Amendments
1988 Amendments. Subsec. (a)(1). Pub.L. 100-525, § 8(*l*), struck out "unmarried and" following "such child is".

Subsec. (b). Pub.L. 100-525, § 9(w), expanded restrictions on applicability of provisions of subsec. (a), which restrictions formerly had applied only to subsec. (a)(1), to cover subsec. (a) in its entirety.

mendments. Subsec. (a)(1). 653 added "unmarried and" uch child is".

1981 Amendments. Subsec. (b). Pub.L. 97-116 substituted "an adopted child only if the child" for "a child adopted while under the age of sixteen years who".

1978 Amendments. Subsec. (a). Pub.L. 95-417 substituted in pars. (1) and (2) "eighteen years" for "sixteen years".

Subsec. (b). Pub.L. 95-417 substituted provisions making subsec. (a)(1) of this section applicable to adopted children for provisions making subsec. (a) of this section inapplicable to adopted children.

Effective Dates
1988 Acts. Section 8(*l*) of Pub.L. 100-525 effective as if included in the enactment of Pub.L. 99-653, see section 309(b)(15) of Pub.L. 102-232, set out as a note under section 1101 of this title.

1981 Acts. Amendment by Pub.L. 97-116 effective on Dec. 29, 1981, see section 21(a) of Pub.L. 97-116, set out as a note under section 1101 of this title.

Repeal
Pub.L. 99-653, § 14, Nov. 14, 1986, 100 Stat. 3658, set out in the credit of this section, was repealed by Pub.L. 100-525, § 8(*l*), Oct. 24, 1988, 102 Stat. 2618. The repeal served to strike out the words "unmarried and" after "while such child is" in subsec. (a)(1) of this section.

Cross references to related statutes

CROSS REFERENCES

Definition of the term—
Alien, see 8 USCA § 1101(a)(3).
Child, as used in subchapters I and II of this chapter, see 8 USCA § 1101(b)(1).
Child, as used in this subchapter, see 8 USCA § 1101(c)(1).
Lawfully admitted for permanent residence, see 8 USCA § 1101(a)(20).
Naturalization, see 8 USCA § 1101(a)(23).
Parent, as used in subchapters I and II of this chapter, see 8 USCA § 1101(b)(2).
Parent, as used in this subchapter, see 8 USCA § 1101(c)(2).
idence, see 8 USCA § 1101(a)(33).
ted States, see 8 USCA § 1101(a)(38).

Digest topic and key number

References to secondary sources

LIBRARY REFERENCES

Administrative Law
Children not requiring naturalization, see West's Federal Practice Manual § 6637.
Naturalized citizens, evidence, see West's Federal Practice Manual § 6519.

American Digest System
Citizens ⊂⇒9.

327

FIGURE 6.19 ANNOTATIONS ACCOMPANYING 8 U.S.C.A. § 1431 *(Continued)*

8 § 1431 ALIENS AND NATIONALITY Ch. 12

Encyclopedias
C.J.S. Citizens § 7 et seq.
3A Am Jur 2d, Aliens and Citizens §§ 1553–1557.

> **References to sections in legal encyclopedias**

WESTLAW ELECTRONIC RESEARCH

WESTLAW guide following the Explanation pages of this volume.

> **Summary of a case interpreting the statute**

Notes of Decisions

Admissibility, evidence 7
Depositions, evidence 8
Due process 2
Evidence 7-10
   Admissibility 7
   Depositions 8
   Objections 9
   Sufficiency of evidence 10
Objections, evidence 9
Presumptions 6
Prior law 1
Reacquisition by parent of foreign citizenship 4
Resumption of parent's American citizenship 5
Sufficiency of evidence 10
Termination of parent's American citizenship 3

> **Subjects discussed in cases interpreting the statute**

or law

...me of a child's birth in Italy in ...R.S. § 1993 pertaining to children ...ut of jurisdiction of the United ...whose fathers might be citizens, provided sole source of inherited citizenship status for foreign-born children of American parents, and such statute did not afford citizenship to the child who had an Italian father, even though child's mother was a native-born United States citizen. Montana v. Kennedy, U.S.Ill. 1961, 81 S.Ct. 1336, 366 U.S. 308, 6 L.Ed.2d 313.

Person who was born in Mexico, his father being citizen of United States and his mother citizen of Mexico, was not a citizen by birth, under § 201(g) of the Nationality Act of 1940, former § 601(g) of this title, where father had not had five years' residence in United States after attaining age of 16 years. Ruiz v. Immigration and Naturalization Service, C.A.6 (Ohio) 1969, 410 F.2d 382.

2. Due process

In proceeding on application for admission to United States by applicants, who were foreign-born Chinese seeking admission into United States as sons of native American citizen father and legally resi-

dent alien mother, giving conclusive weight to blood test evidence by board of special inquiry did not constitute a denial of due process. United States ex rel. Dong Wing Ott v. Shaughnessy, C.A.2 (N.Y.) 1955, 220 F.2d 537, certiorari denied 76 S.Ct. 60, 350 U.S. 847, 100 L.Ed. 754.

Requirement that foreign-born Chinese seeking admission to United States as sons of a native American citizen father and a legally resident alien mother submit to a blood test is justified by lack of reliable written governmental records of birth and parentage, difficulty of access to areas from which claimed family groups come and long absences from family group of citizen father, who is an identifying witness, and that such requirement does not constitute a denial of due process because applied to persons solely of Chinese race. United States ex rel. Dong Wing Ott v. Shaughnessy, C.A.2 (N.Y.) 1955, 220 F.2d 537, certiorari denied 76 S.Ct. 60, 350 U.S. 847, 100 L.Ed. 754.

3. Termination of parent's American citizenship

Mere marriage to an alien, without change of domicile, did not terminate citizenship of an American woman in 1906, even though such woman traveled abroad with her alien husband in 1906. Montana v. Kennedy, U.S.Ill.1961, 81 S.Ct. 1336, 366 U.S. 308, 6 L.Ed.2d 313.

4. Reacquisition by parent of foreign citizenship

One born in Italy after his father, who was Italian citizen by birth, became naturalized American citizen, did not lose his American citizenship on his father's reacquisition of Italian citizenship under Italian nationality law after two years residence in Italy, but became citizen of both nations. Perri v. Dulles, C.A.3 (N.J.) 1953, 206 F.2d 586.

328

The next step is checking the pocket part. The pocket part shows new statutory language that supersedes the language in the main volume. It also shows additional research references.

FIGURE 6.20   POCKET PART ENTRY FOR 8 U.S.C.A. § 1431

ALIENS AND NATIONALITY   **8 § 1431**

Immigration Law Service § 30:104, Regular Employment Abroad.
Immigration Law Service § 30:105, Military Personnel; Proof.
Immigration Law Service § 30:106, Intention to Reside Abroad With Spouse.
Immigration Law Service § 30:107, Effect of Government Restrictions.
Immigration Law Service § 30:108, Residence and Physical Presence Requirements.
Immigration Law Service § 30:109, Other Naturalization Requirements.
Immigration Law Service § 30:110, Basic Requirements; Residence and Physical Presence.
Immigration Law Service § 30:111, Other Requirements.
Immigration Law Service § 30:154, Naturalization Requirements; Proof.
Immigration Law Service § 30:155, Effect of Eligibility Under Other Provisions.
Immigration Law Service § 30:188, Employees of Nonprofit Communications Organizations Residence and Physical Presence Requirements.
Immigration Law Service § 30:189, Other Requirements.
Immigration Law Service § 30:196, Seamen Eligibility.
Immigration Law Service § 30:205, Nationals of United States.
Immigration Law Service § 30:219, When to Apply.
Immigration Law Service § 30:228, Supplementary Information Required of Certain Applicants.
Immigration Law Service § 30:259, Limitation to Persons Residing Within Jurisdiction (Venue).

Immigration Law Service § 36:220, Time as Cr Counts Towards Naturalization.
Immigration Law Service PSD INA § 334, § 334 (8 U.S.C.A. § 1445). Application for Naturalization; Declaration of Intention.
Steel on Immigration Law, 2d § 15:10, Residence Requirements.
Steel on Immigration Law, 2d § 15:11, Special Classes.
U.S. Citizenship and Naturalization Handbook § 6:2, Structure of Ina.
U.S. Citizenship and Naturalization Handbook § 11:1, Overview.
U.S. Citizenship and Naturalization Handbook § 11:2, Overview.
U.S. Citizenship and Naturalization Handbook § 11:3, Requirements.
U.S. Citizenship and Naturalization Handbook § 11:5, in General.
U.S. Citizenship and Naturalization Handbook § 11:6, Requirements.
U.S. Citizenship and Naturalization Handbook § 9:20, Other Bases for Eligibility.
U.S. Citizenship and Naturalization Handbook § 9:59, Jurisdiction to Administer Oath; Generally.
U.S. Citizenship and Naturalization Handbook § 11:10, in General.
U.S. Citizenship and Naturalization Handbook § 11:22, Physical and Legal Custody Requirements.
U.S. Citizenship and Naturalization Handbook § 11:25, in General.
U.S. Citizenship and Naturalization Handbook § 11:26, in General.

Notes of Decisions

9. Continuance of marital relationship

Immigration and Naturalization Service (INS) could not deny a naturalization application based on status as spouse of citizen solely because applicant ceased to reside in marital union with her citizen spouse prior to naturalization but after filing the application; fact that applicant no longer resided with her husband did not change her legal status as "spouse" of a citizen. Ali v. Smith, W.D.Wash.1999, 39 F.Supp.2d 1254. Aliens ⬅ 62(1)

§ 1431. Children born outside the United States and residing permanently in the United States; conditions under which citizenship automatically acquired

(a) A child born outside of the United States automatically becomes a citizen of the United States when all of the following conditions have been fulfilled:

(1) At least one parent of the child is a citizen of the United States, whether by birth or naturalization.

(2) The child is under the age of eighteen years.

(3) The child is residing in the United States in the legal and physical custody of the citizen parent pursuant to a lawful admission for permanent residence.

(b) Subsection (a) of this section shall apply to a child adopted by a United States citizen parent if the child satisfies the requirements applicable to adopted children under section 1101(b)(1) of this title.

(June 27, 1952, c. 477, Title III, ch. 2, § 320, 66 Stat. 245; Oct. 5, 1978, Pub.L. 95–417, § 4, 92 Stat. 917; Dec. 29, 1981, Pub.L. 97–116, § 18(m), 95 Stat. 1620; Nov. 14, 1986, Pub.L. 99–653, § 14, 100 Stat. 3657; Oct. 24, 1988, Pub.L. 100–525, §§ 8(*l*), 9(w), 102 Stat. 2618, 2621; Oct. 30, 2000, Pub.L. 106–395, Title I, § 101(a), 114 Stat. 1631.)

HISTORICAL AND STATUTORY NOTES

Revision Notes and Legislative Reports

2000 Acts. House Report No. 106–852, see 2000 U.S. Code Cong. and Adm. News, p. 1499.

Amendments

2000 Amendments. Pub.L. 106–395, § 101(a), rewrote the section, which formerly read:

47

New statutory language supersedes the language in the main volume.

New annotations follow the text of the statute.

FIGURE 6.20   POCKET PART ENTRY FOR 8 U.S.C.A. § 1431 (Continued)

8 § 1431

ALIENS AND NATIONALITY

"**§ 1431. Children born outside United States of one alien and one citizen parent; conditions for automatic citizenship**

"(a) A child born outside of the United States, one of whose parents at the time of the child's birth was an alien and the other of whose parents then was and never thereafter ceased to be a citizen of the United States, shall, if such alien parent is naturalized, become a citizen of the United States, when—

"(1) such naturalization takes place while such child is under the age of eighteen years; and

"(2) such child is residing in the United States pursuant to a lawful admission for permanent residence at the time of naturalization or thereafter and begins to reside permanently in the United States while under the age of eighteen years.

"(b) Subsection (a) of this section shall apply to an adopted child only if the child is residing in the United States at the time of naturalization of such adoptive parent, in the custody of his adoptive parents, pursuant to a lawful admission for permanent residence."

Effective and Applicability Provisions

2000 Acts. Pub.L. 106–395, Title I, § 104, Oct. 30, 2000, 114 Stat. 1633, provided that: "The amendments made by this title [amending this section and section 1433 of this title and repealing section 1432 of this title] shall take effect 120 days after the date of the enactment of this Act [Oct. 30, 2000] and shall apply to individuals who satisfy the requirements of section 320 or 322 of the Immigration and Nationality Act [this section and section 1433 of this title], on such effective date."

LIBRARY REFERENCES

American Digest System

Citizens ⊜9.
Key Number System Topic No. 77.

Research References

ALR Library

177 ALR, Fed. 459, Illegal Reentry Under § 276 of Immigration and Nationality Act (8 U.S.C.A. § 1326) of Alien Who Has Been Denied Admission, Excluded, Deported, or Removed or Has Departed United States While Order of Exclusion, Deportation.

175 ALR, Fed. 67, Validity, Construction, and Application of 8 U.S.C.A. § 1401(C)-(G), Providing for American Citizenship in Certain Circumstances of Child Born Outside United States, or Found Within United States and of Unknown Parentage.

95 ALR, Fed. 262, Applicability and Effect of Equitable Estoppel Doctrine in Immigration and Naturalization Proceedings.

Encyclopedias

3A Am. Jur. 2d Aliens and Citizens § 8, 1970'S Legislation.

3C Am. Jur. 2d Aliens and Citizens § 2685, Who is a "Child," "Parent," "Father," or "Mother".

3C Am. Jur. 2d Aliens and Citizens § 2877, Definition; Controlling Law; Applicable Rules.

3C Am. Jur. 2d Aliens and Citizens § 2878, "Parent," "Father," "Mother," and "Child" Defined.

3C Am. Jur. 2d Aliens and Citizens § 2879, Permanent Residence Requirement.

3C Am. Jur. 2d Aliens and Citizens § 2880, Where One Parent is Citizen at Child's Birth.

3C Am. Jur. 2d Aliens and Citizens § 2881, Application to Adopted Child.

CJS Aliens § 1821, Automatic Acquisition of Citizenship.

CJS Aliens § 1822, "Parent," "Father," "Mother," and "Child" Defined.

CJS Aliens § 1823, Permanent Residence and Legal Custody Requirements.

CJS Aliens § 1824, One Parent Must be Citizen at Child's Birth.

CJS Aliens § 1825, One Parent Must be Citizen at Child's Birth-Application to Adopted Child.

CJS Aliens § 1828, Eligibility.

Treatises and Practice Aids

Immigration Law and Business § 5:4, Statutory Requirements.

Immigration Law and Defense § 11:9, Special Classes of Applicants-Spouses and Children of Citizens.

Immigration Law and Defense § 7:73, Alienage.

Immigration Law and Defense § 11:17, Derivation of Citizenship by Naturalization of Parent.

Immigration Law and Defense § 11:21, Parent Naturalized on or After December 24, 1952.

Immigration Law and the Family § 6:45, Generally.

Immigration Law and the Family § 15:30, Legitimate Children.

Immigration Law and the Family § 15:31, Adopted Children.

Immigration Law and the Family § 15:32, Naturalization of Children on Application of U.S. Citizen Parent.

Immigration Law and the Family § 15:33, Naturalization of Adults.

Immigration Law Service § 1:9, 1970'S Legislation.

Immigration Law Service § 29:10, Who is a "Child," "Parent," "Father," or "Mother".

Immigration Law Service § 15:401, Treatment of Nationality Claims.

Immigration Law Service § 30:112, Automatic Acquisition of Citizenship.

Immigration Law Service § 30:113, "Parent," "Father," "Mother," and "Child" Defined.

Immigration Law Service § 30:114, Permanent Residence and Legal Custody Requirements.

48

Digest topic and key number

Additional research references

A.L.R. Annotations

Encyclopedia references

FIGURE 6.20   POCKET PART ENTRY FOR 8 U.S.C.A. § 1431 (Continued)

ALIENS AND NATIONALITY

8 § 1431
Note 11

Immigration Law Service § 30:115, One Parent Must be Citizen at Child's Birth.

Immigration Law Service § 30:116, Application to Adopted Child.

Immigration Law Service § 30:116.3, Application Procedures.

Immigration Law Service PSD INA § 101, Section 101 (8 U.S.C.A. § 1101). Definitions.

Immigration Law Service 2d § 1:6, Overview.

Immigration Law Service 2d § 3:71, Family-Sponsored Immigrants.

Steel on Immigration Law, 2d § 1:3, Since 1952.

Steel on Immigration Law, 2d § 15:16, Special Classes-Relatives.

U.S. Citizenship and Naturalization Handbook § 5:2, Automatic Vesting: Lack of Knowledge by Citizen.

U.S. Citizenship and Naturalization Handbook § 5:3, Applicable Law and Common Requirements.

U.S. Citizenship and Naturalization Handbook § 5:4, Children Born Out-Of-Wedlock and Adopted Children.

U.S. Citizenship and Naturalization Handbook § 5:8, Required Residence of Child.

U.S. Citizenship and Naturalization Handbook § 5:11, Last Qualifying Event Between January 13, 1941 and December 23, 1952.

U.S. Citizenship and Naturalization Handbook § 5:12, Last Qualifying Event Between December 24, 1952 and February 26, 2001.

U.S. Citizenship and Naturalization Handbook § 5:13, Last Qualifying Event on or After February 27, 2001 (Or Under 18 Years of Age on 2/27/01).

U.S. Citizenship and Naturalization Handbook App 4-19, Appendix 4-19. Excerpts from Act of November 14, 1986, Pub. L. 99-653, 100 Stat. 3655.

U.S. Citizenship and Naturalization Handbook App 4-27, Appendix 4-27. Child Citizenship Act of 2000, Public Law 106-395, 114 Stat. 1631 (Oct. 30, 2000).

Newer cases interpreting the statute

Notes of Decisions

Children within section   11
Retroactive effect of section   ½

½. Retroactive effect of section

Child Citizenship Act's (CCA) derivative citizenship provision did not operate retrospectively so as to make citizen of adult who, as a child, would have satisfied the CCA's current conditions for derivative naturalization, but did not meet the requirements that were in effect when she was a minor. Drakes v. Ashcroft, C.A.2 2003, 323 F.3d 189. Citizens ⮑ 9

Child Citizenship Act did not operate retroactively to make native of Guatemala born prior to enactment of Act a citizen before he was found in United States, so as to preclude conviction for being found in United States after having been removed as result of conviction for aggravated felony. U.S. v. Arbelo, C.A.11 (Fla.) 2002, 288 F.3d 1262, certiorari denied 123 S.Ct. 256, 537 U.S. 911, 154 L.Ed.2d 192. Aliens ⮑ 56; Citizens ⮑ 9

Child Citizenship Act (CCA) did not apply retroactively to alien's case to confer derivative citizenship upon a 40 year-old child with one citizen parent. Lee v. Ashcroft, E.D.N.Y.2002, 216 F.Supp.2d 51, transferred to court of appeal 268 F.Supp.2d 150, order vacated on reconsideration 2003 WL 21310247.

Child Citizenship Act (CCA) did not apply retroactively to grant alien U.S. citizenship based on his father's naturalization. Chant v. Ashcroft, C.A.9 2003, 71 Fed.Appx. 731, 2003 WL 21782679, Unreported. Citizens ⮑ 9

2. Due process

Congress had rational basis for immigration scheme which assertedly treated adopted alien children of subsequently naturalized parents more favorably than adopted alien children of United States citizen parents by providing for the acquisition of citizenship of alien children adopted before age sixteen by citizen parents, but requiring adoptive parents to apply for a certificate of citizenship on behalf of the child before the child reached eighteen years of age,

and thus, the scheme did not violate the equal protection component of the Due Process Clause; Congress had an interest in requiring affirmative action on the part of adoptive parents to establish the adopted child's connection to the United States. Crider v. Ashcroft, C.A.9 2003, 74 Fed.Appx. 729, 2003 WL 21805240, Unreported. Constitutional Law ⮑ 250.5

11. Children within section

Child Citizenship Act (CCA) did not apply to confer automatic citizenship on alien who was born outside the United States to United States citizen, so as to prevent his removal for allegedly having been convicted of aggravated felonies, where alien was not under 18 years old when the CCA went into effect; CCA applies only to children under 18 years of age on CCA's effective date. Gomez-Diaz v. Ashcroft, C.A.7 2003, 324 F.3d 913. Aliens ⮑ 40; Citizens ⮑ 9

Defendant charged with illegal re-entry after deportation could not benefit from amendment allowing for automatic citizenship of adopted children under 18 years of age, where defendant was not under 18 on or after amendment's effective date. U.S. v. Hodulik, C.A.6 (Tenn.) 2002, 44 Fed.Appx. 656, 2002 WL 1396904, Unreported, certiorari denied 123 S.Ct. 484, 537 U.S. 1013, 154 L.Ed.2d 417.

The Child Citizenship Act (CCA) did not confer automatic citizenship on petitioner who was orphaned and adopted by two United States citizens when he was four years old, as would prevent his removal for having committed an aggravated felony, where petitioner was not under 18 years old when the CCA was enacted, and the CCA only applied to children who were under 18 years old on the Act's effective date. Hughes v. Ashcroft, C.A.9 2001, 255 F.3d 752. Citizens ⮑ 9

Defendant charged with illegal re-entry after deportation could not benefit from amendment allowing for automatic citizenship of adopted children under 18 years of age, where defendant was not under 18 on or after amendment's effective date. U.S. v. Hodulik, C.A.6 (Tenn.) 2002, 44 Fed.Appx. 656, 2002 WL 1396904, Unreport-

49

Reprinted with permission from Thomson West, *United States Code Annotated*, 2004 Cumulative Annual Pocket Part, Title 8, pp. 47–49. © 2004 Thomson West.

The next step is checking each of the noncumulative supplements. This page is from the January 2005 supplement. The supplement shows new annotations but no new statutory language. Because the supplements are noncumulative, all supplements published after the pocket part must be checked for amendments to the statute or new annotations.

FIGURE 6.21 NONCUMULATIVE SUPPLEMENT ENTRY FOR 8 U.S.C.A. § 1431

---

8 § 1429 UNITED STATES CODE ANNOTATED

§ 1429. Prerequisite to naturalization; burden of proof

Notes of Decisions

12. Removal—Generally

District court was precluded from granting naturalization to an alien while removal proceedings were pending against alien. Zayed v. U.S., C.A.6 (Ohio) 2004, 368 F.3d 902. Aliens ⬤ 68(6)

16. Review

Issue of whether district court had jurisdiction, under provision of Immigration and Nationality Act (INA) permitting alien whose application for naturalization had been denied to seek review in district court, to review Attorney General's denial of alien's naturalization petition, given that denial was based on provision of INA stating that no application for naturalization could be considered by Attorney General if there was a removal proceeding pending against applicant, was open question requiring remand, in alien's suit against Attorney General, seeking declaration that he was of good moral character, and that, but for removal proceedings, he was eligible for naturalization; Attorney General had been considering and granting applications to terminate removal proceedings to permit persons to proceed on their naturalization applications in exceptional cases, and because this practice, in face of seemingly clear statutory bar to considering naturalization applications while formal removal attempts were underway, suggested questions that required further development, remand was necessary. Apokarina v. Ashcroft, C.A.3 (Pa.) 2004, 93 Fed.Appx. 469, 2004 WL 742286, Unreported. Aliens ⬤ 68(6)

> **Newer cases interpreting the statute**

§ 1431. Children born outside the United States and residing permanently in the United States; conditions under which citizenship automatically acquired

Notes of Decisions

½. Retroactive effect of section

Child Citizenship Act (CCA) did not apply retroactively to automatically grant derivative citizenship to alien whose father became a citizen; alien was not under 18 years old as of CCA's effective date. Lawal v. Ashcroft, C.A.3 (Pa.) 2004, 89 Fed.Appx. 774, 2004 WL 235036, Unreported. Citizens ⬤ 9

11. Children within section

Naturalization of alien's father did not act to make alien a citizen, even though alien was in his father's legal custody; alien's parents were not legally separated at the time of the naturalization inasmuch as they had never been married. Lawal v. Ashcroft, C.A.3 (Pa.) 2004, 89 Fed.Appx. 774, 2004 WL 235036, Unreported. Citizens ⬤ 9

§ 1439. Naturalization through service in the armed forces

(a) Requirements

A person who has served honorably at any time in the armed forces of the United States for a period or periods aggregating one year, and, who, if separated from such service, was never separated except under honorable conditions, may be naturalized without having resided, continuously immediately preceding the date of filing such person's application, in the United States for at least five years, and in the State or district of the Service in the United States in which the application for naturalization is filed for at least three months, and without having been physically present in the United States for any specified period, if such application is filed while the applicant is still in the service or within six months after the termination of such service.

(b) Exceptions

A person filing an application under subsection (a) of this section shall comply in all other respects with the requirements of this subchapter, except that—

(1) no residence within a State or district of the Service in the United States shall be required;

(2) notwithstanding section 1429 of this title insofar as it relates to deportability, such applicant may be naturalized immediately if the applicant be then actually in the Armed Forces of the United States, and if prior to the filing of the application, the applicant shall have appeared before and been examined by a representative of the Service;

(3) the applicant shall furnish to the Secretary of Homeland Security, prior to any hearing upon his application, a certified statement from the proper executive department for each period of his service upon which he relies for the benefits of this section, clearly showing that such service was honorable and that no discharges from service, including periods of service not relied upon by him for the benefits of this section, were other than honorable (the certificate or certificates herein provided for shall be conclusive evidence of such service and discharge); and

(4) notwithstanding any other provision of law, no fee shall be charged or collected from the applicant for filing the application, or for the issuance of a certificate of naturalization upon being granted citizenship, and no clerk of any State court shall charge or collect any fee for such services unless the laws of the State require such charge to be made, in which case nothing more than the portion of the fee required to be paid to the State shall be charged or collected.

270

Reprinted with permission from Thomson West, *United States Code Annotated*, Pamphlet Number 3 (January 2005), p. 270. © 2005 Thomson West.

In state statutory research, the first step is using the subject index to locate relevant code sections. This example shows what you would find if looked under Assumption of Risk in the General Index to Vernon's *Texas Statutes and Codes Annotated*.

FIGURE 6.22   VERNON'S *TEXAS STATUTES AND CODES ANNOTATED* GENERAL INDEX

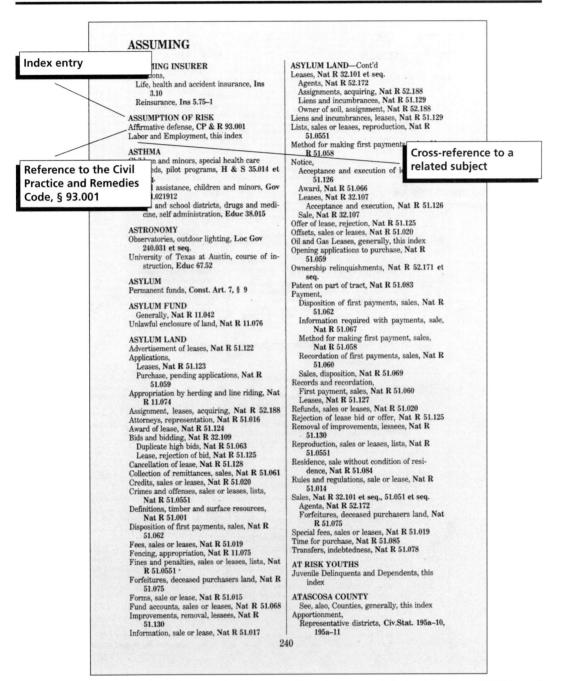

The next step is looking up the statute in the main volume. This code section sets out the affirmative defense of assumption of the risk, and the annotations list a variety of research references.

FIGURE 6.23 TEXAS CIVIL PRACTICE AND REMEDIES CODE § 93.001

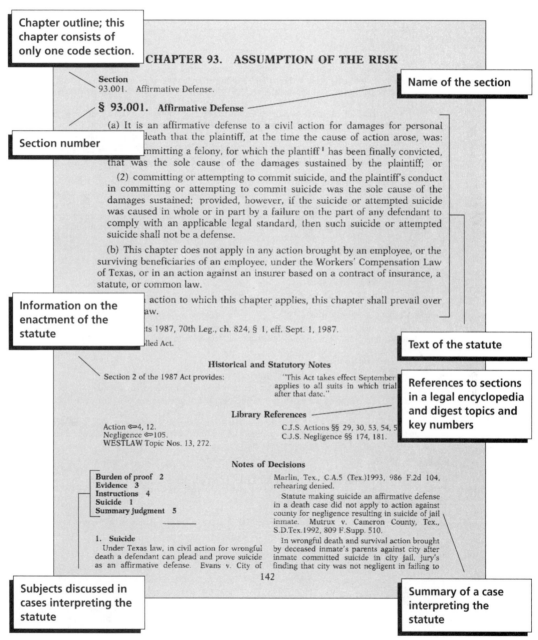

Reprinted with permission from Thomson West, Vol. 4 Vernon's *Texas Codes Annotated*, Civil Practice and Remedies Code, Chapter 93, p. 142 (1997). © 1997 Thomson West.

The next step is checking the pocket part. The pocket part shows new statutory language that supersedes the language in the main volume. The state code may include cumulative or noncumulative supplements in addition to the pocket part. If so, you need to check those supplements to further update your research.

FIGURE 6.24   POCKET PART ENTRY FOR TEXAS CIVIL PRACTICE AND REMEDIES CODE § 93.001

LIABILITY IN TORT   § 93.001
Title 4

    (4) before the health care practitioner conducts the physical examination or medical screening, the patient or, if the patient is a minor or is otherwise legally incompetent, the patient's parent, managing conservator, legal guardian, or other person with legal responsibility for the care of the patient signs a written statement that acknowledges:

      (A) that the health care practitioner is conducting a physical examination or medical screening that is not administered for or in expectation of compensation; and

      (B) the limitations on the recovery of damages from the health care practitioner in connection with the physical examination or medical screening being performed.

Added by Acts 2003, 78th Leg., ch. 749, § 1, eff. Sept. 1, 2003.

§ 91.003. Insurance Required

    (a) Section 91.002 applies only to a health care practitioner who has liability insurance coverage in effect to cover any act or omission to which this chapter applies. The health care practitioner's liability coverage must cover the acts or omissions of the health care practitioner and must be in the amount of at least $100,000 per person and $300,000 for each single occurrence of death or bodily injury and $100,000 for each single occurrence for injury to or destruction of property.

    (b) The coverage may be provided under a contract of insurance or other plan of insurance and may be satisfied by the purchase of a $300,000 bodily injury and property damage combined single-limit policy.

Added by Acts 2003, 78th Leg., ch. 749, § 1, eff. Sept. 1, 2003.

§ 91.004. Applicability

    (a) This chapter does not apply to an act or omission that is intentional, wilfully or wantonly negligent, or done with conscious indifference or reckless disregard for the safety of others.

    (b) This chapter does not:

      (1) limit the liability of a school district to its students, teachers, or staff; or

      (2) affect a school district's liability limits or immunities under Chapter 101.

    (c) This chapter does not apply to a governmental unit or employee of a governmental unit as defined by Section 101.001.

    (d) This chapter does not limit the liability of an insurer or insurance plan in an action under Chapter 21, Insurance Code, or in an action for bad faith conduct, breach of fiduciary or negligent failure to settle a claim.

by Acts 2003, 78th Leg., ch. 749, § 1, eff. Sept. 1, 2003.

**CHAPTER 93. ASSUMPTION OF THE RISK AND CERTAIN
OTHER AFFIRMATIVE DEFENSES**

Section	Section
93.001. Assumption of the Risk: Affirmative Defense.	93.002. Dry Fire Hydrants: Affirmative Defense.

§ 93.001. Assumption of the Risk: Affirmative Defense

    (a) It is an affirmative defense to a civil action for damages for personal injury or death that the plaintiff, at the time the cause of action arose, was:

      (1) committing a felony, for which the plaintiff has been finally convicted, that was the sole cause of the damages sustained by the plaintiff; or

      (2) committing or attempting to commit suicide, and the plaintiff's conduct in committing or attempting to commit suicide was the sole cause of the damages sustained; provided, however, if the suicide or attempted suicide was caused in whole or in part by a failure on the part of any defendant to comply with an applicable legal standard, then such suicide or attempted suicide shall not be a defense.

121

> **New statutory language supersedes the language in the main volume.**

FIGURE 6.24   POCKET PART ENTRY FOR TEXAS CIVIL PRACTICE AND REMEDIES CODE § 93.001
(Continued)

---

§ 93.001   LIABILITY IN TORT
                                                                            Title 4

Annotations follow the statutory text.

(b) This section does not apply in any action brought by an employee, or the surviving beneficiaries of an employee, under the Workers' Compensation Law of Texas, or in an action against an insurer based on a contract of insurance, a statute, or common law.

(c) In an action to which this section applies, this section shall prevail over any other law.

Added by Acts 1987, 70th Leg., ch. 824, § 1, eff. Sept. 1, 1987. Amended by Acts 1997, 75th Leg., ch. 437, § 1, eff. Sept. 1, 1997.

Historical and Statutory Notes

1997 Legislation

Acts 1997, 75th Leg., ch. 437, in the section heading, inserted "Assumption of the Risk:"; throughout the text, substituted "section" for "chapter"; and in subsec. (a)(1), corrected the spelling of "plaintiff".

Research References

Encyclopedias

TX Jur. 3d Negligence § 70, Generally.

TX Jur. 3d Wrongful Death § 26, In General.

Forms

Texas Jurisprudence Pleading & Practice Forms 2d Ed § 17:7, Statutory Assumption Of Risk-Plaintiff Committed Felony.

Texas Jurisprudence Pleading & Practice Forms 2d Ed § 17:8, Statutory Assumption Of Risk-Plaintiff Or Decedent Committed Or Attempted To Commit Suicide.

Texas Jurisprudence Pleading & Practice Forms 2d Ed § 89:21, Answer-Affirmative Defense-Statutory Assumption Of Risk-Decedent Committed Or Attempted Suicide.

Texas Jurisprudence Pleading & Practice Forms 2d Ed § 105:17, Answer-Affirmative Defense-Denial Of Negligence-Assumption Of Risk By Party Committing A Felony.

Texas Jurisprudence Pleading & Practice Forms 2d Ed § 156:80, Answer-Affirmative Defense-Statutory Assumption Of Risk-Plaintiff Committed Felony.

Texas Jurisprudence Pleading & Practice Forms 2d Ed § 178:75, Answer-Affirmative Defense-Statutory Assumption Of Risk-Plaintiff Committed Felony.

Texas Jurisprudence Pleading & Practice Forms 2d Ed § 178:76, Answer-Affirmative Defense-

Statutory Assumption Of Risk-Plaintiff Or Decedent Committed Or Attempted To Commit Suicide.

Texas Jurisprudence Pleading & Practice Forms 2d Ed § 192:35, Assumption Of Risk.

Texas Jurisprudence Pleading & Practice Forms 2d Ed § 192:38, Answer-Affirmative Defense-Assumption Of Risk.

Texas Jurisprudence Pleading & Practice Forms 2d Ed § 199:20, Answer-Allegation-Unforeseeable Criminal Act Of Third Person.

Texas Jurisprudence Pleading & Practice Forms 2d Ed § 128A:56, Answer-Affirmative Defense-Statutory Assumption Of Risk-Plaintiff Committed Felony.

Texas Jurisprudence Pleading & Practice Forms 2d Ed § 128A:57, Answer-Affirmative Defense-Plaintiff's Decedent Committed Or Attempted To Commit Suicide.

Treatises and Practice Aids

TX Practice Guide, Personal Injury 2d CH. 7.V, 7 V. Pleadings.

TX Practice Guide, Personal Injury 2d CH. 12.-II, 12 II. Burden Of Proof; Prima Facie Case Or Defense.

Texas Practice Guide Torts CH 9.A, 9.A. Defenses.

37 Tex. Prac. Series § 471, Defenses.

Notes of Decisions

1. Suicide

Physician who unsuccessfully operated on patient to repair damage caused by self-inflicted injuries established an affirmative defense in action for negligence and wrongful death brought by survivors of the patient, where patient was attempting to commit suicide at the time the causes of action arose, and self-inflicted injuries were the sole cause of the patient's death. Galindo v. Dean (App. 11 Dist. 2002) 69 S.W.3d 623. Health ☞ 766

3. Evidence

Mental health patient's damages arising from the murder she committed were inextricably intertwined with her illegal conduct, and thus, the

unlawful acts rule, and assumption of risk, precluded patient's claims against therapist for breach of contract, violation of the Insurance Code and Deceptive Trade Practices Act, conspiracy to commit commercial bribery, professional negligence, and breach of the duty of good faith and fair dealing, and against doctor for professional negligence. Ward v. Emmett (App. 4 Dist. 2001) 37 S.W.3d 500. Health ☞ 696; Health ☞ 767

5. Summary judgment

Survivors of patient who was treated for self-inflicted injuries failed to present genuine issues of fact as to whether physician who operated on patient contributed to her death; survivors filed

122

F. CHECKLIST FOR STATUTORY RESEARCH

1. LOCATE A STATUTE

- ❐ Use an index to search by subject.
- ❐ Use the popular name table to locate a statute from its popular name.
- ❐ For federal statutes, use the conversion tables to locate a statute using its public law number.
- ❐ In LexisNexis and Westlaw, retrieve statutes from their citations, execute word searches for statutes in the appropriate database (state, federal, or combined), browse the table of contents for the code, or search for an act by popular name. In Westlaw, search by subject using the statutory index.
- ❐ On the Internet, locate statutes on government or general legal research web sites.

2. READ THE STATUTE AND ACCOMPANYING ANNOTATIONS

- ❐ Use research references to find cases, secondary sources, and other research materials interpreting the statute.

3. UPDATE PRINT RESEARCH

- ❐ Check the pocket part accompanying the main volume.
- ❐ Check any cumulative or noncumulative supplements accompanying the code.

4. SPECIAL NOTES

- ❐ In U.S.C.A., update entries to the popular name and conversion tables in the noncumulative supplements.
- ❐ In state codes, check for additional updating tools.
- ❐ In state or federal statutory research, update your research or find additional research references using Shepard's in print or in LexisNexis or KeyCite in Westlaw.
- ❐ In Internet research, check the date of the statute and update your research accordingly.

CHAPTER 7

FEDERAL LEGISLATIVE HISTORY RESEARCH

A. Introduction to federal legislative history

B. Researching federal legislative history in print

C. Researching federal legislative history electronically

D. Citing federal legislative history

E. Sample pages for federal legislative history research

F. Checklist for federal legislative history research

A. INTRODUCTION TO FEDERAL LEGISLATIVE HISTORY

When a legislature passes a statute, it does so with a goal in mind, such as prohibiting or regulating certain types of conduct. Despite their best efforts, however, legislators do not always draft statutes that express their intentions clearly, and it is almost impossible to draft a statute that contemplates every possible situation that may arise under it. Accordingly, lawyers and judges are often called upon to determine the meaning of an ambiguous statute. Lawyers must provide guidance about what the statute permits or requires their clients to do. In deciding cases, judges must determine what the legislature intended when it passed the statute.

If you are asked to analyze an ambiguous statute, you have a number of tools available to help with the task. If the courts have already resolved the ambiguity, secondary sources, statutory annotations, Shepard's Citations, or other research resources can lead you to cases that explain the meaning of the statute.

If the ambiguity has not yet been resolved, however, you face a bigger challenge. You could research similar statutes to see if they shed

light on the provision you are interpreting. You could also look to the language of the statute itself for guidance. You may have studied what are called "canons of construction" in some of your other classes. These canons are principles used to determine the meaning of a statute. For example, one canon provides that statutory terms are to be construed according to their ordinary and plain meaning. Another states that remedial statutes are to be broadly construed, while criminal statutes are to be narrowly construed.[1] Although these tools can be helpful in interpreting statutes, they rarely provide the complete answer to determining the legislature's intent.

One of the best ways to determine legislative intent is to research the paper trail of documents that legislators create during the legislative process. These documents are known as the legislative history of the statute. This chapter discusses various types of documents that make up a statute's legislative history and explains how to locate and use them. At the state level, the types of legislative history documents produced and their ease of accessibility vary widely; therefore, this chapter discusses only federal legislative history.

1. THE PROCESS OF ENACTING A LAW

"Legislative history" is a generic term used to refer to a variety of documents produced during the legislative process; it does not refer to a single document or research tool. Courts consider some legislative history documents more important than others, depending on the type of information in the document and the point in the legislative process when the document was created. Understanding what legislative history consists of, as well as the value of different legislative history documents, requires an understanding of the legislative process. **Figure 7.1** illustrates this process.

The legislative process begins when a bill is introduced into the House of Representatives or the Senate by a member of Congress. After the bill is introduced, it is usually referred to a committee. The committee can hold hearings on the bill to obtain the views of experts and interested parties, or it can refer the bill to a subcommittee to hold hearings. If the committee is not in favor of the bill, it usually takes no action. This ordinarily causes the bill to expire in the committee, although the sponsor is free to reintroduce the bill in a later session of Congress. If the committee is in favor of the bill, it will recommend passage to the full chamber of the House or Senate. The recommendation is presented

---

[1]*See generally* Abner J. Mikva & Eric Lane, AN INTRODUCTION TO STATUTORY INTERPRETATION AND THE LEGISLATIVE PROCESS 114–119 (Aspen Publishers 2d ed. 2002).

FIGURE 7.1 HOW A BILL BECOMES A LAW

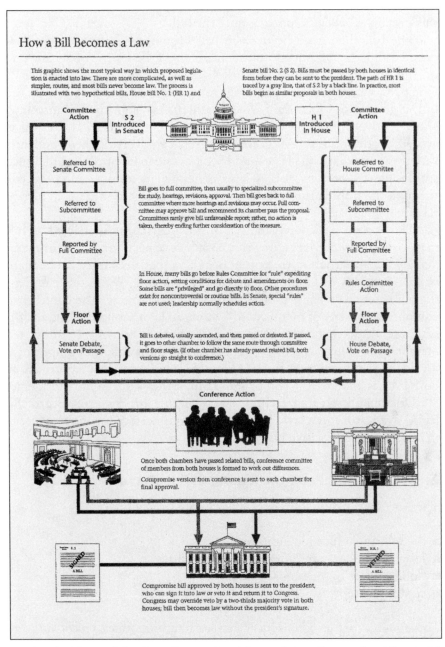

How a Bill Becomes a Law

This graphic shows the most typical way in which proposed legislation is enacted into law. There are more complicated, as well as simpler, routes, and most bills never become law. The process is illustrated with two hypothetical bills, House bill No. 1 (HR 1) and Senate bill No. 2 (S 2). Bills must be passed by both houses in identical form before they can be sent to the president. The path of HR 1 is traced by a gray line, that of S 2 by a black line. In practice, most bills begin as similar proposals in both houses.

Reprinted with permission from Congressional Quarterly Inc., *Congressional Quarterly's Guide to Congress*, CQ Press, 5th Ed. (2000), p. 1093. Copyright © 2000 CQ Press, a division of Congressional Quarterly, Inc.

in a committee report that contains the full text of the bill and an analysis of each provision. Because the committee presents its views in a report, this process is called "reporting out" the bill.

The bill then goes before the full House or Senate, where it is debated and may be amended. The members of the House or Senate vote on the bill. If it is passed, the bill goes before the other chamber of Congress, where the same process is repeated. If both chambers pass the bill, it goes to the President. The President can sign the bill into law, allow it to become law without a signature, or veto it. If the bill is vetoed, it goes back to Congress. Congress can override the President's veto if two-thirds of the House and Senate vote in favor of the bill. Once a bill is passed into law, it is assigned a public law number and proceeds through the publication process described in Chapter 6, on statutory research.

This is a simplified explanation of how legislation is enacted. A bill may make many detours along this path before becoming a law or being defeated. One situation that often occurs is that the House and Senate will pass slightly different versions of the same bill. When this happens, the bill is sent to what is called a conference committee. The conference committee consists of members of both houses of Congress, and its job is to attempt to reconcile the two versions of the bill. If the committee members are able to agree on the provisions of the bill, the compromise version is sent back to both chambers of Congress to be reapproved. If both houses approve the compromise bill, it then goes to the President.

Documents created at each stage of this process constitute the legislative history of a law. The next section describes the major sources that make up a legislative history.

2. SOURCES OF FEDERAL LEGISLATIVE HISTORY

There are four major sources of federal legislative history:

- the bills introduced in Congress
- hearings before committees or subcommittees
- floor debates in the House and Senate
- committee reports.

These sources are listed in order from least authoritative to most authoritative. Although some of these sources are generally considered to have more weight than others, none should be viewed in isolation. Each item contributes to the documentation of the legislature's intent. In fact, you may find that the documents contain information that is either contradictory or equally as ambiguous as the underlying statute. It is rare when an inquiry into legislative history will give you a definitive answer to a question of statutory interpretation. What is more likely is that the documents

will equip you with information you can use to support your arguments for the proper interpretation of the statute.

a. Bills

The bill introduced into Congress, and any later versions of the bill, can be helpful in determining Congressional intent. Changes in language and addition or deletion of specific provisions may shed light on the goal the legislature was attempting to accomplish with the bill. Analysis of changes to a bill, however, requires speculation about the reasons behind the changes. Consequently, this is often considered an insufficient indication of legislative intent unless it is combined with other materials indicating intent to achieve a particular objective.

b. Hearings

Hearings before committees and subcommittees consist of the testimony of experts and interested parties called to give their views on the bill. These documents may contain transcripts of testimony, documents, reports, studies, or any other information requested by or submitted to the hearing committee. Unlike interpretation of different versions of a bill, interpretation of hearings does not require speculation. The individuals or groups providing information usually give detailed explanations and justifications for their positions.

Congress uses hearings to gather information. As a consequence, individuals or groups with opposing views are often represented, and their goal is to persuade Congress to act in a particular way. This results in the inclusion of information both for and against the legislation in the hearing documents. Sometimes it is possible to ascertain whether material from a particular source motivated Congress to act in a particular way, but this is not always the case. Therefore, hearing documents must be used carefully in determining Congressional intent.

c. Floor Debates

Floor debates are another source of legislative history. They are published in a daily record of Congressional proceedings called the *Congressional Record*. Unlike hearings, which include commentary that may or may not have been persuasive to the committee, floor debates consist of statements by the legislators themselves. Thus, the debates can be a good source of information about Congress's intent in passing a bill. Debates may consist of transcripts of comments or exchanges taking place on the floor of Congress. In addition, members of Congress are permitted to submit prepared statements setting forth their views. Statements by a bill's sponsors may be especially useful in determining

legislative intent. Different members of Congress may give different reasons for supporting legislation, however, and they are permitted to amend or supplement their statements after the fact. As a consequence, floor debates are not a definitive source for determining legislative intent.

d. Committee Reports

Committee reports are generally considered to be the most authoritative legislative history documents. They usually contain the committee's reasons for recommending the bill, a section-by-section analysis of the bill, and the views of any committee members who dissent from the committee's conclusions. If a bill is sent to a conference committee to work out compromise language, the conference committee usually prepares a report. This report discusses only the provisions that differed before the House and Senate. It usually contains the agreed-upon language of the bill and an explanation of the compromise.

3. STRATEGIES FOR APPROACHING FEDERAL LEGISLATIVE HISTORY RESEARCH

Your method of researching legislative history will depend on the type of material you need. If you are researching the history of an individual statute, your approach will be different than if you are looking for legislative activity on a particular subject, without regard for whether a statute was passed on the topic.

If you are researching the history of an individual statute, it is important to remember that not all legislation is accompanied by all of the documents described above. A committee might elect not to hold hearings. Or the bill could be amended during floor debate, in which case the amendment would not have any history to be documented elsewhere. In addition, you may not always need to look at all of these documents to resolve your research question. If you are trying to determine Congress's intent in enacting a specific provision within a statute, and a committee report sets out the goals Congress was attempting to accomplish with that provision, you might not need to go any further in your research. Often, however, the committee reports will not discuss the provision you need to interpret. In that case, you may need to delve further into the legislative history, reviewing floor debates or hearings to see if the provision was discussed in either of those sources. In other instances, you may need to compile a complete legislative history.

Your research path will depend largely on the scope of your assignment. You will almost always begin with the statute itself. From there, you should be able to use the bill number, public law number, or *Statutes at Large* citation to locate documents relating to the statute. In most cases, you will probably want to begin by reviewing committee

reports. If the committee reports do not address your question, you will then need to assess which other sources of legislative history are likely to assist you and which research tools provide the most efficient means of accessing those documents. If your research takes you beyond readily accessible committee reports, you may want to consult with a reference librarian for assistance in compiling the relevant documents.

If you are trying to find out about legislative activity on a specific topic, rather than the history of an individual statute, you will need to search by subject. Because most bills are not passed into law, you may find documents relating to bills that have expired. In addition, you may locate documents unrelated to a bill. For example, committees can hold hearings on any subject within their jurisdiction, even if no legislation on the subject has been introduced.

Some research tools lend themselves more easily than others to subject searching, and some are more comprehensive in their coverage than others. Therefore, you will need to determine how much information you need, such as whether you need information on bills that have expired as well as existing legislation, and how far back in time you want to search. Again, you would be well advised to consult with a reference librarian for assistance in developing your research plan for this type of research.

The remainder of this chapter discusses methods for locating legislative history documents. The next section discusses print research tools that are accessible at many law libraries. Unlike some other sources of authority, however, legislative history is often easiest to access through electronic means. In particular, Internet research sites made available by the government and commercial providers may be the most economical and user-friendly ways to locate federal legislative history. A description of print and electronic research tools follows.

B. RESEARCHING FEDERAL LEGISLATIVE HISTORY IN PRINT

Four print sources of legislative history are available in many law libraries:

1. compiled legislative histories containing all of the legislative history documents on a statute
2. *United States Code Congressional and Administrative News*, or U.S.C.C.A.N., which contains selected committee reports on bills passed into law
3. Congressional Information Service (CIS) materials containing committee reports and hearings on microfiche, as well as citations to floor debates in the *Congressional Record*
4. the *Congressional Record*, which contains floor debates on legislation.

You would not necessarily research each of these sources in order. Some documents may be accessible through more than one of these research tools. Therefore, you should assess the scope of your research project to determine which source is most likely to provide the information you need.

1. COMPILED LEGISLATIVE HISTORIES

Legislative histories for major pieces of legislation are sometimes compiled and published as separate volumes. In this situation, an author or publisher collects all of the legislative history documents on the legislation and publishes them in a single place. If a legislative history on the statute you are researching has already been compiled, your work has been done for you. Therefore, if you are researching a major piece of legislation, you should begin by looking for a compiled legislative history.

There are two ways to locate a compiled legislative history. The first is to look in the on-line catalog in your library. Compiled legislative histories can be published as individual books that are assigned call numbers and placed on the shelves. The second is to look for the statute in a reference book listing compiled legislative histories. One example of this type of reference book is *Sources of Compiled Legislative Histories: A Bibliography of Government Documents, Periodical Articles, and Books*, by Nancy P. Johnson. This book will refer you to books, government documents, and periodical articles that either reprint the legislative history for the statute or, at a minimum, contain citations to and discussion of the legislative history. This book is organized by public law number, so you would need to know the public law number of the statute to get started. You should be able to find the public law number following code sections in U.S.C. or an annotated code. Another good reference for compiled legislative histories is *Federal Legislative Histories: An Annotated Bibliography and Index to Officially Published Sources*, by Bernard D. Reams, Jr.

2. UNITED STATES CODE CONGRESSIONAL AND ADMINISTRATIVE NEWS

United States Code Congressional and Administrative News, or U.S.C.C.A.N., is a readily available source of committee reports on bills passed into law. For each session of Congress, U.S.C.C.A.N. publishes a series of volumes containing, among other things, the text of laws passed by Congress (organized by *Statutes at Large* citation) and selected committee reports. References to reports in U.S.C.C.A.N. usually include the year the book was published and the starting page of the document. Thus, to find a report cited as 1996 U.S.C.C.A.N.

FIGURE 7.2   EXCERPT FROM ANNOTATIONS ACCOMPANYING 18 U.S.C.A. § 2441

HISTORICAL AND STATUTORY NOTES

Revision Notes and Legislative Reports

1996 Acts. House Report No. 104–698, see 1996 U.S. Code Cong. and Adm. News, p. 2166.

House Report No. 104–788, see 1996 U.S. Code Cong. and Adm. News, p. 4021.

1997 Acts. House Conference Report No. 105–401, see 1997 U.S. Code Cong. and Adm. News, p. 2896.

References in Text

U.S.C.C.A.N. references tion 101 of the Immigration and Nationality Act, referred to in subsec. (b), is section 101 of Act June 27, 1952, c. 477, Title I, 66 Stat. 166, which is classified to section 1101 of Title 8, Aliens and Nationality.

Codifications

Section 584 of Pub.L. 105–118, which directed that section 2401 of title 18 be amended, was executed to section 2441 of Title 18, despite parenthetical refer-

ence to "section 2401 of Title 18", as the probable intent of Congress.

Amendments

1997   Amendments. Subsec.   (a). Pub.L. 105–118, § 583(1), substituted "war crime" for "grave breach of the Geneva Conventions".

Subsec. (b). Pub.L. 105–118, § 583(2), substituted "war crime" for "breach" each place it appeared.

Subsec. (c). Pub.L. 105–118, § 583(3), rewrote subsec. (c). Prior to amendment, subsec. (c) read as follows: "(c) Definitions.—As used in this section, the term 'grave breach of the Geneva Conventions' means conduct defined as a grave breach in any of the international conventions relating to the laws of warfare signed at Geneva 12 August 1949 or any protocol to any such convention, to which the United States is a party."

14

Reprinted with permission from Thomson West, *United States Code Annotated*, Vol. 18 (2000) p. 14. © 2000 Thomson West.

2166,[2] you would need to locate the 1996 edition of U.S.C.C.A.N., find the volumes labeled "Legislative History," and turn to page 2166. U.S.C.C.A.N. does not reprint all committee reports for all legislation. Nevertheless, U.S.C.C.A.N. is often a good starting place for research into committee reports because it is available at most law libraries and is fairly easy to use.

U.S.C.C.A.N. is a West publication; therefore, you can find cross-references to it in the annotations in U.S.C.A. The cross-references are usually listed in the Historical and Statutory Notes section of the annotations. If the statute has been amended, the Historical and Statutory Notes section will explain the major changes resulting from later enactments, and the legislative history section of the Historical and Statutory Notes will refer you to the year and page number of any committee reports reprinted in U.S.C.C.A.N. **Figure 7.2** shows U.S.C.C.A.N. references in U.S.C.A., and **Figure 7.3** shows the starting page of a committee report in U.S.C.C.A.N.

---

[2]This is not a complete citation. Refer to Section D below for citation rules for U.S.C.C.A.N.

FIGURE 7.3   **STARTING PAGE, HOUSE JUDICIARY COMMITTEE REPORT ON THE WAR CRIMES ACT OF 1996**

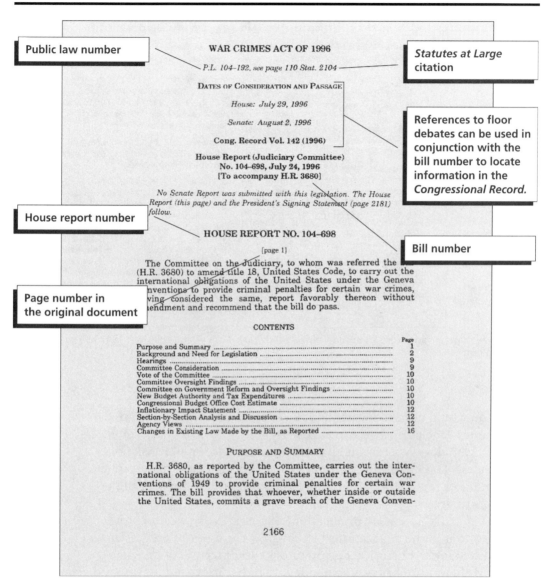

Public law number

WAR CRIMES ACT OF 1996

P.L. 104–192, see page 110 Stat. 2104

Statutes at Large citation

DATES OF CONSIDERATION AND PASSAGE

House: July 29, 1996

Senate: August 2, 1996

Cong. Record Vol. 142 (1996)

House Report (Judiciary Committee)
No. 104–698, July 24, 1996
[To accompany H.R. 3680]

References to floor debates can be used in conjunction with the bill number to locate information in the *Congressional Record.*

No Senate Report was submitted with this legislation. The House Report (this page) and the President's Signing Statement (page 2181) follow.

House report number

HOUSE REPORT NO. 104–698

[page 1]

Bill number

The Committee on the Judiciary, to whom was referred the (H.R. 3680) to amend title 18, United States Code, to carry out the international obligations of the United States under the Geneva Conventions to provide criminal penalties for certain war crimes, having considered the same, report favorably thereon without amendment and recommend that the bill do pass.

Page number in the original document

CONTENTS

	Page
Purpose and Summary	1
Background and Need for Legislation	2
Hearings	9
Committee Consideration	9
Vote of the Committee	10
Committee Oversight Findings	10
Committee on Government Reform and Oversight Findings	10
New Budget Authority and Tax Expenditures	10
Congressional Budget Office Cost Estimate	10
Inflationary Impact Statement	12
Section-by-Section Analysis and Discussion	12
Agency Views	12
Changes in Existing Law Made by the Bill, as Reported	16

PURPOSE AND SUMMARY

H.R. 3680, as reported by the Committee, carries out the international obligations of the United States under the Geneva Conventions of 1949 to provide criminal penalties for certain war crimes. The bill provides that whoever, whether inside or outside the United States, commits a grave breach of the Geneva Conven-

2166

3. CONGRESSIONAL INFORMATION SERVICE

Congressional Information Service (CIS) is another commercial publisher of legislative history documents, but its materials are more comprehensive than those available through U.S.C.C.A.N. CIS compiles, among other documents, committee reports and hearings on microfiche.[3] In addition, CIS provides citations to floor debates published in the *Congressional Record*. CIS is a good resource for finding the complete legislative history of a statute, as well as for searching by subject.

Although CIS compiles legislative history documents on microfiche, the tools for locating these materials are published in books. The CIS finding tools consist of the Index volumes, the Abstracts volumes, and the Legislative Histories volumes. CIS publishes a new set of Index, Abstracts, and Legislative Histories[4] volumes for each calendar year. Monthly softcover booklets containing the Index and Abstracts are published for the current year. For each four-year period from 1970 through 1998, the annual indices have been combined into cumulative indices, e.g., the *1995–1998 Four-Year Cumulative Index*.

The easiest way to locate the complete legislative history of a bill enacted into law is to use the Legislative Histories volumes. These volumes are organized by public law number. If you know the year the law was passed and the public law number, you can look it up in the appropriate volume of CIS Legislative Histories. CIS will list all of the documents in the legislative history, as well as a very brief summary of each document.

After the title of each document, a CIS citation will be listed. This citation indicates the year the document was created and the number assigned to the microfiche containing the document. Microfiche numbers will generally begin with PL for public laws, H for House documents, S for Senate documents, or J for joint documents. The microfiche should be filed in your library by year, and then by document number within each year. The only exception to this concerns references to the *Congressional Record*. CIS does not reproduce the *Congressional Record* as part of this microfiche set. Therefore, although CIS will list citations to floor debates appearing in the *Congressional Record*, you will need to go to the *Congressional Record* itself to read the debates. **Figure 7.4** shows a page from a CIS Legislative Histories volume.

---

[3]CIS also makes this material available electronically through an Internet service called LexisNexis Congressional. Refer to Section C below for a discussion of electronic research sources.

[4]CIS began publishing a separate Legislative Histories volume in 1984. For legislation passed before 1984, the listings of legislative histories appear at the end of the Abstracts volume for each year.

FIGURE 7.4   CIS LEGISLATIVE HISTORIES ENTRY FOR PUB. L. NO. 104-192

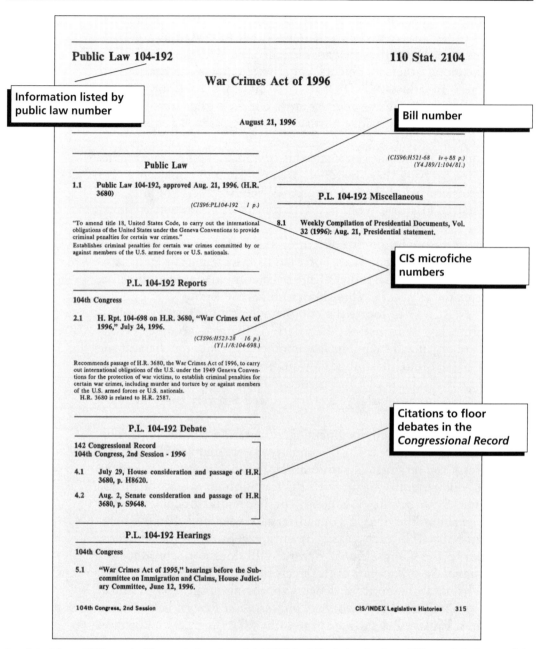

Reprinted from *CIS/Annual* with permission. Copyright 1997 LexisNexis Academic and Library Solutions, a division of Reed Elsevier Inc. All Rights Reserved. *CIS/Annual 1996*, Legislative Histories of U.S. Public Laws (1997), p. 315.

You can also use CIS to search for legislative activity on a particular subject, rather than the history of an individual statute. To locate documents by subject, you can use the Index and Abstracts volumes. The process of locating documents using the Index and Abstracts is similar to that for researching cases with a digest. In digest research, you use the Descriptive-Word Index to find references to the subject volumes in the digest. The summaries in the subject volumes then provide you with citations to the cases themselves. Similarly, to locate documents in CIS, you use the Index to find references to document summaries in the Abstracts, which then lead to the documents themselves on CIS microfiche.

The Index is a regular alphabetical subject index that will refer you to document numbers within the Abstracts. The summaries in the Abstracts will help you assess the content of the documents and target specific pages with useful information. They are especially helpful with hearings because they allow you to determine who testified, what the witness testified about, and where to find the testimony within the document. Once you have located useful information using the Abstracts, you can read the documents in full on microfiche. **Figures 7.5** and **7.6** show CIS Index and Abstracts entries, respectively.

4. CONGRESSIONAL RECORD

The *Congressional Record* is the record of all activity on the floor of the House and Senate. Therefore, it is the source you will use to find floor debates on a bill, regardless of whether the bill was passed into law. There are several ways to locate information in the *Congressional Record*, which are discussed below. First, however, it is important to understand how the *Congressional Record* is organized.

A new volume of the *Congressional Record* is published for each session of Congress. While Congress is in session, the current volume of the *Congressional Record* is published daily as a softcover pamphlet; this is called the daily edition. At the end of each session of Congress, the daily editions are compiled into a hardbound set; this is called the permanent edition.

The material in these two editions should be identical, but the pages in each are numbered differently. The daily edition is separated into different sections, including sections for House (H) and Senate (S) materials, and the pages within each section are numbered separately. In the permanent edition, all of the pages are numbered consecutively. References to the *Congressional Record* will vary, therefore, depending on whether they are to the permanent or daily edition. References to both editions will give the volume and page number, but the page numbering

FIGURE 7.5   CIS INDEX ENTRY

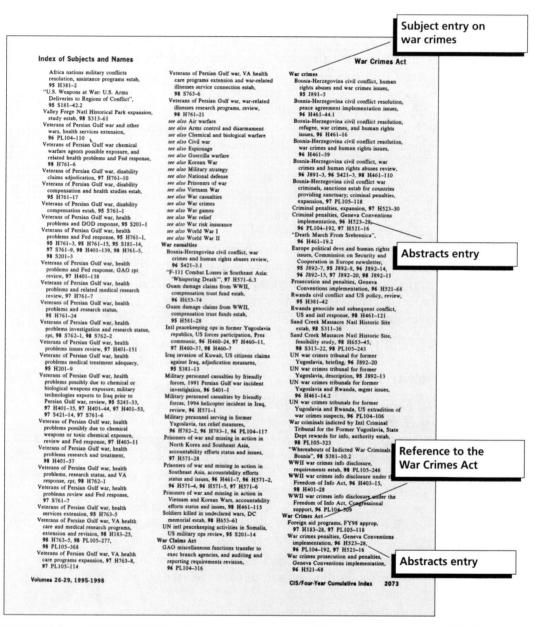

Reprinted from *1995–1998 CIS Four-Year Cumulative Index* with permission. Copyright 1999 LexisNexis Academic and Library Solutions, a division of Reed Elsevier Inc. All Rights Reserved. *1995–1998 CIS Four-Year Cumulative Index* (1999) p. 2073.

FIGURE 7.6 CIS ABSTRACTS ENTRY

Judiciary H523-28

H523-19 ANTI-CAR THEFT IMPROVEMENTS ACT OF 1995.
June 12, 1996. 104-2. 19 p.
H Doc Rm CIS/MF/3
•Item 1008-C; 1008-D.
H. Rpt. 104-618.
*Y1.1/8:104-618.
MC 96-16159.

Recommends passage of H.R. 2803, the Anti-Car Theft Improvements Act of 1995, to amend the Anti Car Theft Act of 1992 to revise the National Motor Vehicle Title Information System (NMVTIS), established to provide State motor vehicle departments with access to the data bases of other States in order to check whether a vehicle had been stolen before issuing the vehicle a new title.
Includes provisions to:
a. Transfer NMVTIS operating authority from DOT to the Department of Justice.
b. Expand NMVTIS to include title information on non-commercial light trucks and vans.
c. Extend NMVTIS implementation deadline to Oct. 1, 1997.

H523-20 CHURCH ARSON PREVENTION ACT OF 1996.
June 17, 1996. 104-2. 11 p.
H Doc Rm CIS/MF/3
•Item 1008-C; 1008-D.
H. Rpt. 104-621.
*Y1.1/8:104-621.
MC 96-16161.

Recommends passage, with an amendment in the nature of a substitute, of H.R. 3525, the Church Arson Prevention Act of 1996, to clarify and expand Federal jurisdiction over offenses relating to destruction of religious property.
Bill responds to 1996 increase in cases of arson against African-American churches.

H523-21 ANTITRUST HEALTH CARE ADVANCEMENT ACT OF 1996.
June 27, 1996. 104-2. 17 p.
H Doc Rm CIS/MF/3
•Item 1008-C; 1008-D.
H. Rpt. 104-646.
*Y1.1/8:104-646.
MC 96-17606.

Recommends passage of H.R. 2925, the Antitrust Health Care Advancement Act of 1996, to modify application of antitrust laws to health care provider sponsored networks (PSNs) and require case-by-case determination on whether PSNs, which include groups of physicians, nurses, hospitals, and other health care entities, are permissible under antitrust laws.
Includes dissenting views (p. 14-17).

H523-22 FAN FREEDOM AND COMMUNITY PROTECTION ACT OF 1996.
June 27, 1996. 104-2. 32 p.
H Doc Rm CIS/MF/3
•Item 1008-C; 1008-D.
H. Rpt. 104-656, pt. 1.
*Y1.1/8:104-656/PT.1.
MC 96-17614.

Volume 27, Number 1-12

Recommends passage, with an amendment in the nature of a substitute, of H.R. 2740, the Fan Freedom and Community Protection Act of 1996, to revise laws relating to relocation of professional football, hockey, and basketball franchises.
Includes provisions to:
a. Extend a limited exemption from antitrust laws to the National Football League, the National Hockey League, and the National Basketball Association to grant those leagues greater control over franchise movement by league members.
b. Require a sports league that approves a franchise relocation to provide an expansion team to the city from which the franchise left.
c. Require sports team owners who breach playing facility contracts with State or local governments to repay all the financial assistance received from that government.
Includes dissenting views (p. 28-32).
H.R. 2740 is similar to H.R. 2699.

H523-23 DEFENSE OF MARRIAGE ACT.
July 9, 1996. 104-2.
45 p. Corrected print.
H Doc Rm CIS/MF/3
•Item 1008-C; 1008-D.
H. Rpt. 104-664.
*Y1.1/8:104-664/CORR.
MC 96-17622.

Recommends passage of H.R. 3396, the Defense of Marriage Act, to define marriage under Federal law as the legal union between one man and one woman, and to allow each State to decide individually what legal status to give to another State's same-sex marriages.
Bill responds to possible issuance by Hawaii of marriage licenses to same-sex couples.
Includes dissenting views (p. 35-44).

H523-24 GOVERNMENT ACCOUNTABILITY ACT OF 1996.
July 16, 1996. 104-2. 11 p.
H Doc Rm CIS/MF/3
•Item 1008-C; 1008-D.
H. Rpt. 104-680.
*Y1.1/8:104-680.
MC 96-17634.

Recommends passage, with an amendment in the nature of a substitute, of H.R. 3166, the Government Accountability Act, to provide that individuals who make false statements to Congress or the judiciary are subject to Federal criminal prosecution.
Bill responds to May 1995 Supreme Court decision in *Hubbard v. U.S.* restricting criminal liability for false statements to statements made to the executive branch.
H.R. 3166 is similar to H.R. 1678.

H523-25 REPEAL OF PROHIBITION ON FEDERAL EMPLOYEES CONTRACTING OR TRADING WITH INDIANS.
July 17, 1996. 104-2. 6 p.
H Doc Rm CIS/MF/3
•Item 1008-C; 1008-D.
H. Rpt. 104-681.
*Y1.1/8:104-681.
MC 96-19218.

Recommends passage of H.R. 3215, to repeal the prohibition barring BIA and Indian Health Service employees from contracting with Indians or purchasing or selling services or property.
H.R. 3215 is similar to S. 325.

H523-26 PUEBLO OF ISLETA INDIAN LAND CLAIMS.
July 22, 1996. 104-2. 6 p.
H Doc Rm CIS/MF/3
•Item 1008-C; 1008-D.
H. Rpt. 104-694.
*Y1.1/8:104-694.
MC 96-19219.

Recommends passage of H.R. 740, to confer jurisdiction on the U.S. Court of Federal Claims to hear and render judgment on claims by the Pueblo of Isleta Indian Tribe of New Mexico against the U.S. for lands taken without adequate compensation to the tribe.

H523-27 CONTINUED PARTICIPATION OF SENIOR JUDGES IN AN IN BANC PROCEEDINGS.
July 23, 1996. 104-2. 5 p.
H Doc Rm CIS/MF/3
•Item 1008-C; 1008-D.
H. Rpt. 104-697.
*Y1.1/8:104-697.
MC 96-19226.

Recommends passage of S. 531, to authorize active circuit judges who take senior status while an in banc case is pending to continue to participate in the pending in banc case.

H523-28 WAR CRIMES ACT OF 1996.
July 24, 1996. 104-2. 16 p.
H Doc Rm CIS/MF/3
•Item 1008-C; 1008-D.
H. Rpt. 104-698.
*Y1.1/8:104-698.
MC 96-19227.

Recommends passage of H.R. 3680, the War Crimes Act of 1996, to implement U.S. obligations under the 1949 Geneva Conventions on the laws of warfare by establishing criminal penalties for war crimes, including murder and torture by or against members of the U.S. armed forces or U.S. citizens.
H.R. 3680 is related to H.R. 2587.

Description of the Committee's report

CIS/INDEX 207

will differ for each edition. Thus, 142 Cong. Rec. H8620[5] refers to volume 142 of the *Congressional Record*, page 8,620 of the House section of the daily edition. The "H" before the page number alerts you that the reference is to the daily edition. By contrast, a citation to 142 Cong. Rec. 11,352 refers to volume 142 of the *Congressional Record*, page 11,352 of the permanent edition. Because the page number contains no letter designation, the reference is to the permanent edition. **Figure 7.7** is an excerpt from the daily edition.

There are several ways to find citations to material in the *Congressional Record*. If you are looking for debates on a specific statute, you will find *Congressional Record* citations in the CIS Legislative Histories volumes. In the listing summarizing the statute's legislative history documents, CIS provides the dates and page numbers of references to the legislation in the *Congressional Record*.

You can also use U.S.C.C.A.N. to find *Congressional Record* references. At the beginning of each report published in U.S.C.C.A.N., you will find a list of the dates when the House and Senate considered the bill, which you can use in conjunction with the bill number to locate material in the daily edition of the *Congressional Record*. At the end of each issue of the daily edition of the *Congressional Record*, you will find a Daily Digest of Congressional activity for that day. If you know the date on which the bill was considered, you can look up the bill number in the Daily Digest to find references to the legislation within that issue of the *Congressional Record*.

The index to the *Congressional Record* will allow you to find information on a piece of legislation or to search by subject. If you are researching the permanent edition of the *Congressional Record*, the index will be published in a separate volume. During the current session of Congress, softcover interim indices for the daily edition are published roughly every two weeks. The interim indices are not cumulative; thus, you would need to check each one to find out if activity on the bill or subject you are researching has taken place.

The index is divided into two sections, one with a subject index, and the other containing the history of bills and resolutions. Either section will refer you to pages with relevant material. In using the section with the history of bills and resolutions, a couple of caveats are in order. First, you will need to know the House and Senate bill numbers of the legislation, not the public law number. A bill cannot be assigned a public law number until it is passed into law, and floor debates, by definition, take place before the passage of a bill. The CIS Legislative Histories volumes and the committee reports in U.S.C.C.A.N. will provide the bill

---

[5]The citations here are not complete. Refer to Section D below for citation rules for the *Congressional Record*.

FIGURE 7.7   CONGRESSIONAL RECORD, DAILY EDITION

Comments on the War Crimes Act in the House of Representatives

Mr. Speaker, H.R. 740, introduced by [ge]ntleman from New Mexico [Mr. [SCHIF]P] and the gentleman from New [Mexi]co [Mr. SKEEN] would permit the [Puebl]o of Isleta Indian Tribe to file a [claim] in the U.S. Court of Federal [Claim]s for certain aboriginal lands ac[quire]d from the tribe by the United [State]s. The tribe was erroneously ad[vise]d by the Bureau of Indian Affairs in [regar]d to this claim, and as a result [neve]r filed a claim for aboriginal lands before the expiration of the statute of limitations.

The court's jurisdiction would apply only to claims accruing on or before August 13, 1946, as provided in the Indian Claims Commission Act.

The Pueblo of Isleta Tribe seeks the opportunity to present the merits of its aboriginal land claims, which otherwise would be barred as untimely. The tribe cites numerous precedents for conferring jurisdiction under similar circumstances, such as the case of the Zuni Indian Tribe in 1978.

An identical bill passed the Senate in the 103d Congress, but was not considered by the House. In the 102d Congress, H.R. 1206, amended to the current language, passed the House, but was not considered by the Senate before adjournment. On June 11, 1996, the Judiciary Committee favorably reported this bill by unanimous voice vote.

Mr. Speaker, I reserve the balance of my time.

Mr. SCOTT. Mr. Speaker, I yield myself such time as I may consume.

Mr. Speaker, I think the bill has been explained that was introduced by the gentleman from New Mexico [Mr. SKEEN] and the gentleman from New Mexico [Mr. SCHIFF]. It is a fair bill, and I would just urge colleagues to support it at this time.

Mr. Speaker, I yield back the balance of my time.

Mr. RICHARDSON. Mr. Speaker, I wish to extend my strong support for H.R. 740 which deals with the Pueblo of Isleta Indian land claims. H.R. 740 comes before Congress for a vote which will correct a 45-year-old injustice. In 1951, the Pueblo of Isleta was given erroneous advice by employees of the Bureau of Indian Affairs regarding the nature of the claim the Pueblo could mount under the Indian Claims Commission Act of 1946. This is documented and supported by testimony. The Pueblo was not made aware of the fact that a land claim could be made based upon aboriginal use and occupancy. As a result, it lost the opportunity to make such a claim.

The Pueblo of Isleta was a victim of circumstances beyond its control, and this bill is an opportunity for us to correct this wrong. No expenditure or appropriations of funds are provided for in this bill; only the opportunity for the Pueblo to make a claim for aboriginal lands which the Isletas believe to be rightfully theirs. This bill may be the last chance for the United States to correct an injustice which occurred many years ago because of misinformation from the BIA.

Therefore, I urge my colleagues to support H.R. 740.

Mr. SMITH of Texas. Mr. Speaker, I have no further requests for time, and I yield back the balance of my time.

The SPEAKER pro tempore. The question is on the motion offered by the gentleman from Texas [Mr. SMITH] that the House suspend the rules and pass the bill, H.R. 740.

The question was taken; and (two-thirds having voted in favor thereof) the rules were suspended and the bill was passed.

A motion to reconsider was laid on the table.

WAR CRIMES ACT OF 1996

Mr. SMITH of Texas. Mr. Speaker, I move to suspend the rules and pass the bill (H.R. 3680) to amend title 18, United States Code, to carry out the international obligations of the United States under the Geneva Conventions to provide criminal penalties for certain war crimes.

The Clerk read as follows:

H.R. 3680

Be it enacted by the Senate and House of Representatives of the United States of America in Congress assembled,

SECTION 1. SHORT TITLE.

This Act may be cited as the "War Crimes Act of 1996".

SEC. 2. CRIMINAL PENALTIES FOR CERTAIN WAR CRIMES.

(a) IN GENERAL.—Title 18, United States Code, is amended by inserting after chapter 117 the following:

"CHAPTER 118—WAR CRIMES

"Sec.
"2401. War crimes.

"§ 2401. War crimes

"(a) OFFENSE.—Whoever, whether inside or outside the United States, commits a grave breach of the Geneva Conventions, in any of the circumstances described in subsection (b), shall be fined under this title or imprisoned for life or any term of years, or both, and if death results to the victim, shall also be subject to the penalty of death.

"(b) CIRCUMSTANCES.—The circumstances referred to in subsection (a) are that the person committing such breach or the victim of such breach is a member of the armed forces of the United States or a national of the United States (as defined in section 101 of the Immigration and Nationality Act).

"(c) DEFINITIONS.—As used in this section, the term 'grave breach of the Geneva Conventions' means conduct defined as a grave breach in any of the international conventions relating to the laws of warfare signed at Geneva 12 August 1949 or any protocol to any such convention, to which the United States is a party."

(b) CLERICAL AMENDMENT.—The table of chapters for part I of title 18, United States Code, is amended by inserting after the item relating to chapter 117 the following new item:

"118. War crimes .... 2401".

The SPEAKER pro tempore. Pursuant to the rule, the gentleman from Texas [Mr. SMITH] and the gentleman from Virginia [Mr. SCOTT] each will control 20 minutes.

The Chair recognizes the gentleman from Texas [Mr. SMITH].

GENERAL LEAVE

Mr. SMITH of Texas. Mr. Speaker, I ask unanimous consent that all Members may have 5 legislative days to revise and extend their remarks on the bill under consideration.

The SPEAKER pro tempore. Is there objection to the request of the gentleman from Texas?

There was no objection.

Mr. SMITH of Texas. Mr. Speaker, I yield myself such time as I may consume.

Mr. Speaker, H.R. 3680 is designed to implement the Geneva conventions for the protection of victims of war. Our colleague, the gentleman from North Carolina, WALTER JONES, should be commended for introducing this bill and for his dedication to such a worthy goal.

□ 1445

Mr. Speaker, the Geneva Conventions of 1949 codified rules of conduct for military forces to which we have long adhered. In 1955 Deputy Under Secretary of State Robert Murphy testified to the Senate that—

The Geneva Conventions are another long step forward towards mitigating the severity of war on its helpless victims. They reflect enlightened practices as carried out by the United States and other civilized countries, and they represent largely what the United States would do, whether or not a party to the Conventions. Our own conduct has served to establish higher standards and we can only benefit by having them incorporated in a stronger body of wartime law.

Mr. Speaker, the United States ratified the Conventions in 1955. However, Congress has never passed implementing legislation.

The Conventions state that signatory countries are to enact penal legislation punishing what are called grave breaches, actions such as the deliberate killing of prisoners of war, the subjecting of prisoners to biological experiments, the willful infliction of great suffering or serious injury on civilians in occupied territory.

While offenses covering grave breaches can in certain instances be prosecutable under present Federal law, even if they occur overseas, there are a great number of instances in which no prosecution is possible. Such nonprosecutable crimes might include situations where American prisoners of war are killed, or forced to serve in the Army of their captors, or American doctors on missions of mercy in foreign war zones are kidnapped or murdered. War crimes are not a thing of the past, and Americans can all too easily fall victim to them.

H.R. 3680 was introduced in order to implement the Geneva Conventions. It prescribes severe criminal penalties for anyone convicted of committing, whether inside or outside the United States, a grave breach of the Geneva Conventions, where the victim or the perpetrator is a member of our Armed Forces. In future conflicts H.R. 3680 may very well deter acts against Americans that violate the laws of war.

Mr. Speaker, I urge my colleagues to support this legislation, and I reserve the balance of my time.

Mr. SCOTT. Mr. Speaker, I yield myself such time as I may consume.

Mr. Speaker, as the gentleman from Texas has fully explained, H.R. 3680 implements this country's international

numbers. Second, be sure to check both the House and Senate listings for activity on the bill; either chamber of Congress could act at any time on a piece of pending legislation.

C. RESEARCHING FEDERAL LEGISLATIVE HISTORY ELECTRONICALLY

As noted earlier in this chapter, electronic sources are often easier to use in locating legislative history than print sources. In particular, Internet sources can be extremely useful in legislative history research. No matter which electronic tool you use, your research strategy will still largely be governed by whether you are looking for information on an individual statute or searching by subject.

As with print research, electronic research into the legislative history of an individual statute is easiest if you have a citation identifying the legislation. Most electronic tools will allow you to search using a public law number, bill number, or *Statutes at Large* citation. Conducting a word search using the popular name of the act is also an effective strategy. Searching simply by topic or with general keywords is the least efficient means of researching for material on an individual statute. It is possible that you could miss important documents if you do not have the correct terms in the search; in addition, you are likely to retrieve material on other pieces of legislation unrelated to your research. By contrast, topic or keyword searching is most effective when you want to find out about legislative activity on a particular subject.

One exception to these general approaches concerns electronic research in the *Congressional Record*. Conducting *Congressional Record* research on-line is easiest if you have the House and Senate bill numbers or the dates and page numbers of *Congressional Record* references to the bill. You can locate this information using the print sources described above or some of the electronic tools described below. You can also conduct a word search using the popular name of the act or general keywords.

More information on electronic searching generally is available in Chapter 10.

1. LEXISNEXIS AND WESTLAW

Both LexisNexis and Westlaw provide access to many legislative history documents. Both services have databases that allow you to search the full text of bills introduced in Congress, selected committee reports and Congressional testimony, and floor debates in the *Congressional Record*. Both also have databases containing compiled legislative histories for certain major pieces of legislation. LexisNexis also provides electronic access to the CIS microfiche set, although it is usually available only to

law firms and other commercial subscribers. Most academic subscriptions to LexisNexis do not allow access to this material, so you may not be able to access it with a student password. You may, however, have access to the same information through LexisNexis Congressional, which is described in the next section.

2. INTERNET SOURCES

Both government and commercial Internet web sites now contain a significant amount of legislative history. Government-operated sites can be used free of charge. One commercial source, LexisNexis Congressional (formerly known as Congressional Universe), is an excellent Internet resource available by subscription. This service provides electronic access to CIS legislative histories. If you are conducting research at a library that maintains a subscription to this service, you can access it through the library's computer network.

Two sources of legislative history provided by the federal government are Thomas, a site maintained by the Library of Congress, and GPO Access, a site maintained by the Government Printing Office (GPO). The Internet addresses for both of these sites are listed in Appendix A. One potential drawback to using either of these sites is that some of their databases do not yet go back very far. As of this writing, some information on these sites dates back only to the early 1990s. For each category of information available, you should be able to determine the period of time covered, and you will want to check this carefully before you begin your research. If you are researching the legislative history of a fairly recent statute, however, these are excellent tools to use. In addition, these sites will become more comprehensive over time as new material is added to them.

Thomas will provide you with the text of bills introduced, House and Senate roll call votes, public laws, the text of the *Congressional Record*, committee reports, and other information on the legislative process. Thomas will also allow you to search in several ways. You can search by public law number, report number, or committee name, or you can conduct word searches. The introductory screens for the Thomas site appear in **Figure 7.8**.

GPO Access also makes some legislative history documents available. Here, you will find the text of bills introduced into Congress, selected reports and hearings, and the *Congressional Record*. You can conduct word searches in any of these databases, and you can include a date restriction if you know the session of Congress you want to research. If you know the bill number, you can enter it as your word search to locate documents related to a specific piece of legislation. **Figure 7.9** shows the introductory screens for the legislative information section of GPO Access.

LexisNexis Congressional, a commercial research service, is both more comprehensive than the government sites and in some ways more

FIGURE 7.8   INTRODUCTORY SCREENS FOR THOMAS

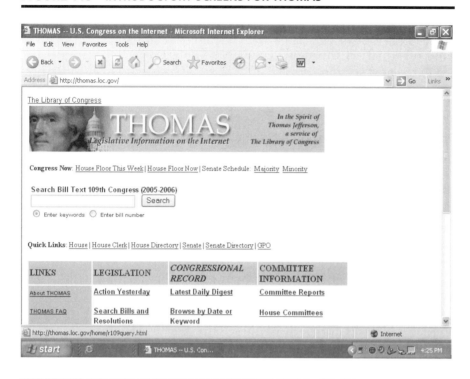

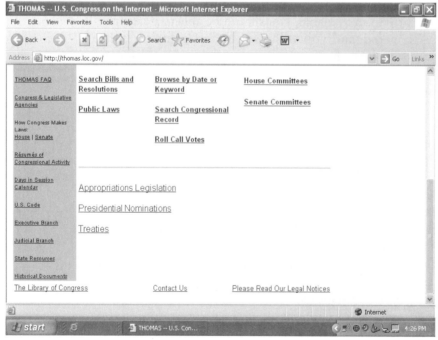

**FIGURE 7.9   INTRODUCTORY SCREENS FOR GPO ACCESS, LEGISLATIVE
INFORMATION**

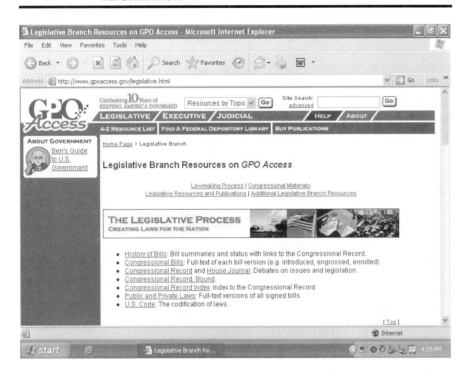

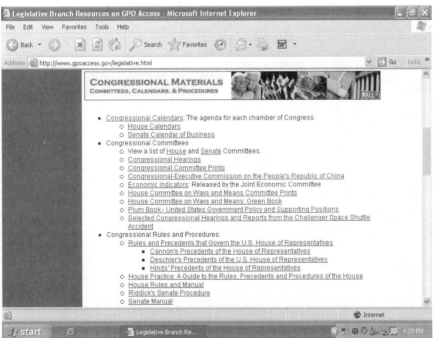

user-friendly. As noted above, LexisNexis Congressional is an electronic version of the CIS microfiche set. Its database includes committee reports, hearings, bills, and the *Congressional Record*. The introductory screen in **Figure 7.10** shows some of the types of information available through this service.

There are two important differences between the CIS legislative history microfiche set and LexisNexis Congressional. First, LexisNexis Congressional does not contain complete information on Congressional hearings. Unlike the CIS microfiche, LexisNexis Congressional includes only the text of prepared statements and transcripts of testimony, but not any attachments or documents submitted to the committee. The second difference concerns access to the *Congressional Record*. Although CIS provides citations to the *Congressional Record* in its Legislative Histories volumes, it does not reproduce the *Congressional Record* as part of the legislative history microfiche set. LexisNexis Congressional, by contrast, does provide electronic access to the *Congressional Record* from 1985 forward.

Within LexisNexis Congressional, you can search the full text of the documents available on-line, or you can search through the CIS Index. The easiest way to locate all of the available documents on a piece of legislation is to search within the Index. Searching this way retrieves the

FIGURE 7.10   INTRODUCTORY SCREEN FOR LEXISNEXIS CONGRESSIONAL

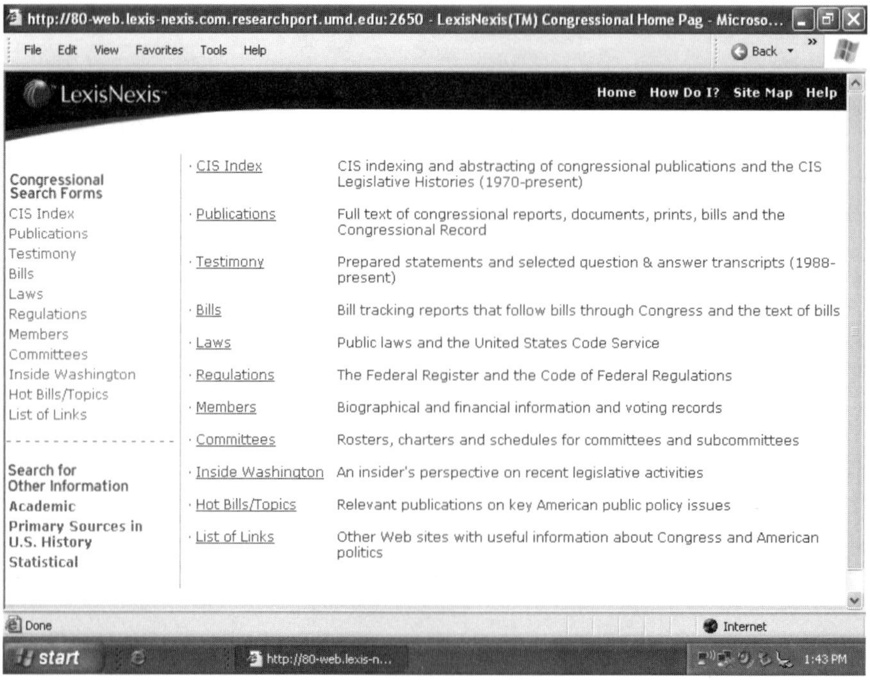

Reprinted with permission of LexisNexis Academic and Library Solutions, LexisNexis Congressional Introductory screen.

same information you would find in the print Index and Abstracts. Your search will first retrieve index entries. You can click on these to retrieve abstracts (summaries) of the documents available, and you can retrieve the full text of a document by clicking on the appropriate link.[6] You can search in the CIS Index by number using the public law number, *Statutes at Large* citation, or bill number. As you can see from **Figure 7.11**, however, other searching options are also available.

Full-text searching, by contrast, requires you to search separate databases for each type of legislative history document (reports, hearings, etc.) that you want to retrieve. If you are compiling the legislative history for one piece of legislation, searching in the CIS Index database is usually preferable to this piecemeal approach. If you are researching legislative activity by subject, however, you may want to conduct full-text searches for each type of document.

LexisNexis Congressional contains a wealth of legislative material beyond what is described here and can be searched using a variety of techniques. If you have any questions about how to find information in this service, the How Do I? option in the top right corner of the screen should lead you in the right direction. In addition, the Help function, which also appears in the top right corner, provides a link to the coverage and update schedule for all of the LexisNexis Congressional databases.

D. CITING FEDERAL LEGISLATIVE HISTORY

Citations to legislative history documents are covered in *ALWD Manual* Rule 15 and *Bluebook* Bluepages B6.1.6 and Rule 13. This chapter discusses citations to committee reports and floor debates because those are the sources you are most likely to cite in a brief or memorandum.

In the *Bluebook*, the examples contained in Rule 13 show some of the Congressional document abbreviations in large and small capital letters. According to Bluepages B13, however, legislative documents in briefs and memoranda should appear in ordinary type.

1. COMMITTEE REPORTS

Using either the *ALWD Manual* or the *Bluebook*, a citation to a committee report consists of four elements: (1) the abbreviation for the type of document; (2) the report number; (3) the pinpoint reference to the cited material; and (4) a parenthetical containing the date of the report.

Although citations to reports in both formats contain the same elements, the document abbreviations, report number, and date differ in

---

[6]Sometimes LexisNexis Congressional will provide a reference to a document that is not contained within its database. If that happens, you can use the citation provided by LexisNexis Congressional to locate the document in the CIS microfiche set.

FIGURE 7.11   SEARCH OPTIONS FOR CONGRESSIONAL PUBLICATIONS IN LEXISNEXIS CONGRESSIONAL

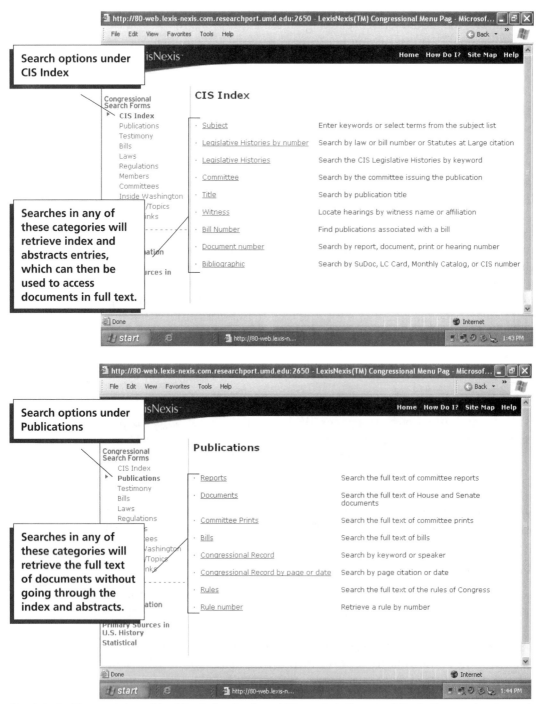

Reprinted with permission of LexisNexis Academic and Library Solutions, LexisNexis Congressional search options.

their presentation, as illustrated in the following examples. Here is an example of a citation to a report issued by the House of Representatives in *ALWD Manual* format:

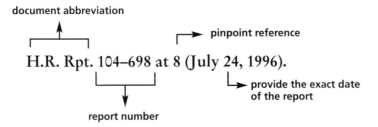

Here is an example in *Bluebook* format:

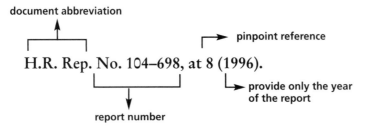

Both the *ALWD Manual* and the *Bluebook* require a parallel citation to U.S.C.C.A.N. if the report is reprinted there. A citation to a report reprinted in U.S.C.C.A.N. consists of six elements: (1) the report citation, as discussed above; (2) a notation that the citation is to a reprint of the document; (3) the year of the U.S.C.C.A.N. volume; (4) the publication name (U.S.C.C.A.N.); (5) the starting page of the report in U.S.C.C.A.N.; and (6) the pinpoint reference to the page in U.S.C.C.A.N. containing the cited material.

Although the elements of a U.S.C.C.A.N. citation in either *ALWD Manual* or *Bluebook* format are the same, the presentation of the citation varies slightly depending on which format you use. Here is an example in *ALWD Manual* format:

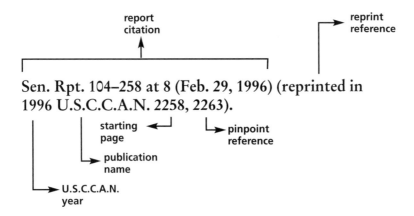

Here is an example in *Bluebook* format:

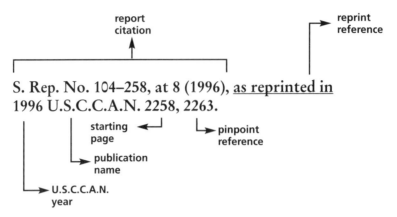

If you locate a report in U.S.C.C.A.N., you can still find the page numbers for the original document. Throughout the report, U.S.C.C.A.N. provides the page numbers of the original document in brackets.

2. FLOOR DEBATES

Floor debates are published in the *Congressional Record*. As explained earlier in this chapter, two versions of the *Congressional Record* are published. The daily edition is published during the current session of Congress, and the permanent edition is published at the close of the session. Both the *ALWD Manual* and the *Bluebook* require citation to the permanent edition if possible. A citation to the permanent edition using either the *ALWD Manual* or the *Bluebook* consists of four elements: (1) the volume number of the *Congressional Record*; (2) the abbreviation Cong. Rec.; (3) the page number with the information cited; and (4) a parenthetical containing the year.

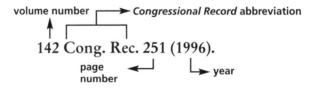

A citation to the daily edition contains the same elements, except that the parenthetical must indicate that the citation is to the daily edition and provide the exact date of the daily edition.

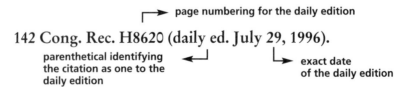

E. SAMPLE PAGES FOR FEDERAL LEGISLATIVE HISTORY RESEARCH

Beginning on the next page, **Figures 7.12** through **7.22** contain sample pages illustrating what you would find if you researched committee reports on the War Crimes Act of 1996 in print using U.S.C.C.A.N. and electronically using Thomas and LexisNexis Congressional.

The first step is locating the statute to find the public law number. U.S.C. or any annotated code will provide the public law number. If you locate the statute in U.S.C.A., the annotations will also provide citations to U.S.C.C.A.N.

FIGURE 7.12   18 U.S.C.A. § 2441 AND ACCOMPANYING ANNOTATIONS

Ch. 118   WAR CRIMES   18 § 2441

Pub.L. 90–321, Title II, § 202(b), May 29, 1968, 82 Stat. 162, added item "42. Extortionate credit transactions".

Pub.L. 90–284, Title I, § 104(b), Title X, § 1002(b), Apr. 11, 1968, 82 Stat. 77, 92, added items "102. Riots" and "12. Civil disorders", respectively.

1965   Amendments. Pub.L. 89–141, § 3, Aug. 28, 1965, 79 Stat. 581, added item "84. Presidential assassination, kidnaping, and assault".

1956 Amendments. Aug. 1, 1956, c. 825, § 2(a), 70 Stat. 798, substituted

"Chapter 3, Animals, birds, fish, and plants" for "Chapter 3, Animals, birds, and fish".

Act July 18, 1956, c. 629, § 202, 70 Stat. 575, added item "68. Narcotics".

Act July 14, 1956, c. 595, § 2, 70 Stat. 540, added item "2. Aircraft and Motor Vehicles".

1949 Amendments. Act May 24, 1949, c. 139, § 1, 63 Stat. 89, struck out the words "constituting crimes" from heading for chapter 21, and inserted "Chapter 50, Gambling—1081".

CHAPTER 118—WAR CRIMES

Sec.
2441. War crimes.

HISTORICAL AND STATUTORY NOTES

Amendments
1996 Amendments. Pub.L. 104–294, Title VI, § 605(p)(2), Oct. 11, 1996, 110

Stat. 3510, redesignated former item 2401 as 2441.

WESTLAW COMPUTER ASSISTED LEGAL RESEARCH

WESTLAW supplements your legal research in many ways. WESTLAW allows you to

● update your research with the most current information

● expand your library with additional resources

● retrieve current, comprehensive history citing references to a case with KeyCite

For more information on using WESTLAW to supplement your research, see the WESTLAW Electronic Research Guide, which follows the Explanation.

---

§ 2441. War crimes

(a) **Offense.**—Whoever, whether inside or outside the United States, commits a war crime, in any of the circumstances described in subsection (b), shall be fined under this title or imprisoned for life or any term of years, or both, and if death results to the victim, shall also be subject to the penalty of death.

(b) **Circumstances.**—The circumstances referred to in subsection (a) are that the person committing such war crime or the victim of such war crime is a member of the Armed Forces of the United

13

Statutory provision

FIGURE 7.12   18 U.S.C.A. § 2441 AND ACCOMPANYING ANNOTATIONS (*Continued*)

---

18 § 2441   **CRIMES**   Part 1

States or a national of the United States (as defined in section 101 of the Immigration and Nationality Act).

(c) **Definition.**—As used in this section the term 'war crime' means any conduct—

(1) defined as a grave breach in any of the international conventions signed at Geneva 12 August 1949, or any protocol to such convention to which the United States is a party;

(2) prohibited by Article 23, 25, 27, or 28 of the Annex to the Hague Convention IV, Respecting the Laws and Customs of War on Land, signed 18 October 1907;

(3) which constitutes a violation of common Article 3 of the international conventions signed at Geneva, 12 August 1949, or any protocol to such convention to which the United States is a party and which deals with non-international armed conflict;

(4) of a person who, in relation to an armed conflict contrary to the provisions of the Protocol on Prohibitions or Restrictions on the Use of Mines, Booby-Traps and Other Devices as amended at Geneva on 3 May 1996 (Protocol II as amended on 3 May 1996), when the United States is a party to such Protocol, willfully kills or causes serious injury to civilians.

(Added Pub.L. 104–192, § 2(a), Aug. 21, 1996, 110 Stat. 2104, § 2401; renumbered § 2441, Pub.L. 104–294, § 605(p)(1), Oct. 11, 1996, 110 Stat. 3510, and amended Pub.L. 105–118, Title V, § 583, Nov. 26, 1997, 111 Stat. 2436.)

> **Public law number of the statute as originally passed**

> **Public law number of an amendment**

> **Annotations provide references to U.S.C.C.A.N.**

HISTORICAL AND STATUTORY NOTES

Revision Notes and Legislative Reports
1996 Acts. House Report No. 104–698, see 1996 U.S. Code Cong. and Adm. News, p. 2166.

House Report No. 104–788, see 1996 U.S. Code Cong. and Adm. News, p. 4021.

1997 Acts. House Conference Report No. 105–401, see 1997 U.S. Code Cong. and Adm. News, p. 2896.

References in Text
Section 101 of the Immigration and Nationality Act, referred to in subsec. (b), is section 101 of Act June 27, 1952, c. Title I, 66 Stat. 166, which is classified to section 1101 of Title 8, Aliens and nationality.

Codifications
Section 584 of Pub.L. 105–118, which directed that section 2401 of title 18 be amended, was executed to section 2441 of Title 18, despite parenthetical refer-

ence to "section 2401 of Title 18", as the probable intent of Congress.

Amendments
1997 Amendments. Subsec. (a). Pub.L. 105–118, § 583(1), substituted "war crime" for "grave breach of the Geneva Conventions".

Subsec. (b). Pub.L. 105–118, § 583(2), substituted "war crime" for "breach" each place it appeared.

Subsec. (c). Pub.L. 105–118, § 583(3), rewrote subsec. (c). Prior to amendment, subsec. (c) read as follows: "(c) Definitions.—As used in this section, the term 'grave breach of the Geneva Conventions' means conduct defined as a grave breach in any of the international conventions relating to the laws of warfare signed at Geneva 12 August 1949 or any protocol to any such convention, to which the United States is a party."

14

To locate a report in U.S.C.C.A.N., locate the edition of U.S.C.C.A.N. for the appropriate year, locate the volumes labeled ``Legislative History," and turn to the page number provided in the annotations. In this case, the committee report is in 1996 U.S.C.C.A.N. beginning on page 2166.

FIGURE 7.13   HOUSE JUDICIARY COMMITTEE REPORT REPRINTED IN U.S.C.C.A.N.

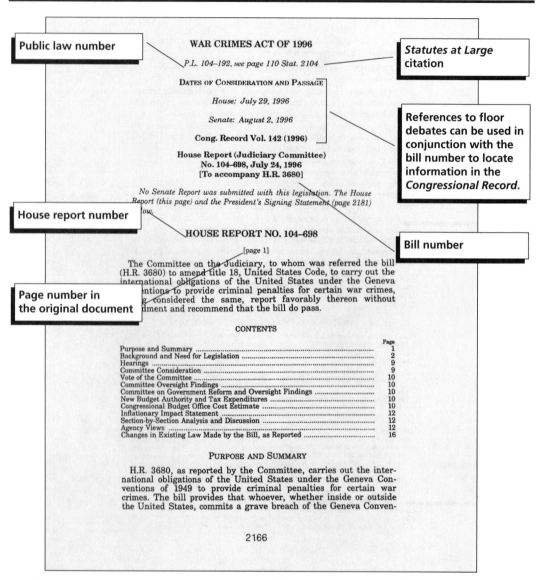

Reprinted with permission from Thomson West, *United States Code Congressional and Administrative News,* 104th Congress-Second Session 1996, Vol. 5 (1997), p. 2166. © 1997 Thomson West.

Reports on this Act are also available through Thomas. Selecting the option to search for committee reports for the 104th Congress brings up a search screen.

FIGURE 7.14   SEARCH SCREEN IN THOMAS

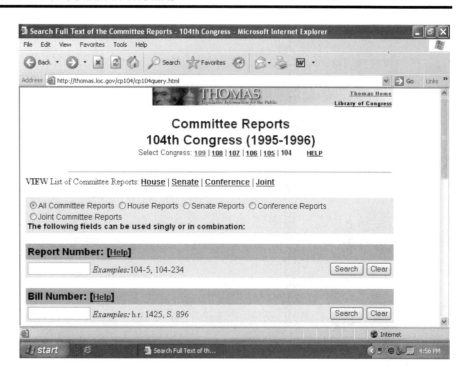

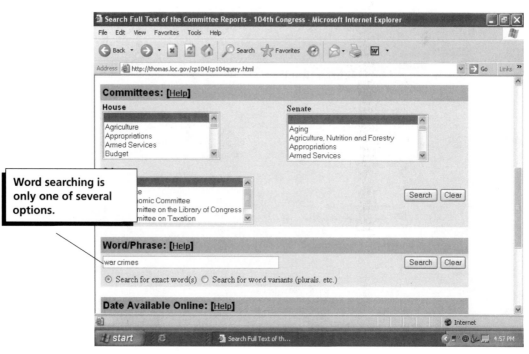

Word searching is only one of several options.

Searching for the terms "war crimes" retrieves the following results. To access the report for the War Crimes Act of 1996, click on the link for that document.

FIGURE 7.15   SEARCH RESULTS IN THOMAS

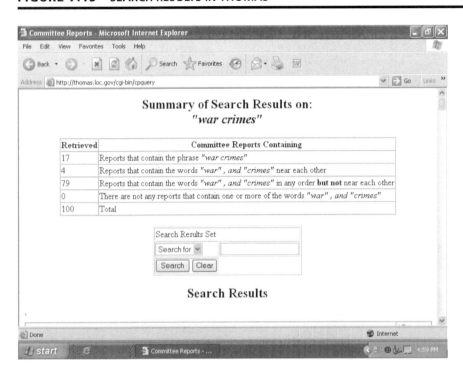

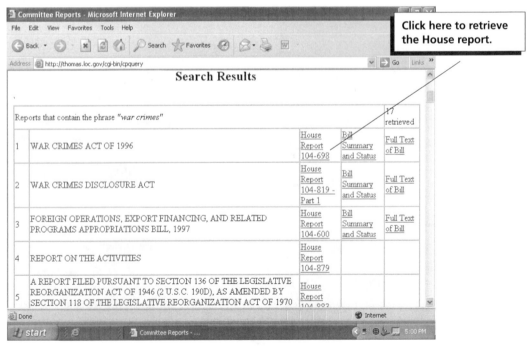

The report begins with a table of contents.

FIGURE 7.16   HOUSE JUDICIARY COMMITTEE REPORT RETRIEVED THROUGH THOMAS

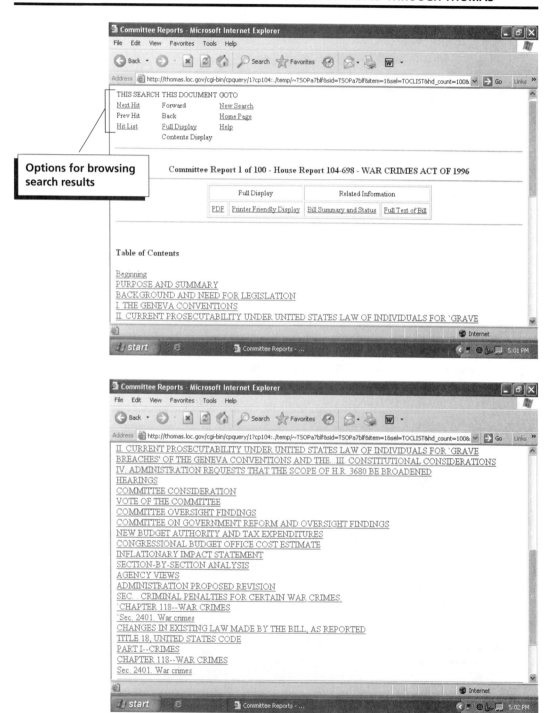

To locate legislative history in LexisNexis Congressional, access the LexisNexis Congressional web site from your library's computer network. Select the option to search in the ``CIS Index.''

FIGURE 7.17   SEARCH OPTIONS, LEXISNEXIS CONGRESSIONAL

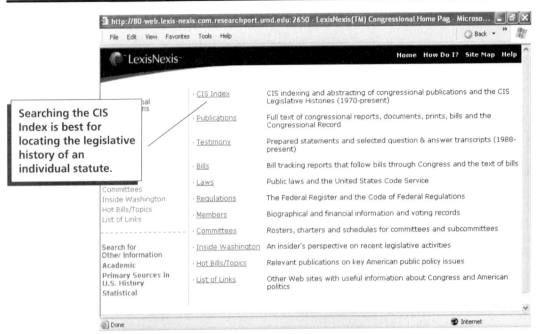

Select the option for "Legislative Histories by number."

FIGURE 7.18   SEARCH OPTIONS, LEXISNEXIS CONGRESSIONAL

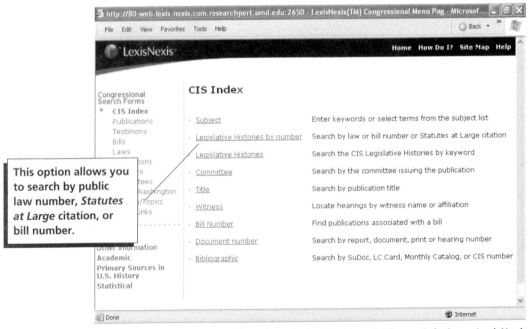

Both figures are reprinted with permission of LexisNexis Academic and Library Solutions, LexisNexis Congressional search options.

Enter the public law number, *Statutes at Large* citation, or bill number.

FIGURE 7.19   SEARCH SCREEN, LEXISNEXIS CONGRESSIONAL

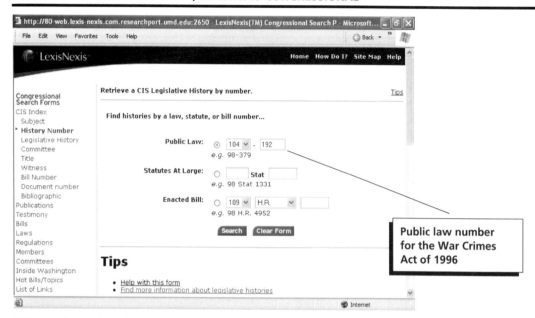

This search produced one document, an entry for the legislative history of the War Crimes Act of 1996. Click on the link to view a list of documents.

FIGURE 7.20   SEARCH RESULTS, LEXISNEXIS CONGRESSIONAL

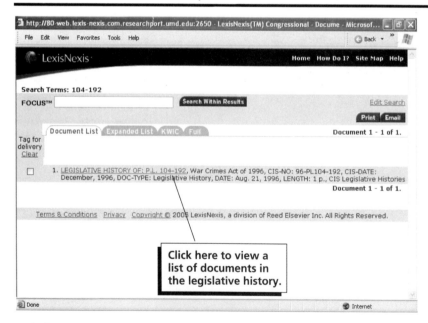

Both figures are reprinted with permission of LexisNexis Academic and Library Solutions, LexisNexis Congressional search screen and search results.

Clicking on the index entry or Full tab takes you to an abstract containing a summary of the bill and a list of documents that make up its legislative history. You can access the full text of a document by clicking on the appropriate link.

FIGURE 7.21   ABSTRACTS ENTRIES FROM LEXISNEXIS CONGRESSIONAL

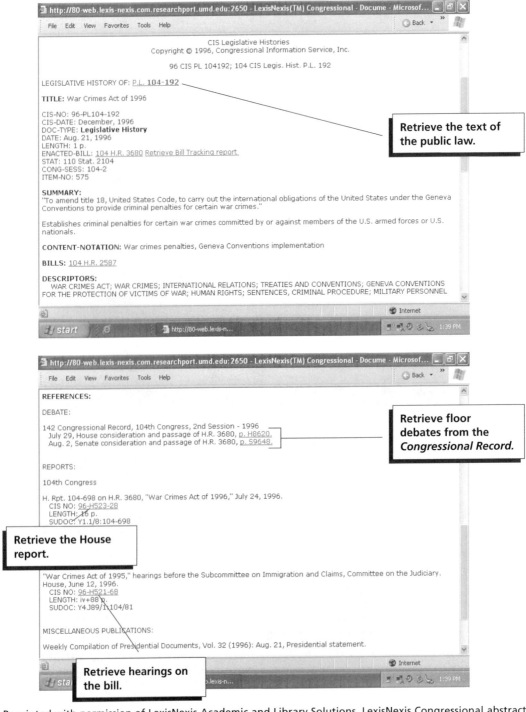

Reprinted with permission of LexisNexis Academic and Library Solutions, LexisNexis Congressional abstract entries.

By following the links, you can retrieve the full text of the House report.

FIGURE 7.22   HOUSE JUDICIARY COMMITTEE REPORT RETRIEVED FROM LEXISNEXIS CONGRESSIONAL

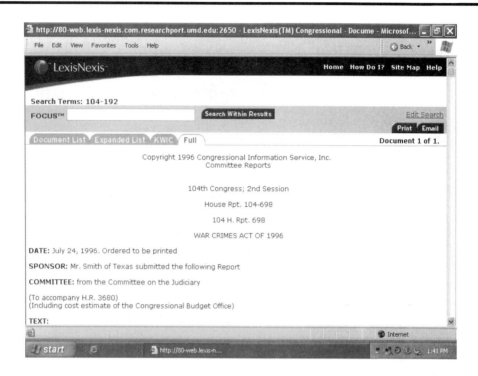

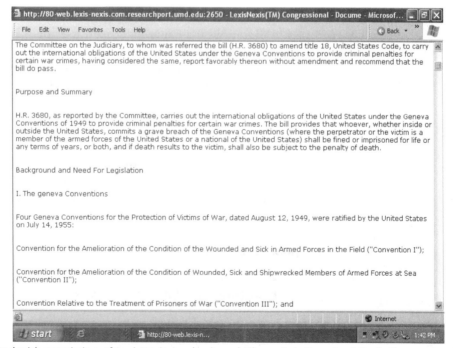

Reprinted with permission of LexisNexis Academic and Library Solutions, LexisNexis Congressional house report.

F. CHECKLIST FOR FEDERAL LEGISLATIVE HISTORY RESEARCH

Because the same legislative documents can be accessed through a variety of print and electronic resources, this section provides both a research checklist and a summary chart in **Figure 7.23** setting out where you can locate legislative history documents.

1. IDENTIFY THE SCOPE OF YOUR RESEARCH

❏ Determine whether you need the history of an individual statute or material on a general subject.

❏ To research the history of an individual statute, begin by locating the statute.

■ The public law number should follow the statute in U.S.C. or an annotated code.

■ To determine Congressional intent, start with committee reports; use U.S.C.C.A.N., a compiled legislative history, the CIS microfiche set, or an electronic source to locate committee reports.

■ For more comprehensive legislative history research, locate hearings, floor debates, and prior versions of the bill in addition to committee reports; use a compiled legislative history, the CIS microfiche set (in conjunction with the *Congressional Record*), or an electronic source to locate a statute's complete legislative history.

❏ To research material on a general subject, use the CIS microfiche set or an electronic source.

❏ If necessary, consult a reference librarian for assistance in determining the appropriate scope of your research and locating necessary documents.

2. LOCATE A COMPILED LEGISLATIVE HISTORY

❏ Search the library's on-line catalog for separately published legislative histories.

❏ Use Johnson, *Sources of Compiled Legislative Histories*, or Reams, *Federal Legislative Histories*.

3. LOCATE COMMITTEE REPORTS IN U.S.C.C.A.N.

❏ Use annotations in U.S.C.A. to locate cross-references to committee reports reprinted in U.S.C.C.A.N.

4. LOCATE COMPLETE LEGISLATIVE HISTORIES IN THE CIS MICROFICHE SET

❒ Look up the public law number in the Legislative Histories volumes (after 1984) to locate listings of all legislative history documents for an individual statute.

❒ Before 1984, locate the same information in the legislative histories section in the annual Abstracts volumes.

❒ Use the Index and Abstracts volumes if you do not have the public law number or need to locate information by subject.

5. LOCATE FLOOR DEBATES IN THE *CONGRESSIONAL RECORD* USING PRINT RESOURCES

❒ Locate references to floor debates using the CIS Legislative Histories volumes or reports reprinted in U.S.C.C.A.N.

❒ Use the *Congressional Record* index to locate information by subject or bill number.

6. SEARCH FOR LEGISLATIVE HISTORY ELECTRONICALLY

❒ Search by public law number, *Statutes at Large* citation, or bill number to locate the legislative history of an individual piece of legislation.

❒ Use subject or word searches to locate information by subject.

❒ Use Westlaw and LexisNexis to locate legislative documents.

❒ Use Thomas or GPO Access for free Internet access to legislative documents.

❒ Use LexisNexis Congressional if your library subscribes to this service for electronic access to the CIS microfiche set.

FIGURE 7.23   RESEARCH SUMMARY FOR FEDERAL LEGISLATIVE HISTORY

TO LOCATE THIS TYPE OF DOCUMENT	USE THIS PRINT RESOURCE	OR THIS ELECTRONIC RESOURCE
Bills	Compiled legislative histories, CIS microfiche	LexisNexis, Westlaw, LexisNexis Congressional, Thomas, GPO Access
Hearings	Compiled legislative histories, CIS microfiche	LexisNexis, Westlaw, LexisNexis Congressional, Thomas, GPO Access
Floor debates	Compiled legislative histories, *Congressional Record*	*Congressional Record* accessed through LexisNexis, Westlaw, LexisNexis Congressional, Thomas, GPO Access
Committee reports	Compiled legislative histories, U.S.C.C.A.N., CIS microfiche	LexisNexis, Westlaw, LexisNexis Congressional, Thomas, GPO Access

FEDERAL ADMINISTRATIVE LAW RESEARCH

A. Introduction to federal administrative law

B. Researching federal regulations in print

C. Researching federal regulations electronically

D. Citing federal regulations

E. Sample pages for federal administrative law research

F. Checklist for federal administrative law research

A. INTRODUCTION TO FEDERAL ADMINISTRATIVE LAW

Administrative agencies exist at all levels of government. Examples of federal administrative agencies include the Food and Drug Administration (FDA), the Environmental Protection Agency (EPA), and the Federal Communications Commission (FCC). Agencies are created by statute, but they are part of the executive branch because they "enforce" or implement a legislatively created scheme. In creating an agency, a legislature will pass what is known as "enabling" legislation. Enabling legislation defines the scope of the agency's mission and "enables" it to perform its functions, which may include promulgating regulations and adjudicating controversies, among other functions. If an agency is empowered to create regulations, those regulations cannot exceed the authority granted by the legislature. Thus, for example, while the FCC may be able to establish regulations concerning television licenses, it would not be able to promulgate regulations concerning the labeling of drugs because that would exceed the authority granted to it by Congress in its enabling legislation.

Federal agencies often create regulations to implement statutes passed by Congress. Sometimes Congress cannot legislate with the level

of detail necessary to implement a complex legislative scheme. In those circumstances, Congress charges an agency with enforcing the statute, and the agency will develop procedures for implementing more general legislative mandates. In the Family and Medical Leave Act, for instance, Congress mandated that an employer allow an employee with a "serious health condition" to take unpaid medical leave. Pursuant to the statute, the Department of Labor has promulgated more specific regulations defining what "serious health condition" means.

In format, a regulation looks like a statute. It is, in essence, a rule created by a government entity, and many times administrative regulations are called "rules." In operation, they are indistinguishable from statutes, although the methods used to create, modify, and repeal them are different from those applicable to statutes. Federal administrative agencies are required to conform to the procedures set out in the Administrative Procedure Act (APA) in promulgating regulations. State agencies may be required to comply with similar statutes at the state level. Without going into too much detail, the APA frequently requires agencies to undertake the following steps: (1) notify the public when they plan to promulgate new regulations or change existing ones; (2) publish proposed regulations and solicit comments on them before the regulations become final; and (3) publish final regulations before they go into effect to notify the public of the new requirements.

Regulations and proposed regulations, along with other information on the executive branch of government, are published daily in the *Federal Register*. After final regulations are published in the *Federal Register*, they are codified in the *Code of Federal Regulations* (C.F.R.). Like U.S.C., the C.F.R. is divided into fifty "Titles." The C.F.R. Titles are subdivided into chapters, which are usually named for the agencies issuing the regulations. Chapters are subdivided into Parts covering specific regulatory areas, and Parts are further subdivided into sections. To find a regulation, you would need to know its Title, Part, and section number. Thus, a citation to 16 C.F.R. § 1210.1 tells you that the regulation is published in Title 16 of the C.F.R. in Part 1210, section number 1210.1. **Figure 8.1** illustrates what a federal regulation looks like.

B. RESEARCHING FEDERAL REGULATIONS IN PRINT

1. LOCATING AND UPDATING REGULATIONS IN PRINT

Researching federal regulations entails two steps:

a. locating regulations
b. updating your research.

FIGURE 8.1 16 C.F.R., BEGINNING OF PART 1210

An individual regulation

Consumer Product Safety Commission

§1210.2

manufactured after October 15, 1979 must be certified as complying with the standard. Cellulose insulation which is sold in bags or other containers is "manufactured" when the insulation is packaged in the bag or other container in which it will be sold. Insulation which is not sold in bags or containers is "manufactured" when the insulation leaves the manufacturing site to be sold.

PART 1210—SAFETY STANDARD FOR CIGARETTE LIGHTERS

Subpart A—Requirements for Child Resistance

Sec.
1210.1   Scope, application, and effective date.
1210.2   Definitions.
1210.3   Requirements for cigarette lighters.
1210.4   Test protocol.
1210.5   Findings.

Subpart B—Certification Requirements

1210.11   General.
1210.12   Certificate of compliance.
1210.13   Certification tests.
1210.14   Qualification testing.
1210.15   Specifications.
1210.16   Production testing.
1210.17   Recordkeeping and reporting.
1210.18   Refusal of importation.

Subpart C—Stockpiling

1210.20   Stockpiling.

SOURCE: 58 FR 37584, July 12, 1993, unless otherwise noted.

Subpart A—Requirements for Child Resistance

AUTHORITY: 15 U.S.C. 2056, 2058, 2079(d).

§1210.1 Scope, application, and effective date.

This part 1210, a consumer product safety standard, prescribes requirements for disposable and novelty lighters. These requirements are intended to make the lighters subject to the standard's provisions resistant to successful operation by children younger than 5 years of age. This standard applies to all disposable and novelty lighters, as defined in §1210.2, that are manufactured or imported after July 12, 1994.

§1210.2 Definitions.

As used in this part 1210:
(a) *Cigarette lighter.* See *lighter.*
(b) *Disposable lighter*—means a lighter that either is:
(1) Not refillable with fuel or
(2)(i) Its fuel is butane, isobutane, propane, or other liquified hydrocarbon, or a mixture containing any of these, whose vapor pressure at 75 °F (24 °C) exceeds a gage pressure of 15 psi (103 kPa), and
(ii) It has a Customs Valuation or ex-factory price under $2.00, as adjusted every 5 years, to the nearest $0.25, in accordance with the percentage changes in the monthly Wholesale Price Index from June 1993.
(c) *Lighter,* also referred to as *cigarette lighter,* means a flame-producing product commonly used by consumers to ignite cigarettes, cigars, and pipes, although they may be used to ignite other materials. This term does not include matches or any other lighting device intended primarily for igniting materials other than smoking materials, such as fuel for fireplaces or for charcoal or gas-fired grills. When used in this part 1210, the term *lighter* includes only the disposable and novelty lighters to which this regulation applies.
(d) *Novelty lighter* means a lighter that has entertaining audio or visual effects, or that depicts (logos, decals, art work, etc.) or resembles in physical form or function articles commonly recognized as appealing to or intended for use by children under 5 years of age. This includes, but is not limited to, lighters that depict or resemble cartoon characters, toys, guns, watches, musical instruments, vehicles, toy animals, food or beverages, or that play musical notes or have flashing lights or other entertaining features. A novelty lighter may operate on any fuel, including butane or liquid fuel.
(e) *Successful operation* means one signal of any duration from a surrogate lighter within either of the two 5-minute test periods specified in §1210.4(f).
(f) *Surrogate lighter* means a device that: approximates the appearance, size, shape, and weight of, and is identical in all other factors that affect child resistance (including operation

Outline of the Part

Citation to the *Federal Register* where the regulations were originally published

Statutory authority for promulgating the regulations

This section describes how to complete these steps using print research resources.

a. Locating Regulations

The C.F.R. is published as a set of softcover books. Once you locate the C.F.R. set, the next question is how to find regulations relevant to your research issue. There are two ways to accomplish this. One way is to use the cross-references to the C.F.R. in U.S.C.S. or U.S.C.A. The other is to go directly to the C.F.R. itself, using a subject index to refer you to relevant C.F.R. provisions.[1]

(1) Using an annotated code

Because regulations are often used to implement statutory schemes, U.S.C.S. and U.S.C.A. frequently contain cross-references to applicable regulations. Thus, if your research leads you to statutes, the annotations are a useful tool to guide you toward regulations that bear on the area of law you are researching. You may recall from Chapter 6 that U.S.C.S. contains more extensive regulatory annotations than U.S.C.A. does. **Figure 8.2** shows C.F.R. cross-references in U.S.C.S. annotations.

(2) Using an index

Another way to locate regulations is to use the CFR Index and Finding Aids. This is a subject index within the C.F.R. set itself. Like all other C.F.R. volumes, it is a softcover book, and it is published annually. **Figure 8.3** shows a page from the CFR Index and Finding Aids.

b. Updating Regulations

The C.F.R. is updated once a year in four separate installments. Titles 1 through 16 are updated on January 1 of each year, Titles 17 through 27 on April 1, Titles 28 through 41 on July 1, and Titles 42 through 50 on October 1. Because a new set of C.F.R. volumes is published annually, the C.F.R. is not updated with pocket parts. Instead, new or amended

---

[1]Subject-matter services used for researching specific subject areas of the law may also contain the text of regulations. Researching with subject-matter services is covered in Chapter 9.

FIGURE 8.2   ANNOTATIONS TO 15 U.S.C.S. § 2056

Reprinted from *United States Code Service, Lawyer's Edition* with permission. Copyright 1996 Matthew Bender Company, Inc., a member of the LexisNexis Group. All Rights Reserved. *United States Code Service,* Title 15 Commerce and Trade §§ 1701-2800 (1996), p. 158.

regulations are published in the *Federal Register.* They are not codified within the C.F.R. until a new set is published. Because agencies can act at any time during the year, updating C.F.R. research is essential. Updating is a two-step process:

- Use the List of CFR Sections Affected to find any *Federal Register* notices indicating that the regulation has been affected by agency action.
- Update from the date of the List of CFR Sections Affected until the present.

(1) Using the List of CFR Sections Affected
The List of CFR Sections Affected (LSA) is a monthly publication listing each C.F.R. section affected by agency action. The LSA is a cumulative publication; thus, you only need to check the most recent issue to determine whether any changes to a regulation have taken place since the date the relevant Title of the C.F.R. was last published.

FIGURE 8.3   INDEX ENTRY, CFR INDEX AND FINDING AIDS

CFR Index

Program performance measures, standards, financial incentives, and penalties, 45 CFR 305

State plan approval and grant procedures, 45 CFR 301

State plan requirements, 45 CFR 302

Child welfare

See also Aid to Families with Dependent Children; Child labor; Child support; Day care; Maternal and child health

Adoption and foster care

General, 45 CFR 1355

Social Security Act—

Title IV-B, fiscal requirements, 45 CFR 1357

Title IV-E, fiscal requirements, 45 CFR 1356

Child abuse and child pornography reporting designations and procedures, 28 CFR 81

Child abuse and neglect prevention and treatment, 45 CFR 1340

Consolidation of grants to insular areas for social programs, 45 CFR 97

Family violence prevention and services programs, 45 CFR 1370

Indian child protection and family violence prevention, 25 CFR 63

Indian child welfare, 25 CFR 23

Indians, financial assistance and social services program, 25 CFR 20

Social services block grants, 45 CFR 96

Children

See Infants and children

Children and Families Administration

See Child Support Enforcement Office; Community Services Office; Family Assistance Office; Refugee Resettlement Office

Illegitimacy ratio decrease, Social Security Act section 403(a)(2) bonus implementation to reward, 45 CFR 283

Temporary Assistance for Needy Families (TANF) Program

Data collection and reporting requirements, 45 CFR 265

Ensuring that recipients work, 45 CFR 261

General accountability provisions, 45 CFR 262

General provisions, 45 CFR 260

High performance bonus awards, 45 CFR 270

Citizens band radio service

Methodology for determining whether State or territory's child poverty rate increase is result of TANF program, 45 CFR 284

Native employment works (NEW) program, 45 CFR 287

Other accountability provisions, 45 CFR 264

State and Federal TANF funds, expenditures, 45 CFR 263

Tribal TANF provisions, 45 CFR 286

China

Income from sources outside U.S., China Trade Act corporations, income taxes, 26 CFR 1 (1.941-1—1.943-1)

Chocolate

See Cacao products

Cigarette lighters

Products subject to other Acts, regulation under Consumer Product Safety Act, 16 CFR 1145

Safety standard, 16 CFR 1210

Cigars and cigarettes

See also Smoking

Customs and Border Protection Bureau, air commerce regulations, aircraft liquor kits, 19 CFR 122

Customs examination, sampling, and testing of merchandise, 19 CFR 151

Internal Revenue Service, statement of procedural rules, 26 CFR 601

Railroad Retirement Board, prohibition of cigarette sales to minors, 20 CFR 368

Tennessee Valley Authority, property management, tobacco products prohibition, 18 CFR 1303

Tobacco products and cigarette papers and tubes

Contraband cigarettes, 27 CFR 646

Exportation without payment of tax or with drawback of tax, 27 CFR 44

Importation, 27 CFR 275

Manufacture, 27 CFR 40

Miscellaneous regulations, 27 CFR 46

Removal without payment of tax for use of United States, 27 CFR 45

Unfair or deceptive advertising and labeling of cigarettes in relation to health hazards of smoking, 16 CFR 408

Citizens band radio service

See Radio

> Reference to C.F.R. Title and Part with regulations on safety standards for cigarette lighters

103

Once you have located the most recent LSA, the first step in using it is checking the time period it covers. This information is on the inside front cover. In the illustration in **Figure 8.4**, the LSA for March 2004 contains changes to Titles 1 through 16 of the C.F.R. from January 2 through March 31, 2004.

The next step is looking up the regulation in the LSA. The LSA is organized numerically by Title number, and within each Title, numerically by Part and section number. If you do not find the Part or section listed in the LSA, there have been no changes to the regulation. If you do find the Part or section listed, the LSA will refer you to the page or pages of the *Federal Register* containing information on the agency's action. **Figure 8.5** is an example of a page from the March 2004 LSA.

The *Federal Register* is a daily publication. It begins on the first business day of the new year with page one and is consecutively paginated from that point on until the last business day of the year. Because the *Federal Register* is consecutively paginated throughout the year, locating an individual page number can be difficult. The LSA has a table in the back listing the range of page numbers contained in each daily issue. You can use this table to identify the precise day on which the change was reported in the *Federal Register*. An example of the table appears in **Figure 8.6**.

Once you know the date of the *Federal Register* issue containing the page with changes to the regulation, you can go directly to that issue and read about the change. **Figure 8.7** shows the page from the *Federal Register* with the notice relevant to 16 C.F.R. Parts 1000-1799, including Part 1210.

(2) Updating beyond the list of CFR sections affected
Although the LSA is published monthly, agency action can affect federal regulations after the latest LSA was published. Therefore, the next step in updating is using the *Federal Register* to update your research from the last day covered by the LSA through the most current issue of the *Federal Register*.

For purposes of illustrating this process, assume that the most current issue of the *Federal Register* is dated April 28, 2004. In the earlier example, the March 2004 LSA provided updates through March 31, 2004, according to the information on the inside front cover. Therefore, you would still need to update your research for the period from April 1 through April 28. To update for this period, you would need to use a table on the inside back cover of the April 28 *Federal Register* called CFR Parts Affected During April. The table of CFR Parts Affected appears in the back of each issue of the *Federal Register* and is cumulative for the current month. Thus, the table in the back of the April 28 issue covers the period from April 1 through April 28.

Remember that the C.F.R. is divided into Titles, Parts, and sections. The cumulative table in the back of the *Federal Register* will not tell you

FIGURE 8.4 INSIDE FRONT COVER, MARCH 2004 LIST OF CFR SECTIONS AFFECTED

FIGURE 8.5 MARCH 2004 LIST OF CFR SECTIONS AFFECTED

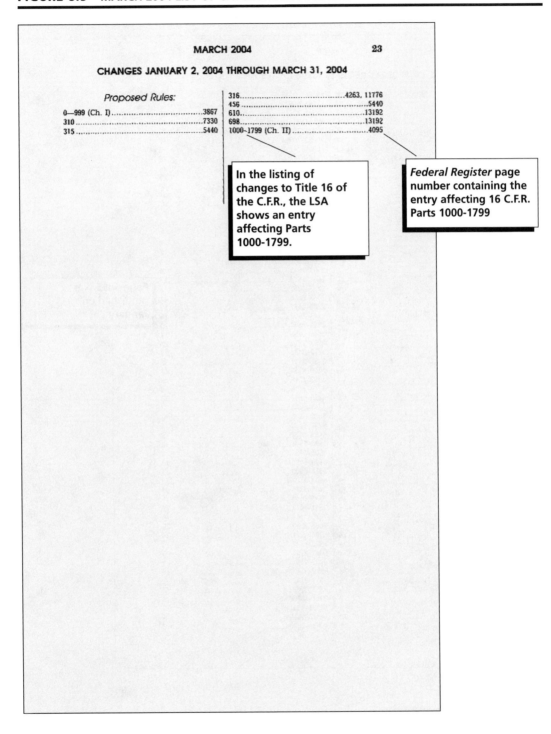

MARCH 2004   23

CHANGES JANUARY 2, 2004 THROUGH MARCH 31, 2004

Proposed Rules:

0—999 (Ch. I)...............................3867	316..4263, 11776
310..7330	456...5440
315..5440	610...13192
	698...13192
	1000–1799 (Ch. II).................................4095

In the listing of changes to Title 16 of the C.F.R., the LSA shows an entry affecting Parts 1000-1799.

Federal Register page number containing the entry affecting 16 C.F.R. Parts 1000-1799

FIGURE 8.6 MARCH 2004 LIST OF CFR SECTIONS AFFECTED, TABLE OF *FEDERAL REGISTER* ISSUE PAGES AND DATES

122   TABLE OF FEDERAL REGISTER ISSUE PAGES AND DATES

Pages	Date		Pages	Date
54123–54325	16		69295–69582	12
54327–54650	17		69583–69939	15
54651–54796	18		69941–70119	16
54797–54978	19		70121–70419	17
54979–55189	22		70421–70687	18
55191–55259	23		70689–70994	19
55261–55298	24		70995–74159	22
55299–55431	25		74161–74465	23
55433–55805	26		74467–74828	24
55807–56135	29		74829–75105	29
56137–56519	30		75107–75383	30
56521–56764	Oct. 1		75385–75795	31
56765–57318	2		**2004**	
57319–57606	3		**69 FR Page**	
57607–57782	6		1–241	Jan. 2
57783–58007	7		243–484	5
58009–58260	8		485–848	6
58261–58574	9		849–1267	7
58575–59078	10		1269–1501	8
59079–59304	14		1503–1645	9
59305–59512	15		1647–1892	12
59513–59704	16		1893–2052	13
59705–59854	17		2053–2288	14
59855–60024	20		2289–2477	15
60025–60279	21		2479–2652	16
60281–60616	22		2653–2824	20
60617–60839	23		2825–2996	21
60841–61096	24		2997–3212	22
61097–61321	27		3213–3482	23
61323–61605	28		3483–3817	26
61607–61731	29		3819–4056	27
61733–61985	30		4057–4218	28
61987–62211	31		4219–4438	29
62213–62350	Nov. 3		4439–4842	30
62351–62502	4		4843–5003	Feb. 2
62503–62729	5		5005–5256	3
62731–63009	6		5257–5458	4
63011–63731	7		5459–5678	5
63733–63981	10		5679–5904	6
63983–64262	12		5905–6138	9
64263–64489	13		6139–6524	10
64491–64798	14		6525–6903	11
64799–64976	17		6904–7103	12
64977–65151	18		7105–7345	13
65153–65382	19		7347–7540	17
65383–65625	20		7541–7677	18
65627–65827	21		7679–7862	19
65829–66000	24		7863–8089	20
66001–66318	25		8091–8321	23
66319–66691	26		8323–8543	24
66693–67011	28		8545–8795	25
67013–67355	Dec. 1		8797–9187	26
67357–67584	2		9189–9513	27
67585–67785	3		9515–9742	Mar. 1
67787–67396	4		9743–9909	2
67397–68231	5		9911–10129	3
68233–68485	8		10131–10311	4
68487–68715	9		10313–10594	5
68717–69000	10		10595–10900	8
69001–69293	11			

Page 4095 was published on January 28.

FIGURE 8.7   *FEDERAL REGISTER,* JANUARY 28, 2004

Federal Register / Vol. 69, No. 18 / Wednesday, January 28, 2004 / Proposed Rules   4095

Commission would not pursue intermediate treasurers.[11] *See Cal. Democratic Party* v. *FEC,* 13 F. Supp. 2d 1031, 1037 (E.D. Cal. 1998) (dismissing individual capacity claims against a former treasurer because "there is no allegation that [the treasurer] violated any personal obligation" and dismissing official capacity claims against him "since [he] is no longer treasurer * * * and thus, is not the appropriate person against whom an official capacity suit can be maintained. * * *").[12]

VII. Proposed Policy

In light of the considerations explained above, the Commission is considering exercising its discretion in enforcement matters by naming treasurers as follows:

1. In all enforcement actions where a political committee is a respondent, name as respondents the committee and its current treasurer "in (his or her) official capacity as treasurer."

2. In enforcement actions where a treasurer has apparently breached a personal obligation owing by virtue of his or her responsibilities under the Act and regulations, or a prohibition that applies to individuals, name that treasurer as a respondent "in (his or her) personal capacity."

The Commission invites comments on this policy that is under consideration. Comments may be submitted on any aspect of the policy being considered, including:

(A) If the Commission adopts the policy, are there certain circumstances that warrant flexibility in applying the policy?

[11] For example, while Treasurer A is the treasurer for Joe Smith for Congress, a violation occurs that subjects A to official and individual liability. Treasurer A would be named in both his official and personal capacities. After the enforcement action has begun, Treasurer A resigns and Treasurer B takes over. The Commission should pursue Treasurer A in his individual capacity, and Treasurer B in her official capacity. If Treasurer B resigns and is succeeded by Treasurer C prior to the conclusion of the enforcement matter, the Commission should then continue to pursue Treasurer A in his individual capacity and pursue Treasurer C in her official capacity. Treasurer B is no longer named in her official capacity.

[12] A deeper examination of the court file indicates that—despite the *California Democratic Party* court's assertion to the contrary"the Commission never actually pled that the treasurer in this case was personally liable. Rather, the complaint references the treasurer "as treasurer" and the treasurer's response to the treasurer's motion to dismiss indicates that the Commission was pursuing the treasurer "in his official capacity." Compl., paragraphs 8, 58–59, Prayer paragraphs 1–5; Resp. to Def. Mot. to Dismiss, p. 21. However, the *California Democratic Party* court's result underscores the need for the Commission to delineate more clearly the capacity in which it pursues treasurers.

(B) Whether, and to what extent, the Commission should consider a treasurer's "best efforts" to comply with the law.

(C) Whether and how to apply the prospective policy in its Administrative Fines program.

Dated: January 23, 2004.

Bradley A. Smith,
Chairman, Federal Election Commission.
[FR Doc. 04–1790 Filed 1–27–04; 8:45 am]
BILLING CODE 6715–01–P

CONSUMER PRODUCT SAFETY COMMISSION

16 CFR Chapter II

Pilot Program for Systematic Review of Commission Regulations; Request for Comments and Information

AGENCY: Consumer Product Safety Commission.

ACTION: Notice of systematic review of current regulations.

SUMMARY: The Consumer Product Safety Commission (CPSC or Commission) is undertaking a pilot program to systematically review its current substantive regulations to ensure, to the maximum practical extent, consistency among them and with respect to accomplishing program goals. The pilot is currently expected to be completed by the end of calendar year 2004. Depending on the results of the pilot, the availability of personnel and fiscal resources, and other priorities for action, the Commission would then develop and implement an expanded systematic review process to address the remainder of its substantive regulations.

The primary purpose of the review is to assess the degree to which the regulations under review remain consistent with the Commission's program policies. In addition, each regulation will be examined with respect to the extent that it is current and relevant to CPSC program goals. Attention will also be given to whether the regulations can be streamlined, if possible, to minimize regulatory burdens, especially on small entities. To the degree consistent with other Commission priorities and subject to the availability of personnel and fiscal resources, specific regulatory or other projects may be undertaken in response to the results of this review.

In the initial, pilot phase of this program the following four regulations will be evaluated: safety standard for walk-behind power mowers, 16 CFR part 1205; requirements for electrically operated toys and other electrically

operated articles intended for u[se by] children, 16 CFR part 1505; sta[ndards for] the flammability of vinyl plastic[s, 16] CFR part 1611; and child-resista[nt] packaging requirements for aspi[rin,] methyl salicylate, 16 CFR 1700.[14(a)(10)] and 1700.14(a)(3), respectively.

The Commission solicits writ[ten] comments from interested perso[ns] concerning the designated regul[ations'] currentness and consistency wi[th] Commission policies and goals, [and] suggestions for streamlining wh[ere] appropriate. In so doing, comme[nters] are requested to specifically add[ress] how their suggestions for change could be accomplished within the various statutory frameworks for Commission action under the Consumer Product Safety Act (CPSA), 15 U.S.C. 2051–2084, Federal Hazardous Substances Act (FHSA), 15 U.S.C. 1261–1278, Flammable Fabrics Act (FFA), 15 U.S.C. 1191–1204; and Poison Prevention Packaging Act (PPPA), 15 U.S.C. 1471–1476.

DATES: Written comments and submissions in response to this notice must be received by March 29, 2004.

ADDRESSES: Comments and other submissions should be captioned "Pilot Regulatory Review Project" and mailed to the Office of the Secretary, Consumer Product Safety Commission, Washington, DC 20207, or delivered to that office, room 502, 4330 East-West Highway, Bethesda, Maryland 20814. Comments and other submissions may also be filed by facsimile to (301) 504–0127 or by e-mail to *cpsc-os@cpsc.gov.*

FOR FURTHER INFORMATION CONTACT: N.J. Scheers, PhD, Director, Office of Planning & Evaluation, U.S. Consumer Product Safety Commission, Washington, DC 20207; telephone (301) 504–7670; e-mail *nscheers@cpsc.gov.*

SUPPLEMENTARY INFORMATION:

A. The Pilot Review Program

The President's Office of Management and Budget has designed the Program Assessment Rating Tool (PART) to provide a consistent approach to rating programs across the Federal government. A description of the PART process and associated program evaluation materials is available online at: *http://www.whitehouse.gov/omb/ budintegration/ part_assessing2004.html.*

Based on an evaluation of the Commission's regulatory programs using the PART, the recommendation was made that CPSC develop a plan to systematically review its current regulations to ensure consistency among them in accomplishing program goals. The pilot review program launched with

> The *Federal Register* entry announces a pilot program for reviewing regulations in 16 C.F.R. Chapter II (Parts 1000-1799), but does not contain changes to the regulations.

which sections have been affected, only which Parts. Therefore, you must know the Part of the C.F.R. containing the section you are updating. If you do not see this Part referenced in the table, no action has been taken during the month to date. If you do see a reference to the Part, however, you have some additional work to do. The table will refer you to page numbers within that month's *Federal Register* with information affecting the C.F.R. Part. You cannot tell from this table which sections within the Part have been affected. Therefore, you must look up each page number reference to see which sections have been affected. When you look up each reference, if you do not find any mention of the section you are researching, your research is complete. If you do find a reference to the section, read about the change to see how it affects your research. **Figure 8.8** shows an excerpt from the table of CFR Parts Affected from the April 28, 2004, *Federal Register*.

Although the *Federal Register* is a daily publication, today's edition is not immediately available in print like a newspaper. It takes time for the daily issues to be printed and distributed. Accordingly, if you want to update your research through the current date without using electronic resources, the final step is contacting the agency directly to find out whether any action has been taken recently or is contemplated in the near future. At the beginning of any *Federal Register* notice regarding rule making, you will find the name and contact information for a person at the agency. In administrative law research, agency staff can be one of your best resources, and you should not hesitate to use e-mail or the telephone as one of your research tools.

FIGURE 8.8 *FEDERAL REGISTER,* APRIL 28, 2004, TABLE OF CFR PARTS AFFECTED DURING APRIL

Reader Aids

Federal Register

Vol. 69, No. 82

Wednesday, April 28, 2004

Cumulative table

CUSTOMER SERVICE AND INFORMATION

Federal Register/Code of Federal Regulations

General Information, indexes and other finding aids	202–741–6000
Laws	741–6000

Presidential Documents

Executive orders and proclamations	741–6000
The United States Government Manual	741–6000

Other Services

Electronic and on-line services (voice)	741–6020
Privacy Act Compilation	741–6064
Public Laws Update Service (numbers, dates, etc.)	741–6043
TTY for the deaf-and-hard-of-hearing	741–6086

ELECTRONIC RESEARCH
World Wide Web

Full text of the daily Federal Register, CFR and other publications is located at: **http://www.gpoaccess.gov/nara/index.html**

Federal Register information and research tools, including Public Inspection List, indexes, and links to GPO Access are located at: **http://www.archives.gov/federal_register/**

E-mail

FEDREGTOC-L (Federal Register Table of Contents LISTSERV) is an open e-mail service that provides subscribers with a digital form of the Federal Register Table of Contents. The digital form of the Federal Register Table of Contents includes HTML and PDF links to the full text of each document.

To join or leave, go to **http://listserv.access.gpo.gov** and select *Online mailing list archives, FEDREGTOC-L, join or leave the list (orchange settings);* then follow the instructions.

PENS (Public Law Electronic Notification Service) is an e-mail service that notifies subscribers of recently enacted laws.

To subscribe, go to **http://listserv.gsa.gov/archives/publaws-1.html** and select *Join or leave the list* (or change settings); then follow the instructions.

FEDREGTOC-L and **PENS** are mailing lists only. We cannot respond to specific inquiries.

Reference questions. Send questions and comments about the Federal Register system to: **fedreg.info@nara.gov**

The Federal Register staff cannot interpret specific documents or regulations.

FEDERAL REGISTER PAGES AND DATE, APRIL

17033–17282	1
17283–17584	2
17585–17898	5
17899–18244	6
18245–18470	7
18471–18800	8
18801–19076	9
19077–19310	12
19311–19752	13
19753–19920	14
19921–20536	15
20537–20804	16
20805–21038	19
21039–21392	20
21393–21688	21
21689–21940	22
21941–22376	23
22377–22716	26
22717–23086	27
23087–23414	28

CFR PARTS AFFECTED DURING APRIL

At the end of each month, the Office of the Federal Register publishes separately a List of CFR Sections Affected (LSA), which lists parts and sections affected by documents published since the revision date of each title.

1 CFR

51	18801

3 CFR

Proclamations:

7785	18465
7766	18467
7767	18469
7768	19077
7769	19307
7770	19751
7771	20537
7772	21683
7773	21685
7774	21687
7775	23085

Executive Orders:

13334	19917

Administrative Orders:

Presidential Determinations:

No. 2004–26 of March 24, 2004	21675
No. 2004–27 of April 6, 2004	21677
No. 2004–28 of April 14, 2004	21679

5 CFR

537	21039

Proposed Rules:

1650	18294
1653	18294
1655	18294
1690	18294

7 CFR

301	21039
319	21941
701	22377
772	18471
905	19079
916	19753
917	19753
925	21689
929	18803
956	22377
979	21947
981	21692
982	19082
983	17844
984	17899
989	21695
1000	21950
1001	21950
1005	21950
1006	21950
1007	21950
1030	21950
1032	21950
1033	21950
1124	21950

1126	21950
1131	21950

Proposed Rules:

28	22458
272	20724
273	20724
301	19950
330	17984
761	20834
762	20834
763	20834
764	20834
765	20834
766	20834
767	20834
768	20834
769	20834
926	19118
929	23330
1033	19292
1124	18834
1150	22690
1160	22690
1205	22690
1207	22690
1209	22690
1210	22690
1215	22690
1216	21430
1218	22690
1219	22690
1220	22690
1230	22690
1240	22690
1250	22690
1260	22690
1280	22690

C.F.R. Title

8 CFR

103	20528

Proposed Rules:

103	18296

9 CFR

1	17899
2	17899
3	17899
53	23087
77	20805
93	21040
94	21042
98	
301	
309	
310	
311	18245
313	18245
318	18245
319	18245
320	18245, 21047
381	21047

C.F.R. Part affected

10 CFR

170	22664

FIGURE 8.9   UPDATING C.F.R. RESEARCH IN PRINT

DATE	JANUARY 2, 2004	JANUARY 2, 2004–MARCH 31, 2004	APRIL 1, 2004–APRIL 28, 2004	APRIL 28, 2004–PRESENT
Source	Title 16, C.F.R.	March 2004 List of CFR Sections Affected (LSA)	April 28, 2004, *Federal Register*	Agency personnel
Use	Locate regulations in the C.F.R. using an annotated code or a C.F.R. index. The date of the C.F.R. is listed on the front cover.	Use the latest monthly issue. Dates of coverage are on the inside front cover. look up the Title and section number of the regulation. If it is listed, use the table in the back to find the date of the *Federal Register* containing the change. Look up the page in the *Federal Register* to locate the change.	Use the latest daily issue. The monthly cumulative table of CFR Parts Affected is in the back of the issue. If the C.F.R. Part is not listed, no changes have taken place during the month to date. If the C.F.R. Part is listed, each page reference must be checked to see which individual sections have been affected.	Contact the agency to find more recent information.

The chart in **Figure 8.9** summarizes the process of updating print research, using the example of a regulation within Title 16 of the C.F.R. published on January 2, 2004, an LSA dated March 31, 2004, and the most current *Federal Register* dated April 28, 2004.

2. SHEPARD'S FOR THE *CODE OF FEDERAL REGULATIONS*

Shepard's is available for the C.F.R., as it is for many other publications. Because the C.F.R. is not annotated,[2] Shepard's can be an invaluable research tool. Shepard's will provide references to cases that have cited the regulation, which can help you determine whether the regulation remains valid and how it has been interpreted. The process of Shepardizing should be familiar to you by now: locate the correct set of Shepard's, in this case, *Shepard's Code of Federal Regulations Citations;* locate the correct volumes by checking the "What Your Library Should Contain" section

---

[2]Some administrative regulations are reproduced as part of the U.S.C.S. and U.S.C.A. sets and may have limited annotations; however, U.S.C.S. and U.S.C.A. do not contain all Titles of the C.F.R.

FIGURE 8.10 SHEPARD'S® ENTRY FOR 16 C.F.R. PART 1210

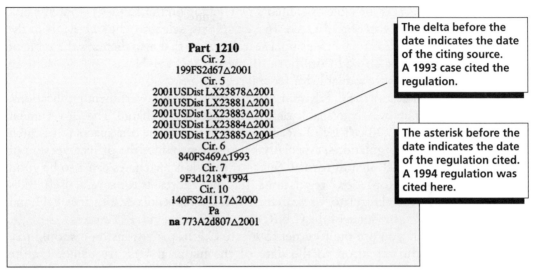

Reproduced by permission of LexisNexis. Further reproduction of any kind is strictly prohibited. From *Shepard's Code of Federal Regulations Citations,* Titles 1–20; 2004, 4th ed., Vol. 1, p. 546.

on the front of the most recent softcover supplement; and check each noncumulative volume for references to the regulation. Shepard's will refer you to cases and secondary sources that cite the regulation. A list of the treatment codes applicable to Shepard's entries for C.F.R. provisions can be found in the front of each volume of *Shepard's Code of Federal Regulation Citations.* A sample entry appears in **Figure 8.10**.

C. RESEARCHING FEDERAL REGULATIONS ELECTRONICALLY

LexisNexis, Westlaw, and the Internet are all excellent sources for regulatory research. The C.F.R. is available in LexisNexis and Westlaw, and it is usually up to date. You can check the date through which the regulation is updated by looking at the heading on the first screen displaying the regulation. The *Federal Register* is also available in both services. Because LexisNexis and Westlaw incorporate changes to regulations as they occur, the versions of the C.F.R. in their databases are not official sources for regulations. If you need the official source, you must use a print or electronic government source for the C.F.R. and *Federal Register.*

Administrative regulations in LexisNexis and Westlaw can be located either in the general administrative materials databases or in the databases for specific subject areas, if regulations have been promulgated in those subject areas. Once you select a database, you can find regulations by

executing a word search using the techniques described in Chapter 10. You can also browse the table of contents of the C.F.R. In Westlaw, you can access the table of contents by clicking on the Table of Contents link near the top of the screen. In LexisNexis, selecting the C.F.R. from the source directory brings up a search screen that also displays the table of contents. In addition, both Shepard's in LexisNexis and KeyCite in Westlaw are available for federal regulations.

Because the C.F.R. and *Federal Register* are government publications, they are widely available on the Internet free of charge. The Government Printing Office's GPO Access service is one of the best places to research federal regulations, especially because it provides the official version of the C.F.R. in .pdf format. Sites for individual agencies can also be good sources for federal regulations. Internet addresses for several useful sites for federal regulatory research are listed in Appendix A. **Figures 8.11** and **8.12** show some of the C.F.R. research options in GPO Access.

If you use the Internet to locate C.F.R. provisions, you should pay careful attention to the date of the material you are using. Unlike LexisNexis and Westlaw, Internet sources of regulations often are no more up to date than the print version of the C.F.R. In GPO Access, for example, the official C.F.R. database is only updated four times per year as the new print editions of the C.F.R. become available, although the *Federal Register* database is updated daily.

GPO Access is testing a new version of the C.F.R. called the *Electronic Code of Federal Regulations* (e-CFR), which makes updating much easier than it used to be. The e-CFR is an unofficial edition of the C.F.R. that incorporates changes to regulations as they are published in the *Federal Register,* in the same way that LexisNexis and Westlaw continually update their C.F.R. databases. Although the e-CFR is not an official source for regulations, it is a useful research tool. By comparing the official C.F.R. text with the e-CFR version, you can determine quickly and easily whether a regulation has been changed since the latest official edition of the C.F.R. was published. If you need an official source and citation for the change, you can then retrieve the *Federal Register* page containing the change in the GPO Access *Federal Register* database.

You can also update C.F.R. research in GPO Access using a process similar to that for updating print C.F.R. research. You may want to refer back to **Figure 8.9** for an overview of the print updating process. Because the e-CFR is a prototype as of this writing, it is possible that it will be changed or discontinued. Further, although no reason exists to doubt the accuracy of the e-CFR, there may be times when, out of an abundance of caution, you want to double check your research. An alternative method of updating in GPO Access requires you to research two sources:

■ Use the List of CFR Sections Affected (LSA) to find any *Federal Register* notices indicating that the regulation has been affected by agency action.

FIGURE 8.11   INTRODUCTORY SCREEN FOR C.F.R. RESEARCH IN GPO ACCESS

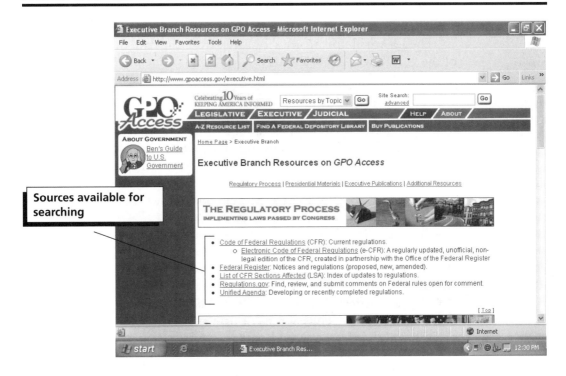

FIGURE 8.12   GPO ACCESS C.F.R. SEARCH OPTIONS

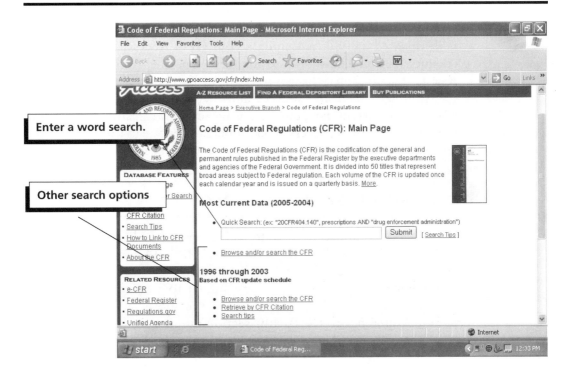

■ Use the Current List of CFR Parts Affected to update from the date of the LSA until the present.

The LSA will update your research from the date the latest volume of the C.F.R. was published through the end of the prior month. Thus, if the latest C.F.R. volume had been published on January 2 and today's date were April 28, the current LSA would be dated March, and it would contain updates from January 2 through March 31. To locate references to a regulation in the LSA, you can search for the regulation's citation in the LSA database, or you can browse the .pdf version of the LSA. If the LSA contains a reference to the regulation, it will provide the page number of the *Federal Register* where the change is published. You can retrieve the *Federal Register* page by citation in the GPO Access *Federal Register* database.

The second updating step requires you to use the Current List of CFR Parts Affected. This table lists all of the C.F.R. Parts affected by changes occurring after the last monthly issue of the LSA through the current date. It is the electronic counterpart to the *Federal Register*'s table of CFR Parts Affected, and it is updated daily from changes published in the *Federal Register*. Thus, if today's date were April 28, the Current List of CFR Parts Affected would contain updates since the March LSA, covering the period from April 1 through April 28. The table lists only the Parts affected by agency action, not individual sections. Therefore, if you find a reference to the C.F.R. Part you are researching in this table, you need to retrieve the relevant page from the *Federal Register* to determine the section or sections within the C.F.R. Part affected by agency action. Because the Current List of CFR Parts Affected is a cumulative table updated daily, it will update your GPO Access C.F.R. research completely. You do not need to conduct a separate search in the *Federal Register* for additional changes to the regulation you are researching.

Although electronic sources allow you to update your research through the current date, contacting agency staff can still be a valuable step in your research process. You should not hesitate to use e-mail or the telephone as a research tool to stay current with an agency's activities.

D. CITING FEDERAL REGULATIONS

Citations to administrative materials are governed by Rule 19 in the *ALWD Manual* and Bluepages B6.1.4 and Rule 14.2 in the *Bluebook*. The citations are the same using either format.

A citation to the C.F.R. is very similar to a citation to a federal statute. It consists of the Title number, the abbreviation C.F.R., the pinpoint reference to the Part or section number, and a parenthetical containing the year. Here are two examples:

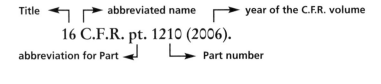

The preceding examples did not involve a regulation commonly known by name. If they had, the citation would have begun with the name of the regulation, pursuant to *ALWD Manual* Rule 19.1 and *Bluebook* Rule 14.2.

Citations to the *Federal Register* are also fairly simple and are the same using either the *ALWD Manual* or the *Bluebook*. They require the volume number, the abbreviation Fed. Reg., the page number, and a parenthetical containing the exact date.

If appropriate, you should also provide a pinpoint reference to the specific page or pages containing the cited material.

E. SAMPLE PAGES FOR FEDERAL ADMINISTRATIVE LAW RESEARCH

Beginning on the next page, **Figures 8.13** through **8.25** contain sample pages from the C.F.R. showing the process of print research into regulations pertaining to safety standards for cigarette lighters, as well as several samples from GPO Access.

The first step is locating relevant regulations. You could use a subject index such as the CFR Index and Finding Aids, as illustrated in this example. You could also use statutory annotations to locate relevant regulations.

FIGURE 8.13   INDEX ENTRY, CFR INDEX AND FINDING AIDS

CFR Index   **Citizens band radio service**

Program performance measures, standards, financial incentives, and penalties, 45 CFR 305
State plan approval and grant procedures, 45 CFR 301
State plan requirements, 45 CFR 302

Child welfare
See also Aid to Families with Dependent Children; Child labor; Child support; Day care; Maternal and child health
Adoption and foster care
General, 45 CFR 1355
Social Security Act—
Title IV-B, fiscal requirements, 45 CFR 1357
Title IV-E, fiscal requirements, 45 CFR 1356
Child abuse and child pornography reporting designations and procedures, 28 CFR 81
Child abuse and neglect prevention and treatment, 45 CFR 1340
Consolidation of grants to insular areas for social programs, 45 CFR 97
Family violence prevention and services programs, 45 CFR 1370
Indian child protection and family violence prevention, 25 CFR 63
Indian child welfare, 25 CFR 23
Indians, financial assistance and social services program, 25 CFR 20
Social services block grants, 45 CFR 96

Children
See Infants and children

Children and Families Administration
See Child Support Enforcement Office; Community Services Office; Family Assistance Office; Refugee Resettlement Office
Illegitimacy ratio decrease, Social Security Act section 403(a)(2) bonus implementation to reward, 45 CFR 283
Temporary Assistance for Needy Families (TANF) Program
Data collection and reporting requirements, 45 CFR 265
Ensuring that recipients work, 45 CFR 261
General accountability provisions, 45 CFR 262
General provisions, 45 CFR 260
High performance bonus awards, 45 CFR 270

Methodology for determining whether State or territory's child poverty rate increase is result of TANF program, 45 CFR 284
Native employment works (NEW) program, 45 CFR 287
Other accountability provisions, 45 CFR 264
State and Federal TANF funds, expenditures, 45 CFR 263
Tribal TANF provisions, 45 CFR 286

China
Income from sources outside U.S., China Trade Act corporations, income taxes, 26 CFR 1 (1.941-1—1.943-1)

Chocolate
See Cacao products

Cigarette lighters
Products subject to other Acts, regulation under Consumer Product Safety Act, 16 CFR 1145
Safety standard, 16 CFR 1210

Cigars and cigarettes
See also Smoking
Customs and Border Protection Bureau, air commerce regulations, aircraft liquor kits, 19 CFR 122
Customs examination, sampling, and testing of merchandise, 19 CFR 151
Internal Revenue Service, statement of procedural rules, 26 CFR 601
Railroad Retirement Board, prohibition of cigarette sales to minors, 20 CFR 368
Tennessee Valley Authority, property management, tobacco products prohibition, 18 CFR 1303
Tobacco products and cigarette papers and tubes
Contraband cigarettes, 27 CFR 646
Exportation without payment of tax or with drawback of tax, 27 CFR 44
Importation, 27 CFR 275
Manufacture, 27 CFR 40
Miscellaneous regulations, 27 CFR 46
Removal without payment of tax for use of United States, 27 CFR 45
Unfair or deceptive advertising and labeling of cigarettes in relation to health hazards of smoking, 16 CFR 408

Citizens band radio service
See Radio

> Reference to C.F.R. Title and Part with regulations on safety standards for cigarette lighters

103

The next step is locating C.F.R. sections. In this example, you can find applicable sections within the C.F.R. by looking in the volume with Title 16 and locating Part 1210. If you were interested in researching the definition of a cigarette lighter, you might want to read 16 C.F.R. § 1210.2.

FIGURE 8.14 16 C.F.R. PART 1210

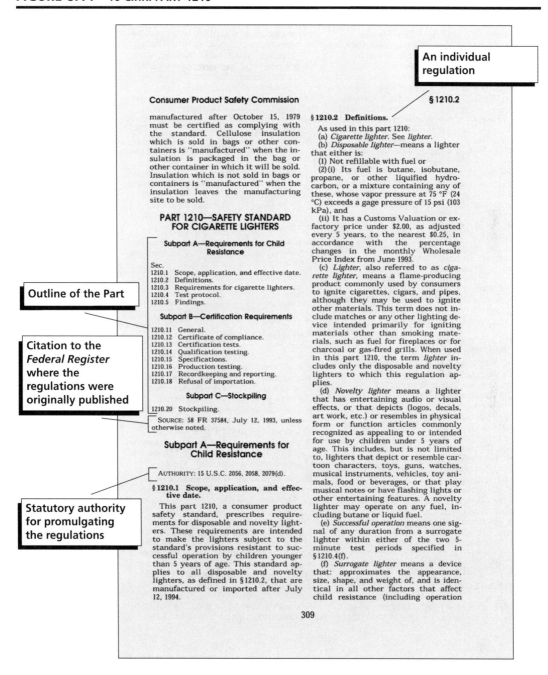

An individual regulation

Outline of the Part

Citation to the *Federal Register* where the regulations were originally published

Statutory authority for promulgating the regulations

Consumer Product Safety Commission

manufactured after October 15, 1979 must be certified as complying with the standard. Cellulose insulation which is sold in bags or other containers is "manufactured" when the insulation is packaged in the bag or other container in which it will be sold. Insulation which is not sold in bags or containers is "manufactured" when the insulation leaves the manufacturing site to be sold.

PART 1210—SAFETY STANDARD FOR CIGARETTE LIGHTERS

Subpart A—Requirements for Child Resistance

Sec.
1210.1 Scope, application, and effective date.
1210.2 Definitions.
1210.3 Requirements for cigarette lighters.
1210.4 Test protocol.
1210.5 Findings.

Subpart B—Certification Requirements

1210.11 General.
1210.12 Certificate of compliance.
1210.13 Certification tests.
1210.14 Qualification testing.
1210.15 Specifications.
1210.16 Production testing.
1210.17 Recordkeeping and reporting.
1210.18 Refusal of importation.

Subpart C—Stockpiling

1210.20 Stockpiling.

SOURCE: 58 FR 37584, July 12, 1993, unless otherwise noted.

Subpart A—Requirements for Child Resistance

AUTHORITY: 15 U.S.C. 2056, 2058, 2079(d).

§ 1210.1 Scope, application, and effective date.

This part 1210, a consumer product safety standard, prescribes requirements for disposable and novelty lighters. These requirements are intended to make the lighters subject to the standard's provisions resistant to successful operation by children younger than 5 years of age. This standard applies to all disposable and novelty lighters, as defined in § 1210.2, that are manufactured or imported after July 12, 1994.

§ 1210.2

§ 1210.2 Definitions.

As used in this part 1210:
(a) *Cigarette lighter.* See *lighter.*
(b) *Disposable lighter*—means a lighter that either is:
(1) Not refillable with fuel or
(2)(i) Its fuel is butane, isobutane, propane, or other liquified hydrocarbon, or a mixture containing any of these, whose vapor pressure at 75 °F (24 °C) exceeds a gage pressure of 15 psi (103 kPa), and
(ii) It has a Customs Valuation or exfactory price under $2.00, as adjusted every 5 years, to the nearest $0.25, in accordance with the percentage changes in the monthly Wholesale Price Index from June 1993.
(c) *Lighter,* also referred to as *cigarette lighter,* means a flame-producing product commonly used by consumers to ignite cigarettes, cigars, and pipes, although they may be used to ignite other materials. This term does not include matches or any other lighting device intended primarily for igniting materials other than smoking materials, such as fuel for fireplaces or for charcoal or gas-fired grills. When used in this part 1210, the term *lighter* includes only the disposable and novelty lighters to which this regulation applies.
(d) *Novelty lighter* means a lighter that has entertaining audio or visual effects, or that depicts (logos, decals, art work, etc.) or resembles in physical form or function articles commonly recognized as appealing to or intended for use by children under 5 years of age. This includes, but is not limited to, lighters that depict or resemble cartoon characters, toys, guns, watches, musical instruments, vehicles, toy animals, food or beverages, or that play musical notes or have flashing lights or other entertaining features. A novelty lighter may operate on any fuel, including butane or liquid fuel.
(e) *Successful operation* means one signal of any duration from a surrogate lighter within either of the two 5-minute test periods specified in § 1210.4(f).
(f) *Surrogate lighter* means a device that: approximates the appearance, size, shape, and weight of, and is identical in all other factors that affect child resistance (including operation

309

FIGURE 8.14   16 C.F.R. PART 1210 *(Continued)*

---

§ 1210.3   16 CFR Ch. II (1–1–04 Edition)

and the force(s) required for operation), within reasonable manufacturing tolerances, to, a lighter intended for use by consumers; has no fuel; does not produce a flame; and produces an audible or visual signal that will be clearly discernible when the surrogate lighter is activated in each manner that would normally produce a flame in a production lighter. (This definition does not require a lighter to be modified with electronics or the like to produce a signal. Manufacturers may use a lighter without fuel as a surrogate lighter if a distinct signal such as a "click" can be heard clearly when the mechanism is operated in each manner that would produce a flame in a production lighter and if a flame cannot be produced in a production lighter without the signal. *But see* § 1210.4(f)(1).)

(g) *Model* means one or more cigarette lighters from the same manufacturer or importer that do not differ in design or other characteristics in any manner that may affect child-resistance. Lighter characteristics that may affect child-resistance include, but are not limited to, size, shape, case material, and ignition mechanism (including child-resistant features).

§ 1210.3 Requirements for cigarette lighters.

(a) A lighter subject to this part 1210 shall be resistant to successful operation by at least 85 percent of the child-test panel when tested in the manner prescribed by § 1210.4.

(b) The mechanism or system of a lighter subject to this part 1210 that makes the product resist successful operation by children must:

(1) Reset itself automatically after each operation of the ignition mechanism of the lighter,

(2) Not impair safe operation of the lighter when used in a normal and convenient manner,

(3) Be effective for the reasonably expected life of the lighter, and

(4) Not be easily overriden or deactivated.

§ 1210.4 Test protocol.

(a) *Child test panel.* (1) The test to determine if a lighter is resistant to successful operation by children uses a panel of children to test a surrogate

lighter representing the production lighter intended for use. Written informed consent shall be obtained from a parent or legal guardian of a child before the child participates in the test.

(2) The test shall be conducted using at least one, but no more than two, 100-child test panels in accordance with the provisions of § 1210.4(f).

(3) The children for the test panel shall live within the United States.

(4) The age and sex distribution of each 100-child panel shall be:

(i) 30 +or- 2 children (20 +or- 1 males; 10 +or- 1 females) 42 through 44 months old;

(ii) 40 +or- 2 children (26 +or- 1 males; 14 +or- 1 females) 45 through 48 months old;

(iii) 30 +or- 2 children (20 +or- 1 males; 10 +or- 1 females) 49 through 51 months old.

NOTE: To calculate a child's age in months:

1. Subtract the child's birth date from the test date.

	Month	Day	Year
Test Date	8	3	94
Birth Date	6	23	90
Difference	2	-20	4

2. Multiply the difference in years by 12 months.

4 years × 12 months = 48 months.

3. Add the difference in months.

48 months + 2 months = 50 months.

4. If the difference in days is greater than 15 (e.g. 16, 17), add 1 month.

If the difference in days is less than -15 (e.g., -16, -17) subtract 1 month.

50 months - 1 month = 49 months.

If the difference in days is between -15 and 15 (e.g., -15, -14, ... 14, 15), do *not* add or subtract 1 month.

(5) No child with a permanent or temporary illness, injury, or handicap that would interfere with the child's ability to operate the surrogate lighter shall be selected for participation.

(6) Two children at a time shall participate in testing of surrogate lighters. Extra children whose results will not be counted in the test may be used if necessary to provide the required partner for test subjects, if the extra children are within the required age range and a parent or guardian of each such child has signed a consent form.

To begin updating § 1210.2, locate the most recent List of CFR Sections Affected (LSA), which in this example is the LSA for March 2004. Look on the inside front cover to see the dates covered.

FIGURE 8.15 INSIDE FRONT COVER, MARCH 2004 LIST OF CFR SECTIONS AFFECTED

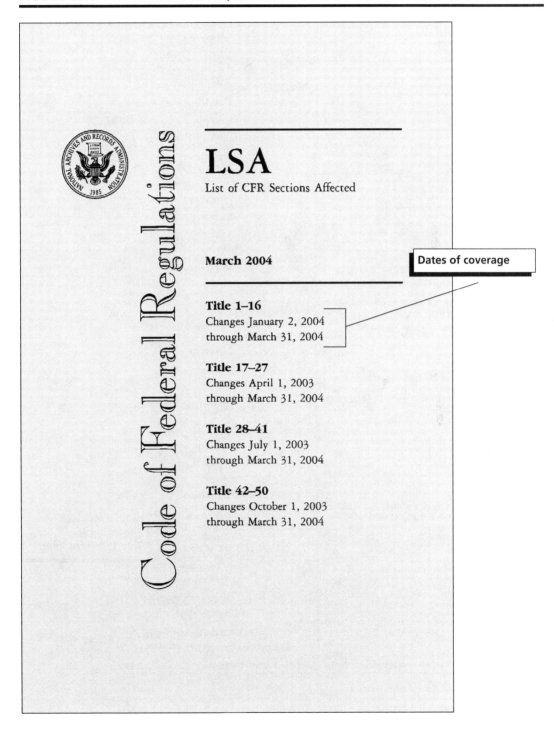

Code of Federal Regulations

LSA
List of CFR Sections Affected

March 2004

Dates of coverage

Title 1–16
Changes January 2, 2004
through March 31, 2004

Title 17–27
Changes April 1, 2003
through March 31, 2004

Title 28–41
Changes July 1, 2003
through March 31, 2004

Title 42–50
Changes October 1, 2003
through March 31, 2004

Look up the regulation within the LSA. If the regulation is not listed, the agency has not taken action affecting it. If the regulation is listed, the page of the *Federal Register* containing the change will be listed.

FIGURE 8.16   MARCH 2004 LIST OF CFR SECTIONS AFFECTED

---

22   LSA—LIST OF CFR SECTIONS AFFECTED

CHANGES JANUARY 2, 2004 THROUGH MARCH 31, 2004

TITLE 14 *Proposed Rules:—Con.*

7713, 7714, 7715, 8578, 8579, 8581, 8582, 8583, 8585, 8586, 10389, 11825, 12992, 12993	
73	552, 5099, 8884, 15746
77	5101
91	2529, 6218
119	2529, 6218
121	282, 551, 2529, 2970, 6216, 6218
135	551, 2529, 2970, 6218
136	2529, 6218
145	2970
183	2970
400—499 (Ch. III)	8575

TITLE 15—COMMERCE AND FOREIGN TRADE

Chapter VII—Bureau of Industry and Security, Department of Commerce (Parts 700—799)

711.7 Added; interim	2502
730 Authority citation revised	5687
730.8 (c) revised	5687
730 Supplement No. 3 amended	5687
732.3 (d)(4) amended	3005
(h)(2) revised	5687
732 Supplement Nos. 1 and 2 revised	5687
734 Authority citation revised	5690, 5929
734.1 (a) amended	5690
734.3 (a)(3) revised	5929
(b)(4) amended	5690
734.4 (a) and (c) introductory text revised; (b) removed	5929
(d) introductory text revised	5690
736.2 (b)(3)(i) amended	5690
738 Supplement No. 1 amended	3005
740 Supplement No. 1 amended	3005
740.2 (a)(9) added	5930
740.4 Amended	5690
740.5 Amended	5690
740.6 (a) amended	5690
740.9 (a)(2)(viii)(B) amended	5690
740.12 (b)(5)(iii) amended	5690
740.13 (a)(1) amended	5690
742 Authority citation revised	16479
742.6 (a)(2) revised	16480
745 Supplement No. 2 amended	12790
746 Authority citation revised	5690

746.2 (a)(1)(ii) amended	5690
746.4 (b)(2) introductory text, (ii)(B) and (c)(2)(vii)(A) amended	5690
746.7 Introductory text revised	5690
746 Supplement No. 1 removed	3005
746.1 (d) removed	3005
748 Authority citation revised	5690
748.2 (a) amended	5690
750 Authority citation revised	5691
750.7 (c)(1)(viii) revised	5691
752 Authority citation revised	5691
752.3 (a)(2) and (3) revised	5691
764 Authority citation revised	7870
764.5 (e) revised	7870
766.3 (a) revised	7870
766.18 (f) added	7870
766 Supplement No. 1 added	7870
774 Supplement No. 1, Category 0 (ECCN 0A018, 0A918, 0A988, 0E018, 0E918) amended	16480
Supplement No. 1, Category 1 (ECCN 1C351 and 1C352) amended	12791
Supplement No. 1, Category 1 (ECCN 1C353) amended	12792
Supplement No. 1, Category 7 (ECCN 7A994 and 7E994) amended	5930
Supplement No. 1, Category 8 (ECCN 8A018, 8A918) amended	16481
Supplement No. 1, Category 9 (ECCN 9A991) amended	5930

Proposed Rules:

740	
742	
748	
754	1685
772	1685

> The listing for Title 15 begins here.

TITLE 16—COMMERCIAL PRACTICES

Chapter I—Federal Trade Commission (Parts 0—999)

304 Policy statement	9943
310.4 (b)(3)(iv) revised	16373
456 Policy statement	5451
602.1 (c)(2) and (3) added	6530
603 Added; interim	8535

FIGURE 8.16   MARCH 2004 LIST OF CFR SECTIONS AFFECTED *(Continued)*

MARCH 2004   **23**

CHANGES JANUARY 2, 2004 THROUGH MARCH 31, 2004

Proposed Rules:

0—999 (Ch. I) 3867	316..4263, 11776
310 7330	456 5440
315 5440	610..13192
	698..13192
	1000–1799 (Ch. II) 4095

In the listing of changes to Title 16 of the C.F.R., the LSA shows an entry affecting Parts 1000-1799.

Federal Register page number containing the entry affecting 16 C.F.R. Parts 1000-1799

A table in the back of the LSA indicates the date on which the relevant *Federal Register* page was published.

FIGURE 8.17 MARCH 2004 LIST OF CFR SECTIONS AFFECTED, TABLE OF *FEDERAL REGISTER* ISSUE PAGES AND DATES

---

122   TABLE OF FEDERAL REGISTER ISSUE PAGES AND DATES

54123–54325	16	69295–69582	12
54327–54650	17	69583–69939	15
54651–54796	18	69941–70119	16
54797–54978	19	70121–70419	17
54979–55189	22	70421–70687	18
55191–55259	23	70689–70994	19
55261–55298	24	70995–74159	22
55299–55431	25	74161–74465	23
55433–55805	26	74467–74828	24
55807–56135	29	74829–75105	29
56137–56519	30	75107–75383	30
56521–56764	Oct. 1	75385–75795	31
56765–57318	2	**2004**	
57319–57606	3	**69 FR Page**	
57607–57782	6	1–241	Jan. 2
57783–58007	7	243–484	5
58009–58260	8	485–848	6
58261–58574	9	849–1267	7
58575–59078	10	1269–1501	8
59079–59304	14	1503–1645	9
59305–59512	15	1647–1892	12
59513–59704	16	1893–2052	13
59705–59854	17	2053–2288	14
59855–60024	20	2289–2477	15
60025–60279	21	2479–2652	16
60281–60616	22	2653–2824	20
60617–60839	23	2825–2996	21
60841–61096	24	2997–3212	22
61097–61321	27	3213–3482	23
61323–61605	28	3483–3817	26
61607–61731	29	3819–4056	27
61733–61985	30	4057–4218	28
61987–62211	31	4219–4438	29
62213–62350	Nov. 3	4439–4842	30
62351–62502	4	4843–5003	Feb. 2
62503–62729	5	5005–5256	3
62731–63009	6	5257–5458	4
63011–63731	7	5459–5678	5
63733–63981	10	5679–5904	6
63983–64262	12	5905–6138	9
64263–64489	13	6139–6524	10
64491–64798	14	6525–6903	11
64799–64976	17	6904–7103	12
64977–65151	18	7105–7345	13
65153–65382	19	7347–7540	17
65383–65625	20	7541–7677	18
65627–65827	21	7679–7862	19
65829–66000	24	7863–8089	20
66001–66318	25	8091–8321	23
66319–66691	26	8323–8543	24
66693–67011	28	8545–8795	25
67013–67355	Dec. 1	8797–9187	26
67357–67584	2	9189–9513	27
67585–67785	3	9515–9742	Mar. 1
67787–67396	4	9743–9909	2
67397–68231	5	9911–10129	3
68233–68485	8	10131–10311	4
68487–68715	9	10313–10594	5
68717–69000	10	10595–10900	8
69001–69293	11		

Page 4095 was published on January 28.

Look up the page number within the *Federal Register* to determine how the regulation was changed.

FIGURE 8.18 *FEDERAL REGISTER,* JANUARY 28, 2004

Federal Register / Vol. 69, No. 18 / Wednesday, January 28, 2004 / Proposed Rules   4095

Commission would not pursue intermediate treasurers.[11] *See Cal. Democratic Party* v. *FEC,* 13 F. Supp. 2d 1031, 1037 (E.D. Cal. 1998) (dismissing individual capacity claims against a former treasurer because "there is no allegation that [the treasurer] violated any personal obligation" and dismissing official capacity claims against him "since [he] is no longer treasurer * * * and thus, is not the appropriate person against whom an official capacity suit can be maintained. * * *").[12]

VII. Proposed Policy

In light of the considerations explained above, the Commission is considering exercising its discretion in enforcement matters by naming treasurers as follows:

1. In all enforcement actions where a political committee is a respondent, name as respondents the committee and its current treasurer "in (his or her) official capacity as treasurer."

2. In enforcement actions where a treasurer has apparently breached a personal obligation owing by virtue of his or her responsibilities under the Act and regulations, or a prohibition that applies to individuals, name that treasurer as a respondent "in (his or her) personal capacity."

The Commission invites comments on this policy that is under consideration. Comments may be submitted on any aspect of the policy being considered, including:

(A) If the Commission adopts the policy, are there certain circumstances that warrant flexibility in applying the policy?

[11] For example, while Treasurer A is the treasurer for Joe Smith for Congress, a violation occurs that subjects A to official and individual liability. Treasurer A would be named in both his official and personal capacities. After the enforcement action has begun, Treasurer A resigns and Treasurer B takes over. The Commission should pursue Treasurer A in his individual capacity, and Treasurer B in her official capacity. If Treasurer B resigns and is succeeded by Treasurer C prior to the conclusion of the enforcement matter, the Commission should then continue to pursue Treasurer A in his individual capacity and pursue Treasurer C in her official capacity. Treasurer B is no longer named in her official capacity.

[12] A deeper examination of the court file indicates that—despite the *California Democratic Party* court's assertion to the contrary—the Commission never actually pled that the treasurer in this case was personally liable. Rather, the complaint references the treasurer "as treasurer" and the Commission's response to the treasurer's motion to dismiss indicates that the Commission was pursuing the treasurer "in his official capacity." Compl., paragraphs 8, 58–59, Prayer paragraphs 1–5; Resp. to Def. Mot. to Dismiss, p. 21. However, the *California Democratic Party* court's result underscores the need for the Commission to delineate more clearly the capacity in which it pursues treasurers.

(B) Whether, and to what extent, the Commission should consider a treasurer's "best efforts" to comply with the law.

(C) Whether and how to apply the prospective policy in its Administrative Fines program.

Dated: January 23, 2004.

Bradley A. Smith,
Chairman, Federal Election Commission.

[FR Doc. 04–1790 Filed 1–27–04; 8:45 am]
BILLING CODE 6715–01–P

CONSUMER PRODUCT SAFETY COMMISSION

16 CFR Chapter II

Pilot Program for Systematic Review of Commission Regulations; Request for Comments and Information

AGENCY: Consumer Product Safety Commission.

ACTION: Notice of systematic review of current regulations.

SUMMARY: The Consumer Product Safety Commission (CPSC or Commission) is undertaking a pilot program to systematically review its current substantive regulations to ensure, to the maximum practical extent, consistency among them and with respect to accomplishing program goals. The pilot is currently expected to be completed by the end of calendar year 2004. Depending on the results of the pilot, the availability of personnel and fiscal resources, and other priorities for action, the Commission would then develop and implement an expanded systematic review process to address the remainder of its substantive regulations.

The primary purpose of the review is to assess the degree to which the regulations under review remain consistent with the Commission's program policies. In addition, each regulation will be examined with respect to the extent that it is current and relevant to CPSC program goals. Attention will also be given to whether the regulations can be streamlined, if possible, to minimize regulatory burdens, especially on small entities. To the degree consistent with other Commission priorities and subject to the availability of personnel and fiscal resources, specific regulatory or other projects may be undertaken in response to the results of this review.

In the initial, pilot phase of this program the following four regulations will be evaluated: safety standard for walk-behind power mowers, 16 CFR part 1205; requirements for electrically operated toys and other electrically

operated articles intended for children, 16 CFR part 1505; standard for the flammability of vinyl plastic, 16 CFR part 1611; and child-resistant packaging requirements for aspirin, methyl salicylate, 16 CFR 1700, and 1700.14(a)(3), respectively.

The Commission solicits written comments from interested persons concerning the designated regulations' currentness and consistency with Commission policies and goals, suggestions for streamlining where appropriate. In so doing, commenters are requested to specifically address how their suggestions for change could be accomplished within the various statutory frameworks for Commission action under the Consumer Product Safety Act (CPSA), 15 U.S.C. 2051–2084, Federal Hazardous Substances Act (FHSA), 15 U.S.C. 1261–1278, Flammable Fabrics Act (FFA), 15 U.S.C. 1191–1204; and Poison Prevention Packaging Act (PPPA), 15 U.S.C. 1471–1476.

DATES: Written comments and submissions in response to this notice must be received by March 29, 2004.

ADDRESSES: Comments and other submissions should be captioned "Pilot Regulatory Review Project" and mailed to the Office of the Secretary, Consumer Product Safety Commission, Washington, DC 20207, or delivered to that office, room 502, 4330 East-West Highway, Bethesda, Maryland 20814. Comments and other submissions may also be filed by facsimile to (301) 504–0127 or by e-mail to *cpsc-os@cpsc.gov.*

FOR FURTHER INFORMATION CONTACT: N.J. Scheers, PhD, Director, Office of Planning & Evaluation, U.S. Consumer Product Safety Commission, Washington, DC 20207; telephone (301) 504–7670; e-mail *nscheers@cpsc.gov.*

SUPPLEMENTARY INFORMATION:

A. The Pilot Review Program

The President's Office of Management and Budget has designed the Program Assessment Rating Tool (PART) to provide a consistent approach to rating programs across the Federal government. A description of the PART process and associated program evaluation materials is available online at: *http://www.whitehouse.gov/omb/budintegration/part_assessing2004.html.*

Based on an evaluation of the Commission's regulatory programs using the PART, the recommendation was made that CPSC develop a plan to systematically review its current regulations to ensure consistency among them in accomplishing program goals. The pilot review program launched with

> The *Federal Register* entry announces a pilot program for reviewing regulations in 16 C.F.R. Chapter II (Parts 1000-1799), but does not contain changes to the regulations.

Update beyond the LSA with the *Federal Register.* In this example, the most recent *Federal Register* is dated April 28, 2004. The table of CFR Parts Affected During April appears in the back of the *Federal Register* and is cumulative for the month to date.

FIGURE 8.19   *FEDERAL REGISTER,* APRIL 28, 2004, TABLE OF CFR PARTS AFFECTED DURING APRIL

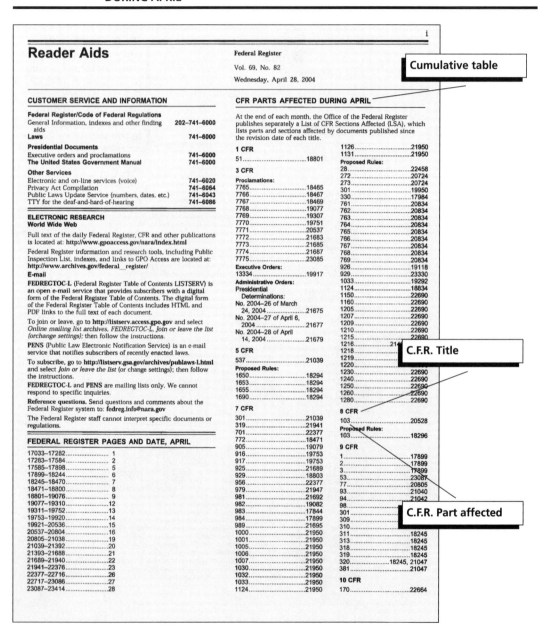

The table shows a reference to 16 C.F.R. Part 1210 on page 19762. The table does not indicate which section was affected, so the reference must be checked to see if § 1210.2 was changed.

FIGURE 8.20 *FEDERAL REGISTER,* **APRIL 28, 2004, TABLE OF CFR PARTS AFFECTED DURING APRIL**

16 C.F.R. Part 1210 was affected by action reported on page 19762.

ii **Federal Register** / Vol. 69, No. 82 / Wednesday, April 28, 2004 / Reader Aids

171 22664
Proposed Rules:
9 22737
71 21978

11 CFR

Proposed Rules:
110 .... 18301, 18841

12 CFR

3 22382
208 22382
225 22382
229 19921
325 22382
335 19085
567 22382
609 21699
.... 21699
.... 21699
.... 21699
.... 21699
.... 21699
.... 18808
[Propos]ed Rules:
.... 21978
.... 23380
.... 19123, 23380
303 20558
334 23380
571 23380
701 21439
705 21443
717 23380
742 21439
1710 19126

13 CFR

102 21952

14 CFR

11 22385
23 22717
25 .... 18246, 19311, 22720
39 .... 17033, 17034, 17901, 17903, 17905, 17906, 17909, 17911, 17913, 17914, 17915, 17917, 17918, 17919, 17921, 17924, 17925, 18250, 19313, 19618, 19756, 19758, 19759, 20539, 20809, 20811, 20815, 20817, 20818, 21049, 21393, 21395, 21397, 21401, 21402, 21699, 21701, 22386, 22388, 22389, 22392, 23090, 23093, 23095, 23098, 23099
71 .... 17283, 19314, 19315, 19316, 19317, 19318, 19319, 19922, 19923, 20820, 20821, 20822, 20823, 21404, 22394, 22395, 22396, 22397, 22398, 22599, 22730
73 .... 18471, 21053
77 22732
91 21953
97 17284
121 19761
135 18472
1260 21703
Proposed Rules:
39 .... 17072, 17073, 17076, 17077, 17080, 17082, 17084, 17086, 17088, 17091, 17095, 17097, 17101, 17103, 17105, 17107, 17109, 17111, 17113, 17115, 17610, 17984, 17987, 17989, 17991, 17993, 17996, 18304, 18306, 18843, 18845, 18848, 19132, 19135, 19777, 19950, 19952, 19954, 19956, 20566, 21444, 21766, 21768, 21771, 21774, 22459, 22461, 22743, 22745, 23161
61 21073
71 .... 18308, 18309, 18508, 19359, 19360, 19958, 19960, 19961, 19962, 19963, 20834, 20835, 20837, 21447, 21448, 21449, 23161
91 21073
119 21073
121 21073
135 21073
136 21073
399 21450

15 CFR

738 21055
740 21055
774 17926

16 CFR

316 21024
1210 19762
Proposed Rules:
316 18851
603 23370
613 23370
614 23370
682 21388
801 18686
802 18686
803 18686

17 CFR

200 21057
232 .... 21954, 22704
239 .... 22300, 22704
249 22704
259 22704
269 22704
274 .... 22300, 22704
Proposed Rules:
30 17998
230 21650
232 17864
239 21650
240 .... 17864, 21650
249 .... 17864, 21650

18 CFR

Proposed Rules:
1 21777

19 CFR

Proposed Rules:
24 18296

20 CFR

404 19924
641 19014
Proposed Rules:
404 18310

21 CFR

Ch. 1 17285
1 .... 19763, 19765, 19766
20 19766
173 17297
201 18255
206 18728
250 18728
312 17927
314 18728
520 21956
522 17585
573 19320
600 18728
601 18728
606 18255
610 18255
807 18472
1308 17034
Proposed Rules:
Ch. 1 17615
101 20838
201 21778
208 21778
209 21778

22 CFR

126 18810

24 CFR

Proposed Rules:
30 19906
200 21036
203 19906
320 19746

25 CFR

Proposed Rules:
30 20839
37 20839
39 20839
42 20839
44 20839
47 20839

26 CFR

1 .... 17586, 21405, 22399
Proposed Rules:
1 .... 17117, 17477, 18314, 21454, 22463
20 20840
301 .... 17117, 20840

27 CFR

9 20823

28 CFR

803 21058
804 21059

29 CFR

35 17570
541 22122
1952 .... 20826, 20828
1981 17587
4022 19925
4044 .... 19925, 22599
Proposed Rules:
1910 17774
1917 19361
1918 19361
1926 .... 20840, 22748

30 CFR

75 17480
925 19927
931 19321
Proposed Rules:
200 19137
917 21075

31 CFR

1 17298
103 .... 19093, 19098
240 17272

32 CFR

199 17035
719 20540
725 20540
727 20541
752 20542
1602 20542
1605 20542
1609 20542
1656 20542
2001 17052
Proposed Rules:
519 18314

33 CFR

101 17927
104 17927
117 .... 17055, 17057, 17595, 17597, 18473, 19103, 19325, 20544, 21061, 21062, 21064, 21956, 22733
147 .... 19933, 21065
165 .... 18473, 19326, 21067, 23101
167 18476
334 .... 20545, 20546, 20547
402 18811
Proposed Rules:
100 18002
110 .... 17119, 20568
117 .... 17122, 17616, 17618, 18004, 22749
165 .... 18794, 18797, 21981, 22751, 22753
334 20570

34 CFR

99 21670

36 CFR

223 18813
400 17928
Proposed Rules:
13 17355
242 19964
292 21796

37 CFR

1 21704
401 17299

38 CFR

20 .... 19935, 21068
Proposed Rules:
3 22757
4 22757
17 21075

39 CFR

111 .... 17059, 22401
Proposed Rules:
111 .... 19363, 20841, 21455, 22464

40 CFR

9 .... 19105, 22402
51 21604
52 .... 17302, 17929, 18815, 19937, 19939, 20548, 21711, 21713, 21715, 21717, 21731, 22441, 22443, 22445, 22447, 23103, 23109, 23110

Page 19762 discusses adjusted customs value for cigarette lighters.

FIGURE 8.21   *FEDERAL REGISTER,* APRIL 14, 2004

Contact information

Action affecting 16 C.F.R. Part 1210

Effective date

Information on the change

Summary

19762   Federal Register / Vol. 69, No. 72 / Wednesday, April 14, 2004 / Rules and Regulations

Good Cause for "No Notice"

Sections 553(b)(3)(B) and 553(d)(3) of the Administrative Procedures Act (APA) (5 U.S.C. 553(b)(3)(B) and 553(d)(3)) authorize agencies to dispense with certain notice procedures for rules when they find good cause exists to do so. Under section 553(b)(3)(B), the requirements of notice that notice and public comment on this change to the compliance date are both impracticable and contrary to the public interest. Notice and comment are impracticable in this instance because they would defeat the need for the rule change. Air carriers using certain equipment are unable to comply with the regulation because of a parts availability problem beyond their control. The FAA would not be able to accomplish notice and comment rulemaking until after the compliance date in the current regulation. Further, the FAA finds that the carriage of AEDs on commercial aircraft represent a significant benefit to the flying public, and delaying implementation of the rule for availability of an approved battery is contrary to that interest when little safety risk is involved for a short time.

Good Cause for Immediate Adoption

Section 553(d) of the APA requires that rules become effective no less than 30 days after their issuance. Paragraph (d)(1) allows an agency to make a rule effective immediately if it is relieving in nature. This final rule extends a compliance date, relieving the requirement to have equipment installed that may not be available. Accordingly, this rule is effective on issuance.

List of Subjects in 14 CFR Part 121

Air carriers, Aircraft, Airmen, Alcohol abuse, Aviation safety, Charter flights, Drug abuse, Drug testing, Reporting and recordkeeping requirements, Safety, Transportation.

The Amendment

■ In consideration of the foregoing, the Federal Aviation Administration amends part 121 of Title 14, Code of Federal Regulations (14 CFR Part 121) as follows:

PART 121—OPERATING REQUIREMENTS: DOMESTIC, FLAG, AND SUPPLEMENTAL OPERATIONS

■ 1. The authority citation for part 121 continues to read as follows:

Authority: 49 U.S.C. 106(g), 40113, 40119, 44101, 44701–44702, 44705, 44709–44711, 44713, 44716–44717, 44722, 44901, 44903–44904, 44912, 46105.

■ 2. Amend Appendix A, Automated External Defibrillators, paragraph 2, to read as follows:

Appendix A to Part 121—First Aid Kits and Emergency Medical Kits

*   *   *   *   *

Automated External Defibrillators

*   *   *   *   *

2. On and after April 30, 2005, meet FAA Technical Standard Order requirements for power sources for electronic devices used in aviation as approved by the Administrator.

*   *   *   *   *

Issued in Washington, DC, on April 8, 2004.

Marion C. Blakey,
Administrator.
[FR Doc. 04–8512 Filed 4–12–04; 10:16 am]
BILLING CODE 4910–13–P

CONSUMER PRODUCT SAFETY COMMISSION

16 CFR Part 1210

Safety Standard for Cigarette Lighters; Adjusted Customs Value for Cigarette Lighters

AGENCY: Consumer Product Safety Commission.

ACTION: Final rule.

SUMMARY: The Commission has a safety standard requiring that disposable and novelty lighters meet specified requirements for child-resistance. The rule defines disposable lighters, in part, as refillable lighters that use butane or similar fuels and have a Customs Value or ex-factory price below a threshold value (initially set at $2.00). The standard provides that the initial $2.00 value adjusts every 5 years for inflation as measured by the percentage change since June 1993 in the appropriate Wholesale Price Index for which cigarette lighters are a part, as published by the Department of Labor's Bureau of Labor Statistics ("BLS") (now referred to as the Producer Price Index for Miscellaneous Fabricated Products). The adjustment is rounded to the nearest $0.25 increment. With this notice, the Commission adds to the rule a statement that the import value adjusted to $2.25 when the June 2003 Index was finalized by BLS in November 2003. This information was also conveyed to the public by a Commission press release issued January 5, 2004.

This notice also makes a technical correction to change the term "Wholesale Price Index" to "Producer Price Index for Miscellaneous Fabricated Products."

DATES: This rule is effective April 14, 2004.

FOR FURTHER INFORMATION CONTACT: Vogel, Office of Compliance, Consumer Product Safety Commission, Washington, DC 20207; telephone 504–7599; e-mail *jvogel@cpsc.gov.*

SUPPLEMENTARY INFORMATION:

Background

In 1993, the Commission issued a standard that required disposable and novelty lighters to meet certain requirements for child-resistance. The standard defines disposable lighters as those that either are (1) non-refillable or (2) use butane or similar fuels and have "a Customs Valuation or ex-factory price under $2.00, as adjusted every 5 years, to the nearest $0.25, in accordance with the percentage changes in the monthly Wholesale Price Index from June 1993 . . . " 16 CFR 1210.2(b)(2)(ii).

Thus, the rule provides for the $2.00 threshold to adjust in accordance with inflation. The rule provides for adjustment to be rounded to the nearest twenty-five cents. Adjustment did not occur in 1998 because change in the Index since June 1993 was not sufficient to warrant an adjustment.

The name of the Wholesale Price Index has changed to the Producer Price Index. The Index that includes cigarette lighters is the Producer Price Index for Miscellaneous Fabricated Products (hereafter "the Index"). The Bureau of Labor Statistics generally releases the Index figures for the month of June in July, and the figures are subject to revision for four months.

Adjustment to $2.25 occurred as of November 2003. This figure is based on an 8% increase since June 1993 in the Index rounded to the nearest twenty-five cents.

The staff was concerned that there could be confusion about the exact amount and timing of the increase without specific notice from the Commission. So, on January 5, 2004, the Commission issued a press release notifying the public of the change in the price of lighters included in the cigarette lighter standard due to the adjustment and indicating that the adjustment would be enforced prospectively from March 1, 2004 (available on CPSC's Web site at *http://www.cpsc.gov/cpscpub/prerel/prhtm104/04060.html*). To provide enhanced notice to those subject to the standard of this and any future

Reading through the *Federal Register,* page 19763 shows a revision to 16 C.F.R. § 1210.2. The updating process is now complete. An e-mail or telephone call to the agency would confirm that no further action on § 1210.2 has taken place.

FIGURE 8.22   *FEDERAL REGISTER,* APRIL 14, 2004

Federal Register / Vol. 69, No. 72 / Wednesday, April 14, 2004 / Rules and Regulations   **19763**

adjustments, the Commission is adding a statement to the standard that states the adjusted $2.25 value.

This notice also makes a technical correction to change the term "Wholesale Price Index" to "Producer Price Index" and notes that the specific Producer Price Index currently applicable to cigarette lighters is the Producer Price Index for Miscellaneous Fabricated Products.

The Administrative Procedure Act

Section 553(b)(3)(B) of the Administrative Procedure Act ("APA") authorizes an agency to dispense with notice and comment procedures when the agency, for good cause, finds that those procedures are "impracticable, unnecessary, or contrary to the public interest." This amendment adds a statement to inform the public of an adjustment that has occurred automatically according to the terms of the cigarette lighter regulation. Accordingly, the Commission finds that notice and comment is unnecessary.

The APA also authorizes an agency, "for good cause found and published with the rule," to dispense with the otherwise applicable requirement that a rule be published in the **Federal Register** at least 30 days before its effective date. 5 U.S.C. 553(d)(3). The Commission hereby finds that a 30 day delay of the effective date is unnecessary because this amendment informs the public of an adjustment that has occurred automatically in accordance with the requirements of the cigarette lighter standard.

List of Subjects in 16 CFR Part 1500

Cigarette lighters, Consumer ...tion, Fire prevention, Hazardous ...ls, Infants and children, ...g, Packaging and containers, ...ing and recordkeeping ...ments.

...rdingly, 16 CFR part 1210 is ...ded as follows:

PART 1210—SAFETY STANDARD FOR CIGARETTE LIGHTERS

■ 1. The authority for part 1210 continues to read as follows:

Authority: 15 U.S.C. 2056, 2058, 2079(d).

■ 2. Revise § 1210.2(b)(2)(ii) to read as follows:

§ 1210.2   Definitions.

*   *   *   *   *

(b) * * *

(2) * * *

(ii) It has a Customs Valuation or ex-factory price under $2.00, as adjusted every 5 years, to the nearest $0.25, in accordance with the percentage changes

in the appropriate monthly Producer Price Index (Producer Price Index for Miscellaneous Fabricated Products) from June 1993. The adjusted figure, based on the change in that Index since June 1993 as finalized in November 2003, is $2.25.

Dated: April 6, 2004.

Todd Stevenson,
Secretary, Consumer Product Safety Commission.

[FR Doc. 04–8400 Filed 4–13–04; 8:45 am]

BILLING CODE 6355–01–P

DEPARTMENT OF HEALTH AND HUMAN SERVICES

Food and Drug Administration

21 CFR Part 1

[Docket No. 2002N–0278]

Prior Notice of Imported Food Under the Public Health Security and Bioterrorism Preparedness and Response Act of 2002; Reopening of Comment Period

AGENCY: Food and Drug Administration, HHS.

ACTION: Interim final rule; reopening of comment period.

SUMMARY: The Food and Drug Administration (FDA) is reopening for 30 days the comment period for FDA's prior notice interim final rule (IFR) that published in the **Federal Register** of October 10, 2003 (68 FR 58974). The prior notice interim final rule requires the submission to FDA of prior notice of food, including animal feed, that is imported or offered for import into the United States. FDA is taking this action consistent with its statement in the preamble of the prior notice IFR (68 FR 58974 at 59023) that it would reopen the comment period for an additional 30 days in March 2004, to ensure that those who comment on this interim final rule would have had the benefit of our outreach and education efforts and would have had some experience with the systems, timeframes, and data elements of the prior notice system.

DATES: Submit written or electronic comments by May 14, 2004.

ADDRESSES: Submit written comments to the Division of Dockets Management (HFA–305), Food and Drug Administration, 5630 Fishers Lane, rm. 1061, Rockville, MD 20852. Submit electronic comments to *http://www.fda.gov/dockets/ecomments.*

FOR FURTHER INFORMATION CONTACT: May D. Nelson, Center for Food Safety and Applied Nutrition (HFS–24), Food and

Drug Administration, 5100 Paint Branch Pkwy., College Park, MD 20740, 301–436–1722.

SUPPLEMENTARY INFORMATION:

I. Background

On October 10, 2003, FDA issued an IFR to implement new section 801(m) of the Federal Food, Drug, and Cosmetic Act (FD&C Act) (21 U.S.C. 381(m)), added by section 307 of the Public Health Security and Bioterrorism Preparedness and Response Act of 2002 (Bioterrorism Act), which required prior notification of imported food to begin on December 12, 2003. The prior notice IFR requires the submission to FDA of prior notice of food, including animal feed, that is imported or offered for import into the United States (68 FR 58974). The interim final rule requires that the prior notice be submitted to FDA electronically via either the Customs and Border Protection (CBP) Automated Broker Interface (ABI) of the Automated Commercial System (ACS) or the FDA Prior Notice System Interface (FDA PN System Interface) (21 CFR 1.280). Food imported or offered for import without adequate prior notice is subject to refusal and, if refused, must be held (21 CFR 1.283).

Under section 801(m)(2)(A) of the FD&C Act, FDA is to choose timeframes that "shall be no less than the minimum amount of time necessary for the Secretary [of Health and Human Services] to receive, review, and appropriately respond to such notification* * *" Using this standard, the prior notice IFR requires that the information must be submitted and confirmed electronically as facially complete by FDA for review no more than 5 days and no less than 8 hours (for food arriving by water), 4 hours (for food arriving by air or land/rail), and 2 hours (for food arriving by land/road) before the food arrives at the port of arrival (21 CFR 1.279). However, when we issued the interim final rule, FDA committed to exploring ways to increase integration of advance electronic notification processes with CBP and to reduce prior notice timeframes. Indeed, we stated in the preamble to the interim final rule (68 FR 58974 at 58995) that, by March 12, 2004, FDA and CBP would publish a plan, including an implementation schedule, to achieve the goal of a uniform, integrated system and to coordinate timeframes for import prior notice information while fulfilling the Bioterrorism Act mandates for air and truck modes of transportation with timeframes finalized by CBP when they finalize their rule entitled "Required

---

> After the explanation, the revised regulation is set forth.

You can update C.F.R. research in GPO Access using the electronic versions of the LSA and *Federal Register* and the Current List of CFR Parts Affected. You can also use the unofficial e-CFR to find regulatory changes.

FIGURE 8.23   e-CFR SEARCH SCREEN AND RESULTS

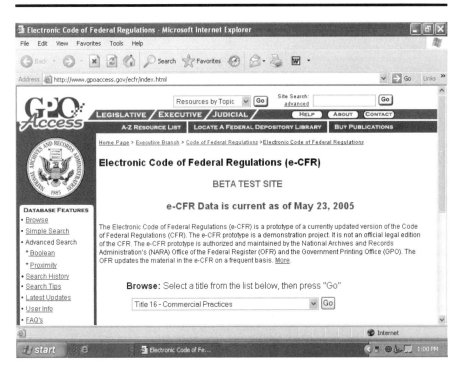

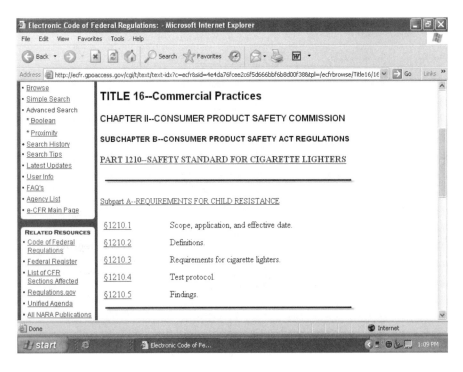

The regulation is displayed in textual form.

FIGURE 8.24   EXCERPT FROM THE e-CFR VERSION OF 16 C.F.R. § 1210.2

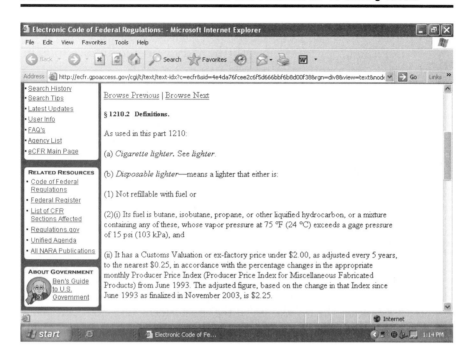

At the end of the regulation, you will find a reference to the change to the regulation that appears in the *Federal Register.*

FIGURE 8.25   EXCERPT FROM THE e-CFR VERSION OF 16 C.F.R. § 1210.2

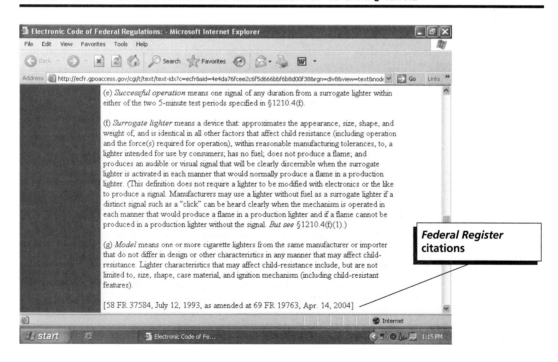

F. CHECKLIST FOR FEDERAL ADMINISTRATIVE LAW RESEARCH

1. LOCATE PERTINENT REGULATIONS

❏ Use the cross-references to the C.F.R. in the annotations in U.S.C.S. and U.S.C.A.

❏ Use a subject index, such as the CFR Index and Finding Aids or CIS Index to the *Code of Federal Regulations*.

❏ Use LexisNexis and Westlaw by executing word searches in the databases for the C.F.R. or specific subject areas or by browsing the table of contents.

❏ Use GPO Access or other Internet web sites to locate regulations.

2. UPDATE PRINT RESEARCH WITH THE LIST OF CFR SECTIONS AFFECTED (LSA), *FEDERAL REGISTER,* AND TABLE OF CFR PARTS AFFECTED

❏ To update from the date of the C.F.R. volume through the end of the prior month:

■ Look up the regulation in the most recent LSA to locate page numbers in the *Federal Register* reflecting changes to the regulation.

■ Use the table in the back of the LSA to find the date of the *Federal Register* issue containing the change.

■ Read the material in the *Federal Register* to see how it affects the regulation.

❏ To update from the end of the prior month to the present:

■ Use the cumulative table of CFR Parts Affected on the inside back cover of the latest issue of the *Federal Register.*

■ If the Part in which the section appears is listed, look up each page number referenced in the table to see if the section has been affected.

3. UPDATE GPO ACCESS RESEARCH WITH THE e-CFR OR THE ELECTRONIC VERSIONS OF THE LSA, *FEDERAL REGISTER,* AND CURRENT LIST OF CFR PARTS AFFECTED

❏ Compare the official C.F.R. text with the e-CFR version to determine whether the regulation has been amended; locate *Federal Register* notices as necessary for an official citation or additional information.

❏ Alternatively, use the electronic version of the LSA, *Federal Register,* and Current List of CFR Parts Affected:

- To update from the date of the C.F.R. volume through the end of the prior month, look up the regulation in the most recent electronic LSA to locate page numbers in the *Federal Register* reflecting changes to the regulation.
- Retrieve the *Federal Register* page containing the change in the *Federal Register* database.
- Read the material in the *Federal Register* to see how it affects the regulation.
- To update from the end of the prior month to the present, use the cumulative Current List of CFR Parts Affected.
- If the Part in which the section appears is listed, look up each page number referenced in the table to see if the section has been affected.

4. CONTACT THE AGENCY FOR ADDITIONAL INFORMATION ON RECENT OR PROPOSED REGULATORY CHANGES

5. USE SHEPARD'S IN PRINT OR IN LEXISNEXIS, OR KEYCITE IN WESTLAW, TO UPDATE YOUR RESEARCH OR LOCATE RESEARCH REFERENCES

CHAPTER 9

SUBJECT-MATTER SERVICE RESEARCH

A. Introduction to subject-matter services

B. Researching subject-matter services in print, CD-ROM, and Internet formats

C. Subject-matter research in LexisNexis and Westlaw

D. Citing subject-matter services

E. Sample pages for print subject-matter service research

F. Checklist for subject-matter service research

A. INTRODUCTION TO SUBJECT-MATTER SERVICES

Many research tools are organized by type of authority and jurisdiction. Some, however, are organized by subject. They may contain only one type of authority, such as cases, but include authority from many jurisdictions. Alternatively, they may collect multiple types of authority from multiple jurisdictions in a defined subject area. These services may also compile information not available in other sources, including cases not reported in general case reporters or news and analysis in the field not available elsewhere. As a consequence, if you are researching an area of law for which subject-matter services are available, complete research requires that you consult them.

Unlike the other chapters in this book, this chapter will not take you step-by-step through the process of using different types of subject-matter services. Subject-matter services are published by many different commercial publishers. As a consequence, no uniform method of organization or research process applies to all of them. Instead, each one contains its own explanation of how to use the service. This chapter, therefore, focuses on more general information about these

resources, rather than on step-by-step instructions. The sample pages in Section E show the process for researching materials relating to the Americans with Disabilities Act so you can see how two of these services are organized.

1. OVERVIEW OF SUBJECT-MATTER SERVICES

Subject-matter research services are often called "looseleaf" services. This is because many of them are actually published in looseleaf binders. By putting the information in a binder, the publisher is able to update individual pages or sections as necessary. Not all services are published in binders, however. They are available in many formats, including bound print volumes, CD-ROMs, and Internet databases. Thus, this chapter refers to them as subject-matter services, rather than looseleaf services.

A subject-matter service may contain some or all of the following types of information:

- news or analysis of current events in the field
- statutory material, including
    federal statutes
    state statutes
    legislative history of pertinent statutes
- administrative materials, including
    federal regulations and agency decisions
    state regulations and agency decisions
- cases, including
    federal cases
    state cases

A few subject-matter services contain all of this information, but most contain some combination of these items. Some, but by no means all, of the areas for which subject-matter services are available include environmental law, tax, bankruptcy, government contracts, intellectual property, employment and labor law, and securities law. Some of the best known publishers of subject-matter services are the Bureau of National Affairs (BNA), CCH, Inc. (CCH), Clark Boardman Callaghan (CBC), Matthew Bender (MB), Pike & Fischer (P & F), and Research Institute of America (RIA).

The statutes, regulations, and legislative history documents contained in a subject-matter service could be located through other resources, such as an annotated code or LexisNexis Congressional. The advantage of the subject-matter service, however, is that it compiles all of this information in one place, which makes using it easier and more

efficient than researching each item individually. This is especially true because many subject-matter services focus on complex, highly regulated areas of the law for which it might be difficult to compile all of the relevant information.

Many of the cases in a subject-matter service could also be located through digests or other general legal research resources, but again, the compilation of material from many different jurisdictions makes the subject-matter service easier to use. In addition, some of the opinions reported in the service may not be reported elsewhere, so the service may give you access to cases you would not have been able to locate in other sources.

In short, "one-stop shopping" and access to authority not published elsewhere make subject-matter services an invaluable research tool.

2. LOCATING SUBJECT-MATTER SERVICES

Locating a subject-matter service is not unlike locating a treatise—it is much easier to find if you already know what you are looking for. The difficult part is figuring out whether a subject-matter service exists for your research issue when you have not previously conducted research in that area of law.

One quick place to check for subject-matter services is the *Bluebook*. Table T.15 contains an alphabetical list of some of the more commonly used services.

Another place to look is in a directory of subject-matter services. Two that are especially helpful are *Legal Looseleafs in Print* and *Directory of Law-Related CD-ROMs*, both of which are compiled and edited by Arlene L. Eis. These reference books list subject-matter services by publisher, title, and subject. Both of these publications, plus *Legal Newsletters in Print*, are indexed electronically in a subscription service called LawTRIO. If your library subscribes to this service, you should be able to access it from the library's computer network. Sample entries from LawTRIO appear in **Figures 9.1, 9.2,** and **9.3**. Once you know the name of a pertinent subject-matter service, you can locate it using your library's on-line catalog or computer network.

B. RESEARCHING SUBJECT-MATTER SERVICES IN PRINT, CD-ROM, AND INTERNET FORMATS

Although no uniform process applies to using subject-matter services, this section provides some general information that may help you get started with your research.

FIGURE 9.1   SEARCH SCREEN FOR THE LAWTRIO DATABASE

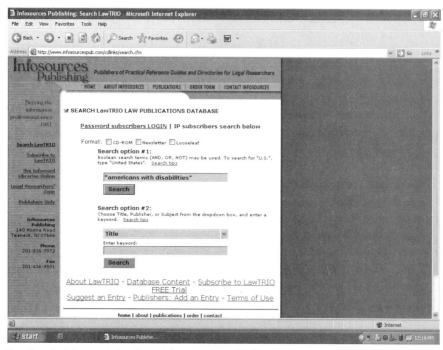

Reprinted with permission from Arlene L. Eis and Infosources Publishing (2005).

FIGURE 9.2   SEARCH RESULT IN THE LAWTRIO DATABASE

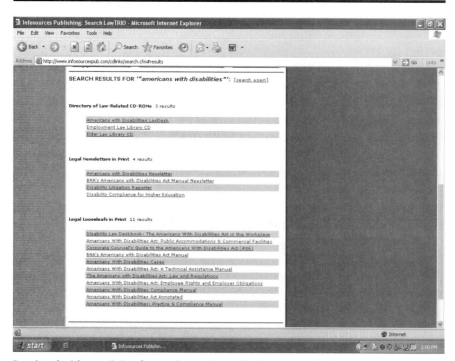

Reprinted with permission from Arlene L. Eis and Infosources Publishing (2005).

FIGURE 9.3   ENTRY FOR A LOOSELEAF SERVICE IN THE LAWTRIO DATABASE

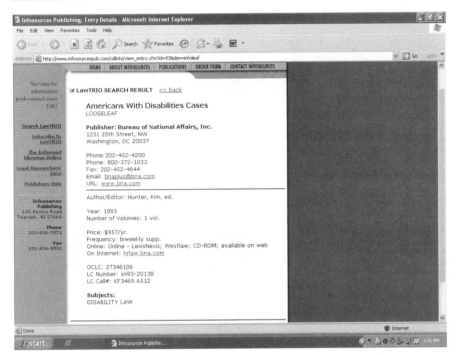

Reprinted with permission from Arlene L. Eis and Infosources Publishing (2005).

1. PRINT RESOURCES

In print form, most subject-matter services have a section at the beginning of the binder or in the front of a bound volume entitled "Overview" or "How to use this service." This section should first explain the scope of the service. Does it contain statutes, cases, news bulletins, or some combination of materials? Knowing the scope will help you determine how the service fits with your overall research strategy. This section should also explain how to find and update material within the service, and some contain sample research problems illustrating the research process. Subject-matter services that contain cases are often organized in a digest format similar to the format of West digests, although they do not use the West topic and key number system. Regardless of how they are organized, however, all subject-matter services have some type of indexing method that you can use to locate information.

2. CD-ROM AND INTERNET RESOURCES

Some subject-matter services are available in CD-ROM format. A growing number of publishers are also making their products available through subscriptions to databases available via the Internet.

Your library may have special terminals for using CD-ROM resources, or these services may be accessible through the library's computer network. Internet services should also be accessible through the library's computer network, although you may need a password to retrieve information. A reference librarian will be able to give you instructions for accessing the Internet version of any subject-matter service available at your library.

As with the print versions of these services, the CD-ROM and Internet versions vary in their scope, organization, and searching options. Like other electronic research tools, they require you to execute searches to retrieve information contained within the database. Chapter 10 explains general techniques that you can use to search effectively in CD-ROM and Internet subject-matter services. Accordingly, you may want to review Chapter 10 in conjunction with this chapter. Whenever you use a CD-ROM or Internet subject-matter service for the first time, you should plan to spend some time reviewing the printed manual or reading through the help function to use the features of the service effectively.

C. SUBJECT-MATTER RESEARCH IN LEXISNEXIS AND WESTLAW

Both LexisNexis and Westlaw have databases devoted to subject areas of the law. You will find them in the Westlaw directory under "Topical Practice Areas" and in the LexisNexis source directory under "Area of Law—By Topic." These databases allow you to search cases, statutes, regulations, secondary sources, and other materials in a subject area, instead of by jurisdiction. Once within the database for a subject area, you can limit your search to a particular jurisdiction. Thus, for example, if you were to select the database for Labor & Employment, you could search all jurisdictions in that subject area, or you could choose to search only materials for an individual state. In addition, some of the subject-matter services published by BNA, CCH, and other publishers are available in the LexisNexis and Westlaw subject-area databases.

D. CITING SUBJECT-MATTER SERVICES

Citations to subject-matter services contain the same elements using either the *ALWD Manual* or the *Bluebook*, although as noted below, abbreviations for some items within the citation will vary depending on which format you use. In the *ALWD Manual*, subject-matter service citations are governed by Rule 28, and in the *Bluebook*, they are governed by Rule 19.

A citation to a subject-matter service consists of six components: (1) the title of the item; (2) the volume of the service; (3) the abbreviated

title of the service; (4) the abbreviated name of the publisher of the service in parentheses; (5) the pinpoint reference to the subdivision in the service where the cited item begins; and (6) a parenthetical containing the date and, for case citations, the jurisdiction and level of court deciding the case. The *ALWD Manual* always requires the exact date of the item. The *Bluebook* requires the exact date for items from a looseleaf service, but just the year for items from a bound service. When citing cases, be sure to refer to the rules for case citations, as well as those for subject-matter services.

The following example shows how to cite a case reported in a subject-matter service in *ALWD Manual* format.

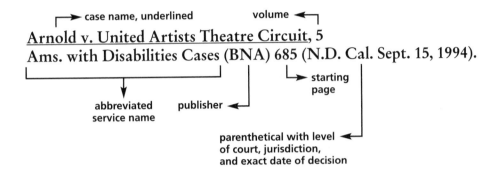

Determining the abbreviated name of the service requires you to use Appendix 3 in the *ALWD Manual.* For the example above, Appendix 3 abbreviates "American" (singular) as "Am." but directs you to add an "s" to form an abbreviation of the plural form of the word. Appendix 3 does not abbreviate any other words in the title of the service. Thus, the service is cited as Ams. with Disabilities Cases.

Using the *Bluebook*, the citation is similar, but not identical. The name of the service is abbreviated slightly differently. Also, because *Americans with Disabilities Cases* is a bound service, only the year is necessary for the date:

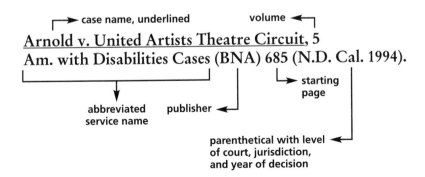

Determining the proper abbreviation for the name of the service requires you to use two Tables. Rule 19 refers you to Table T.15, which contains abbreviations for commonly used services. *Americans with*

Disabilities Cases is not listed in Table T.15. If a publication does not appear in Table T.15, Rule 19.1 directs you to use the periodical abbreviations in Table T.13 to determine the abbreviation for the service. Table T.13 abbreviates "Americans" (plural) as "Am." Table T.13 does not abbreviate any other words in the title of the service. Thus, the service can be abbreviated as Am. with Disabilities Cases.

E. SAMPLE PAGES FOR PRINT SUBJECT-MATTER SERVICE RESEARCH

Figures 9.4 through **9.11** illustrate some of the features of two different print subject-matter services, the *Americans with Disabilities Act Manual* (hereinafter ADA Manual) and *Americans with Disabilities Cases* (hereinafter A.D. Cases[1]), both published by BNA. These services are also available electronically through LexisNexis, Westlaw, and BNA.

The ADA Manual is a three-binder set containing, among other items, news, the full text of the federal Americans with Disabilities Act (ADA), federal regulations, summaries of state disability laws, technical assistance and resources for employers and businesses, and summaries of disability cases from federal and state courts.

BNA's A.D. Cases is a reporter service that publishes the full text of disability decisions. The A.D. Cases service also has its own digesting system. The finding tool for locating cases in the reporter is the Cumulative Digest and Index. Each Cumulative Digest and Index volume covers a specific period of time, so you would need to use several volumes to research cases over a period of years.

Like many other BNA reporter services, the A.D. Cases service divides material into different topics called "classifications," and each classification is assigned a number. You can find a classification number applicable to your research issue in two ways. In the front of each volume of the Cumulative Digest and Index, you will find an "Outline of Classifications," which is similar to the key number outline at the beginning of a West digest topic. You can review this outline to locate classification numbers. Each volume of the Cumulative Digest and Index also contains an alphabetical subject index called the "Topic Finder," which will refer you to classification numbers.

Once you have identified classification numbers relevant to your research, you can look them up within the Cumulative Digest and Index to locate case summaries, just as you would find case summaries under key numbers in a West digest. The Cumulative Digest and Index will give you the full citations to the cases, which you can find in the A.D. Cases reporter volumes. The cases in the A.D. Cases reporter volumes also contain "headnotes" listing the applicable classification numbers.

---

[1]This is not the correct abbreviation for a citation to this service. See Section D above for a discussion of citation rules for subject-matter services.

In BNA's *Americans with Disabilities Act Manual,* you would begin by reviewing the information in the "Overview" section to see what is included in the service and how it is organized.

FIGURE 9.4   EXCERPT FROM THE OVERVIEW, *BNA'S AMERICANS WITH DISABILITIES ACT MANUAL*

No. 153
10.0003

How to Use ADAM

Overview

The Americans with Disabilities Act of 1990 prohibits discrimination against people with disabilities in employment, state and local government services, public accommodations, and telecommunications. To that end, the ADA's five sections, or titles, cover employment, state and local governments and transportation, public accommodations, telecommunications, and miscellaneous provisions. The ADA is modeled in large part on the Rehabilitation Act of 1973, which prohibits discrimination on the basis of disability by federal contractors and subcontractors and employers that receive federal funds.

BNA's *Americans with Disabilities Act Manual* provides detailed information and practical guidance on all aspects of the ADA, allowing subscribers to:

- keep up-to-date on laws, regulations, and cases;
- monitor emerging trends in disability law; and
- simplify and speed research.

For full text of disability-related cases, consult BNA's *Americans with Disabilities Cases,* which also provides headnotes of the issues addressed in each case.

How ADAM Is Organized

Identifies finding tools for this service

...sletter contains news on the ADA and its ...ation, regulatory and legal developments, case summaries, and articles relevant to disabilities issues.

Index and Table of Cases
The index, which is updated three times a year, organizes the manual's contents by subject and cross-references subject areas to other relevant sections. A table of cases allows rapid location of pertinent court decisions.

Tab 20–Employment (Title I)
This section addresses issues covered under Title I, the employment section of the ADA, such as coverage, definition of disability, prohibited actions, reasonable accommodation, exceptions and defenses, and interaction of the ADA with other laws and programs.

Tab 25–State & Local Governments/Transportation (Title II)

Describes an individual section

...tion covers prohibitions against discrimina...te and local governments and explains ac...standards for public transportation services. ...n addresses issues such as coverage, program accessibility, communications with people with disabilities, administrative requirements, accessibility requirements for vehicles, and paratransit services.

Tab 30–Public Accommodations (Title III)
This section covers prohibitions against discrimination by private entities in places of public accommodation, such as hotels, restaurants, stores, theaters, and

other service establishments. Issues such as accessibility standards for buildings and facilities, barrier removal, examinations and courses, auxiliary aids and services, service animals, and direct threat exceptions are addressed.

Binder 2

Tab 35–Telecommunications (Title IV)
This section covers Title IV, which requires that people with speech and/or hearing disabilities have equal access to telecommunication systems. The section includes information on telecommunications relay services, hearing-aid-compatible telephones, and TRS telephone numbers.

Tab 50–Policy & Practice
This section discusses ADA requirements in the areas of recruiting and selection, interviewing and testing, workplace accommodations, and evacuation planning for employees with disabilities, and includes sample policies and forms for ADA compliance.

Tab 70–Statutes/Regulations
This section includes the full text of the ADA and other federal laws, agency regulations implementing the ADA, and policy guidance documents issued by the Equal Employment Opportunity Commission and other agencies.

Binder 3

Tab 80–State Disability Laws
This section includes summaries of state laws that prohibit discrimination on the basis of disability.

10–21–04   Copyright © 2004 by The Bureau of National Affairs, Inc.

FIGURE 9.4   **EXCERPT FROM THE OVERVIEW, *BNA'S AMERICANS WITH DISABILITIES ACT MANUAL* (Continued)**

10:0004   OVERVIEW

Tab 90–Technical Assistance & Resources

This section includes Technical Assistance Manuals for Titles I, II, and III of the ADA issued by the Equal Employment Opportunity Commission and the Justice Department; directories of ADA-related federal offices and information sources; sample forms, policies, and job descriptions; and information on disability-related tax incentives.

Reproduced with permission from *BNA's Americans with Disabilities Act Manual,* pp. 10:0003–0004. Copyright 2004 by The Bureau of National Affairs, Inc. (800-372-1033) http://www.bna.com.

Once you know the scope of the service, you could use the Master Index to find sections and pages with information on various topics.

FIGURE 9.5   EXCERPT FROM THE MASTER INDEX, *BNA'S AMERICANS WITH DISABILITIES ACT MANUAL*

INDEX - 1

MASTER INDEX

BNA'S AMERICANS WITH DISABILITIES ACT MANUAL

(Covers through Supplement No. 155)

How to Use This Index

This topical index provides references to the material in **BNA's AMERICANS WITH DISABILITIES ACT MANUAL**. The number preceding the colon in each citation indicates the tabbed divider, and the number following the colon gives the page number in that tabbed divider on which the information may be found, e.g., 70:0101.

Editor's Notes [*Ed. Note:*] clarify the scope of a particular heading and, where appropriate, refer the researcher to related headings. The phrase "et seq." after a page citation indicates a series of three or more pages relating to the subject entry.

Federal act and law references include in parentheses detailed section numbers (e.g., §12102(2)) to facilitate research. Federal regulation references include in parentheses the Code of Federal Regulations title and regulation number (e.g., 29 CFR 1630.2(k)).

This index is arranged alphabetically word-by-word. For example, the heading DRUG TESTING precedes the heading DRUGSTORES. Moreover, hyphenated words are treated as two separate words, not as single words. For example, CHECK-OUT AISLES precedes the heading CHECKLISTS. Also, it is important to note that most headings appear in plural form.

To help researchers locate quickly the text of federal acts and laws, the phrase "Full text" with its tab and page citation is printed first under certain subject headings. See example below:

REHABILITATION ACT
Full text, 70:0301 et seq.

Cross-references assist users by linking related information within the index. They refer researchers from one topic heading to another topic heading or to a subheading under another topic heading where relevant information is found. They also suggest related topic headings.

Types of cross-references are:

- *See* .... all information at other location
- *See also* .... more information at other location
- *See generally* .... all related information at other location
- *See now* .... change of terminology or agency name

Cross-references to another main topic heading are indicated by the use of CAPITAL LETTERS. The word *"subheading"* may be included in the cross-reference to pinpoint the exact subentry language used for particular information. Internal cross-references are also used to link one subheading to another under the same topic heading. The phrase *"this heading"* appears at the end of these cross-references.

This index, which is updated every four months, provides in-depth analysis of disability law topics. The *NEWSLETTER* is indexed separately, and that index is filed with the newsletters.

See also the Table of Cases for a listing of court decisions.

A

ACCESS BOARD
See ARCHITECTURAL AND TRANSPOR-TATION BARRIERS COMPLIANCE BOARD (ACCESS BOARD)

ACCESS ROUTES
See ACCESSIBILITY GUIDELINES (ADAAG), *subheading:* Routes

ACCESS TO INFORMATION
See also CONFIDENTIALITY
Federal contractor records, OFCCP regulation (41 CFR 60-741.81), 70:0331

ACCESSIBILITY GUIDELINES (ADAAG)
See also ACCESSIBILITY REQUIRE-MENTS; *specific facilities*
Ed. Note: The revised guidelines released by the U.S. Access Bd. are reprinted beginning at 30:0201. These guidelines are advisory

only until adopted by federal agencies. Current provisions are located at Tab 70.
Current guidelines, full text, Appx. A to 28 CFR Part 36, 70:0201 et seq.
—Advisory committee recommendations, Spl-Supp (11/14/96)
—Overview, 70:0199-0200
Revised ADA-ABA guidelines, advisory, 30:0201 et seq.
—Appendices, 30:0277 et seq.
—DOJ advance notice of proposed rulemaking, 30:0601 et seq.
—Monetary impacts on new construction and alterations, 30:0270
—Overview, 30:0199-0200
Additions
—Current provisions, generally (ADAAG 4.1.5), 70:0212
—Definition (ADAAG 3.5), 70:0204 et seq.
—DOJ technical assistance manual, 90:0938
—Revised ADA-ABA provisions, advisory, 30:0232

—State and local government facilities (ADAAG 4.1.5), 70:2229
Adults, provisions based on (ADAAG 2.1), 70:0203
Airports (ADAAG 10.4), 70:0274
Alarms. See ALARMS
Alterations
—Amusement rides (ADAAG 15.1.2, A15.1.2), 70:2519, 2545
—Bus stops (ADAAG 10.2.2), 70:0271
—Curb ramps (ADAAG 4.1.6(3)(a)), 70:0214
—Definition (ADAAG 3.5), 70:0204 et seq.
—Detention and correctional facilities, DOL advance notice of proposed rulemaking, 30:0606, 0615
—DOJ regulation (28 CFR 36.406), 70:0162
—DOJ technical assistance manual, 90:0939
—Dressing rooms (ADAAG 4.1.6(3)(h)), 70:0215
—Escalators (ADAAG 4.1.6(1)(f)), 70:0213
—Exceptions (ADAAG 4.1.6(1)(i-k)), 70:0213-14
—Generally (ADAAG 4.1.6), 70:0213 et seq.
—Monetary impacts of new rules, 30:0270

If you were interested in researching "Public Accommodations," you might review the section that describes the ADA's public accommodation requirements.

FIGURE 9.6   **EXCERPT FROM PUBLIC ACCOMMODATIONS, *BNA'S AMERICANS WITH DISABILITIES ACT MANUAL***

Cross-reference to a C.F.R. Part with relevant regulations. Regulations can be located in the C.F.R. or within this service.

No. 161
30:0001

Introduction to Title III

Overview

Title III of the Americans with Disabilities Act prohibits discrimination on the basis of disability by private entities in places of public accommodation—facilities open to the public, including certain mixed-use and commercial facilities. According to Title III, places of public accommodation must remove barriers to access and must provide appropriate alternative services when physical barriers cannot be removed.

Title III is enforced by the Justice Department under regulations at 28 C.F.R. Part 36. DOJ has issued a Technical Assistance Manual to help employers and businesses comply with the law.

This chapter defines public accommodations and covers compliance and new construction and alteration requirements.

Title III Basics

Who Is Covered?

Title III prohibits disability-based discrimination in the "full and equal enjoyment" of goods, services, privileges, advantages, or accommodations of any place of public accommodation by anyone who owns, leases, leases to, or operates a place of public accommodation 12182(a)).

Textual description of ADA statutory and regulatory provisions on public accommodations

tities are considered public accommodations operations "affect commerce" among states, tate and a foreign country, or between same state but through another state or try (42 U.S.C. § 12181(1)).

andlord who owns a public accommodation nt who operates a public accommodation are subject to the ADA's requirements. A lease or contract may be used to determine the extent of each party's responsibility. However, allocations made in a lease or other contract are effective only between the parties; both landlord and tenant remain fully liable for ADA compliance (28 C.F.R. § 36.201(b)).

Federal government facilities are not covered by the ADA, but are covered by the 1973 Rehabilitation Act.

What Is a Public Accommodation?

Title III covers public accommodations—that is, facilities that are open to the public but are owned or operated by private entities—meaning nongovernmental bodies. Public facilities and services of state and local governmental bodies are covered by Title II.

The term "public accommodations" encompasses a wide range of facilities, including, but not limited to:

• hotels, motels, and other places of lodging, unless they contain five rooms or less for rental and are occupied by the proprietor as a residence;

• restaurants, bars, and other establishments serving food or drink;

• theaters, concert halls, stadiums, and other places of entertainment;

6-16-05

• stores, shopping centers, and service establishments such as laundromats, dry-cleaners, banks, and professional offices;

• public transportation stations;

• parks, zoos, and other places of recreation;

• daycare centers and social service establishments; and

• health spas and other places of exercise (28 C.F.R. § 36.104).

A foreign-flag cruise ship operating in U.S. waters is both a public accommodation and a transportation service that is generally subject to the requirements of Title III of the ADA, the U.S. Supreme Court held in *Spector v. Norwegian Cruise Line Ltd.*, U.S., No. 03-1388, 6/6/05.

Title III's requirements do not apply when they are not "readily achievable" or when they pose "a significant risk to the health or safety of others" that cannot be eliminated by modifications, the court said. Any modifications that would interfere with the internal affairs of foreign ships, as prohibited by maritime law, are not required by Title III, the court said.

Other Applications of Title III

A place of public accommodation or physical barrier to enter a public accommodation is not necessarily needed for a Title III claim. For instance, the law applies to courses and examinations related to licensing and certification for professional or trade purposes (36 C.F.R. § 36.309).

In addition, Title III has been applied to an automated telephone answering system used in selecting contestants for a television game show (*Rendon v. Valleycrest Productions Ltd.*, 294 F.3d 1279, 13 AD Cases 404 (11th Cir. 2002)).

Whether Internet access to a company's products is covered under Title III was addressed by one federal district court, which dismissed claims that the goods and services offered by an airline at its "virtual ticket counters" are inaccessible to blind customers using

Copyright © 2005 by The Bureau of National Affairs, Inc.

3

Working either from the Master Index or the cross-references in the discussion of public accommodations, you could find regulations defining public accommodation.

FIGURE 9.7 28 C.F.R. PT. 36, REPRINTED IN *BNA'S AMERICANS WITH DISABILITIES ACT MANUAL*

No. 132
70:0151

Justice Department Public Accommodations Regulations

Following is the text of regulations (28 C.F.R. Part 36) issued by the Justice Department to implement Title III of the Americans with Disabilities Act.

PART 36—NONDISCRIMINATION ON THE BASIS OF DISABILITY BY PUBLIC ACCOMMODATIONS AND IN COMMERCIAL FACILITIES

28 C.F.R. Part 36

Table of Contents

Subpart A—General

Section
36.101 Purpose.
36.102 Application.
36.103 Relationship to other laws.
36.104 Definitions.
36.105-36.199 [Reserved]

Subpart B—General Requirements
36.201 General.
36.202 Activities.
36.203 Integrated settings.
36.204 Administrative methods.
36.205 Association.
36.206 Retaliation or coercion.
36.207 Places of public accommodations located in private residences.
36.208 Direct threat.
36.209 Illegal use of drugs.
36.210 Smoking.
36.211 Maintenance of accessible features.
36.212 Insurance.
36.213 Relationship of subpart B to subparts C and D of this part.
36.214-36.299 [Reserved]

Subpart C—Specific Requirements
36.301 Eligibility criteria.
36.302 Modifications in policies, practices, or procedures.
36.303 Auxiliary aids and services.
36.304 Removal of barriers.
36.305 Alternatives to barrier removal.
36.306 Personal devices and services.
36.307 Accessible or special goods.
36.308 Seating in assembly areas.
36.309 Examinations and courses.
36.310 Transportation provided by public accommodations.
36.311-36.399 [Reserved]

Subpart D—New Construction and Alterations
36.401 New construction.
36.402 Alterations.
36.403 Alterations: Path of travel.

36.404 Alterations: Elevator exemption.
36.405 Alterations: Historic preservation.
36.406 Standards for new construction and alterations.
36.407 Temporary suspension of certain detectable warning requirements.
36.408-36.499 [Reserved]

Subpart E—Enforcement
36.501 Private suits.
36.502 Investigations and compliance reviews.
36.503 Suit by the Attorney General.
36.504 Relief.
36.505 Attorneys Fees.
36.506 Alternative means of dispute resolution.
36.507 Effect of unavailability of technical assistance.
36.508 Effective date.
36.509-36.599 [Reserved]

Subpart F—Certification of State Laws or Local Building Codes
36.601 Definitions.
36.602 General rule.
36.603 Filing a request for certification.
36.604 Preliminary determination.
36.605 Procedure following preliminary determination of equivalency.
36.606 Procedure following preliminary denial of certification.
36.607 Effect of certification.
36.608 Guidance concerning model codes.
Appendix A to Part 36—Standards for Accessible Design
Appendix B to Part 36—Preamble to Regulation on Nondiscrimination on the Basis of Disability by Public Accommodations and in Commercial Facilities (Published July 26, 1991)

Authority: 5 U.S.C. 301; 28 U.S.C. 509, 510; 42 U.S.C. 12188(b); Pub. L. 101-410, 104 Stat. 890, as amended by Pub. L. 104-134, 110 Stat. 1321.

Subpart A—General

Sec. 36.101. Purpose.

The purpose of this part is to implement title III of the Americans with Disabilities Act of 1990 (42 U.S.C. 12181),

which prohibits discrimination on the basis of disability by public accommodations and requires places of public accommodation and commercial to be designed, constructed, and in compliance with the accessibil dards established by this part.

Regulation

Sec. 36.102. Application.

(a) *General.* This part applies to any —

(1) Public accommodation;

(2) Commercial facility; or

(3) Private entity that offers examinations or courses related to applications, licensing, certification, or credentialing for secondary or postsecondary education, professional, or trade purposes.

(b) *Public accommodations.*

(1) The requirements of this part applicable to public accommodations are set forth in subparts B, C, and D of this part.

(2) The requirements of subparts B and C of this part obligate a public accommodation only with respect to the operations of a place of public accommodation.

(3) The requirements of subpart D of this part obligate a public accommodation only with respect to —

(i) A facility used as, or designed or constructed for use as, a place of public accommodation; or

(ii) A facility used as, or designed and constructed for use as, a commercial facility.

(c) *Commercial facilities.* The requirements of this part applicable to commercial facilities are set forth in subpart D of this part.

(d) *Examinations and courses.* The requirements of this part applicable to private entities that offer examinations or courses as specified in paragraph (a) of this section are set forth in Sec. 36.309.

1-16-03

BNA's *Americans with Disabilities Cases* (A.D. Cases) is a reporter service. You can locate cases in A.D. Cases using the Cumulative Digest and Index accompanying that service. The "Introduction" in the front of each volume of the Cumulative Digest and Index explains how to locate cases.

FIGURE 9.8   CUMULATIVE DIGEST AND INDEX, BNA'S A.D. CASES

Description of the organization of A.D. Cases

INTRODUCTION

This Americans with Disabilities Cases Cumulative Digest and Index (CDI) volume organizes, under AD Cases classification numbers (e.g., ▸333.29), concise descriptions of case holdings on points of disability law.

Case references (e.g., 6 AD Cases 1865) are to volumes and page numbers of cases reported in Americans with Disabilities Cases volumes 1-6, covering the period 1974 - August 18, 1997.

The Outline of Classifications (page 1) provides descriptions of the classification numbers. Scope notes under the descriptions of the classification number indicate other classification numbers where related cases may be found. Additionally, an Outline in Brief is provided at the beginning of each section. A Star (★) appearing after a classification number in the Outline in Brief indicates that there are no reported cases for the period covered.

The Topic Finder (page 51) is an alphabetical arrangement by descriptive words and phrases of all material covered in the classification scheme. References in the Topic Finder are to classification numbers.

The Table of Cases (page 1869) lists court decisions by both forward and reverse titles, and indicates the court or agency that handed down the opinion, the history of the case, official parallel citations, and the volume and page number where the case appears in AD Cases volumes.

Instructions for researching begin here.

RESEARCHING BY SUBJECT

1. Turn first to the Topic Finder to locate your subject. Note the classification number and turn to it in the Cumulative Digest and Index (CDI) to find concise descriptions of all decisions on point.

2. Alternatively, turn to the Outline of Classifications. A quick survey of the main sections will lead you to the general subject in which you are interested. Note the applicable classification number(s), turn to the CDI, and proceed to the description of the decisions.

RESEARCHING BY CASE NAME

Turn to the Table of Cases to get the page citation in AD Cases volumes, and proceed to the volume and page indicated. Related decisions may be obtained by using the classification numbers assigned to the headnotes appearing at the start of every decision. Proceed to the CDI using these classification numbers.

v

FIGURE 9.8   CUMULATIVE DIGEST AND INDEX, BNA'S A.D. CASES *(Continued)*

ORDER OF DIGESTS

Rulings of law in the Cumulative Digest and Index volumes are grouped under the various classification numbers by tribunal in the following order:

1. Supreme Court of the United States.

2. United States Court of Appeals, in order of circuit number (including Court of Appeals for the District of Columbia and Court of Appeals for the Federal Circuit).

3. Federal District Courts, in alphabetical order of states in which courts are sitting, U.S. Court of Federal Claims, U.S. Bankruptcy Courts, and Judicial Panel on Multi-district Litigation (JPML).

4. State, county, and city courts, in alphabetical order of states.

5. EEOC decisions.

Under each tribunal, rulings appear in the order of the volume and page where the case was reported in AD Cases.

CITATIONS

Each entry in the CDI is followed by the name of the case, the tribunal that made the ruling, the date of the decision, and the volume and page number where the case can be found in AD Cases.

vi

Reproduced with permission from *Americans with Disabilities Cases Cumulative Digest and Index,* Table of Cases, Vol. 1–6 (1974–1997), pp. v–vi. Copyright 2002 by The Bureau of National Affairs, Inc. (800-372-1033) http://www.bna.com.

A.D. Cases organizes cases according to "classification numbers." One way to locate classification numbers is through the "Topic Finder," an alphabetical subject index near the beginning of each volume of the Cumulative Digest and Index.

FIGURE 9.9 A.D. CASES TOPIC FINDER

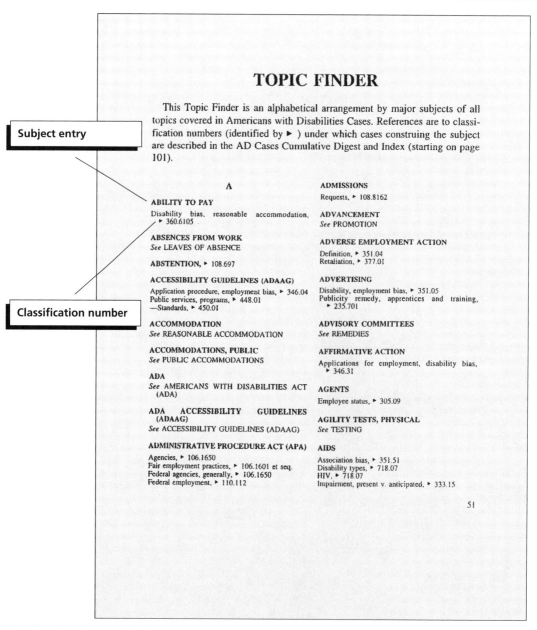

TOPIC FINDER

This Topic Finder is an alphabetical arrangement by major subjects of all topics covered in Americans with Disabilities Cases. References are to classification numbers (identified by ▶) under which cases construing the subject are described in the AD Cases Cumulative Digest and Index (starting on page 101).

Subject entry

Classification number

A

ABILITY TO PAY
Disability bias, reasonable accommodation, ▶ 360.6105

ABSENCES FROM WORK
See LEAVES OF ABSENCE

ABSTENTION, ▶ 108.697

ACCESSIBILITY GUIDELINES (ADAAG)
Application procedure, employment bias, ▶ 346.04
Public services, programs, ▶ 448.01
—Standards, ▶ 450.01

ACCOMMODATION
See REASONABLE ACCOMMODATION

ACCOMMODATIONS, PUBLIC
See PUBLIC ACCOMMODATIONS

ADA
See AMERICANS WITH DISABILITIES ACT (ADA)

ADA ACCESSIBILITY GUIDELINES (ADAAG)
See ACCESSIBILITY GUIDELINES (ADAAG)

ADMINISTRATIVE PROCEDURE ACT (APA)
Agencies, ▶ 106.1650
Fair employment practices, ▶ 106.1601 et seq.
Federal agencies, generally, ▶ 106.1650
Federal employment, ▶ 110.112

ADMISSIONS
Requests, ▶ 108.8162

ADVANCEMENT
See PROMOTION

ADVERSE EMPLOYMENT ACTION
Definition, ▶ 351.04
Retaliation, ▶ 377.01

ADVERTISING
Disability, employment bias, ▶ 351.05
Publicity remedy, apprentices and training, ▶ 235.701

ADVISORY COMMITTEES
See REMEDIES

AFFIRMATIVE ACTION
Applications for employment, disability bias, ▶ 346.31

AGENTS
Employee status, ▶ 305.09

AGILITY TESTS, PHYSICAL
See TESTING

AIDS
Association bias, ▶ 351.51
Disability types, ▶ 718.07
HIV, ▶ 718.07
Impairment, present v. anticipated, ▶ 333.15

51

Once you have identified useful classification numbers, you can find case summaries by looking up the classification numbers in the digest section of the Cumulative Digest and Index. Because each volume of the Cumulative Digest and Index covers only a certain period of time, you may need to look through several volumes to complete your research.

FIGURE 9.10   CASE SUMMARIES, A.D. CASES CUMULATIVE DIGEST AND INDEX

AD CDI   ENFORCEMENT   ▶575.01

▶ 567.01 In general

U.S. Courts of Appeals

NLRB's decision that employer, which provides transportation services to elderly and disabled clients, violated §8(2)(1) of LMRA by its work rule providing for immediate dismissal of employees who discuss problems and complaints about employer with passengers does not violate ADA or Minn. Vulnerable Adults Act, since decision does not prevent employer from taking steps to protect passengers with disabilities. —*Handicabs Inc. v. National Labor Relations Bd.* (CA 8, 9/11/96) 5 AD Cases 1484

U.S. District Courts

Blind couple who were refused boarding by tour bus driver because of their guide dog lack standing to seek injunctive relief against tour bus company, there being no real and immediate threat that they will be subject to repeated injury by tour bus company, as they have not shown that they are likely to use same buses in near future or that, if they do use them, company is likely to violate their rights under ADA again. —*O'Brien v. Werner Bus Lines Inc.* (DC EPa, 2/26/96) 5 AD Cases 444

Blind couple who seek injunction against tour bus company whose driver refused to let them board with their guide dog have not shown likelihood that they are going to use company's buses in near future, where record does not show that couple used its buses regularly or even on occasion before incident.—*Id.*

Blind couple who seek injunctive relief against tour bus company whose driver refused to let them board with their guide dog have not shown that company is likely to violate their rights under ADA again, where company president immediately recognized error, apologized to couple, and took corrective measures by addressing issue with his drivers through memorandum, individual communication, discussion at drivers' meetings, and drivers' handbook.—*Id.*

Tour bus company's evidence of its efforts to instruct its drivers on its non-biased policy regarding disabled passengers shifts burden in summary judgment proceeding to blind couple, who had not been allowed to board tour bus because of their guide dog, to provide evidence that those efforts are inadequate, such as by showing that incidents of bias have occurred following its efforts, by introducing expert testimony of inadequacy of those efforts, or by showing pattern of past conduct so permeated with bias that inadequacy of simple corrective procedures is obvious.—*Id.*

▶ 575.   Enforcement

▶ 575.01 In general

U.S. Courts of Appeals

Lower court was warranted in concluding ... gulation concerning duty of newly public facility to provide wheel-with lines of sight over standing spectators required only substantial compliance rather than 100% compliance, where DOJ never indicated in technical assistance manual whether every wheelchair location must be afforded view over standing spectators. —*Paralyzed Veterans of America v. D.C. Arena L.P.* (CA DC, 7/1/97) 6 AD Cases 1614

Doubts about scope of injunction that disabled individuals who seek total ban on smoking at all of two companies' fast-food restaurants could be entitled to do not justify dismissal of ADA action in view of fact that they have alleged cognizable claims, at least with respect to restaurants that they expect to visit.

—*Staron v. McDonald's Corp.* (CA 2, 4/4/95) 4 AD Cases 353

Beer brewery did not establish that proposed modification of its blanket "no animals" policy to permit guide dogs to accompany blind visitors on its public brewery tour would either fundamentally alter its nature or would jeopardize safety, and it was thus required to make modification under ADA. —*Johnson v. Gambrinus Co./Spoetzl Brewery* (CA 5, 3/27/97) 6 AD Cases 1115

Lower court had no duty to delineate exact nature of changes that beer brewery make before concluding that it ADA in not modifying its blanket "no animals" policy to allow guide dog to accompany blind visitor on its public brewery tour, where visitor met his burden of showing that modification of policy is reasonable in run of cases, and it therefore must make modification unless it can establish affirmative defense.—*Id.*

For Guidance see Introduction   1527

[Classification numbers]

[Case summary]

Reproduced with permission from *Americans with Disabilities Cases Cumulative Digest and Index,* Table of Cases, Vol. 1–6 (1974–1997), p. 1527. Copyright 2002 by The Bureau of National Affairs, Inc. (800-372-1033) http://www.bna.com.

The full text of cases summarized in the Cumulative Digest and Index appears in the A.D. Cases reporter volumes.

FIGURE 9.11   *ARNOLD v. UNITED ARTISTS THEATRE CIRCUIT*

ARNOLD v. UNITED ARTISTS THEATRE CIRCUIT   5 AD Cases 685

YOUNG v. ST. LUKE'S-ROOSEVELT HOSPITAL CTR.

U.S. District Court,
Southern District of New York

SONJA YOUNG, Plaintiff v. ST. LUKE'S-ROOSEVELT HOSPITAL CENTER, Defendant, No. 95 CIV 6077(HB), March 25, 1996

AMERICANS WITH DISABILITIES ACT

Amendment of complaint ▸108.7221 ▸708.01

Former employee, to avoid dismissal of her ADA action, must amend complaint by providing statements or other documentation from former supervisor and from emergency room doctor who treated her for epiglottal attack that focuses on nature and severity of her bronchitis and upper respiratory impairment, duration or expected duration of bronchitis, and its permanent or long-term impact on her health; among matters that would be relevant would be number of absences that she took in five-year period before her last absence, length of those absences, and type of treatment that she received.

Sonja Young, New York, N.Y., plaintiff pro se.

Michael L. Stevens and Jennifer Pitarresi (Arent, Fox, Kintner, Plotkin & Kahn), Washington, D.C., for defendant.

Full Text of Opinion

HAROLD BAER, Jr., District Judge: — Plaintiff Sonja Young filed this employment discrimination claim pursuant to the Americans with Disabilities Act ("ADA") of 1990. Defendants St. Luke's-Roosevelt Hospital Center moves this Court pursuant to Fed. R. Civ. Pro. 12(b)(6) to dismiss plaintiff's complaint.

Papers having been filed and oral argument having been heard on these motions on March 21, 1996 and due deliberation having been had, defendant St. Luke's motion to dismiss plaintiff's complaint is held in abeyance. Plaintiff has thirty days from the date hereof to amend her complaint and submit additional information in support of her claim. Should the plaintiff fail to do so within this thirty day period the motion will be granted.

During this thirty day period, plaintiff will obtain statements or other

documentation from her former supervisor during her employment at St. Luke's from the 1988 to 1993 and from a doctor who treated her in the emergency room for an epiglottal attack. Defendant is to provide plaintiff with the addresses of these former St. Luke's employees as soon as conveniently possible. Plaintiff should focus her inquiry on three areas. First, the nature and severity of her bronchitis and upper respiratory impairment. Instances regarding how many absences due to bronchitis plaintiff took from 1988 to 1993 prior to her twelve day absence in 1993, this to evidence how debilitating the attacks were. Second, the duration or expected duration of plaintiff's bronchitis. The length of plaintiff's prior absences in the 1988 to 1993 period and what type of treatment plaintiff received would be relevant. Third, the permanent or long term impact, or the projected permanent or long term impact of or resulting from the bronchitis and upper respiratory infections to plaintiff's health.

Unless plaintiff provides the Court with additional information obtained from these or other prospective witnesses within the thirty day period, defendant's motion to dismiss plaintiff's claim will be granted.

SO ORDERED.

ARNOLD v. UNITED ARTISTS THEATRE CIRCUIT

U.S. District Court,
Northern District of California

CONNIE ARNOLD, et al., Plaintiffs v. UNITED ARTISTS THEATRE CIRCUIT, INC., Defendant, No. C 93-0079 TEH, April 26, 1994; Memorandum Opinion and Order September 15, 1994

AMERICANS WITH DISABILITIES ACT

1. Title III — Class action ▸519.01 ▸575.01 ▸700.38

Action under Title III of ADA challenging movie theater company's alleged failure to comply, in both existing and new theaters, with regulations concerning seating for wheelchair users and other mobility-impaired persons satisfies requirements for certification of class, where number of persons af-

> The case begins here.

FIGURE 9.11 *ARNOLD v. UNITED ARTISTS THEATRE CIRCUIT (Continued)*

5 AD Cases 686   ARNOLD v. UNITED ARTISTS THEATRE CIRCUIT

fected by alleged access violations at more than 70 theaters numbers in thousands, company's accommodations at particular theaters are very likely to affect all wheelchair users or semi-ambulatory persons in same way, class representatives possess same interests and rely on same legal theories as other members of proposed class, and they have no individual claims different from those of other class members.

2. Title III — Class action ►575.01 ►700.38

Class action under Title III of ADA challenging movie theater company's alleged failure to comply, in both existing and new theaters, with regulations concerning seating for wheelchair users and other mobility-impaired persons will be certified under Rule 23(b)(2) of Federal Rules of Civil Procedure, even though damages are sought [under] state law, since class is remarkably [h]ogeneous in that all members [chall]enging company's refusal to [add c]ertain architectural features [at] its various theaters that af[fect all] of them in almost precisely [same wa]y.

[...] **action** ►575.01 ►700.38

[...] [a]mbulatory persons cannot be included within class of persons who can challenge movie theater company's alleged failure to comply, in both existing and new theaters, with regulations concerning seating for wheelchair users and other mobility-impaired persons, since Title III of ADA does not impose any specific requirements regarding semi-ambulatory seating.

4. Bifurcation ►575.01

Class action under Title III and state law against movie theater company for allegedly failing to comply with regulations concerning seating for wheelchair users and other mobility-impaired persons will be bifurcated, with issues of liability, injunctive and declaratory relief, and damages for named class representatives being tried in first phase and damages for other class members being tried in second phase.

5. Title III ►503.01

Showing of intent to discriminate is not element of cause of action under Title III of ADA.

6. Enforcement ►575.01

Use of separate juries to hear liability and classwide damages phases of class action under Title III of ADA is constitutionally permissible.

Lawrence W. Paradis (Miller Starr & Regalia), Oakland, Calif., and Elaine Feingold, Berkeley, Calif., for plaintiffs Connie Arnold and Ann Cupulo.

Lawrence W. Paradis (Miller Starr & Regalia), Oakland, Calif., and Brad Seligman, Berkeley, Calif., for plaintiffs Howard Ripley, Julianna Cyril, Cynde Soto, and Cyrus Berlowitz.

Peter I. Ostroff (Sidley & Austin), Los Angeles, Calif., Michael W. O'Neil, Orinda, Calif., for defendant United Artists Theatre Circuit, Inc.

David H. Raizman, Los Angeles, Calif., for California Assn. of Persons with Handicaps and California Foundation of Independent Living Centers, amici curiae.

Jane C. Pandell and Randy Wright (Pandell Norvich & Borsuk), Walnut Creek, Calif., for Raad/Uesugi & Associates, Stan Stanovich, and Heidenfrost/Harowits & Associates.

Patrick M. Glenn (Hanson Bridgett Marcus Vlahos & Rudy), San Francisco, Calif., for Irwin Seating Co.

Stephen Goldberg (Spierer Woodward Denis & Furstman), Redondo Beach, Calif., and Thomas L. Wolf (Myer Swanson & Adams, Colo., for Proctor Co.

Timothy L. McInerney & Dillon, P.C.), Oakland, Tolladay Construction Co.,

Full Text of Opinion

THELTON E. HENDERSON, Chief Judge: — This case is a suit by disabled persons who use wheelchairs or who walk using aids such as crutches, brought against United Artists Theatre Circuit, Inc. ("United Artists" or "UA"). Plaintiffs charge that defendant's movie theaters do not afford disabled persons full and equal access to their accommodations, in violation of California and federal law.

Plaintiffs have filed motions seeking certification of the suit as a class action under Rule 23(b)(2) of the Federal Rules of Civil Procedure ("Rules") and bifurcation of the trial. The Court heard oral argument on this matter on March 7, 1994. After consideration of the parties' written and oral arguments, the Court, for the reasons set forth below, GRANTS plaintiffs' motion for certification of this suit as a Rule 23(b)(2) class action, and GRANTS plaintiffs' motion for bifurcation of the trial.

I. PLAINTIFFS' MOTION FOR CLASS CERTIFICATION

A. NATURE OF THE MOTION

Plaintiffs seek certification of this lawsuit as a class action under subpart

> AD Cases headnote with a classification number. This does not correspond to a West topic or key number.

> The opinion begins here.

F. CHECKLIST FOR SUBJECT-MATTER SERVICE RESEARCH

1. LOCATE A SUBJECT-MATTER SERVICE FOR YOUR RESEARCH ISSUE

❏ Look in Table T.15 in the back of the *Bluebook.*

❏ Check a reference source such as the LawTRIO database or print sources such as *Legal Looseleafs in Print* or *Directory of Law-Related CD-ROMs.*

❏ Locate subject area databases in LexisNexis and Westlaw.

2. DETERMINE HOW TO USE THE SERVICE

❏ In print services, look for the "Overview" or "How to use this service" section.

❏ In CD-ROM and Internet services, follow the service's instructions for locating information.

❏ In LexisNexis and Westlaw, execute word searches or use other available search options.

ELECTRONIC LEGAL RESEARCH

As Chapter 1 explains, legal research can be accomplished using both print and electronic research tools. Frequently, you will use some combination of these tools in completing a research project. Although print and electronic resources are often used together, this chapter introduces you to some search techniques unique to electronic research. Earlier chapters discussed both print and electronic research in the context of individual types of authority, such as cases or statutes. This chapter explains some of the basics of electronic searching that can be used effectively in a number of services, regardless of the type of authority you need to locate. In doing so, it focuses on research in Westlaw and LexisNexis, two of the most commonly available commercial services containing a wide variety of legal authority. Although Westlaw and LexisNexis are featured in this chapter, they are only two of many electronic research services available, and you should be able to adapt the techniques described here to other electronic research services.

This chapter describes electronic search techniques in general terms and provides few specific commands for executing them. Electronic research providers update their services regularly, thus making it impossible to describe commands with any accuracy. In fact, you will likely receive training through your law school on the use of at least Westlaw and LexisNexis, if not other electronic services, and those training sessions will cover the commands necessary to execute the functions in those services.

In addition, print or on-line instructions should be available for any electronic service you use, and these instructions should contain up-to-date information for executing search commands. A single instruction session on any electronic service cannot convey all of the nuances involved in researching with it, so you should plan to review additional instructional material for any electronic service you learn to use.

A. INTRODUCTION TO ELECTRONIC LEGAL RESEARCH

1. OVERVIEW OF ELECTRONIC LEGAL RESEARCH SERVICES

Electronic legal research services can be divided into three categories. Fee-based services charge individual users a fee every time the service is used. Subscription services charge the subscriber for access, but individual users ordinarily are not charged for researching in the service. Publicly available services are those available for free on the Internet. Appendix A contains the Internet addresses for a number of publicly available research sites, including those discussed in this chapter and elsewhere in this text. A brief overview of some popular electronic legal research services follows.

a. Fee-Based Services

WESTLAW AND LEXISNEXIS. As noted earlier, Westlaw and LexisNexis are two of the most commonly available electronic services for conducting legal research. Both of these services contain the full text of a broad range of primary and secondary authorities.

LOISLAW. Loislaw is similar to Westlaw and LexisNexis, in that it contains the full text of many legal authorities. It also contains treatises on a number of subjects and has its own citator service, GlobalCite. Although Loislaw has less comprehensive coverage than either Westlaw or LexisNexis, it can be a cost-effective alternative to those services if it contains the information you need. Loislaw is available on the Internet.

VERSUSLAW. VersusLaw is similar to Loislaw. It also offers access to the full text of a range of legal authorities, and like Loislaw, it can be a cost-effective alternative to Westlaw and LexisNexis. As of this writing, however, its coverage is also less comprehensive than that of Westlaw and LexisNexis. VersusLaw is available on the Internet.

b. Subscription Services

LEXISNEXIS CONGRESSIONAL. This service is described in more detail in Chapter 7, on federal legislative history research. It is a subscription service available at many law libraries. LexisNexis Congressional

contains a wealth of legislative information, including federal statutes, Congressional documents generated during the legislative process, administrative regulations, and news about activities taking place on Capitol Hill.

INDEX TO LEGAL PERIODICALS AND LEGALTRAC. These are index services, meaning that they will generate lists of citations to authority. Although they primarily provide citations to legal periodicals, they also provide access to the full text of selected documents. These services are described in more detail in Chapter 3.

SUBJECT-MATTER SERVICES. Chapter 9 discusses research in defined subject areas of the law using specialized subject-matter services. A number of subject-matter services are available electronically, either on the Internet or in CD-ROM format. The techniques for drafting searches described in this chapter can be used effectively in many electronic subject-matter services.

c. Publicly Available Services

WEB SITES OPERATED BY GOVERNMENT OR PRIVATE ENTITIES. Government web sites can provide access to local, state, and federal legal information. Some examples of useful sites for federal law include Thomas, which is maintained by the Library of Congress, and GPO Access, a site operated by the Government Printing Office. These services are described in Chapters 7 and 8. Many courts also maintain web sites where they publish the full text of opinions, local court rules, and other useful information. In addition, web sites operated by trade, civic, educational, or other groups may provide useful information in their specialized fields.

LEGAL RESEARCH WEB SITES. A number of Internet sites collect legal information, and these can be useful research sources. Examples of legal research web sites include FindLaw and American Law Sources On-line. In addition, several law schools have developed "virtual law library" sites, such as Cornell Law School's Legal Information Institute.

INTERNET SEARCH ENGINES. A search engine is a point of entry into the Internet. It is a service that allows you to execute a search or query to locate publicly available Internet sites, much as you would search for individual documents in Westlaw or LexisNexis. Services such as Google, AltaVista, and Yahoo process queries by searching throughout the Internet for web sites that contain some or all of the terms specified. Another service, LawCrawler, limits its searches to law-related web sites, and a service known as MetaCrawler has a function that links several search engines together. This allows you to run your search through several search engines simultaneously.

An Internet search engine is not likely to be an effective tool for locating individual legal authorities. It may, however, help you locate government, educational, legal research, or other web sites with useful information.

2. OVERVIEW OF ELECTRONIC SEARCH TECHNIQUES

Before you undertake the process of electronic research, you need to assess the search options available to you. This will help you decide whether electronic research is your best option or whether print resources are a better choice. Chapter 11, on creating a research plan, touches on this issue. This section explains four techniques for searching electronically and compares them with techniques for print research.

The four primary methods of locating information in an electronic research service are: (1) retrieving a document when you know its citation; (2) browsing a publication's table of contents; (3) searching by subject; and (4) searching for documents that contain words relevant to your research issue, otherwise known as "word searching." These are not the only ways of researching electronically, but they are the most common.

If you have a citation to a document contained in an electronic service's database, you can retrieve it using its citation. There is not much difference from a process perspective between retrieving a document in print or electronically using its citation. Your decision about how to obtain the document will probably turn on other considerations. Print resources are often more economical to use and easier to read than computer resources. In addition, many secondary sources are only available in print. By contrast, electronic resources can be more up to date than print materials and can give you access to documents unavailable in your library's print collection.

Browsing a publication's table of contents is another way to search. Often you can follow links, or drill down, through a publication's table of contents to view the text of individual sections of the document. Table of contents searching usually is not available for every publication in a service's database, but statutory codes and selected secondary sources can often be searched this way. From a process perspective, there is not much difference between browsing a table of contents in print and browsing it electronically. The same considerations that affect whether to use a print or an electronic source for citation searching will also influence your decision about which type of source to use for table of contents searching.

Another option is searching by subject. With this technique, you ordinarily select a subject from an alphabetical menu of topics and then select the source or type of authority that you want to search for information on the subject. To select a subject, you can drill down through

menu options for general subjects to more specific subtopics. If you do not know which subject is most relevant to your research, many services will allow you to execute a search within the menu options to identify relevant subjects or subtopics. After you drill down through the menu options, you will often also have the choice of adding a word search to further refine the search.

Searching electronically by subject combines aspects of searching a print table of contents and a print index. The menu options you can select will usually be broad subjects like those in a table of contents, but you will usually be able to drill down through the menu options to specific subtopics like entries in a print index. Electronic subject searching can be an effective search technique when you know the general subject area you want to search. In addition, you can often use electronic subject searches to search several publications simultaneously, whereas with print research you must search one publication at a time.

There are, however, limitations on electronic subject searching. The content and organization of subject categories vary by service, as do the precision and accuracy with which authorities are assigned to the categories. You should also be aware that many services will not allow you to search for all types of authority by subject. Subject searching may be limited to cases and selected secondary sources. Therefore, if you need to search for a type of authority that is not searchable by subject, or if you need to tailor your search more specifically, using a print index or electronic word search may be more effective.

Electronic word searching is available for virtually any source contained in an electronic service's database. It is most like searching in a print index, although there are significant differences between researching with word searches and print indices. Most print indices are organized around subjects or concepts, rather than individual words in a document. This distinguishes them from electronic word searches, which locate documents based on individual terms, rather than by subject. Obviously, there is a fair amount of overlap between subjects or concepts and the words used to express them, and some entries in a print index are generated from specific terms or key words within the document. Nevertheless, electronic word searching and print index searching are not identical.

For example, if you were trying to find information on cars in a book that uses the term "automobile" instead of "car," you still might find the word "car" in the index, perhaps with a cross-reference to an entry for "automobile." If you researched the same publication in electronic form, a word search for the term "car" would not retrieve any information because the word search is limited to the exact terms you specify. This difference is one of the main factors that will determine whether you should use a word search. Word searches can be very effective for locating unique terms, but electronic subject searching (if it is

available for the authority you need to locate) and print index searching can be better choices for searching by topic.

Experienced researchers rarely rely exclusively on either print or electronic research to complete a research project. Electronic research can be especially useful for locating one or two good "hits," or relevant documents, which you can then use as a springboard into other avenues of research. Understanding electronic search techniques will help you determine the mix of print and electronic research appropriate for your research project.

3. OVERVIEW OF THE ELECTRONIC RESEARCH PROCESS

Electronic research, like print research, is a process. You need to follow an organized plan to research effectively using electronic research tools. Effective electronic searching usually involves the following four steps.

a. Selecting a Service

You want to choose the service or services most likely to contain the information you need. In addition, although you may not be concerned with the cost of research while you are in law school, in practice, selecting a cost-effective service is also an important consideration.

b. Selecting a Search Technique

Once you have selected a service, you will probably have several options for searching for authority, including citation, table of contents, subject, and word searching. To search effectively, you must decide which method is most likely to retrieve the information you need. If you decide to use a word search, you will also need to construct a query that will retrieve the information you need.

c. Selecting a Database in Which to Execute a Search

After you select a search technique (and construct a word search if necessary), you are ready to sign on to a service and execute a search. Most of the time, you will not search through the entire contents of the service. The majority of services divide their contents into databases based on subjects, such as torts or criminal law, or on the sources of information they contain, such as federal cases or cases from an individual state. These databases may be called databases, but they may also have other names, such as sources, libraries, files, infobases, or something similar. To retrieve information, you will need to select a database in which to execute the search.

d. Reviewing the Search Results

Once you have executed a search, you will need to manipulate the results in a way that allows you to determine whether the search has been successful. You may need to view a list of documents retrieved, read the text of individual documents, find specific terms within a document, or use links to other documents. You may also need to refine the search to improve the search results.

Following these steps is not always a linear process. You might decide first on your search technique, which could influence the service you select. Even if you follow the steps in order initially, you may repeat some of them based on the search results. For example, after reviewing your search results, you might go back to the second step and select a different search technique. A single search is unlikely to retrieve exactly the desired information, except when you are retrieving a document you need from its citation. One provider offers the following explanation of the search process in the context of word searching:

> Searching is a process, not an event. This should be your mantra when using [electronic research services]. Searching . . . is not about spending time and mental energy formulating the "golden query" that retrieves your desired information in a single stroke. In practice, good online searching involves formulating a succession of queries until you are satisfied with the results. As you view results from one search, you will come across additional leads that you did not identify in your original search. You can incorporate these new terms into your existing query or create a new one. After each query, evaluate its success by asking:
> - Did I find what I was looking for?
> - What better information could still be out there?
> - How can I refine my query to find better information?
>
> Issuing multiple queries can be frustrating or rewarding, depending on how long it takes you to identify the key material you need to answer your research problem.[1]

Sections B and C below discuss the electronic research process in greater detail. Section B discusses how to conduct electronic research effectively. Section C discusses some additional electronic research tools that may be useful for specific types of electronic research.

---

[1]VersusLaw, Inc. Research Manual, Part 1, Electronic Searching Strategy, http://www.versuslaw.com; *select* Help, Legal Research, Legal Research Manual, Part 1 (accessed June 13, 2005).

B. CONDUCTING EFFECTIVE ELECTRONIC LEGAL RESEARCH

1. SELECTING AN ELECTRONIC LEGAL RESEARCH SERVICE

Because many electronic legal research services exist, you must determine which service or services you should consult for your research project. Two important considerations are scope and cost.

The scope of the service is clearly a paramount consideration. You want to be sure to choose a service that contains the type of material you need. The more you know about your research issue, the easier this will be. For example, if you know you need to retrieve a United States Supreme Court case from the last term, you could research in Westlaw, LexisNexis, Loislaw, VersusLaw, or a publicly available legal research site containing Supreme Court decisions. If you know you need to research federal administrative regulations, you could research in Westlaw, LexisNexis, Loislaw, VersusLaw, LexisNexis Congressional, or GPO Access. Conversely, if you do not know the precise jurisdiction or type of authority you need, you might limit yourself to Westlaw or LexisNexis because those services contain a broad range of authorities.

After you have identified services with the proper scope of information, you should consider the cost of use. The cost of electronic research is something you might not notice as a law student because most, if not all, of the cost is subsidized. In practice, however, cost is an important consideration. You cannot use research services for which your client cannot or will not pay. Even if your client is willing and able to pay for some electronic research, you may not have unlimited ability to use fee-based services.

Of course, just because a service is fee-based does not mean it is a bad research option. It can be less expensive to locate authority through a fee-based service than it is to purchase books that would rarely be used, and some tasks can be accomplished more quickly through electronic research. In those situations, increased efficiency can justify the cost of using a fee-based service. You should not shy away from fee-based services simply because using them costs money. You should, however, be aware of cost issues and select the most cost-effective research options for your client, whether they are print or electronic, fee-based or free of charge.

It is difficult to generalize about the cost of fee-based services because many pricing options exist. Generally speaking, use of Westlaw and LexisNexis will result in the most direct expense to your client. Although some large organizations negotiate flat rates for use of these services, more frequently, charges will be based on the amount of time spent on-line, the number of searches executed, or both. Premiums may be charged for accessing certain sources, especially those containing

multiple types of authority, and separate charges for printing or downloading information also may apply. Loislaw and VersusLaw charge for use of their services as well, but their rates are generally lower than those for Westlaw and LexisNexis. Therefore, if the scope of information available in one of those services is sufficient to meet your research needs, you might choose one of them over Westlaw or LexisNexis.

Because pricing varies widely among fee-based services, it is important to investigate cost issues before you get on-line. Regardless of the method of billing, efficient searching can reduce the cost associated with the use of fee-based services. Cost-cutting strategies for searching efficiently in Westlaw and LexisNexis are discussed below. These strategies can be used when searching in other fee-based services as well.

Subscription and publicly available services are economical choices for your client if they will give you the information you need. Although charges for access to subscription services are usually paid by the subscriber, rather than the user, users can be charged for printing or downloading information. Publicly available services on the Internet are the least expensive option because they involve only the cost of access to the Internet.

If scope and cost do not dictate which service you should use, use the service with which you are most familiar. The more familiar you become with a service, the more comfortable you will feel using it and the more efficient you will be. Although you should try to gain experience using as many services as possible while you are in law school, you may find in practice that you gravitate toward certain services that meet your research needs on a regular basis.

Once you have selected a service, you are ready to begin searching for information. As noted earlier, you can retrieve a document from its citation, browse a publication's table of contents, search by subject, or execute a word search. If you choose table of contents or subject searching, you may be able to refine your search by adding word search terms. Because word searching is the most technically complex way to search, it is discussed in detail below. To locate information using a word search, you will need to construct a search, select a database in which to execute the search, and review the results. The following sections discuss each of these steps. After the discussion of the steps necessary for effective word searching, you will find additional techniques for effective Westlaw and LexisNexis research.

2. CONSTRUCTING A WORD SEARCH

In word searching, the computer will search for the words in your query and retrieve documents containing the requested information. Most electronic services recognize two types of word searches: Boolean searches (sometimes called terms and connectors searches) and natural

FIGURE 10.1 **WESTLAW SEARCH SCREEN**

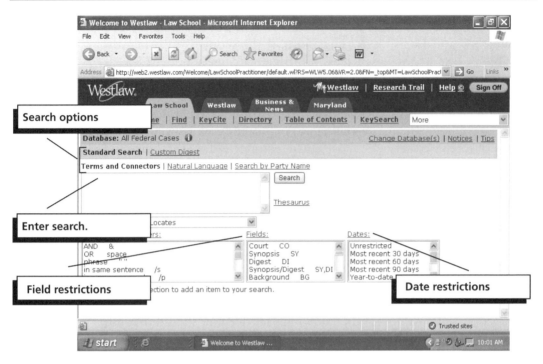

Reprinted with permission from Thomson West, from Westlaw, search screen. © 2005 Thomson West.

language searches. **Figures 10.1** and **10.2** show the search screens from Westlaw and LexisNexis, respectively. The search features identified in these figures are explained in this section.

a. Boolean Searching

Boolean searching retrieves information based on the relationships among words in a document. Using specific commands, you can ask the computer to locate documents that contain certain words in defined relationships to other words. For example, you could search for documents that contain both the term "ice cream" and the term "sundae." Alternatively, you could search for documents that contain either the term "ice cream" or the term "sundae," but not necessarily both. In a Boolean search, the computer looks for documents containing the precise terms you identify, in the precise relationships you request.

(1) Boolean search commands

In Boolean searching, you define the relationships among the terms in the search using "connectors." The most common connectors are AND and OR. AND retrieves documents containing all of the specified terms. OR retrieves documents containing any one of the specified terms. In addition

FIGURE 10.2   LEXISNEXIS SEARCH SCREEN

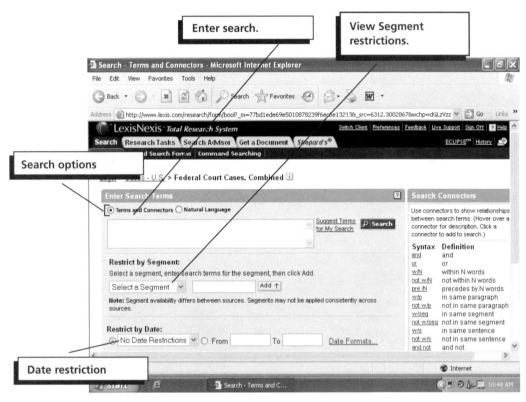

Reprinted with permission of LexisNexis, from LexisNexis, search screen.

to indicating relationships among words within the document as a whole, connectors can also indicate more specific relationships, such as terms appearing within a certain number of words of each other (/N), or within the same paragraph (/P) or sentence (/S). Some services use the connectors ADJ (for adjacent) or NEAR to indicate words in proximity to each other, instead of allowing you to specify the proximity. The help function or search tips section of the service should indicate how close adjacent or near terms have to be to be captured by the search. Connectors can also be used to exclude terms. For example, the AND NOT connector allows you to search for documents that include one term and exclude another. The chart in **Figure 10.3** shows some of the more common connectors.

You can search for individual terms within a Boolean search, or you can search for phrases. The way you indicate that terms should be searched together as a phrase will depend on the service you are using. In some services, such as LexisNexis, words in a sequence are automatically treated as a phrase unless separated by a connector. In a search for ICE CREAM, therefore, LexisNexis would search for the phrase ICE

FIGURE 10.3 BOOLEAN SEARCH CONNECTORS

CONNECTOR OR COMMAND	WESTLAW	LEXISNEXIS	OTHER SERVICES OR SEARCH ENGINES
Search for terms as a phrase.	"Place phrase in quotation marks."	Create a phrase by joining words in sequence without a connector.	Options vary by service; single or double quotation marks are common ways to denote a phrase.
Segregate terms and connectors within a search.	(Place in parentheses.)	(Place in parentheses.)	Options vary by service; parentheses are often used to segregate parts of a search.
Search for terms in the alternative.	Connect terms with **or;** leave a space between terms.	Connect terms with or.	Connect terms with or; other options vary by service.
Search for, or exclude, terms in proximity to each other. (**n** = a specific number)	Term1 **+n** Term2 (Term1 appears a certain number of words before Term2.) Term1 **/n** Term2 (Term1 appears within a certain number of words of Term2; Term1 can occur before or after Term2.) Term1 **/s** Term2 (Term1 appears within the same sentence as Term2.) Term1 **/p** Term2 (Term1 appears within the same paragraph as Term2.)	Term1 **/n** Term2 (Term1 appears within a certain number of words of Term2; Term1 can occur before or after Term2.) Term1 **pre/n** Term2 (Term1 appears a certain number of words before Term2.) Term1 **not /n** Term2 (Term1 does not appear within a certain number of words of Term2.) Term1 **/s** Term2 (Term1 appears within the same sentence as Term2; can also be used to exclude terms, using **not /s.**) Term1 **/p** Term2 (Term1 appears within the same paragraph as Term2; can also be used to exclude terms, using **not /p.**)	Often, proximity is indicated with **/n, /s,** or **/p,** depending on the service. Some services use **adj** (for adjacent) or **near** (for nearby terms).
Search for all terms.	Connect terms with **and** or **&.**	Connect terms with **and** or **&.**	Connect terms with **and;** other options vary by service.
Exclude terms.	Connect terms with **but not** or **%**	Connect terms with **and not.**	Options vary by service.

CREAM as a single unit. Other services automatically treat words in a sequence as though they have a particular connector between them. Westlaw, for example, automatically applies the OR connector between words in a sequence. A Westlaw search for ICE CREAM operates as a search for ICE OR CREAM. Other services may automatically apply the AND, ADJ, or NEAR connectors between words in a sequence. In services that automatically apply a particular connector, you can usually create a phrase using quotation marks or some other type of punctuation. You can search for a phrase in Westlaw by placing the words in quotation marks: "ICE CREAM".

Most searches contain several terms and several connectors. When the search is executed, Boolean logic will process the connectors in a specific sequence. In Westlaw and LexisNexis, the OR connector is processed first, followed by the proximity connectors (/N, /P, /S), the AND connector, and finally, the exclusion connectors (AND NOT, BUT NOT). It is important to understand this hierarchy of connectors to create an effective search.

If you executed a search for ICE AND CREAM OR SUNDAE, the search for the terms CREAM OR SUNDAE would be processed first. After documents with one or the other of those terms were identified, the search for the term ICE would begin. In effect, the query would be processed as a search for ICE AND CREAM OR ICE AND SUNDAE. This is probably not the intended search, and it could miss documents containing the terms you want or retrieve irrelevant documents.

Here, you probably intended to search for the phrase "ice cream" or the term "sundae." There are two ways you could have modified this search to achieve that result. One is by searching for "ICE CREAM" as a phrase, instead of connecting the words with AND. That would result in a search for the phrase "ICE CREAM" or the term "SUNDAE," which was the intended search.

Another way to vary the search would have been to segregate the ICE AND CREAM portion of the search. In Westlaw or LexisNexis, you can accomplish this by placing a portion of the search in parentheses: (ICE AND CREAM) OR SUNDAE. The terms within parentheses would be treated as a separate unit. Thus, the AND connector would apply only to the terms within the parentheses. In this example, adding parentheses would result in a search for the terms ICE AND CREAM as a unit, and then in the alternative, for the individual term SUNDAE. This again would achieve the intended search result. The chart in **Figure 10.3**, containing common connectors, lists them in the order in which they are processed in Boolean searches in Westlaw and LexisNexis.

The hierarchy of connectors, as well as the precise connectors and punctuation used to create a search, can vary in any given service. You should consult the help or search tips function when you are using a

service for the first time to make sure you use the appropriate search commands.

(2) Constructing a basic Boolean search

Once you understand the concept of Boolean searching, your next task is creating an effective search that is tailored to find the information you need. Constructing a basic search involves three steps:

- developing the initial search terms
- expanding the breadth and depth of the search and adding wildcard characters
- adding connectors and parentheses to clarify the relationships among the search terms.

In developing the initial search terms, you should use the process described in Chapter 2. Think about the problem in terms of the parties, any places or things, potential claims and defenses, and the relief sought. You may recall the example factual scenario in Chapter 2, which involved the issue of whether a hotel operator is liable in negligence to a guest whose wrist was broken during a robbery that took place on the hotel premises. To develop a Boolean search on this issue, you might begin with the following words:

hotel negligence guest robbery

Having identified the relevant terms, your next step would be expanding the search. This can be done in two ways. First, unless you are searching for terms of art that need to appear precisely as written to be useful, you need to expand the breadth and depth of the search, as explained in Chapter 2. Expanding the breadth of the search involves generating synonyms and terms related to the initial search terms. Expanding the depth involves expressing the terms with varying degrees of abstraction. Recall that a Boolean search is limited to the exact terms you identify. If an object, idea, concept, or action is expressed in a document using different terminology, a Boolean search will not locate it. Therefore, it is especially important to expand your search terms with this type of searching.

The second way to expand your search is to use wildcard characters. Wildcard characters substitute for variable letters within a word. Westlaw and LexisNexis use two wildcard characters: the asterisk (*) to substitute for individual letters, and the exclamation point (!) to substitute for variable word endings. Thus, in the example above, you might change NEGLIGENCE to NEGLIGEN! to expand the search to include negligence, negligent, negligently, and any other variation on the word.

Although many services use wildcard characters, the functions of the characters are not standard. For example, the asterisk (*) in some

services is used for variable word endings, not the exclamation point (!). You should review the search commands in any service with which you are unfamiliar. In addition, some services will not search for plurals, which means you need to use wildcard characters to capture them, e.g., hotel! for hotel or hotels, wom*n for woman or women. Both Westlaw and LexisNexis will search for plural forms of words automatically if they end in "s" or "es." Westlaw will also automatically search for irregular plurals, such as "mice" or "children," but LexisNexis will not.

The example search might be expanded in the following ways:

> hotel motel inn! lodg! negligen!
> guest visitor tourist robbery theft crim!

Now that a series of terms has been developed and expanded, the next step is identifying the appropriate relationships among the terms using connectors and, if appropriate, parentheses. The closer the connections you require among the terms, the more restrictive the search will be, and the broader the connections, the more open the search will be. For example, the AND connector, which requires only that both words appear somewhere within the same document, will retrieve more documents than a proximity connector such as /P, which requires the words to appear within the same paragraph. Parentheses should be used to group categories of terms that you want to search together.

In the example search, the terms might be connected as follows:

> (hotel or motel or inn! or lodg!) /p
> negligen! /p (guest or visitor or tourist) and
> (robbery or theft or crim!)

The parentheses group related terms together within the search. Thus, the terms relating to the premises (hotel, motel, inn, etc.) will be searched together, as will the terms relating to the injured party and the cause of the injury. The query will then proceed to the relationships among the groups of terms (within the same paragraph or document).

The /P proximity connector is used in the example search to connect the terms relating to the premises, the legal theory, and the injured party. Hotels can be involved in many types of claims, so requiring the premises terms to appear within the same paragraph as the legal theory (NEGLIGEN!) helps target cases involving hotel negligence. Because hotels can be subject to liability in negligence to many parties, requiring terms relating to the injured party to occur within the same paragraph also helps focus the search. By contrast, the terms relating to the act that caused the injury could occur anywhere within the document and still be relevant to the search. Therefore, the AND connector is used for that part of the search.

(3) Constructing a more sophisticated search

In addition to allowing you to search for terms within the body of a document, some services will allow you to limit your search to individual components of the document, such as words in the title, the name of the author, or the date of the document. Although you will not always use this search option, it is an important feature to understand.

In Westlaw, the document components are called "fields"; in LexisNexis, they are called "segments." Both services will allow you to add field or segment restrictions using menu options or by typing commands into the search. The chart in **Figure 10.4** sets out some of the more common fields and segments recognized in Westlaw and LexisNexis.

In the example search, the search results could be limited to cases from a particular jurisdiction or time period. In the hypothetical set out in Chapter 2, the hotel was located in Illinois. Therefore, you might want to limit your search to cases from courts in Illinois. You could do that in Westlaw by choosing the option for "Court" under the "Fields" section on the search screen or typing the field command CO for court, and then typing the search terms in parentheses:

(hotel or motel or inn! or lodg!) /p
negligen! /p (guest or visitor or tourist) and
(robbery or theft or crim!)
and co(Ill!)

The same connectors and commands that apply to other Boolean searches also apply to field and segment searches. Therefore, in the Westlaw search above, ILL is followed by an exclamation point so that Westlaw will search for both the abbreviation Ill. and the full word Illinois.

As another example, you can search for a document by name or title by limiting the search to terms within the name or title. If you wanted to search for the United States Supreme Court case of *Roe v. Wade*, you could search in LexisNexis using the query ROE AND WADE. This search, however, would retrieve every case within the database that ever mentioned Roe v. Wade, which could be hundreds or even thousands of cases. The search would be more successful with a segment restriction. A search for NAME(ROE AND WADE) would limit the search to cases in which the terms ROE and WADE both appear only in the name of the document.

b. Natural Language Searching

Boolean searching requires you to understand various commands and connectors, and as a consequence, can be challenging to master. Another way to execute a word search is to use what is called "natural language" searching. This is what many Internet search engines use as their default search option. It is also available in Westlaw, LexisNexis, and other electronic research services.

FIGURE 10.4   FIELD AND SEGMENT COMMANDS IN WESTLAW AND LEXISNEXIS

DOCUMENT COMPONENT	WESTLAW FIELD COMMAND	LEXISNEXIS SEGMENT COMMAND
title	TI	NAME or TITLE (depending on the source)
author	AU	AUTHOR
date	The Westlaw search screen contains a separate section for date restrictions.	The LexisNexis search screen contains a separate section for date restrictions.
attorney	AT	COUNSEL
court	CO	COURT
opinions written by a particular judge	JU (retrieves any opinion written by that judge)	WRITTENBY (retrieves any opinion written by that judge) OPINIONBY (retrieves majority or plurality opinions) CONCURBY (retrieves concurring opinions) DISSENTBY (retrieves dissenting opinions)
terms occurring within a concurring opinion	CON	CONCUR
terms occurring within a dissenting opinion	DIS	DISSENT

With natural language searching, you simply enter your search as a question, without concern for connectors, parentheses, or wildcard characters. The computer converts the terms in the question into a search format to retrieve documents. In Westlaw and LexisNexis, natural language searching retrieves a fixed number of documents. In LexisNexis, you can manually increase or decrease that number by clicking on "Preferences" along the top of the screen. In Westlaw, you can change the default option by selecting "More" and then "Options" from the pull-down menu.

To construct a natural language search, you begin by developing the initial query. The example search might look like this:

> Is a hotel liable in negligence if a guest is injured
> during a robbery that occurs on the premises?

Like a Boolean search, a natural language search will be limited to the terms you specify. Therefore, the initial search must be expanded:

> Is a hotel, motel, inn, innkeeper, or lodging liable
> in negligence if a guest, visitor, or tourist is injured
> during a robbery, theft, or crime that occurs on the premises?

Both Westlaw and LexisNexis have additional options for refining a natural language search. Natural language searching can be helpful if you are researching an area of law with which you are unfamiliar. If you know some relevant terms, but are uncertain about how to construct an effective Boolean query, you can use a natural language search as a starting point. If the search retrieves relevant authorities, you can use them as an access point into other electronic search functions, such as the table of contents for a code or the Custom Digest or Search Advisor functions for case research. In addition, reading the authorities that the search retrieves can give you enough knowledge about the subject to construct an effective Boolean search.

Although natural language searching can be a useful way to get started with some research projects, it is not likely to be effective as your sole electronic searching technique. The program that converts the question into a search is not perfect. The results can be inconsistent, especially because you do not specify the connectors used to define the relationships among the search terms or add parentheses to group terms together. Boolean searching offers more flexibility in tailoring the search to your needs. You will generally get better search results if you work on becoming proficient in Boolean search techniques.

3. Selecting a Database in Which to Execute the Search

Once you have constructed a word search, you are ready to execute it in the electronic service you have chosen to use. As noted earlier, most services divide their contents into databases based on subjects or on the sources of information they contain. Therefore, you will need to select the database in which to execute your search. Selecting *a* database is not difficult. What is more challenging is selecting *the best* database to obtain the information you need.

Generally speaking, you should select the narrowest database that contains all of the information you need. For example, if you were researching Maryland statutes on-line, you should not choose a data-base that contains statutes from all fifty states. Instead, if possible, search a database that contains only Maryland statutes. Searching in an overly broad database requires you to sort through information that is not rele-vant to your search, making it difficult to determine whether your search was successful. Choosing a database tailored to your research needs will improve the efficiency of your electronic searching.

4. REVIEWING THE SEARCH RESULTS

Sometimes when you execute a word search, the results may not be quite what you expected. Specifically, you may retrieve too many documents, not enough documents, or documents that simply are not useful in resolving your research issue.

If your word search does not retrieve useful information, consider the following options:

- searching in a narrower or broader database
- subtracting less essential terms or expanding the breadth and depth of the search
- excluding terms from the search (AND NOT or BUT NOT can be used as connectors in a Boolean search or as part of a textual query with natural language searching).

In a Boolean search, you have additional options for revising your search:

- making the proximity connectors more restrictive or less restrictive
- subtracting or adding wildcard characters
- subtracting or adding field or segment restrictions.

You may need to browse some of the documents you have retrieved to see why the search was not successful. For example, if you conducted a Boolean search for cases involving diving accidents and included the term DIV! in your search, you could be retrieving cases concerning divestiture of assets or diversity jurisdiction in addition to cases about diving and divers. Browsing can also help you identify additional terms that should be added to your search.

If the search seems completely off the mark, you might not be searching in an appropriate database or for the correct terms. In that case, you may need to consult secondary sources to obtain background information on your research issue, and print resources organized by subject may prove easier to use at this stage of your research. Chapter 3 discusses the use of secondary sources. In addition, Chapter 11, on

creating a research plan, discusses ways to improve your research results if your initial efforts prove fruitless.

5. RESEARCHING EFFECTIVELY IN WESTLAW AND LEXISNEXIS

This section provides some information on how to retrieve and refine the results of a word search in Westlaw and LexisNexis. It also provides some techniques for cost-effective Westlaw and LexisNexis searching.

a. Search Results in Westlaw

To retrieve information using a word search in Westlaw, you must select a database and execute your search. Westlaw will automatically display a list of documents retrieved. You can view the text of a document by selecting it from the list.

The Term function provides another way to browse your search results. Term will move the cursor forward or backward to each occurrence of one of your search terms. Instead of browsing the full text of a document, you can use Term to jump to passages that are likely to have relevant information. Once you select a document, use the Term arrows at the bottom of the screen to jump to the search terms in the document.

After you have browsed your search results, you may want to refine your query, which you can do in a couple of ways. The first is to edit your query, which allows you to change or add terms or field restrictions to the search. If you edit the query, Westlaw will execute the edited search within the original database you selected. You can also choose to run the search in a different database. If the search has retrieved too many documents, another alternative is to use the Locate command. Locate allows you to search for terms within the documents retrieved in the initial query. In effect, it operates as a search within a search. A Locate request can be submitted using Boolean or natural language searching. Once you have executed a Locate request, the citation list will show only the documents containing the Locate term(s), and the Term function will move the cursor to the Locate term(s). An example of a Westlaw search result screen appears in **Figure 10.5**.

b. Search Results In LexisNexis

Word searching in LexisNexis requires you to select a Source in which to search. After you select a Source, you can execute a Boolean or natural language search.

Once you have executed your search, LexisNexis offers four options for viewing the results: Full, KWIC, Cite, and Custom. Full retrieves the full text of each document. KWIC displays portions of the document containing your search terms, along with the immediately surrounding

FIGURE 10.5   WESTLAW SEARCH RESULTS

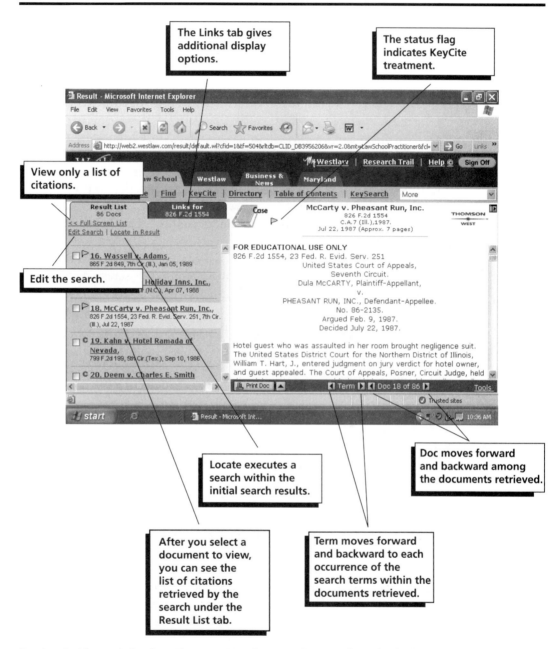

The Links tab gives additional display options.

The status flag indicates KeyCite treatment.

View only a list of citations.

Edit the search.

Doc moves forward and backward among the documents retrieved.

Locate executes a search within the initial search results.

After you select a document to view, you can see the list of citations retrieved by the search under the Result List tab.

Term moves forward and backward to each occurrence of the search terms within the documents retrieved.

Reprinted with permission from Thomson West, from Westlaw, search results display. © 2005 Thomson West.

text. In both Full and KWIC formats, your search terms will be highlighted. When you are viewing a document in Full or KWIC, you can move to the previous or next document using the arrows above the title of the document, and you can use Term to move to each occurrence of one of your terms. Cite displays a list of citations to the documents

retrieved by the search. From the citation list, you can view individual documents in Full or KWIC format by clicking on the citation. Custom allows you to customize the information in the search results display.

LexisNexis offers several ways to refine your search results if necessary. One way is by editing the initial search. Another option is the FOCUS function, which is similar to Locate in Westlaw. By selecting FOCUS, you can search for new terms within the documents retrieved by the initial search.

LexisNexis also has a search function called More Like This. You may be familiar with this function if you have used other Internet search engines. This function creates a new search using terms within a document you have retrieved. Thus, if you found a document that was especially helpful, the More Like This function would allow you to specify key terms from the document and use them to conduct another search in the same or another Source. A related search option is More Like Selected Text. This option allows you to select terms from a document to use as a search in the same or another Source. An example of a search result screen displaying a document in Full format appears in **Figure 10.6**.

c. Cost-Effective Searching in Westlaw and LexisNexis

If you conduct research in Westlaw or LexisNexis, advance planning will allow you to take advantage of strategies to make your research as cost-effective as possible:

- Construct word searches and plan your research path in advance.
- Use research assistance provided by Westlaw and LexisNexis.
- Execute your searches in a way that takes into account the way you are being billed.
- Determine charges for printing or downloading information.

The strategies discussed here can be applied to other fee-based services as well.

(1) Construct word searches and plan your research path in advance

One of the best ways to cut costs is to draft your word searches and plan your research path before you get on-line. No matter how you are being billed, a thoughtful search strategy defined before you sign on is more likely to lead to useful results. This involves writing out your word searches and deciding which databases to search in advance.

Writing out your word searches in advance allows you to generate a list of terms and refine your search before you start incurring charges. Deciding in advance which databases you plan to search will also allow you to search quickly and efficiently. Recall that searching the narrowest database that meets your research needs makes evaluating

FIGURE 10.6   LEXISNEXIS SEARCH RESULTS

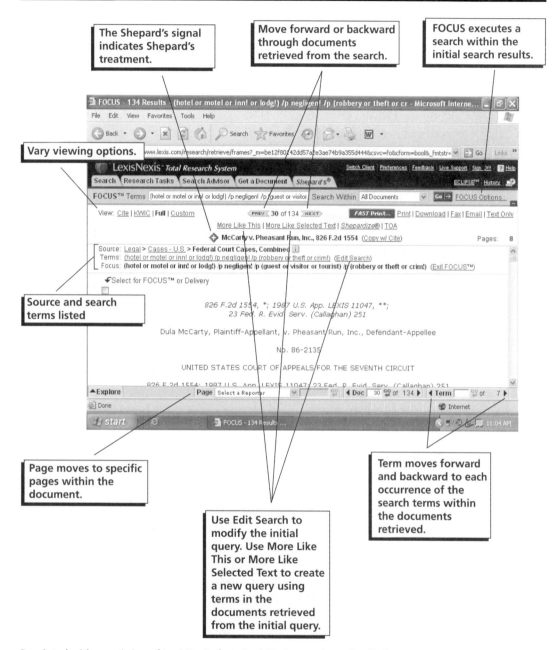

The Shepard's signal indicates Shepard's treatment.

Move forward or backward through documents retrieved from the search.

FOCUS executes a search within the initial search results.

Vary viewing options.

Source and search terms listed

Page moves to specific pages within the document.

Use Edit Search to modify the initial query. Use More Like This or More Like Selected Text to create a new query using terms in the documents retrieved from the initial query.

Term moves forward and backward to each occurrence of the search terms within the documents retrieved.

Reprinted with permission of LexisNexis, from LexisNexis, search results display.

your search results easier, which in turn reduces the amount of time you spend on-line. In addition, Westlaw and LexisNexis charge a premium for access to databases that contain multiple types of authority, such as those containing all federal or state cases. Deciding in advance which databases have the most appropriate information for your search,

instead of automatically searching in the premium databases, will make your research more cost effective.

Advance planning also makes keeping notes of your search process easier. As noted in Chapter 11, on creating a research plan, it is important to keep track of your research process as you search for authority. If you have written out your word searches and intended research path, you will not have to keep as many notes while you are searching on-line. Of course, you may change your strategy based on what your searches retrieve, and you will need to keep notes of your revised searches as you execute them. At a minimum, however, you should begin with a search mapped out.

(2) Use research assistance

Another way to cut costs is to use the research assistance provided by Westlaw and LexisNexis. Both of these services employ research attorneys to provide assistance to users. You can obtain live help on-line or telephone assistance through their toll-free numbers. If you are unsure about whether your strategy is likely to be effective, you may want to contact the provider for assistance. The research attorneys will help you create word searches and select appropriate databases to search to maximize your search results.

(3) Execute searches to account for the billing structure

Once you have signed on to Westlaw or LexisNexis, some search options may be more cost effective than others. If you are being charged by the amount of time you spend on-line, you want to work as quickly as possible to minimize your costs. In that situation, it is especially important that you draft your planned word searches before you sign on because you do not want to spend time thinking up your search once you have started accruing charges. You also want to execute your searches quickly without spending a lot of time browsing documents. It is often more economical to print a list of the citations retrieved by your search so you can review the documents in hard copy off-line. If it turns out that your search was not effective, you can get back on-line to try again.

If you are being charged by the number of word searches you execute, you will often be able to modify your initial search at no additional cost. In that case, when you draft word searches in advance, you may want to devise relatively broad searches, along with potential narrowing modifications. You can then execute the broad searches, browse documents on-line, and execute modifications to narrow the results if necessary. This will allow you to maximize your search results at a lower cost than executing a series of new word searches.

(4) Determine charges for printing or downloading information

Regardless of the overall billing structure for use of Westlaw or LexisNexis, it is often more cost efficient to photocopy materials from

hard copy available in the library than it is to print or download information on-line. Even in law school, you may be charged for printing or downloading. Therefore, whether you are at work or at school, be sure to investigate printing and downloading costs before you get on-line.

C. ADDITIONAL ELECTRONIC RESEARCH RESOURCES ∎

1. ALERT OR CLIPPING SERVICES

Sometimes your work on a research project will be done in a few days, but other times it will extend over a longer period of time. In law school, you might work on a moot court brief or scholarly paper for several weeks or even an entire semester. In legal practice, work on individual cases often extends over months or years. When you are working on an issue over a period of time, one electronic resource that may be useful to you is an alert or clipping service. These services automatically run searches through electronic databases and notify you when relevant new information is added to a database. These services allow you to stay up-to-date on developments affecting your research while you are working on a project.

Many news services offer automatic updates on general news topics and current events. Providers of legal information also frequently offer alert or clipping services. Free services, such as Law.com, offer free daily updates on top legal stories. Fee-based services will often allow you to draft specific queries to update your research on a schedule you specify. You can specify the database(s) in which to run the search, the frequency with which the search is to be run, and the manner in which the search results will be delivered to you. You may have the option to run the search daily, weekly, monthly, or on some other schedule. You can also often choose from a range of delivery options for the search results, including e-mail or fax delivery. Once you access the service, a menu of options will set out the choices available to you.

Westlaw offers several alert services. The two that are most likely to be of use to you in law school are KeyCite Alert and WestClip. KeyCite Alert notifies you when new information is added to the KeyCite entries for cases, statutes, federal regulations, or certain federal administrative agency decisions. When you view the KeyCite entry for an authority, you can click on the KeyCite Alert link to create a KeyCite Alert entry. You can also access KeyCite Alert directly by clicking on the KeyCite link at the top of the screen. WestClip allows you to draft a word search to be run periodically in the database(s) you specify and delivers the search results to you. After you run a search, you can create a WestClip entry by clicking on the "Add Search to WestClip" link at the top of the

list of citations. To access WestClip without first running a search, use the pull-down menu in the top right corner of the screen.

LexisNexis also has two alert services. *Shepard's* Alert is similar to KeyCite Alert. It notifies you when new information is added to the Shepard's entries for cases, statutes, or federal regulations. When you view the Shepard's entry for an authority, you can click on the "Save as *Shepard's* Alert" link to create a *Shepard's* Alert entry, or you can access *Shepard's* Alert directly by clicking on the Alerts tab at the top of the screen. LexisNexis also has a service that is similar to WestClip. This service used to be called ECLIPSE but is now called simply Alert. It runs your search in specific Sources at specified intervals and delivers the search results to you. You must run a search before you can save it as an Alert entry. After you run a search, click on the "Save as Alert" link at the top of the screen.

Other services also offer clipping services. LoisLaw's clipping service is called LawWatch, and VersusLaw's service is called AdvanceLink. You should look for alert or clipping services in any electronic resource you use.

2. BLOGS AND OTHER PUBLICLY AVAILABLE INTERNET SOURCES

Legal research used to be accomplished primarily, if not exclusively, in a limited universe of research sources produced by legal publishers. As more and more information becomes available via the Internet, however, the range of sources available for researching legal issues continues to grow. Government, educational, nonprofit, trade, and civic organizations that are engaged in public education efforts make useful information on many areas of the law available via their web sites. In addition, web logs, or blogs as they have come to be known, are becoming an increasingly important source of information both in our culture as a whole and in legal research. A blog, as you are no doubt aware, is a web site on which the author posts information on a defined topic. Blogs on virtually every topic exist, including many legal topics. You can even find blogs on legal research. Law-related blogs are sometimes called blawgs.

Publicly available web sites and blogs are most likely to be useful to you when you are looking for information on a specific topic. If you find a relevant web site or blog, it may provide you with background information on the topic, references to significant legal authorities, news about legislative initiatives pending at the local, state, or federal level, and links to other sites with useful information. For example, if you were asked to research a problem in bankruptcy, you might want to spend some time looking over the web site for the American Bankruptcy Institute. The screen reproduced in **Figure 10.7** shows some of the kinds of information you would find there. If you were unfamiliar with

FIGURE 10.7   ONLINE RESOURCES, AMERICAN BANKRUPTCY INSTITUTE WEB SITE

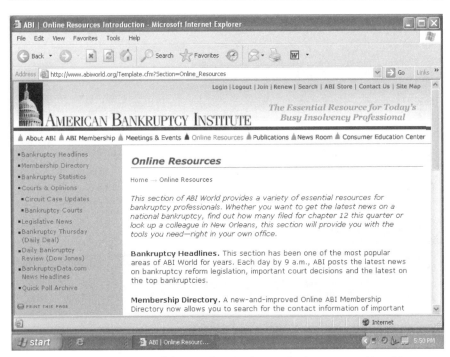

Reprinted with the permission of the American Bankrutpcy Institute, www.abiworld.org.

bankruptcy law, this site might be a good starting point for familiarizing yourself with the topic.

As another example, if you were researching an issue regarding the liability of a manufacturer of an herbal dietary supplement for an injury to a person who ingested the supplement, you might want to locate a blog on alternative medicine. **Figure 10.8** shows a portion of an entry in CAMLaw, a blog devoted to legal issues in complementary and alternative medicine. If you located entries relevant to your research issue, they might provide useful information to familiarize you with the area of law and get you started on your research.

If you are following a number of blogs, either to research a specific issue or to stay up-to-date with developments in the field, you may want to use an RSS feed reader. An RSS feed reader delivers blog headlines to your computer along with links to the full articles so that you do not have to visit each blog in which you are interested to see if new, relevant information has been posted. In a sense, RSS feed readers act like alert services for blogs.

Blogs and other sources of publicly available information are simply new types of secondary sources. When viewed this way, their role in legal research becomes clear. The caveats described in Chapter 3, on

FIGURE 10.8   ENTRY FROM THE CAMLAW BLOG

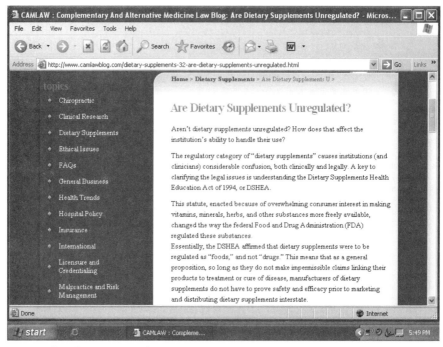

Reprinted with permission from Complementary and Alternative Medicine Law Blog (CAMLaw Blog), www.camlawblog.com, © 2004, lexBlog, Inc.

secondary source research in more traditional legal sources, also apply to blogs and publicly available web sites: Use them to obtain background information on an area of law and to obtain citations to primary authority. Do not rely on them as authoritative sources of legal rules or as official sources of primary authority.

To make sure you use blogs and other publicly available Internet sites appropriately, you should plan to undertake four steps: (1) locate useful information; (2) assess the credibility of the source of the information; (3) save or print a copy of the information you are using; and (4) verify and update any legal authorities you locate through the source. In the following discussion of these four steps, you will find references to Internet sites that may be useful to you. The web site addresses for all these sites appear in Appendix A at the end of this text.

To locate useful information, you could use a general search engine, such as Google, or a specialized search engine, such as Google Scholar for scholarly publications or LawCrawler for law-related web sites. You can also use a directory such as Blawg, a directory of law-related blogs.

Once you have located useful information, you must assess the credibility of the source. Anyone with the necessary equipment can post information on the Internet. Much information available on the Internet is inaccurate or out-of-date. Many individuals and groups post information on the Internet to advance their social or policy agendas. Therefore, you need to make a separate assessment of how much weight to give to information posted on an individual's or organization's blog or web site. The sites you visit should contain information you can use to assess the sources' credibility. The authors of many blogs will provide biographical information to help you assess their expertise. Most sites sponsored by organizations or entities include information about the group, such as its history and mission.

If you find useful information on a blog or publicly available web site, be sure to save or print a copy of the page. Internet sites can change at any moment; the information most helpful to you could change or disappear altogether at any time. If you find that information you accessed earlier is no longer available, you can try to find it in an Internet archive, such as the Internet Archive Wayback Machine, which stores copies of sites for future reference. You cannot count on finding an archived version of a web page that has been changed, moved, or deleted. The better practice, therefore, is to save or print useful information as you locate it.

If you find references to legal authorities through blogs or publicly available web sites, the last step is verifying and updating your research. You should not assume that the authorities you have located are correct, complete, or up-to-date. Use the information you have found as a springboard into more traditional avenues of legal research to make sure that you have located all pertinent information and that the legal authority you cite is authoritative.

D. CITING AUTHORITY OBTAINED FROM ELECTRONIC LEGAL RESEARCH SERVICES

Much of the information you locate through electronic services will also be available in print format. Both the *ALWD Manual* and the *Bluebook* require that you cite the print format if possible. This is not as difficult as it might seem. Many electronic services provide all the information you need for a print citation, including page numbers. For cases, statutes, and other materials available only in electronic format, the following rules apply. This chapter does not contain complete explanations about citing cases, statutes, and other authorities. More information about citing each of these types of authority is included in the chapters devoted to those sources.

1. CASES

Citations to cases available only in Westlaw or LexisNexis are similar, but not identical, in *ALWD Manual* and *Bluebook* format. *ALWD Manual* Rule 12.12 provides that the citation must contain the following three components: (1) the case name; (2) the database identifier, including the year, the name of the database, and the unique document number; and (3) a parenthetical containing the jurisdiction and court abbreviations and the full date. A pinpoint reference can be provided with "at *" and the page number. Here is an example:

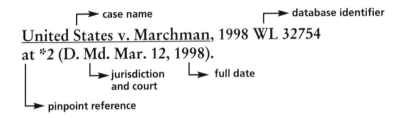

A *Bluebook* citation is the same, except that Bluepages B5.1.3 requires that the docket number for the case be included in the citation and that a comma appear before the pinpoint reference. Here is an example:

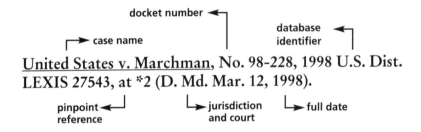

2. STATUTES

Statutory provisions retrieved from Westlaw or LexisNexis should be cited the same way print materials are cited, with additional information in the parenthetical indicating which electronic service was accessed and the date through which the service was updated. Electronic statutory citations are covered in *ALWD Manual* Rule 14.5 and *Bluebook* Rule 18.1.2. The examples in the *Bluebook* and the *ALWD Manual* use slightly different wording to convey the updating information. Also, the *Bluebook* examples show LEXIS in all capital letters, whereas the *ALWD Manual* does not. Otherwise, the

citations are the same using either format. Here is an example in *ALWD Manual* format:

8 U.S.C.A. § 1431 (West, Westlaw current through Pub. L. No. 109-15).

Here is an example in *Bluebook* format:

N.Y. Penal Law § 190.05 (McKinney, LEXIS through ch. 77, May 31, 2005).

3. MATERIALS AVAILABLE ON THE INTERNET

Both the *ALWD Manual* and the *Bluebook* discourage citations to information on the Internet if it is available in print form because of the transient nature of many Internet sites. If you are citing something available in both print and electronic form that you obtained from an electronic source, both the *ALWD Manual* and the *Bluebook* generally require that you provide the print citation, supplemented with additional information indicating the electronic source.

In the *ALWD Manual*, Rule 38 provides general guidance on citing electronic sources, and Rule 40 covers citations to information available only on the Internet. According to Rule 40, a citation to an authority available only via the Internet consists of up to five components: (1) the author of the item or owner of the web site; (2) the title of the item, underlined or italicized; (3) a pinpoint reference if one is available; (4) the URL; and (5) the date, which could be the date of the item, the date the site was updated, or the date you accessed the site, depending on the material you are citing. Here is an example of a citation to a news report in *ALWD Manual* format:

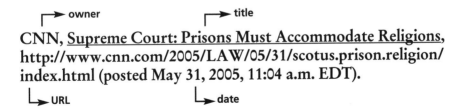

CNN, <u>Supreme Court: Prisons Must Accommodate Religions</u>, http://www.cnn.com/2005/LAW/05/31/scotus.prison.religion/ index.html (posted May 31, 2005, 11:04 a.m. EDT).

In the *Bluebook*, information on Internet citations appears in Rule 18.2. Rule 18.2.1 provides general guidance on citing information available on the Internet. The rest of Rule 18.2 (18.2.2-18.2.4) discusses how to construct different types of Internet citations. To cite a source

available only via the Internet in *Bluebook* format, you must combine the requirements of Rule 18.2.1 with those in 18.2.2-18.2.4. The *Bluebook* does not provide specific formats for Internet citations to all forms of authority. In many cases, you will need to format the citation by analogizing to the rules applicable to similar print sources.

For example, an Internet news report is analogous to a print newspaper article. Applying the principles in Rule 18.2, as well as those for newspaper articles in Bluepages B9.1.4, you could cite the news report this way:

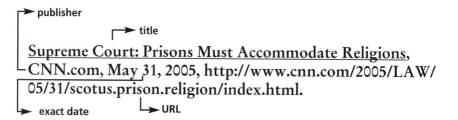

E. SAMPLE PAGES FOR ELECTRONIC LEGAL RESEARCH

Sample search screens for Westlaw and LexisNexis appear earlier in this chapter and throughout the text. Earlier chapters also contain sample search screens for several of the services outlined at the beginning of this chapter, including the Index to Legal Periodicals and LegalTrac (Chapter 3), Thomas and LexisNexis Congressional (Chapter 7), and GPO Access (Chapter 8). Therefore, the sample pages in **Figures 10.9** through **10.12** illustrate some of the services not highlighted elsewhere: FindLaw and Cornell Law School's Legal Information Institute.

FindLaw organizes legal information by category.

FIGURE 10.9   INTRODUCTORY SCREENS FOR FINDLAW

Reprinted with permission. © 2005 FindLaw, Inc., from http://www.findlaw.com.

Selecting the category for "Cases & Codes" brings up these options. You can choose a subcategory in which to execute a search.

FIGURE 10.10   SEARCH OPTIONS IN FINDLAW

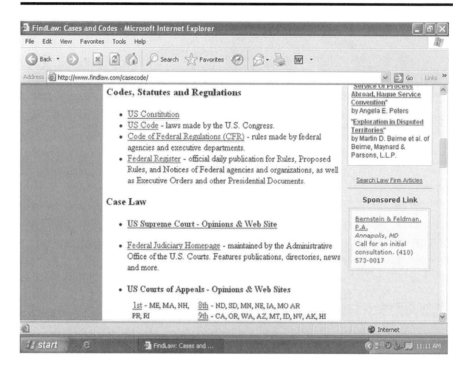

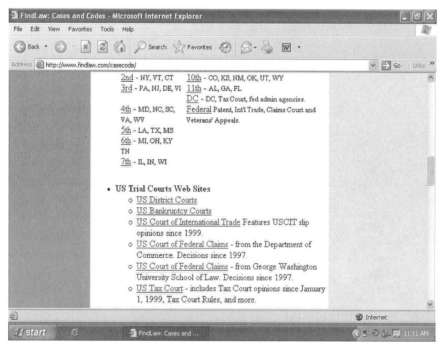

Reprinted with permission. © 2005 FindLaw, Inc., from http://www.findlaw.com/casecode.

Cornell Law School's Legal Information Institute contains a variety of legal information.

FIGURE 10.11 INTRODUCTORY SCREEN, LEGAL INFORMATION INSTITUTE

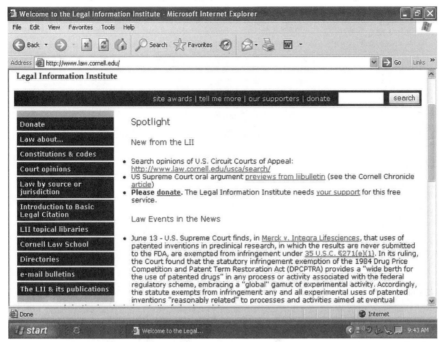

Reprinted with permission. © 2005 Cornell Law School, from http://www.law.cornell.edu.

The category for "Law by source or jurisdiction" will allow you to search for federal, state, foreign, or international law. You can execute word searches in the subcategories of information.

FIGURE 10.12   SEARCH OPTIONS IN LEGAL INFORMATION INSTITUTE

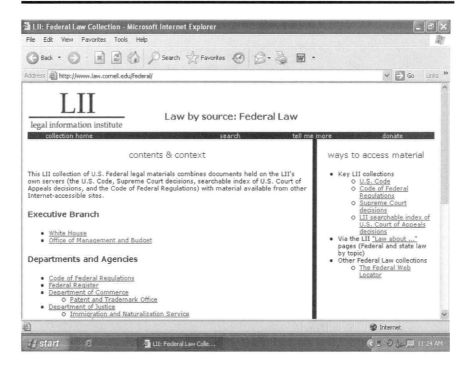

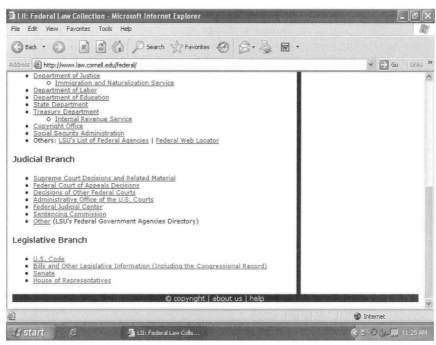

Reprinted with permission. © 2005 Cornell Law School, from http://www.law.cornell.edu.

F. CHECKLIST FOR ELECTRONIC LEGAL RESEARCH

1. SELECT AN ELECTRONIC RESEARCH SERVICE

- ❐ Consider the scope of coverage of the service.
- ❐ Consider the cost of the service.

2. SELECT A SEARCH TECHNIQUE

- ❐ Search techniques:
  - Retrieving a document from its citation
  - Browsing a publication's table of contents
  - Searching by subject
  - Conducting a word search
- ❐ For word searches, construct an effective Boolean search:
  - Develop the initial search terms.
  - Expand the breadth and depth of the search and add wildcard characters.
  - Specify the relationships among the terms using connectors and parentheses.
  - Use a field or segment restriction to target useful authorities.
- ❐ Natural language searching may also be available.

3. SELECT A DATABASE TO SEARCH AND REVIEW THE RESULTS

- ❐ Search the narrowest database that contains the information you need.
- ❐ Browse documents or review a citation list to evaluate your search results.
- ❐ Refine word searches if necessary.
  - Search in a narrower or broader database.
  - Subtract or add terms.
  - Make the proximity connectors more restrictive or less restrictive.
  - Subtract or add wildcard characters.
  - Subtract or add connectors that exclude terms.
  - Subtract or add field or segment restrictions.

4. RESEARCH EFFECTIVELY IN WESTLAW AND LEXISNEXIS

- ❐ In Westlaw:
  - Browse search results from the list of citations or using the Term function.

- Refine word searches by editing the search or using the Locate function.

❏ In LexisNexis:

- Browse documents in Full or KWIC using the Term function, view a list of citations in Cite, or customize the display using Custom.
- Refine word searches by editing the query or using the FOCUS, More Like This, or More Like Selected Text functions.

❏ In both services, search cost effectively.

- Construct word searches and plan your research path in advance.
- Use research assistance provided by Westlaw and LexisNexis.
- Execute searches to account for the billing structure.
- Determine charges for printing or downloading information.

5. USE ADDITIONAL TOOLS FOR EFFECTIVE ELECTRONIC RESEARCH

❏ Use an alert or clipping service to keep research up-to-date.

- In Westlaw, use KeyCite Alert and WestClip.
- In LexisNexis, use *Shepard's* Alert and Alert.

❏ Use blogs or other publicly available Internet sources.

- Locate useful sites to obtain background information on a topic or citations to primary authority.
- Assess the credibility of the source.
- Save or print copies of useful pages.
- Verify and update any legal authorities you locate.

Developing a Research Plan

A. Introduction to research planning

B. Creating a research plan

C. Finding help

D. Sample research plans

E. Research checklists

A. INTRODUCTION TO RESEARCH PLANNING

When you get a research assignment, you might be tempted to begin the project by going directly to the library to see what authority you can find. In fact, searching for authority right away is not the best way to start. Thought and planning before you head for the library will help you in several ways. You will research more efficiently if you have a coherent research plan to follow. You will also research more accurately. Searching haphazardly can cause you to miss important authorities, and nothing is more disconcerting than feeling as though you came across relevant authority by accident. Following an organized plan will help ensure that you check all the appropriate places for authority on your issue and will give you confidence that your research is correct and complete.

B. CREATING A RESEARCH PLAN

Creating a research plan requires three steps: (1) obtaining preliminary information about the problem; (2) writing out a plan to follow in the library; and (3) working effectively in the library. Each of these steps is discussed in turn.

1. OBTAINING PRELIMINARY INFORMATION

When you first receive a research assignment, you might feel like you do not know enough to ask very many questions about it. While this might be true as far as the substance of the problem is concerned, you need to determine the scope of your project by obtaining some preliminary information from the person making the assignment. Specifically:

■ **HOW MUCH TIME DO I HAVE FOR THIS ASSIGNMENT?**

The amount of time you have affects your overall approach, as well as your time management with other projects you have been assigned.

■ **WHAT FINAL WORK PRODUCT SHOULD I PRODUCE?**

You should determine whether you are expected to produce a memorandum, pleading, brief, or informal report of your research results. To a certain extent, this also will be a function of the amount of time you have for the project.

■ **ARE THERE ANY LIMITS ON THE RESEARCH MATERIALS I AM PERMITTED TO USE?**

As a matter of academic integrity, you want to make sure you use only authorized research tools in a law school assignment. In practice, some clients might be unable or unwilling to pay for research completed with tools requiring additional fees, such as LexisNexis or Westlaw research.

■ **WHICH JURISDICTION'S LAW APPLIES?**

This is a question the person giving you the assignment might not be able to answer. There will be times when the controlling jurisdiction will be known. In other cases, it will be up to you to determine whether an issue is controlled by federal or state law, and if it is a question of state law, which state's law applies.

■ **SHOULD I RESEARCH PERSUASIVE AUTHORITY?**

Again, the person making the assignment might not be able to answer this question. You could be asked to focus exclusively on the law of the controlling jurisdiction to answer your research question, or you could specifically be asked to research multiple jurisdictions. If either of those requirements applies to your research, you certainly want to know that before you go to the library. What is more likely, however, is that you will simply be asked to find the answer to a question. If the law of the controlling jurisdiction answers the question, you might not need to go further. If not, you will need to research persuasive authority. Understanding the scope of the assignment will help you focus your efforts appropriately.

In your research class, there will be many parts of the assignment that your professor will expect you to figure out on your own as part of learning about the process of research. In a practice setting, however, you might also ask the following questions:

■ **DO YOU KNOW OF ANY SOURCES THAT ARE PARTICULARLY GOOD FOR RESEARCHING IN THIS AREA OF LAW?**

Practitioners who are experienced in a particular field might know of research sources that are especially helpful for the type of research you are doing, including looseleaf or other subject-matter services.

■ **WHAT BACKGROUND ON THE LAW OR TERMS OF ART SHOULD I KNOW AS I BEGIN MY RESEARCH?**

In a law school assignment, you might be expected to identify terms of art on your own. In practice, however, the person giving you the research assignment might be able to give you some background on the area of law and important terms of art to help you get started on your research.

■ **SHOULD I CONSULT ANY WRITTEN MATERIALS OR INDIVIDUALS WITHIN THE OFFICE BEFORE GOING TO THE LIBRARY?**

Again, in law school, it would be inappropriate to use another person's research instead of completing the assignment on your own. In practice, however, reviewing briefs or memoranda on the same or a similar issue can give you a leg up on your research. In addition, another person within the office might be considered the "resident expert" on the subject and might be willing to act as a resource for you.

2. WRITING OUT A PLAN

Once you have preliminary information on your research project, you are ready to start writing out a plan to take you through the research process. The written plan should have the following components:

■ an initial issue statement
■ a list of potential search terms
■ an outline of the sources you plan to consult, including the order in which you plan to consult them and whether you expect to use print or electronic tools for each source.

a. Developing an Initial Issue Statement and Generating Search Terms

The starting points for your written plan are developing an initial issue statement and generating possible search terms. The issue statement does

not need to be a formal statement like one that would appear at the beginning of a brief or memorandum. Rather, it should be a preliminary assessment of the problem that helps define the scope of your research. For example, an initial issue statement might say something like, "Can the plaintiff recover from the defendant for destroying her garden?" This issue statement would be incomplete in a brief or memorandum because it does not identify a specific legal question and might not contain enough information about the facts. At this point, however, you do not know which legal theory or theories might be successful, nor do you know for certain which facts are most important. What this question tells you is that you will need to research all possible claims that would support recovery.

Alternatively, you might be asked to research a narrower question such as, "Can the plaintiff recover from the defendant *in negligence* for destroying her garden?" This issue statement again might be insufficient in a brief or memorandum, but for purposes of your research plan, it gives you valuable information. Your research should be limited to liability in negligence; intentional torts or contract claims are beyond the scope of this project.

Although this might seem like an exercise in the obvious, the discipline of writing out a preliminary issue statement can help you focus your efforts in the right direction. If you are unable to write a preliminary issue statement, that is an indication that you are not sure about the scope of the assignment and may need to ask more questions about what you should be trying to accomplish.

Once you have written your initial issue statement, you are ready to generate a list of possible search terms. Chapter 2 discusses how to do this, and the techniques described in that chapter should be employed to develop search terms in your research plan.

b. Identifying Research Sources

Once you have a preliminary view of the problem, the next step in creating an effective research plan is identifying potential research sources. First, you need to determine which research sources are likely to have relevant information. Then, you must determine the order in which you want to research those sources.

Chapter 1 discusses three general categories of authority: mandatory primary authority, persuasive primary authority, and secondary authority. You need to decide which of these categories of authority provides a good starting point for your research, and then, within each category, which specific authorities you should consult. The best way to do this is to begin with what you know, identify what you do not yet know, and determine the best ways to fill in the blanks.

For many research projects, your ultimate goal will be to produce a written document, such as a brief or memorandum, describing and

applying primary mandatory authority relevant to the issue. If this type of authority does not exist or does not fully resolve the question, then you will also probably need to discuss primary persuasive authority, secondary authority, or both. Although this is not what you will be asked to do in every research project, this section will illustrate the process of writing a research plan based on this goal. As you will see, this process can be adapted for other types of research projects that you might be asked to complete.

The process of identifying what you know, identifying what you do not yet know, and determining how best to fill in the blanks can be applied to two components of the project: the search for primary mandatory authority, and the search for persuasive authority. You might not be able to write out a complete research plan for both components of the project before going to the library. At a minimum, however, you should try to map out your search for primary mandatory authority. If a search for persuasive authority becomes necessary, you can then rework your plan to include those sources.

(1) Searching for primary mandatory authority

Beginning with the search for primary mandatory authority, the flowchart in **Figure 11.1** illustrates the process you might undertake.

As you can see from the flowchart, there are several places where you might consult secondary sources and several points at which you might make the jump into researching individual primary authorities, depending on how much information you have about your issue when you begin your research.

When you are ready to begin researching individual primary authorities, you need to decide the order in which to consult those sources. There are a couple of ways to do this. If you have consulted secondary sources, you should have a sense of whether the issue is a common-law issue governed by case law or an issue to which statutes, regulations, and other types of authority might apply. This information will help you determine the best starting point for researching individual primary authorities.

Once you have located some type of primary mandatory authority on the issue, whether through secondary sources or some other avenue, you can use that as a springboard to other primary authorities. As noted in the flowchart, for example, a case will contain headnotes that can lead you into the digest to locate other cases. The cases should also cite relevant statutory and regulatory provisions. Statutory annotations can lead you to legislative history, regulations, secondary sources, and cases. Of course, it is possible that the sources you consult initially will not lead you to other primary authorities. In that case, you might want to search independently in primary sources to make sure you have located all of the relevant authority.

FIGURE 11.1 FLOWCHART FOR DETERMINING YOUR RESEARCH PATH

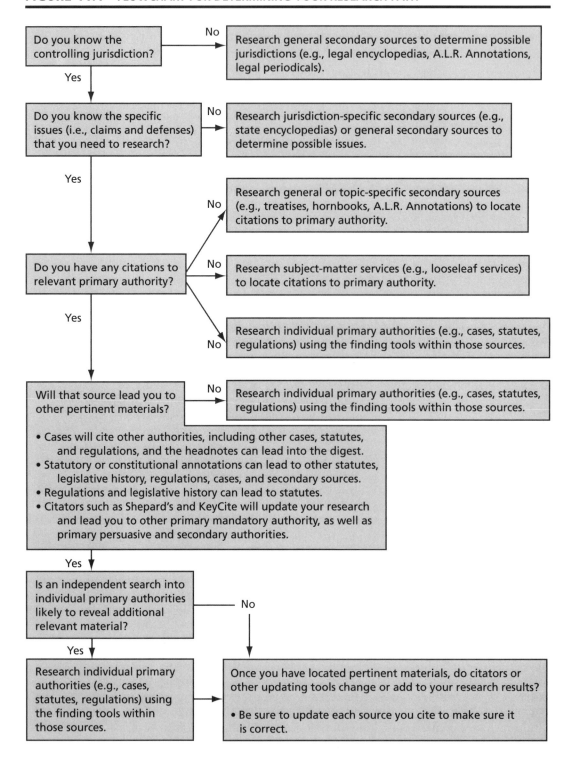

(2) Searching for persuasive authority

As you conduct your research, you might determine that you need to search for persuasive authority to analyze your research issue thoroughly. As in your search for primary mandatory authority, in your search for persuasive authority, you should begin with what you know, identify what you do not yet know, and determine the best ways to fill in the blanks.

The first thing you need to know is why you are searching for persuasive authority. Persuasive authority can serve a variety of purposes in your analysis of a research question. Here are four common reasons why you would want to research persuasive authority:

- When you want to buttress an analysis largely resolved by primary mandatory authority.
- When the applicable legal rules are clearly defined by primary mandatory authority, but the specific factual situation has not arisen in the jurisdiction. You might want to try to locate factually analogous cases from other jurisdictions.
- When the applicable rule is unclear and you want to make an analogy to another area of law to support your analysis.
- When the issue is one of first impression in the controlling jurisdiction for which no governing rule exists. In this case, you might want to find out how other jurisdictions have addressed the issue, or if no jurisdiction has faced the question, whether any commentators have analyzed the issue.

In each of these situations, you might want to research persuasive authority consisting of non-mandatory primary authority from within the controlling jurisdiction, such as cases or statutes in an analogous area of law; primary authority from other jurisdictions; or secondary authorities analyzing the law.

Once you have determined why you need to research persuasive authority, you should review the material you have already located. In your search for primary mandatory authority, you might already have identified some useful persuasive authority. Secondary sources consulted at the beginning of your research could contain persuasive analysis or useful citations to primary persuasive authority. Secondary sources often identify key or leading authorities in an area of law, and that might be enough to meet your needs. A citator might also have identified useful persuasive authority. If the authorities you have already located prove sufficient, you should update your research to make sure everything you cite remains authoritative and, if appropriate, end your search for persuasive authority.

On the other hand, you might review the results of your research and determine that you need to undertake a separate search for persuasive

authority. When you first reviewed secondary sources and used citators, it might not have been with an eye toward locating persuasive authority. Therefore, you might want to take a second pass at these sources. In addition, the persuasive authority you ran across early in your research might not be the best material for you to cite; a more focused research effort could yield more pertinent material.

If you determine that you need to conduct a separate search for persuasive authority, your next step will be deciding the best research path to follow. The flowchart in **Figure 11.2** illustrates several research avenues for locating persuasive authority. Your research path will vary according to a number of factors, including the amount of time you have, the resources available in your library, and the type of work product you are expected to produce. Therefore, the flowchart is intended simply to illustrate options that would be available to you, not to establish a definitive path for locating each type of authority.

One thing you might notice as you review the flowchart is that secondary sources play an important role in locating persuasive authority. Unless you know the precise jurisdiction from which you plan to cite persuasive authority, and the precise type of authority you need to locate (cases, statutes, etc.), beginning your search for persuasive authority in primary sources is not likely to be efficient in most cases. Secondary sources are key to determining which jurisdictions are likely to have relevant authority and which types of authority are likely to be helpful to you.

c. Deciding Between Print and Electronic Sources

One additional decision you will need to make in formulating a research plan is whether to conduct your research using print research tools, electronic tools, or both. For many research projects, a combination of the two will be necessary for complete, accurate, and efficient research. Some sources can be accessed more easily in one format or the other. In addition, if an initial search for a particular type of authority is unfruitful, you might want to switch from print sources to electronic, or vice versa. For purposes of this discussion, electronic sources include LexisNexis and Westlaw, as well as CD-ROM and Internet resources that might be available in your library.

Generally speaking, you will want to use print research sources in the following circumstances:

■ **WHEN YOU ARE SEARCHING FOR MATERIAL NOT AVAILABLE ON-LINE.** For example, although a number of secondary sources are available in electronic form, many others are not. Many treatises and hornbooks and a number of legal periodicals are not included in electronic research tools. LexisNexis and Westlaw in particular do not include all legal periodicals in their databases, and their coverage is limited to articles published after 1980.

FIGURE 11.2 FLOWCHART FOR RESEARCHING PERSUASIVE AUTHORITY

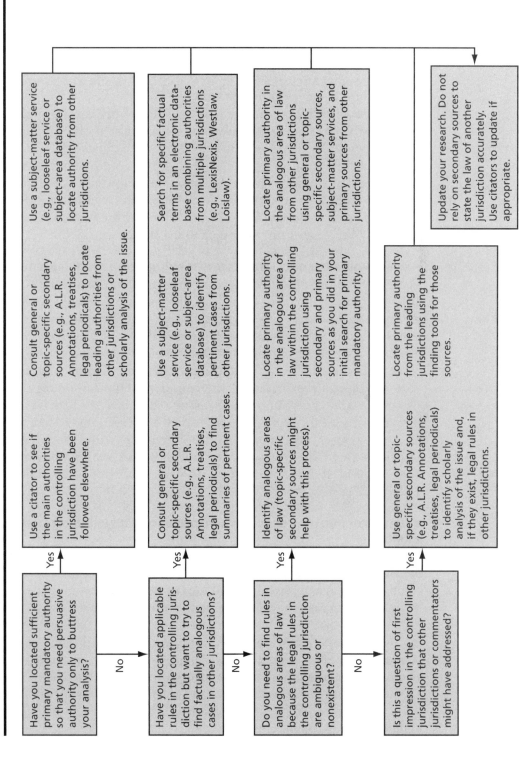

■ **WHEN YOU NEED GENERAL INFORMATION ON A TOPIC ABOUT WHICH YOU ARE UNFAMILIAR.**

It is difficult to draft an effective word search if you have little or no information about your topic, and electronic subject searching is not available in all services or for all types of authority. Searching by subject in print resources may be more effective in this situation.

■ **WHEN YOUR SEARCH TERMS ARE GENERAL OR THE SUBJECT OF YOUR RESEARCH INVOLVES BROAD CONCEPTS.**

A computer search for terms such as "negligence" or "equal protection" will probably retrieve too many documents to be useful because the computer will retrieve every document in the database that contains those terms. By contrast, these general topics could be useful search terms in a print index. The print index may subdivide these general topics into subtopics so that you can target pertinent authorities. It may also limit its references to key authorities under the topic, rather than referring you to every authority containing those terms.

■ **WHEN YOU ARE CONDUCTING STATUTORY OR REGULATORY RESEARCH.**

There are two reasons why researching statutes and regulations can be difficult to do on-line. First, an electronic word search will search only for the terms you specify. A word search that does not include the precise statutory or regulatory language will not be effective. A print index, by contrast, is organized by subject and will contain cross-references that can help direct you to the correct terms or concepts. Second, you will often need to review the complete statutory or regulatory scheme to analyze your research issue. This can be difficult to do through piecemeal research into individual code sections or regulations on the computer, although it has become easier to do through search functions that allow you to see outlines and tables of contents. Nevertheless, statutory and regulatory research are often easiest to accomplish in print.

■ **WHEN YOU NEED TO READ AUTHORITIES LOCATED THROUGH OTHER MEANS.**

It is difficult to read material on a computer screen. Although it is possible to print material retrieved from the computer, cost considerations could make that a poor choice, and the format of the computer printout might not be as easy to read as the print version.

By contrast, electronic sources can be a better option under some circumstances. As a general matter, many experienced researchers find electronic research most effective for locating one or two good "hits," or relevant authorities, which they can then use as an entry point into other research tools. Electronic research is most likely to be effective under the following circumstances:

■ **WHEN THE MATERIAL YOU NEED IS NOT AVAILABLE IN PRINT.**

The scope of the print collection will vary from library to library; thus, some material you need might only be available in electronic form. In addition, some subject-matter services are available only in CD-ROM format or on the Internet. Even if material is available in print in your library, some material might be easier to access in electronic form. For example, legislative history research is often easier to conduct via the Internet using LexisNexis Congressional or Thomas than in the microfiche format available in many libraries.

■ **WHEN YOU HAVE UNIQUE SEARCH TERMS OR ARE SEARCHING FOR PROPER NAMES.**

If you have unique search terms, electronic sources can be a good search option because electronic word searches will search for the precise terms you need, whereas print sources organized by subject might not index those terms. Searches for proper names can also be accomplished effectively in electronic resources.

■ **WHEN YOU NEED TO UPDATE YOUR RESEARCH.**

Not all computer resources are more up to date than print resources, but many are. Updating your research can often be quickly and efficiently accomplished using electronic sources.

When these circumstances do not apply to your research, you will have a choice between print or electronic sources. The amount of time you have for your research, cost considerations, and your level of comfort with the research tools available will inform your choice about which resources to use.

3. WORKING IN THE LIBRARY

a. Keeping Track: Effective Note Taking

Once you have created your research plan, you are ready to go to the library to begin your search for authority. Keeping effective notes as you work in the library is important for several reasons. It will make your research more efficient. You will know where you have already looked, so you can avoid repeating research steps. This is especially critical if you will be working on the project for an extended period of time or if you are working with other people in completing the research. You will also have all of the information you need for proper citations. Moreover, if it happens that your project presents novel or complex issues for which there are no definitive answers, careful note taking will allow you to demonstrate that you undertook comprehensive research to try to resolve those issues.

Note taking is an individualized process, and there is no single right way to do it. Your personal preferences will largely dictate the method

you use. Some people use binders, folders, or pads of paper. Others take notes electronically by creating files and folders on a computer or taking notes with a PDA. Having said that, however, many people find their notes easiest to follow if the notes are organized around topics or issues, rather than by type of authority or individual source. Then within each topic or issue, specific information on each authority can be noted. Regardless of the method you use for keeping notes, you should try to keep each of the following items of information on each source you use:

Source or database

Citation	This does not need to be in proper citation form, but enough information for a proper citation should be included here.
Method of locating the source	This could include references to a secondary source that led you to this authority or the search terms you used in an index or electronic database.
Summary of relevant information	This might be a few sentences or a few pages, depending on the source and its relevance; specific page or section numbers should be noted, and all quotations should be marked clearly here to avoid inadvertent plagiarism later.
Updating information	Note whether the source has been updated and the method of updating, e.g., "updated w/'06 pocket part."

This might not be the only information you need to note. For example, in case research, you might also want to note separately the topics and key numbers in the most important cases. At a minimum, however, you should keep track of these pieces of information. Once you find a method of note taking that is effective for you, you might be able to create a form or template that you use for each source you locate.

As you work through your research plan, be sure to keep notes on computer research as well as print research. On the computer, it is easy to follow a series of links until you lose track of where you have gone. Both LexisNexis and Westlaw will save your research trails so you can retrace your steps later, but they do not save this information indefinitely, and other electronic research services may not save this information at all. Although most web browsers will give you at least limited ability to retrace your steps, your computer might not save this information in a useful format. Therefore, it is important to keep notes on your electronic research while you are doing it.

There is a constant tension as you are researching between keeping written notes on the material you locate and photocopying or printing the material itself. Most people copy more than they need, and many students use copying as a procrastination technique, promising themselves that they will read the information later. Excessive printing or copying does not improve your research. Certainly, having copies of key authorities is important for accurate analysis, quotation, and citation. Facing a huge, disorganized stack of paper, however, can be demoralizing, especially because most of the information will probably prove to be irrelevant in the end if you have not made thoughtful choices about what to copy or print.

The fact is that you will not know for certain at the beginning of your research what should be copied and what should not. Only as you begin to understand the contours of the legal issue will the relevance (or irrelevance) of individual legal authorities become apparent to you. Therefore, you should conduct some research before you begin copying material, and as you delve into the research, you might find that you need to go back and copy material you bypassed originally. As you copy each item, make sure all of the necessary information for a proper citation is included, and make a note at the beginning indicating why you copied the item. You might also want to note directly on the copy the steps you took to update the source.

b. Deciding When to Stop

Deciding when your research is complete can be difficult. The more research you do, the more comfortable you will be with the process, and the more you will develop an internal sense of when a project is complete. In your first few research assignments in law school, however, you will probably feel uncertain about when to stop because you will have little prior experience to draw upon in making that decision.

One issue that affects a person's sense of when to stop is personal work style. Some people are anxious to begin writing and therefore stop researching after they locate a few sources that seem relevant. Others put off writing by continuing to research and research, thinking that the answer will become apparent if they just keep looking a little bit more. Being aware of your work style will help you determine whether you have stopped too soon or are continuing your research beyond what is necessary for the assignment.

Of course, the amount of time you have and the work product you are expected to produce will affect the ending point for your research. If you are instructed to report back in half an hour with your research results, you know when you will need to stop. In general, however, you will know that you have come full circle in your research when, after following a comprehensive research path through a variety of sources,

the authorities you locate start to refer back to each other and the new sources you consult fail to reveal significant new information.

The fact that a few of the sources you have located appear relevant does not mean it is time to stop researching. Until you have explored other potential research avenues, you should continue your work. It might be that the authorities you initially locate will turn out to be the most relevant, but you cannot have confidence in that result until you research additional authorities. On the other hand, you can always keep looking for one more case or one more article to support your analysis, but at some point, the benefit of continuing to research will be too small to justify the additional effort. It is unlikely that one magical source exists that is going to resolve your research issue. If the issue were clear, you probably would not have been asked to research it. If you developed a comprehensive research strategy and followed it until you came full circle in your research, it is probably time to stop.

C. FINDING HELP

Even if you follow all of the steps outlined in this chapter, from time to time, you will not be able to find what you need. The two most common situations that arise are not being able to find any authority on an issue and finding an overwhelming amount of information.

1. WHAT TO DO IF YOU ARE UNABLE TO FIND ANYTHING

If you have researched several different sources and are unable to find anything, it is time to take a different approach. You should not expect the books to fall open to the material you need, and blind alleys are inevitable if you approach a problem creatively. Nevertheless, if you find that you really cannot locate any information on an issue, consider the following possibilities:

■ **MAKE SURE YOU UNDERSTAND THE PROBLEM.**
One possibility is that you have misunderstood a critical aspect of the problem. If diligent research truly yields nothing, you might want to go back to the person who gave you the assignment to make sure you correctly noted all of the factual information you need and have understood the assignment correctly.

■ **RETHINK YOUR SEARCH TERMS.**
Have you expanded the breadth and depth of your search terms? You might be researching the right concepts but not have expressed them in a way that yields information in print indices or computer databases. Expanding your search terms will allow you to look not only more

widely for information, but also more narrowly. For example, if you have searched unsuccessfully under "moving vehicles" for authority involving transportation equipment, you might need to move to more concrete terms, such as "automobiles" or "cars."

In addition, you might need to rethink search terms directed to applicable legal theories. If you have focused on a theory of recovery for which you have not been able to locate authority, you might need to think about other ways to approach the problem. Try not to become so wedded to a legal theory that you pursue it to the exclusion of other viable claims or defenses.

■ **GO BACK TO SECONDARY SOURCES.**

If you did not consult secondary sources originally, you might want to take that route to find the information you need. The material on the issue might be scattered through many digest topics or statutory sections so that it is difficult to locate without secondary sources that compile the relevant information. In addition, the search terms that seemed applicable when you started your research might, in fact, not be helpful. Secondary sources can help point you in the right direction.

Another difficulty is that you might be looking for the wrong type of authority. Are you sure this is a question of state law? Might statutes as well as cases apply to the situation? Secondary sources can help you determine what type of primary authority is likely to be relevant to the situation.

Finally, secondary sources can help you determine whether you are facing a question of first impression. If the controlling jurisdiction simply has not faced this question yet, secondary sources should direct you to jurisdictions that have. If no jurisdiction has resolved the issue, legal periodicals might direct you to arguments and analogies that could be made.

2. WHAT TO DO IF YOU FIND AN OVERWHELMING AMOUNT OF MATERIAL

The same research options that will help you if you are unable to find any material will also help you if you find an overwhelming amount of material. Making sure you understand the problem, of course, is critical. Rethinking your search terms to narrow your approach can also help. If you located information primarily using computer word searches, you might want to try searching by subject, using either print or electronic research tools, because searching by subject instead of by terms in the document might help you focus on relevant authority. Consulting secondary sources, however, is probably the most useful strategy. Synthesizing large amounts of authority is difficult. Secondary sources can help you identify the key authorities and otherwise limit the scope of the information on the issue.

Another consideration here is the scope of your research. If much of the authority you have located is secondary authority or primary persuasive authority, you might need to refocus on primary mandatory authority from the controlling jurisdiction. If the controlling jurisdiction has a sufficient amount of authority for thorough analysis of the issue, you might not need to cite persuasive authority. You might also need to narrow your scope by limiting the legal theories you are considering. If some are clearly more viable than others and you already have an overwhelming amount of authority, you might want to focus on the theories that seem to provide your client with the best chances of prevailing.

D. SAMPLE RESEARCH PLANS

The research plans in **Figures 11.3** through **11.6** are intended to help you develop a coherent research strategy for four common types of research: state common-law research, state statutory research, federal statutory research, and federal and state procedural research. These plans are representative samples of how you could approach the research process and may provide a useful starting point for your own research planning.

1. STATE COMMON-LAW RESEARCH

FIGURE 11.3 FLOWCHART FOR STATE COMMON-LAW RESEARCH

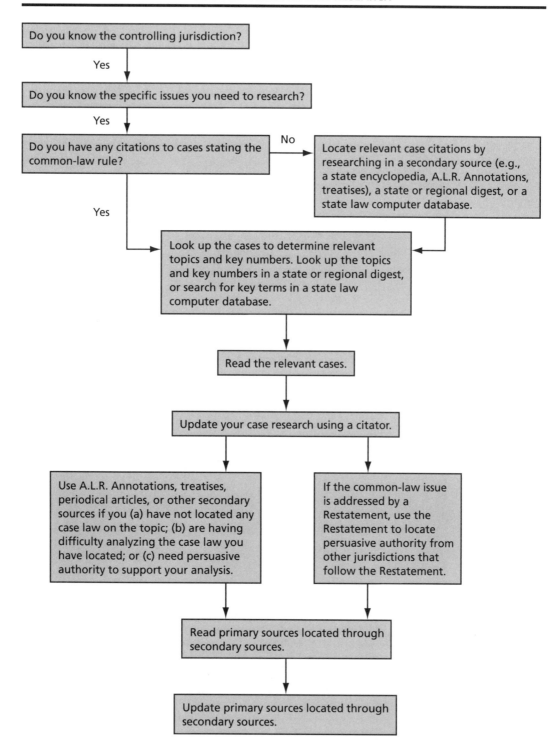

2. STATE STATUTORY RESEARCH

FIGURE 11.4 FLOWCHART FOR STATE STATUTORY RESEARCH

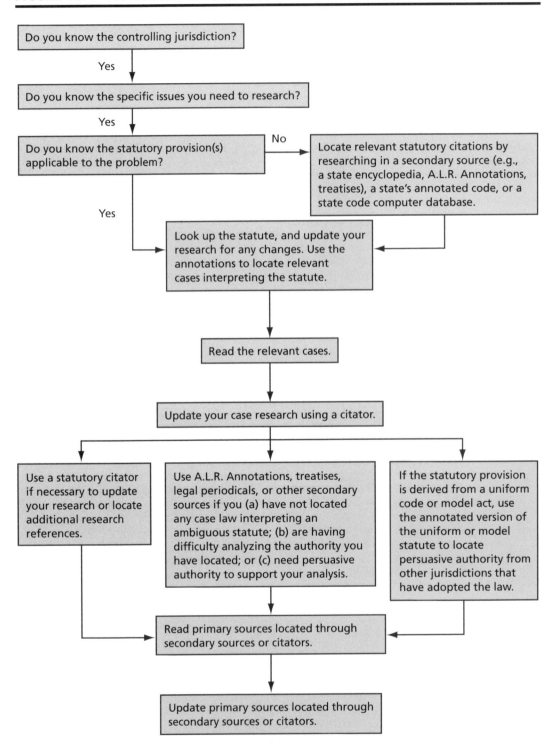

3. FEDERAL STATUTORY RESEARCH

FIGURE 11.5   FLOWCHART FOR FEDERAL STATUTORY RESEARCH

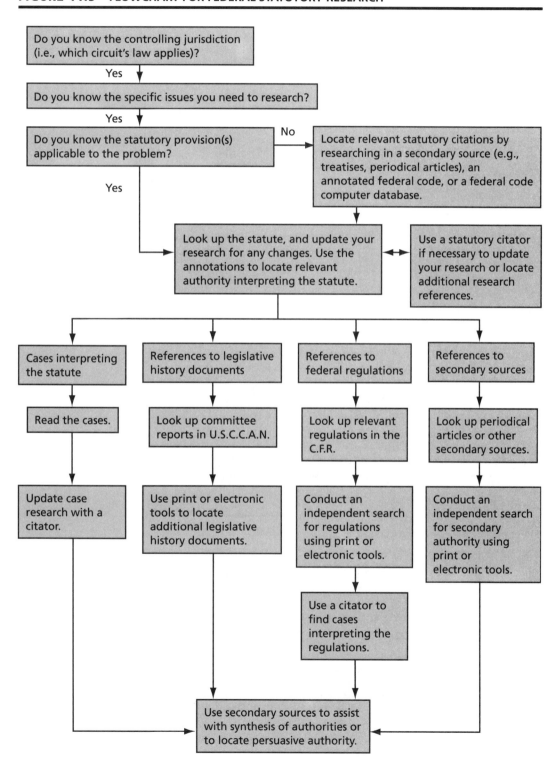

4. FEDERAL OR STATE PROCEDURAL RESEARCH

FIGURE 11.6   FLOWCHART FOR RESEARCHING RULES OF PROCEDURE

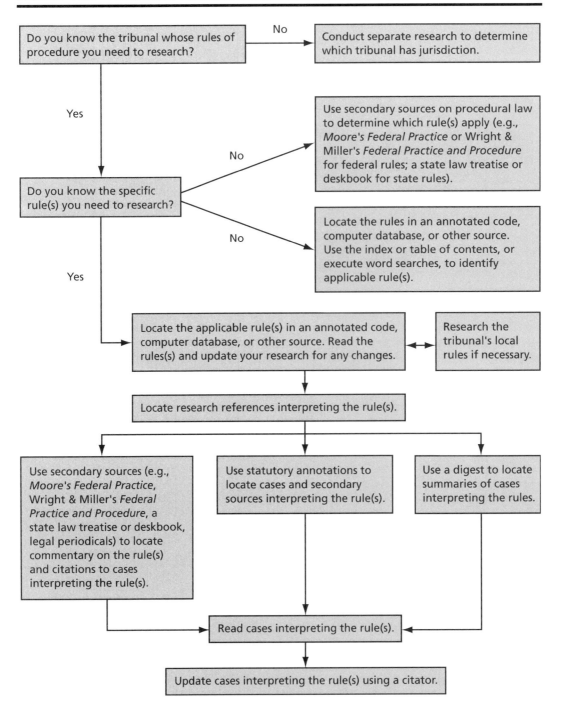

E. RESEARCH CHECKLISTS

1. Checklist for Developing an Effective Research Plan

1. OBTAIN PRELIMINARY INFORMATION ON THE PROBLEM

❏ Determine the due date, work product expected, limits on research tools to be used, controlling jurisdiction (if known), and whether persuasive authority should be located (if known).

❏ If permitted, find out useful research tools, background on the law or terms of art, and whether other written materials or individuals with special expertise should be consulted.

2. WRITE OUT A PLAN

❏ Develop a preliminary issue statement.

❏ Generate a list of search terms.

❏ Identify the type and sequence of research sources to consult by identifying what you know, what you do not yet know, and how best to fill in the blanks.

- Locate primary mandatory authority first.
- Locate persuasive authority later, if necessary:

  - to buttress an analysis largely resolved by primary mandatory authority
  - to locate factually analogous cases from other jurisdictions
  - to make an analogy to another area of law when the applicable rule is unclear
  - to locate commentary or applicable rules from other jurisdictions on an issue of first impression.

- Determine the best mix of print and electronic research tools for your research project.

3. WORK EFFECTIVELY IN THE LIBRARY

❏ Keep effective notes.

❏ Stop researching when your research has come full circle.

❏ Find help if you need it.

- If you are unable to find anything or find too much material, make sure you understand the problem, rethink your search terms, consult secondary sources, and reevaluate the legal theories you are pursuing.

2. MASTER CHECKLIST OF RESEARCH SOURCES

The following is an abbreviated collection of the research checklists that appear at the end of the preceding chapters in this book. This master checklist may help you develop your research plan. It may also be useful to you while you are conducting research.

Secondary Source Research

1. LEGAL ENCYCLOPEDIAS

❑ Use for very general background information and limited citations to primary authority, but not for in-depth analysis of a topic.

❑ Locate information in print by using the subject index or table of contents, locating relevant sections in the main volumes, and updating with the pocket part.

❑ Use LexisNexis and Westlaw to access Am. Jur. 2d.; use Westlaw to access C.J.S.

2. TREATISES

❑ Use for an in-depth discussion and some analysis of an area of law and for citations to primary authority.

❑ Locate treatises in print through the on-line catalog; locate information within a treatise by using the subject index or table of contents, locating material in the main volumes, and updating with the pocket part.

❑ Use LexisNexis and Westlaw to access selected treatises.

3. LEGAL PERIODICALS

❑ Use for background information, citations to primary authority, in-depth analysis of a narrow topic, or information on a conflict in the law or an undeveloped area of the law.

❑ Locate citations to periodical articles by using the *Index to Legal Periodicals and Books* (ILP) and *Current Law Index* (CLI) print indices, or the LegalTrac and ILP electronic indices.

❑ Use LexisNexis and Westlaw to access periodical articles.

❑ Use HeinOnline to locate the full text of legal periodicals in .pdf format.

❑ Selected periodicals may be available on the Internet.

4. *AMERICAN LAW REPORTS*

❑ Use A.L.R.3d, A.L.R.4th, A.L.R.5th, A.L.R.6th, A.L.R. Fed., or A.L.R. Fed. 2d for an overview of an area of law and citations to primary authority.

❏ Locate material in A.L.R. by using the A.L.R. Index, locating material in the main volumes, and updating with the pocket part.

❏ Use LexisNexis and Westlaw to locate A.L.R. Annotations.

5. RESTATEMENTS

❏ Use for research into common-law subjects and to locate mandatory and persuasive authority from jurisdictions that have adopted a Restatement.

❏ Locate information within a print Restatement by using the subject index or table of contents to find Restatement sections in the Restatement volumes, locating case summaries in the noncumulative Appendix volumes, and updating the Appendix volumes with the pocket part.

❏ Use LexisNexis and Westlaw to access selected Restatements.

6. UNIFORM LAWS AND MODEL ACTS

❏ Use to interpret a law adopted by a legislature and to locate persuasive authority from other jurisdictions that have adopted the law.

❏ Locate in print using *Uniform Laws Annotated, Master Edition* (ULA).

❏ Locate information in the ULA set by using the *Directory of Uniform Acts and Codes: Tables and Index*, locating relevant provisions in the main volumes, and updating with the pocket part.

❏ Use LexisNexis and Westlaw to access selected uniform laws and model acts.

Case Research

1. SELECT A PRINT DIGEST

❏ Use federal, state, regional, or combined digests.

2. LOCATE TOPICS AND KEY NUMBERS IN A PRINT DIGEST

❏ Work from a case on point, the Descriptive-Word Index, or the topic entry.

3. READ THE CASE SUMMARIES IN THE PRINT DIGEST

❏ Use the court and date abbreviations to target appropriate cases.

4. UPDATE PRINT DIGEST RESEARCH

❑ Check the pocket part and any cumulative or noncumulative interim pamphlets.
❑ If necessary, check the closing table and mini-digests.

5. ELECTRONIC CASE RESEARCH

❑ Use Westlaw and LexisNexis to conduct word searches for cases.
❑ In Westlaw, use the Custom Digest function to search by digest topic and key number or the KeySearch function to search by subject.
❑ In LexisNexis, use the Search Advisor function to search by subject.
❑ Selected cases may be available on the Internet.

Research with Shepard's Citations and Other Citators

1. LOCATE THE CORRECT SET OF SHEPARD'S IN PRINT

❑ Use a state or regional set of Shepard's for state cases.
❑ Use federal Shepard's for federal cases.

2. LOCATE THE CORRECT VOLUMES WITHIN THE PRINT SET

❑ Check the most recent supplement for the section "What Your Library Should Contain."

3. LOCATE THE ENTRIES FOR THE CASE WITHIN EACH VOLUME LOCATED IN STEP 2

4. INTERPRET THE ENTRIES

❑ Case history appears first, followed by citing sources.
❑ History and treatment codes signal how the history cases and citing sources treated the original case.
❑ Headnote references signal the proposition for which a citing source refers to the original case.

5. CHECK CASE CITATIONS ELECTRONICALLY

❑ To Shepardize a case in LexisNexis, enter the citation in Shepard's and interpret the entries as in Step 4.
❑ In Westlaw, use KeyCite by entering the citation.

Statutory Research

1. LOCATE A STATUTE

❑ Use a subject index, popular name table, or for federal statutes, the conversion tables.
❑ Use LexisNexis and Westlaw to access state and federal statutes.

❑ On the Internet, locate statutes on government or general legal research web sites.

2. **READ THE STATUTE AND ACCOMPANYING ANNOTATIONS**

3. **UPDATE PRINT RESEARCH**

❑ Check the pocket part and any cumulative or noncumulative supplements.

4. **SPECIAL NOTES**

❑ In U.S.C.A., update entries to the popular name and conversion tables in the noncumulative supplements.
❑ In state codes, check for additional updating tools.
❑ In state or federal statutory research, update or find research references using Shepard's in print or in LexisNexis or KeyCite in Westlaw.
❑ In Internet research, check the date of the statute and update your research accordingly.

Federal Legislative History Research

1. **IDENTIFY THE SCOPE OF YOUR RESEARCH**

❑ Determine whether you need to find the history of a particular statute or material on a general subject.

2. **LOCATE A COMPILED LEGISLATIVE HISTORY**

❑ Use the library's on-line catalog; Johnson, *Sources of Compiled Legislative Histories*; or *Reams, Federal Legislative Histories*.

3. **LOCATE COMMITTEE REPORTS IN U.S.C.C.A.N.**

❑ Use annotations in U.S.C.A. to locate cross-references to U.S.C.C.A.N.

4. **LOCATE COMPLETE LEGISLATIVE HISTORIES IN THE CIS MICRO-FICHE SET**

❑ Use the Legislative Histories volumes or Index and Abstracts.

5. **LOCATE FLOOR DEBATES IN THE *CONGRESSIONAL RECORD* USING PRINT SOURCES**

❑ Locate references to floor debates using the CIS Legislative Histories volumes or reports reprinted in U.S.C.C.A.N.
❑ Use the *Congressional Record* index to search by subject or bill number.

6. SEARCH FOR LEGISLATIVE HISTORY ELECTRONICALLY

❑ Use LexisNexis Congressional, Thomas, GPO Access, LexisNexis, and Westlaw to access a range of legislative history documents.

Federal Administrative Law Research

1. LOCATE PERTINENT REGULATIONS

❑ Use statutory cross-references or a subject index to locate federal regulations in the C.F.R. in print.
❑ Use LexisNexis, Westlaw, GPO Access, or other Internet sites to access C.F.R. provisions electronically.

2. UPDATE PRINT RESEARCH WITH THE LIST OF CFR SECTIONS AFFECTED (LSA), *FEDERAL REGISTER*, AND TABLE OF CFR PARTS AFFECTED

❑ Update from the date of the C.F.R. volume through the end of the prior month by using the most recent LSA to find *Federal Register* references affecting the regulation.
❑ Update from the end of the prior month to the present by using the cumulative table of CFR Parts Affected in the most recent issue of the *Federal Register.*

3. UPDATE GPO ACCESS RESEARCH WITH THE e-CFR OR THE ELECTRONIC VERSIONS OF THE LSA, *FEDERAL REGISTER*, AND CURRENT LIST OF CFR PARTS AFFECTED

4. CONTACT THE AGENCY FOR ADDITIONAL INFORMATION ON RECENT OR PROPOSED REGULATORY CHANGES

5. USE SHEPARD'S IN PRINT OR IN LEXISNEXIS, OR KEYCITE IN WESTLAW, TO UPDATE YOUR RESEARCH OR LOCATE RESEARCH REFERENCES

Subject-Matter Service Research

1. LOCATE A SUBJECT-MATTER SERVICE FOR YOUR RESEARCH ISSUE

❑ Use Table T.15 in the back of the *Bluebook*, a reference source such as the LawTRIO database or print sources such as *Legal Looseleafs in Print* or *Directory of Law-Related CD-ROMs,* or subject area databases in LexisNexis and Westlaw.

2. DETERMINE HOW TO USE THE SERVICE

❑ In print services, look for the "Overview" or "How to use this service" section.

❒ In CD-ROM and Internet services, follow the service's instructions.

❒ In LexisNexis and Westlaw, execute word searches or use other available search options.

Electronic Legal Research

1. SELECT AN ELECTRONIC RESEARCH SERVICE

❒ Consider the scope of coverage and cost.

2. SELECT A SEARCH TECHNIQUE

❒ Search techniques: retrieving a document from its citation; browsing a publication's table of contents; searching by subject; conducting a word search.

❒ For word searches, construct an effective Boolean search by developing the initial search, expanding the breadth and depth of the search, using connectors and parentheses, and using a field or segment restriction.

❒ Natural language searching may also be available.

3. SELECT A DATABASE TO SEARCH AND REVIEW THE RESULTS

❒ Search the narrowest appropriate database.

❒ Browse documents or review a citation list to evaluate your search results.

❒ Refine the search if necessary.

4. RESEARCH EFFECTIVELY IN WESTLAW AND LEXISNEXIS

❒ In Westlaw, browse documents using the list of citations or Term function; refine word searches by editing the search or using the Locate function.

❒ In LexisNexis, browse documents in Full or KWIC using the Term function, view a list of citations in Cite, or customize the display using Custom; refine word searches by editing the query or using the FOCUS, More Like This, or More Like Selected Text functions.

❒ In both services, use search strategies for cost effectiveness.

5. USE ADDITIONAL TOOLS FOR EFFECTIVE ELECTRONIC RESEARCH

❒ Use an alert or clipping service to keep research up-to-date.

❒ Use blogs or other publicly available Internet sources by locating useful sites, assessing the credibility of the source, saving or printing copies of useful pages, and verifying and updating legal authorities.

SELECTED INTERNET
RESEARCH RESOURCES

FEDERAL GOVERNMENT WEB SITES

FedWorld
http://www.fedworld.gov
> Provides access to a wide range of federal government information.

FirstGov
http://www.firstgov.gov
> The U.S. government's official portal to a wide range of government resources.

GPO Access
http://www.gpoaccess.gov
> Contains Congressional bills, hearings, and reports, as well as a weekly compilation of Presidential documents. The *Code of Federal Regulations, Federal Register*, and *United States Code* are also included.

Library of Congress
http://www.loc.gov
> Search the on-line catalog of the Library of Congress, and locate a wealth of legal and general information.

Thomas
http://thomas.loc.gov
> The Library of Congress's on-line source for legislative information. This site contains committee reports, the *Congressional Record,* and other legislative history documents.

United States House of Representatives
http://www.house.gov
> The site for the House of Representatives.

United States Senate
http://www.senate.gov
> The site for the Senate.

United States Supreme Court
http://www.supremecourtus.gov
> The site for the U.S. Supreme Court.

The White House
http://www.whitehouse.gov
> The site for the White House.

LAW LIBRARY WEB SITES

These sites can be used to search for a wide range of legal authorities, including state and federal cases and statutes, administrative materials, secondary sources, and legal news.

Cornell Law School's Legal Information Institute
http://www.law.cornell.edu

Emory Law Library Electronic Reference Desk
http://www.law.emory.edu/erd/index.html

The Indiana University School of Law WWW Virtual Library-Law
http://www.law.indiana.edu/v-lib/index.html

Washburn University School of Law WashLaw Legal Research on the Web
http://www.washlaw.edu

GENERAL LEGAL RESEARCH WEB SITES

Like the law library web sites, these sites provide access to a wide range of legal materials. Some can be accessed free of charge; others are fee-based services. Subscription services are not listed here. You should be able to access any services to which your library subscribes from the library's computer network.

Free Services

All Law
http://www.alllaw.com

American Bar Association's Lawlink Legal Research Jumpstation
http://www.abanet.org/lawlink/home.html

American Law Sources On-line
http://www.lawsource.com

CataLaw
http://www.catalaw.com

FindLaw
http://www.findlaw.com

Heiros Gamos
http://www.hg.org

LawGuru
http://www.lawguru.com

LLRX.com
http://www.llrx.com

Rominger Legal
http://www.romingerlegal.com

Fee-based Services

Loislaw
http://www.loislaw.com

LexisNexis
http://www.lexis.com

VersusLaw
http://www.versuslaw.com

Westlaw
http://www.westlaw.com

INTERNET SEARCH ENGINES

Search engines can be used to locate web sites on the Internet. You undoubtedly know of many general search engines. Those listed here are specialized search engines.

Google Scholar
http://www.scholar.google.com
    Searches scholarly literature.

LawBot
http://www.megalaw.com
   Searches for legal web sites.

LawCrawler
http://www.lawcrawler.com
   Searches for legal information.

MetaCrawler
http://www.metacrawler.com
   Allows you to excute a search through multiple search engines simultaneously.

OTHER WEB SITES OF INTEREST

Association of Legal Writing Directors (ALWD)
http://www.alwd.org
   Contains updates and information on the *ALWD Citation Manual*.

Blawg
http://www.blawg.org
   Contains a directory of law-related blogs.

Introduction to Basic Legal Citation
http://www.law.cornell.edu/citation
   Provides tips on using the *Bluebook*.

Internet Archive Wayback Machine
http://www.archive.org
   Contains archived web pages. To see what a web site displayed on a date in the past, enter the URL for the site, and select the date.

Law.com
http://www.law.com
   Contains legal news, employment listings, and other legal information.

Lawyers Weekly USA
http://www.lawyersweeklyusa.com
   Contains legal news, classified advertisements, and selected court opinions. This site also has links to regional on-line newspapers.

Martindale-Hubbell
http://www.martindale.com
   Search for individual lawyers, firms, or government agencies employing attorneys.

Index

---

*References to figures and tables are in **boldface**.*